PATRONAGE AND HUMANIST LITERATURE IN THE AGE OF THE JAGIELLONS

To Dr Skalicka,
with best wishes
and many thanks
from your patient,
Jacqueline Glomski

PATRONAGE AND HUMANIST LITERATURE IN THE AGE OF THE JAGIELLONS

Court and Career in the Writings of Rudolf Agricola Junior, Valentin Eck, and Leonard Cox

JACQUELINE GLOMSKI

UNIVERSITY OF TORONTO PRESS
Toronto Buffalo London

Toronto Buffalo London
Printed in Canada

ISBN 978-0-8020-9300-4

Printed on acid-free paper

Library and Archives Canada Cataloguing in Publication

Glomski, Jacqueline
Patronage and humanist literature in the age of the Jagiellons : court and career in the writings of Rudolf Agricola Junior, Valentin Eck, and Leonard Cox / by Jacqueline Glomski.

Includes bibliographical references and index.
ISBN 978-0-8020-9300-4 (bound)

1. Authors and patrons – Europe – History – 16th century. 2. Agricola, Rudolph, ca. 1490–1521 – Criticism and interpretation. 3. Eck, Valentin, 1494?–ca. 1556 – Criticism and interpretation. 4. Cox, Leonard, fl. 1527 – Criticism and interpretation. 5. European literature – Renaissance, 1450–1600 – History and criticism. 6. Humanism in literature. I. Title.

PN731.G56 2007 809′.031 C2007-902828-4

This book has been published with the help of a grant from The Scouloudi Foundation in association with the Institute of Historical Research, London (UK).

University of Toronto Press acknowledges the financial support for its publishing activities of the Government of Canada through the Book Publishing Industry Development Program (BPIDP).

University of Toronto Press acknowledges the financial assistance to its publishing program of the Canada Council for the Arts and the Ontario Arts Council.

Contents

Acknowledgments

The writing of this book was complicated by the extreme rarity of copies of the works of Rudolf Agricola Junior, Valentin Eck, and Leonard Cox – in many cases extant only in unique copies in libraries scattered throughout central and northern Europe. Moreover, when I started my project, bibliographical work was sketchy on Cox and Eck, and had only recently been carried out on Agricola Junior. I am extremely grateful to Stanisław Siess-Krzyszkowski at the Jagiellonian University's Estreicher Bibliographical Unit for help in locating books that I would otherwise never have found.

I should also like to extend my sincere thanks to the staff of the libraries of which I made use: the British Library (Slavonic and East European Collections; Humanities 2 and Rare Books); the Jagiellonian Library, Jagiellonian University, Cracow (Rare Books); the Emeryk Hutten Czapski Museum, Cracow; the Czartoryski Library, Cracow; the Ossoliński Library, Wrocław (Rare Books); the University of Wrocław Library (Rare Books); the Polish National Library, Warsaw; the University of Warsaw Library (Rare Books); the University of Szczecin Library; the Hungarian Academy of Sciences Libraries, Budapest; the National Széchényi Library, Budapest; and the University of London libraries (Warburg Institute, Institute of Historical Research, Institute of Germanic Studies, School of Slavonic and East European Studies, and King's College).

Also helpful to me were the libraries that supplied microfilm and photocopies: Österreichische Nationalbibliothek, Stadtsbibliothek Berlin, Universitetsbibliotek Uppsala, Kórnik Library (Polish Academy of Sciences), Bayerische Staatsbibliothek, Štátny oblastný archív Bytča, and the University of Toronto Library.

Furthermore, I thank the British Academy for grants that enabled me to begin research during the academic year 1999–2000 and the Warburg Institute for release from my duties. During that year, I was kindly received in Warsaw by the Institute of Literary Research at the Polish Academy of Sciences, the Centre for Studies on the Classical Tradition at the University of Warsaw, and the Department of Classical Studies at the University of Warsaw; in Cracow by the Institute of Polish Philology at the Jagiellonian University; in Szczecin by the Institute of Polish Philology at the University of Szczecin; in Budapest by the Institute of Literary Scholarship at the Hungarian Academy of Sciences; and in Louvain by the Seminarium Philologiae Humanisticae at the Katholieke Universiteit Leuven.

I am very grateful to colleagues who read drafts of the chapters: Alejandro Coroleu, Péter Farbaky, John Flood, Robert Frost, Katarzyna Morawska-Muthesius, Erika Rummel, and Piotr Urbański. I am also grateful to colleagues who answered questions or gave advice: Eckhard Bernstein, Gábor Borbély, Andrew Breeze, Karl Heinz Burmeister, Arthur Burns, Elwira Buszewicz, Anne Duggan, Gabriella Erdélyi, James Estes, Albert Gorzkowski, Brenda Hosington, László Jankovits, Jill Kraye, Karen Lambrecht, Charles Lohr, Nicholas Mann, Mieczysław Markowski, David Marsh, Elizabeth McCutcheon, Dorothea McEwan, Halina Mieczkowska, David Money, Cristina Neagu, Howard Norland, Natalia Nowakowska, Klára Pajorin, Jan Papy, Martyn Rady, Stella Revard, Grażyna Rolak, Dirk Sacré, Helena Saktorová, Marcell Sebők, Jeffrey Chipps Smith, Mary Stevens, Hanna Szabelska, Blanka Szeghyová, Ewa Truskolaska, Gábor Tüskés, Andrea Velich, Zofia Wawrykiewicz, Piotr Wilczek, Dieter Wuttke, and Janet Zmroczek. As usual, any errors or omissions remain my own.

This book is dedicated to my spouse, Lorne Whiteway, with thanks for his attentive reading of my manuscript and for his support over the last twenty years.

Illustrations

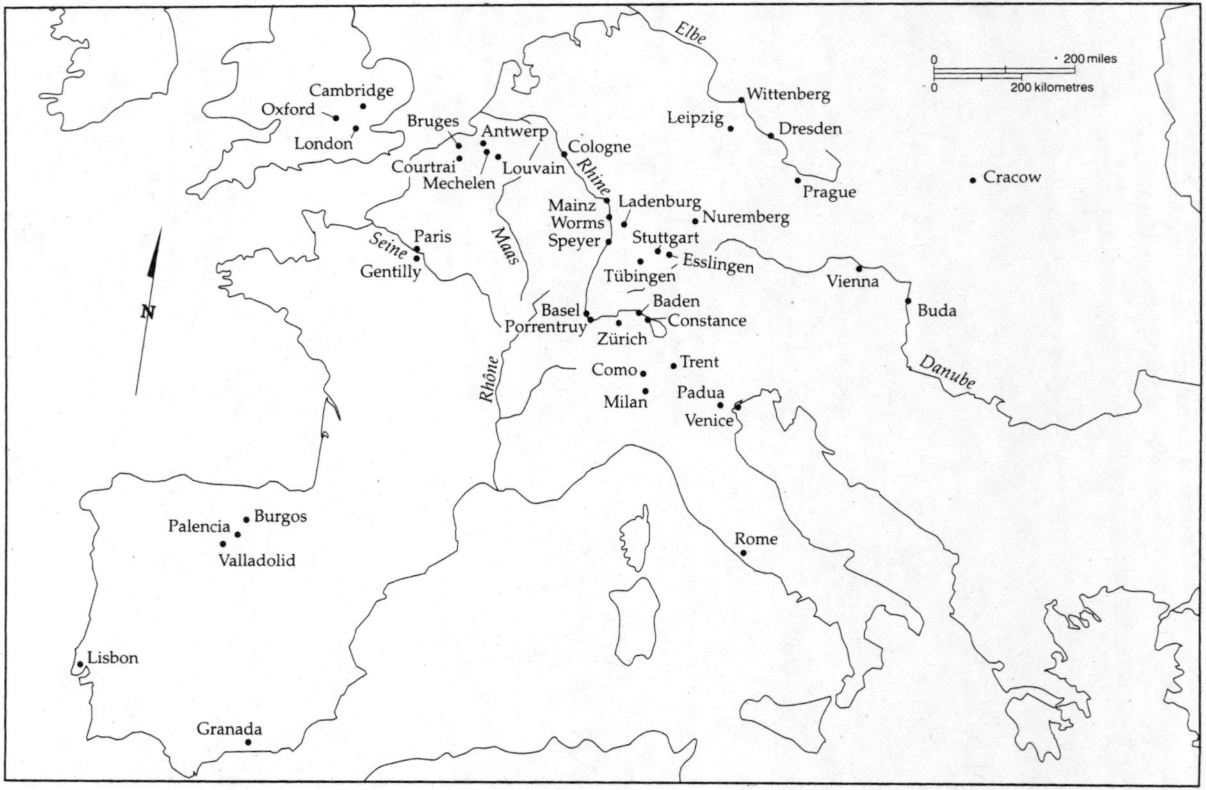

Map 1. Western and central Europe in the sixteenth century. (Cartography Office, Department of Geography, University of Toronto)

Map 2. East central Europe in the early sixteenth century. (Cartography Office, Department of Geography, University of Toronto)

Hymnus de diuo
presule et Mar
tyre Stanislao: tutelari Polo
niæ patrono, per Rudolfum Agricolam poe/
tam a Cæsare laureatum æditus.

161

Fig. 1. Rudolf Agricola Junior, *Hymnus de diuo praesule et martyre Stanislao* (title-page). Cracow, 1519. (Zakład Narodowy im. Ossolińskich, Wrocław)

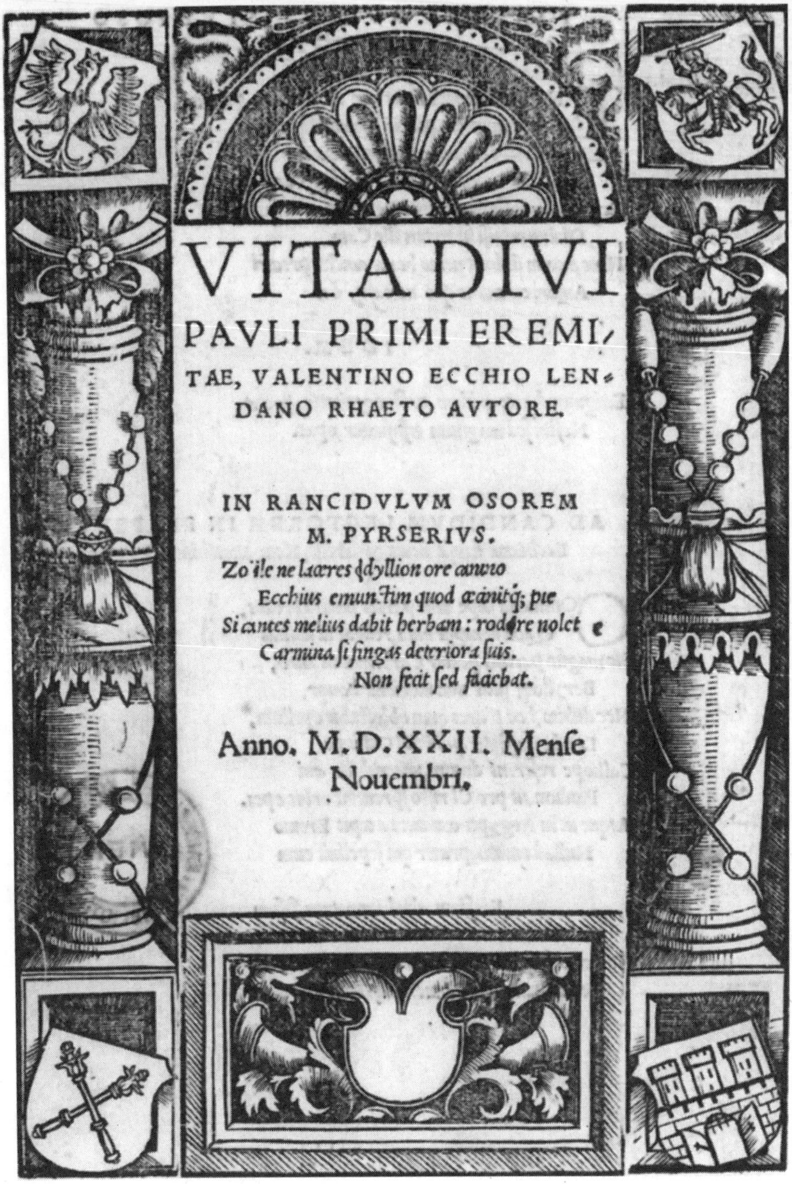

VITA DIVI
PAVLI PRIMI EREMI-
TAE, VALENTINO ECCHIO LEN-
DANO RHAETO AVTORE.

IN RANCIDVLVM OSOREM
M. PYRSERIVS.
Zo'ile ne lacres ꝗdyllion ore canoro
Ecchius emunctim quod cecinitq; pie
Si cantes melius dabit herbam: rodere nolet
Carmina si fingas deteriora suis.
Non scit sed faciebat.

Anno. M.D.XXII. Mense
Nouembri.

Fig. 2. Valentin Eck, *Vita diui Pauli primi eremitae* (title-page). Cracow, 1522. (Österreichische Nationalbibliothek, Vienna)

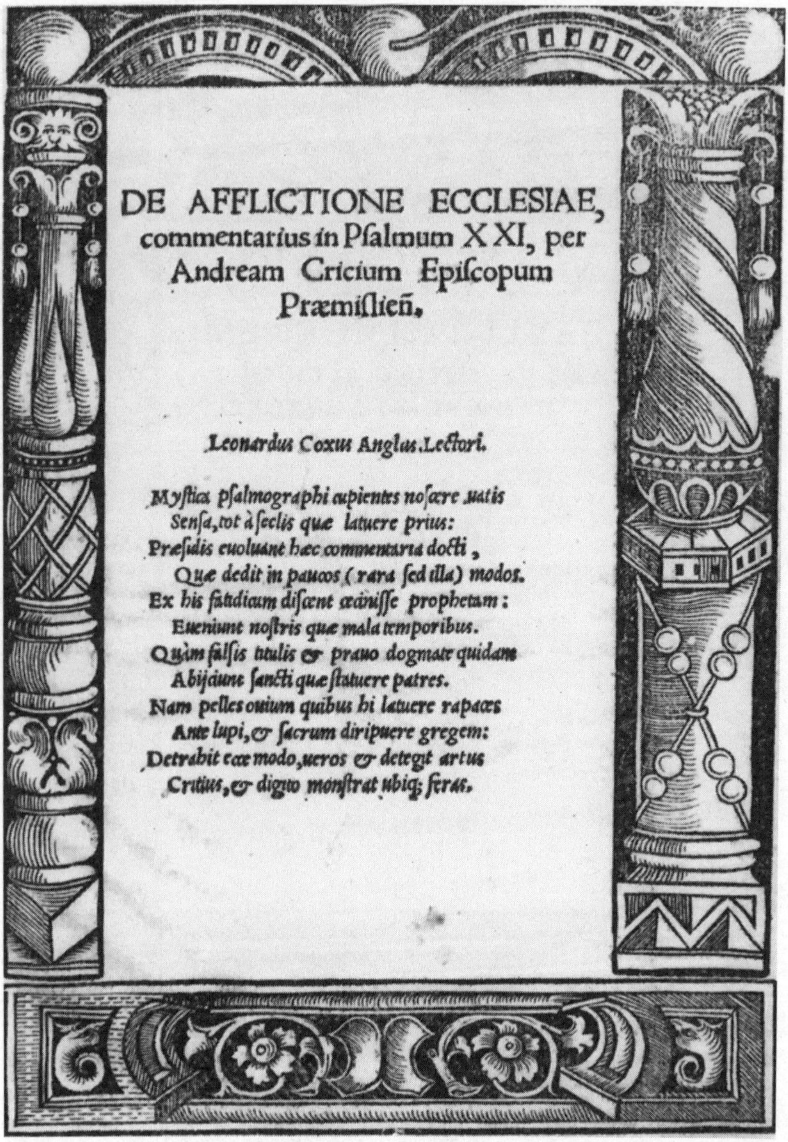

DE AFFLICTIONE ECCLESIAE,
commentarius in Psalmum XXI, per
Andream Cricium Episcopum
Præmislieñ.

Leonardus Coxus Anglus Lectori.

Mystica psalmographi cupientes noscere uatis
Sensa, tot à seclis quae latuere prius:
Præsidis euoluant hæc commentaria docti,
Quæ dedit in paucos (rara sed illa) modos.
Ex his fatidicum discent cecinisse prophetam:
Eueniunt nostris quæ mala temporibus.
Quum falsis titulis & prauo dogmate quidam
Abijciunt sancti quæ statuere patres.
Nam pelles ouium quibus hi latuere rapaces
Ante lupi, & sacrum diripuere gregem:
Detrahit eas modo, ueros & detegit artus
Critius, & digito monstrat ubiq; feras.

Fig. 3. Andreas Cricius (Andrzej Krzycki), *De afflictione Ecclesiae, commentarius in Psalmum XXI* (title-page with commendatory verse by Leonard Cox). Cracow, 1527. (Biblioteka Jagiellońska, Cracow)

PATRONAGE AND HUMANIST LITERATURE IN THE AGE OF THE JAGIELLONS

Introduction

Without patrons and their financial resources, most of the art of early modern Europe would never have come into existence.[1] Patronage not only controlled how much art and literature was produced at that time, but influenced its content and style. During the Middle Ages, the patron-client relationship had attained an intellectual level where, by the dawn of the early modern era, the typical patron was capable of expressing specifically his or her expectations for the finished artistic product and possessed a clear understanding of the technological aspects of that product's completion. The client, on the other hand, had arrived at a comprehension of the character and complexity of his artistic activity and had developed an ability to communicate his role in the process of artistic creation.[2] The client was always working to please his patron, and although the final determination of content and style rested on his creative abilities, he had to keep in mind the patron's tastes and intentions. In the early modern period, art and literature played a key role in the construction of high-profile images for wealthy and powerful patrons. A work of art celebrated the patron's achievements, not so much the talent of the artist.[3]

The patrons of the Renaissance were well aware of the value of the arts as propaganda, of both a temporal and a lasting nature. The function of the artist was to create works that would boost a patron's prestige and promote his or her power and authority. In early modern Europe, conspicuous spending was the chief method of displaying status. Even if, in the Christian culture of the times, wealth was justifiable only if directed to charitable ends, and art was often commissioned in the context of religious duty, the quest for fame was still the motivating factor in patronizing the arts. Philanthropy was not a characteristic of the Renaissance patron. It was fame the patron sought, and it was fame the works of an artist or writer could provide.[4]

The patronage system in early modern Europe not only spawned art of all forms, but also fostered the artistic and literary styles that have come to be identified as 'Renaissance' or 'humanist.' When a new style came into vogue, the involvement of a wealthy and politically influential patron was usually behind its development.[5] East central Europe offered no exception to this process, especially Poland, where a sole member of the ruling Jagiellon family, King Sigismund I, can be considered responsible for the introduction of the Renaissance style in art into his kingdom. The Jagiellons had emerged, at the end of the fifteenth century, as a formidable dynasty that was vying for power with the Habsburgs and restraining the Turks and Tartars from attacking the eastern boundaries of Christian Europe. The art that Sigismund I sponsored at his court in Cracow, from early in the sixteenth century, and that his magnates and nobles subsequently adopted, was international and served the needs of a dynasty with a quasi-imperial outlook, one that ruled a multi-ethnic state and had a broad European perspective.[6] The Latin literature printed at Cracow during Sigismund's reign (1506–48) reflected not only the aesthetic tastes of its patrons, but also the political tensions of east central Europe, on both a domestic and an international level, precisely because it came into existence through the support of some of the most influential people of the region.

The Latin literature printed at Cracow during the period 1510–30 is especially significant in the context of the artistic and literary patronage of the time because the characteristic forms of Renaissance culture took root at Cracow during these years. The Latin literature of the first third of the sixteenth century emerged as a result of the first wave of humanism, fostered by the scholars Filippo Buonaccorsi[7] and Conrad Celtis during their stays in Cracow at the end of the fifteenth century. The taste for a literature based on the imitation of the classics was established during the years 1510–30, and it made possible the flowering of Renaissance literature in Poland at mid-century, as represented by the Latin (and Polish) writings of the poet Jan Kochanowski (1530?–84). In the early sixteenth century, Cracow was an international centre of culture, the site of both a renowned university that attracted nearly half its students from abroad and a booming printing industry that (since no press at Buda existed at this time) served to disseminate learning throughout the region east of Vienna. The writings of the wandering scholars who passed through Cracow reveal that the city functioned as a training ground for humanists who went to work in the provinces of east central Europe and so spread throughout the region the learning they had received at Cracow.

In this book I attempt to identify the aesthetic and rhetorical norms of early humanist writing in the age of the Jagiellons by considering that writing as a product of the patronage system. The tensions inherent in the patron-client relationship shaped a literature that sprang from the negotiation between the tastes of a powerful and wealthy elite and the pens of poor, scholarly Latinists – a literature, therefore, that was wedged between court and *collegium*. My study relies on examples from the work of three itinerant scholar-poets, Rudolf Agricola Junior (*c.* 1490–1521), Valentin Eck (*c.* 1494–1556?), both originally from southern Germany, and Leonard Cox (*c.* 1495–*c.* 1549), an Englishman, who were associated with the courts of Cracow and/or Vienna and/or Buda and who were active in the German-speaking humanist circles operating at the University of Cracow. Of the wandering humanist scholars resident in Cracow during the period 1510–30, it is these three men who have left us the most prominent record of literary and scholarly activity. The Warsaw classicist Tadeusz Bieńkowski referred to them as the three most enterprising humanists of the times, around whom others seemed to gather, and called for more research on their writings.[8]

Yet, in spite of the importance of Agricola Junior, Eck, and Cox as authors of panegyric and political poetry written for the Jagiellonian royals and their magnates, and as organizers of humanist studies at Cracow and disseminators of Renaissance humanist philosophical ideas and of the principles for the writing of Latin poetry and prose throughout east central Europe, their work has attracted only sporadic attention. This may simply be because the writings of Agricola Junior, Eck, and Cox are not regarded as belonging to any national literature. Although Agricola Junior and Eck were born on the shores of Lake Constance, they never returned to Germany after leaving the University of Leipzig.[9] Agricola Junior died in Cracow, having spent his adult life there, except for a three-year stay in Vienna. Eck, after finishing his studies at Cracow, went to live in the Hungarian kingdom. Both

Agricola Junior and Eck travelled through Moravia. Cox, interrupting his stay in Cracow to teach for four years in Hungary, worked for nearly ten years in east central Europe before returning to England.[10] Since the laying of bio-bibliographical foundations in the late nineteenth century by the Silesian scholar Gustav Bauch and the American Frederic Ives Carpenter,[11] only sketchy information on Agricola Junior, Eck, and Cox has appeared, scattered through German, Austrian, Swiss, Hungarian, Czech, Slovakian, Polish, and English historiography.[12] Up to now, there has been no attempt to produce a synthetic study of the works of Agricola Junior, Eck, and Cox. Furthermore, only recently have bibliographies of Agricola Junior's and Eck's writings been compiled,[13] and the biographies of Eck and Cox updated,[14] with research into primary sources.

The question here is, of course, whether the neo-Latin literature printed at Cracow should be considered part of the corpus of Polish literature (or German, or Slovakian, or Hungarian, for that matter, if the nationality of the author is taken into account) written in Latin, or whether it should be treated as a supranational, European literature, existing separately, but on the same basis as the national literatures.[15] In the historiography of Polish literature, this question was avoided until the second half of the twentieth century; before then, the few studies undertaken on neo-Latin writers aimed mostly at tracing the citations of Greek and Roman authors in the early modern text or at analysing the metre of the neo-Latin writer in comparison with his classical model, an approach that, as philologically rigorous as it may be, is limited in that it does not explore the sense of the early modern text, that is, its meaning for contemporary society.[16]

As a resolution to this problem, Piotr Urbański, in his book on the seventeenth-century neo-Latin poet Maciej Kazimierz Sarbiewski, suggests that the analysis of neo-Latin literature should be carried out against the intellectual-cultural background of its epoch, conscious both of the literary norms that neo-Latin authors absorbed from the reading of classical texts and of those they took from contemporary aesthetics.[17] The reception of Renaissance literary norms at Cracow in the 1510s and 1520s, when the Polish elite began to favour the Italianate style in art and literature, was complex because the norms of this style, which was itself based on a renewal of the classics, were absorbed directly from Italy as well as mediated through Hungary and Germany. Unless scholars can accommodate in their views the historical context in which the humanist Latin literature of east central Europe was created, this literature will never be thoroughly understood.

All this means that very little has been written to explain how the neo-Latin literature printed at Cracow in the sixteenth century arose as part of the patronage system, even though patronage was the factor that enabled the production of this literature in the first place.[18] Although it is impossible to know exactly how the writings of the itinerant poets of east central Europe were received and read during their lifetimes, their work can be properly appreciated only if it is analysed against the social and political phenomenon of patronage. As an attempt, then, to place humanist literature in its historical context, my book builds upon the suggestions of Eckhard Bernstein, who, considering the central European humanists of the early sixteenth century as a social group, has examined their consolidated actions and aspirations, and characterized them as 'outsiders' who aspired to achieve the status of 'insiders,' that is, to be accepted as teachers, scholars, and writers at the courts, at the universities, and in town governments of the region.[19] My book also takes into account Christine Treml's study of the central European humanists from a sociological perspective, which analysed their forms of communication and their notions of friendship and of morality and behaviour. Furthermore, the results of my research agree with the findings of Albert Schirrmeister, that the *poetae* successfully exploited the patronage system.[20] Finally, my book owes a debt to the work done by the art historians Thomas DaCosta Kaufmann, Andreas Tönnesmann, and Péter Farbaky, as well as by the Jagiellonian research unit at Geisteswissenschaftliches Zentrum Geschichte und Kultur Ostmitteleuropas in Leipzig on the patronage and politics of the Jagiellonian monarchs and their magnates in relation to the visual arts of the early sixteenth century.[21] It is my hope that, as a culmination of my research on Agricola Junior, Eck, and Cox over the past fifteen years,[22] my book can convincingly argue the significance of their work (in particular) and of early humanism at Cracow (in general) to an anglophone audience.

An examination of the work of Rudolf Agricola Junior, Valentin Eck, and Leonard Cox shows that humanist writers of east central Europe formed a specific identity for their patrons and portrayed, with a humanist slant, the accomplishments of these dignitaries in poetry and prose, while at the same time representing their own role in the conferring of fame upon their patrons. Their writing supported the political ambitions of those people who sustained the imperial pretensions of King Sigismund in order to maintain his influence in the region, which extended from the Baltic to the Black Sea, and to ensure that the Jagiellons remained as European monarchs of the first rank.

As did the writing of their predecessors, especially the poet Paulus Crosnensis (a Ruthenian who studied in Germany, taught at the University of Cracow, and was patronized by a Hungarian nobleman), the work of these three foreign 'newcomers' gives historians a comprehensive view of the process by which intellectual and cultural trends, in this case the conventions of Renaissance humanist Latin, seeped into and spread across east central Europe in the early sixteenth century. Although the writings of the domestic authors of the times, such as Johannes Dantiscus and Andrzej Krzycki, were inspired by Italian trends and are examples of how these trends came into Poland, their work was generally confined to court circles and did not affect the humanist literary groups congregating on the fringes of the University of Cracow, who would go back to their towns of origin, or move on to take up work in other provincial centres, and continue writing and teaching.[23]

My book views the work of Agricola Junior, Eck, and Cox from the position of the poet-clients and demonstrates how they used the panegyric and political poetry they wrote in honour of their patrons not only to advance these patrons, but also to advance themselves and their own humanist cause. I will begin my study with an examination of the writer's strategies for career building, based on the images he used to represent himself vis-à-vis his patrons and his writing. Regarding Agricola Junior, Eck, and Cox as educators who took their academic knowledge of the *ars uersificandi* to the service of the court, I will then analyse their panegyric poetry and explore how, in glorifying the qualities and deeds of their patrons, they turned them, by using a specific rhetoric to create the image of a great man who would support their own goals, into 'humanist heroes.' I will look, moreover, at the public image of the Polish and Hungarian kings and ecclesiastical and lay dignitaries formed by Rudolf Agricola Junior and Valentin Eck in their occasional and political poetry, and will assess the poets' role in producing propaganda that furthered the politics of their patrons. I will demonstrate how the poets stressed their own function in the creation of everlasting fame for the Jagiellonian royals and their magnates in order to create an image of their indispensability at court, and how they promoted their own ideas along with the political program of the dignitaries they praised, through their manipulation of their patrons' images in conformity with their own philosophy of the ideal ruler. The goal of my book, a study of the functioning and the products of literary patronage under the Jagiellons in the early sixteenth century, is to signal the importance of the writings of Agricola Junior, Eck, and Cox as a body of literature that was capable of expressing political aspirations and cultural concepts at national and regional levels, but that up to now has been considered marginal or ephemeral, and been unjustifiably overlooked.

ONE

Patronage and Humanist Literature at Cracow, 1510–1530: The Careers of Rudolf Agricola Junior, Valentin Eck, and Leonard Cox

DYNASTIC POLITICS AND ARTISTIC PATRONAGE IN EARLY SIXTEENTH-CENTURY POLAND: THE INTRODUCTION OF THE NEW STYLE

The early years of the sixteenth century ushered Poland into its Golden Age. When King Sigismund I[1] ascended the throne in 1506, he infused Polish politics with a vigour and flair that secured Poland[2] a place on the highest rung of European monarchies.[3] Sigismund was a firm governor and an astute negotiator who organized the defence of his vast borders and pursued a policy of peace at home. He was also a refined and learned man who promoted a cultural life among his magnates. Sigismund brought the institution of artistic patronage on the Italian model to Poland by employing artists on his castle staff, and through his patronage he introduced Renaissance Italian art into Poland.[4] He was not the first Jagiellonian patron of art – in this role he followed his father and his elder brothers – but his initiative prompted 'a tremendous artistic revolution' at Cracow at the beginning of the sixteenth century.[5] The new art forms, once planted on Polish soil, were able to flourish owing to a favourable economic climate, characterized by prosperous landlords who were enjoying increased demands in the export market for their agricultural products, and by wealthy urban patricians and merchants who were thriving as a result of their interests in banking and mining.[6]

Sigismund's patronizing of the arts on a grand scale at Cracow most likely began with a concern to create an image of himself and his family that befitted a European power. He understood that the advancement of the dynasty's prestige was one means of legitimizing the dynasty's rule. The legitimization of his family's authority in Poland would have been important to Sigismund because his own family had foreign roots. The Jagiellonian dynasty had come into being in 1386, with the marriage of Jogaila, the grand duke of Lithuania, to Jadwiga, the unmarried queen of Poland and last of her line; Jogaila accepted Christianity and became known as Władysław Jagiełło.

Sigismund's artistic projects were sparked by a need to express his family's imperial pretensions, that is, its intent to establish its influence in the whole of east central Europe, especially in relation to the Habsburg dynasty. Sigismund's father, Casimir Jagiellon, who ruled Poland-Lithuania from 1447 to 1492, had raised Poland to one of the two great powers of central Europe during the last quarter of the fifteenth century. He emerged triumphant from the struggles for the crowns of Bohemia and Hungary in 1471, when his eldest son, Vladislav Jagiellon, was elected king of Bohemia after the death of Jiří Poděbrady, and in 1490, when Vladislav was elected king of Hungary after the death of Matthias Corvinus. The Jagiellons now held territory extending from the Baltic Sea to the Adriatic coast, and from Prague in the west almost to Moscow in the east. Vladislav II sat on the thrones of Bohemia and Hungary until his death in 1516. In the meantime, his younger brothers, Jan Olbracht (1492–1501), Alexander (1501–6), and Sigismund (1506–48) were ruling Poland-Lithuania. Having witnessed the extinction of the influence of the Luxemburg and Anjou families in central Europe and having replaced the Bohemian and Hungarian 'national' kings, the Jagiellons were left to face the Habsburgs, whose greatest success in penetrating east central Europe would come from arranging strategic marriages.

Emperor Maximilian I, in control of the Habsburgs' Austrian holdings since his father's death in 1493, had first attended to diplomacy in the West by marrying his son Philip to Juana of Aragon, an act that established the possibility that a male offspring of the marriage would inherit, as Charles V eventually did, thereby bringing Spain under Habsburg control. But Maximilian also had pretensions in the East. He coveted the Bohemian and Hungarian thrones for his family, but the Poles (together with the Hungarians) stood in his way. During the years 1505–7, Maximilian increased his influence at the Buda court and succeeded in obtaining a secret agreement with Vladislav II to have his grandchildren married to Vladislav's children, thus creating the prospect of a

Habsburg succession to the Hungarian throne. Maximilian then supported the enemies of the Jagiellons by encouraging the hostilities of the Teutonic Knights and the Muscovites towards Poland. In the winter of 1512–13, the Muscovite army, assisted by the Habsburgs, laid siege to towns along the Lithuanian border. In the meantime, the Teutonic Knights, also with help from Maximilian, were preparing an uprising, which would erupt into the war of 1519–21 in Prussia.

By 1514, Sigismund, as a result of losses on his Lithuanian frontier, had concluded that he should negotiate with Maximilian not only in order to avoid an open confrontation with him, but, even more, in order to continue his campaign in the East unhampered. A meeting of the three monarchs, Sigismund I, Vladislav II, and Maximilian I, known as the Congress of Vienna, took place in July 1515, at which negotiations begun by Vladislav II in 1506, to have his daughter Anna marry the emperor's grandson Ferdinand and his son Louis marry the emperor's granddaughter Maria, were concluded. The agreements permitted the expansion of the Habsburgs' influence beyond the Danube and eventually the integration of the Jagiellonian realms into the network of Habsburg alliances. For Sigismund, though, the Congress of 1515 was a positive accomplishment, in that the emperor backed down from his compact with the Muscovites and assumed responsibility for elaborating an agreement between them and the Poles. In 1517 an envoy sent from Vienna, Baron Sigismund von Herberstein, would achieve an agreement with Moscow.

Yet Sigismund, by trying to save his Lithuanian positions in the East, had resigned from his interests in the West. The pro-Habsburg faction in Hungary would push its country towards war with Turkey. Unaware of the extent of the military power possessed by the Turks, the Hungarians were slaughtered when they met them in battle at Mohács in August 1526. Vladislav II's son, Louis II, was killed, and his brother-in-law, Ferdinand Habsburg, would succeed him as king of Hungary.

Art historians have concluded that Sigismund was conscious that his political efforts needed to be accompanied by a campaign of cultural activity and renewal of the arts. The king understood that the claim to rule and the advancement of the dynasty could not be credibly represented through political and military means alone and that an image of power had to be promoted as well, through art patronized by the monarch.[7] Sigismund began his career as a patron even before his ascent to the throne.[8] His first project saw him commissioning Francesco Fiorentino, an Italian artist summoned to Cracow from Hungary, to sculpt an architectural surround for the niche tomb of his deceased brother Jan Olbracht, which was completed in 1505. The arch, full of allusions to Roman triumphal glory, amounted to a turning point in the history of Polish art. Not only was it the first piece of art in the Italian Renaissance style to be completed at Cracow, but its iconography hinted at Sigismund's reasons for the introduction of a new style into Poland – to stress his family's imperial aspirations to cross-border rule in east central Europe.[9]

Sigismund's next project saw Fiorentino undertaking the first phase of the reconstruction of the royal castle on Wawel Hill, on which he worked until his death in 1516. The renovation work would be continued from 1524 until 1529 by a certain Master Benedikt, and then by the Florentine Bartolommeo Berrecci from 1530 until his death in 1537.[10] These architects gave the castle a distinctive arcaded courtyard, the earliest surviving example of an arcaded courtyard with Italianate forms in central Europe.[11] At the same time as the castle was being renovated, Sigismund commissioned Berrecci to execute the most important and influential work of art produced in early sixteenth-century Poland: the Sigismund chapel in the Wawel cathedral, which was to house the graves of Sigismund and his son Sigismund August and to remain as a monument to the glory of the Jagiellons and the magnificence of Poland's 'Golden Age.' The cube-shaped chapel, with niches in its walls for the effigies of the kings, was surmounted by a windowed drum, finished with a half-elliptical dome, which was itself surmounted by a high, round lantern. On the exterior, the lantern was topped with a crown; the surface of the dome was covered in silvered metal sheets.[12] The interior of the chapel was filled with sculpture exhibiting both pagan and religious images of kingship and employing various motifs of triumph.[13] The mausoleum was intended as propaganda to justify Sigismund's claim to be the ideal monarch, and as a testimony to his *magnificentia*.[14]

There is no question of Sigismund's commitment to patronage of the arts. His architectural projects occupied him throughout most of his reign. The king pressed on with work on Wawel castle, even when it was hampered by a fire in 1536, until the middle of the century. The construction of the exterior of the Sigismund chapel alone took thirteen years, and the whole work was not finished until 1538, when the interior was completed. Moreover, in order to carry out these projects, Sigismund needed to borrow money from the Cracow bankers Johann and Severin Boner, who became his contractors for the castle renovation and the building of the chapel.[15]

Sigismund's choice of the Italian style evidently stemmed from his contact with Italian artists during his stay at his brother Vladislav's court in Buda in the 1490s, where Italian art had been favoured since the reign of Vladislav's predecessor, Matthias Corvinus, long before Sigismund's marriage to the Milanese princess Bona Sforza in 1518. According to art historians, his subsequent predilection for Italian art was no accident. Sigismund was following cultural trends only in as much as the option for the 'new style' was a means of self-assertion in political and social competition. During the first half of the sixteenth century, Italianate architecture, evocative of 'the modern' and connotative of wealth and power, was employed as a means of demonstrating rank, even as a political manifesto, by princely patrons throughout central Europe.[16]

By mid-century, Sigismund's wealthier subjects would be imitating his patronage of architecture and sculpture. Magnates, affluent burghers, and high-ranking clergymen would begin erecting or remodelling private residences and public buildings in the Italian Renaissance style or in the hybrid, so-called Gothic-Renaissance style that would last long into the sixteenth century. This latter was an amalgamation that resulted from the interaction of Polish patrons, who were, of course, familiar with the patronage of their Hungarian counterparts, with German and Italian artists. King Sigismund's predecessors at Cracow had favoured a flamboyant Gothic, epitomized by the work of Veit Stoss in the town church of St Mary. After the arrival of the Italians, some of whom had come to Cracow via Hungary, the German artists stayed on, dominating in some media but working alongside the Italians in others.[17] A similar trend took hold in the literature of the period: many of the writers patronized by the Polish elite were Germans who imitated Italian-Latin literature, combining it with native, northern elements, and also exhibiting an awareness of Hungarian-Latin writing. Such hybrid forms demonstrate that the Renaissance in Poland, although it was influenced chiefly by Italian culture, was, in reality, a multinational phenomenon.

So, following the example of his king, Justus Ludovicus Decius, royal secretary and monetary adviser, would, in 1535, employ the workshop of the royal architect Bartolommeo Berrecci to build an Italianate villa for himself, in a wood near Cracow that he named 'Wola Justowska.' The Cracow town square itself was transformed by the remodelling of the town houses of the important merchant families, a transformation that entailed the use of Renaissance ornaments. Severin Boner, for example, added a Renaissance parapet to the roof of his house on the market square. The ornamentation has been attributed to the sculptor known as 'il Padovano,' an Italian working in Poland during the middle of the sixteenth century. The parapet must have been completed by Severin's death in 1549, in which case it pre-dates the parapet of the famous Cracow Cloth Hall, standing in the middle of the square, by at least six years.[18] Furthermore, the mixing of Gothic and Italianate forms resulted in a type of grand castle, modelled on work done at Wawel, which spread throughout the southern and central regions of Poland.[19] Examples were the castles of the Boner family at Ogrodzieniec (1530–45), of Archbishop Maciej Drzewicki's family at Drzewica (from before 1527 to 1535), and of Grand-Chancellor Krzysztof Szydłowiecki's family at Szydłowiec (before 1526) and at Ćmielów (1519–31).[20]

Sculptures in the Italian style, especially for memorial chapels, also proved popular. In as early as 1516 the archbishop of Gniezno, Jan Łaski, commissioned a series of tomb slabs from Johannes Fiorentinus, an Italian who was active in Hungary. Łaski made a trip in 1516 to Hungary as ambassador of King Sigismund, and there met with the Hungarian primate Tamás Bakócz, who was building a chapel at Esztergom; Łaski presumably became acquainted with the work of Johannes at that time. The slabs, executed in red Hungarian marble, served as memorials for Łaski and his ecclesiastical benefactors and relatives. This type of slab, a wreath with a coat of arms in the middle, was afterwards frequently imitated in Poland, an example being the tomb of Archbishop Maciej Drzewicki (d. 1535) in Gniezno.[21]

In many cases, it has been difficult to identify the artists responsible for the execution of Italianate sculpture in Poland and therefore to know the details of the patron-client relationship. For example, Berrecci erected a funerary chapel for Piotr Tomicki, bishop of Cracow and vice-chancellor of the kingdom, while he was working on the chapel for the king. Yet Tomicki's tomb, housed within the chapel and previously ascribed to Padovano – it is known that Tomicki did commission a tabernacle intended for the Wawel cathedral from Padovano in 1533 – might be the work of Berrecci.[22] Berrecci's workshop was probably responsible for the execution of the sepulchral monument (1521) of the Cracow bishop Jan Konarski.[23] The sculptor of the tomb (1533–6) of the grand-chancellor, Krzysztof Szydłowiecki, in the collegiate church at Opatów, considered to be one of the most original works of Renaissance sepulchral art in east central Europe, was most likely from the workshop of Giovanni Cini, yet another Italian artist active in Poland in the middle of the sixteenth century.[24]

LITERARY PATRONAGE AT CRACOW I: THE SUPPORTERS OF HUMANIST LATIN

Sigismund's patronage in other areas did not match his sponsorship of architecture and the visual arts, his only other major interest being music.[25] Sigismund never advanced the cause of literature as an art form, leaving it to the Polish nobles and the court of his wife Bona to make a more substantial contribution to the development of literature and humanism in Poland.[26] This may have been a practical choice rather than a personal one: in spite of the Renaissance poets' claim that they were able to immortalize their patrons, the powerful elite had traditionally preferred the visual arts, especially architecture with its imposing form, which they saw as conferring lasting fame.

Nevertheless, Sigismund understood the value of literature for the purposes of political propaganda. He supported the writings of his secretaries Justus Ludovicus Decius, Johannes Dantiscus, and Andrzej Krzycki,[27] which chronicled his military campaigns against the Teutonic Knights, the Muscovites, and the Walachians, and which reported on his suppression of the Gdańsk uprising. Aside from these three poets, an international coterie of writers emerged to celebrate the major events of Sigismund's early reign: his marriages (1512 and 1518), his victory over the Muscovites at Orsha (1514), and his participation in the Congress of Vienna (1515). Furthermore, cycles of poems grew up around the protracted struggles with the Teutonic Knights and the Turks.[28]

The masterpiece of all the Sigismundan literary propaganda was Decius's three-part history in honour of the ruling dynasty,

De uetustatibus Polonorum, De Iagellonum familia, De Sigismundi regis temporibus (Cracow, 1521).[29] Decius's writing created an image of Sigismund and the Jagiellonian dynasty as a European power of the first rank; his use of the Italian Renaissance style, in this case the conventions of Latin humanist literature, served to express the political and social ambitions of the Jagiellonian monarchs. The innovation of Decius's writing is signalled, furthermore, by his book's being the first to chronicle contemporary Polish events.[30]

It has been said that Decius's history was intended for the highest class of Polish society, and thus for a small circle of educated readers.[31] Yet, even in the late medieval period, Polish chronicles composed in Latin functioned partially as illustrations for a foreign audience of the position of Poland and its monarchy in Europe,[32] and it is most probable that Decius's work was intended as political propaganda directed not only at a Polish audience (in its legitimization of the rule of an ethnically foreign, and originally pagan, line), but also at an international readership (in its presentation of a tough Polish-Lithuanian stance in the face of an ever-expanding Habsburg empire).[33] Written in Latin, the book could reach beyond the Cracow elite to the extensive territories ruled over by Sigismund and his nephew Louis II. Latin, moreover, was the linguistic glue that bound Poland-Lithuania to the rest of central Europe, and to the West.

In his work, Decius represented the Jagiellonian family as a dynasty of European standing, ruling over a vast multi-ethnic kingdom, allied to the West. Decius preceded the history of Sigismund's reign (*De Sigismundi regis temporibus*) with a geopolitical and cultural description of Poland, giving the location of the country and listing its regions and their geographic boundaries. He named the Roman Catholic bishoprics and their incumbents, and also mentioned the minority religions, such as the pagan, Jewish, and Greek Orthodox. He explained the ranks of the Polish dignitaries (the palatines, castellans, etc.) and of the royal offices (grand-chancellor, vice-chancellor, marshal, and treasurer). He noted that the nobles generally spoke three or four languages and, above all, Latin. Decius pointed out that the business of the royal chancellery was recorded in Latin. The Poles, like the Italians, learned Latin easily, and, because of this, were better educated than most other nations. Besides Latin, almost all the nobles spoke German and Hungarian, and often Italian. Lithuanian and Ruthenian were also commonly heard.[34] Decius found it advantageous to include information on his own background as an Alsatian immigrant.

Decius's glorification of Sigismund as sovereign, lawgiver, and warrior, and as a member of a dynasty and the bearer of a historical tradition, was enhanced by the woodcut illustrations included in the book. The title-page to the complete work contains a border in which, at the top, the Polish army is shown slaying the eastern hordes and, at the bottom, the Polish eagle is displayed entwined with an 'S' (for 'Sigismundus'). The third section of the history, that dedicated to the reign of Sigismund, has its own title-page, on which there appears a portrait of the king. This was the first official portrait of Sigismund in which he was depicted as *rex armatus* – shown in a right-facing profile, wearing armour, with a crown on his head and a sword and sceptre in his hands, and surrounded by the coats of arms of the provinces of his realm.[35] Below the portrait is a laudatory epigram composed by the Viennese professor of poetics Philipp Gundel.[36] The next two folios contain a large portrait of Sigismund's son and heir, Sigismund August, as well as a portrait of his queen, Bona, each with verses by Gundel. Between the two portraits is a magnificent two-page spread of the Jagiellon family tree, in which each member of the family is represented by a miniature woodcut portrait.

These woodcuts along with those printed in Matthias de Mechovia's *Chronica Polonorum*, produced during the years 1519–21, were the first illustrations in Polish books to depart from the Gothic and to exhibit the new style in the graphic arts.[37] Furthermore, the woodcut portraits of Sigismund I that appeared in *De Sigismundi regis temporibus* and in the king's official statutes issued in 1524 (in which, in the first edition, Sigismund wears, instead of armour, a royal brocaded coat with fur trim and holds a sceptre and, instead of a sword, an orb) were almost certainly based on official portraits of Emperor Maximilian (which in turn had been inspired by Italian state portraits), showing a right-facing profile of the emperor dressed in knight's armour with a coronation cape on top and a crown on his head, and holding a sceptre and sword – insignia symbolizing responsibility towards the state, law and order, and military and administrative authority. Although the transfer to the woodcuts of Sigismund of the iconographical formula employed to represent Maximilian may well have been due to a lack of any other 'ready' formula to represent the Polish ruler, it may also have borne some underlying message, that is, it may have asserted the sovereignty of Polish rule in relation to the emperor.[38]

Just as Sigismund used Latin literature to promote his policies and enhance his prestige, so the Polish magnates, church dignitaries, and wealthy townsmen patronized the new literature with a view to self-aggrandizement. But, as Sigismund – unlike Emperor Maximilian – exhibited no interest in fostering graphic media as an art form, it was left to the Polish elite to fill in this gap in royal patronage. This group took on the task of promoting humanist culture at Cracow in the first quarter of the sixteenth century and became the principal supporters of young scholar-poets.[39] Their patronage of literature was often part of assistance to learning in general, with patrons either building schools, establishing tutorial groups at their courts, or financing lectures at the University of Cracow, all venues where the exponents of humanism taught. In thanks for their support, these literary patrons had educational treatises and handbooks and editions of classical and Italian neo-Latin authors dedicated to them, and they became the subjects of numerous panegyric and occasional poems.

The Cracow elite opted for a literary style based on the renewal of the classics and on the emulation of Italian neo-Latin literature. Italian humanism first crept into Poland through ecclesiastical contacts at the councils of Constance and Basel,[40] and then gained a foothold in Cracow at the end of the fifteenth century largely thanks to the energies of an Italian academic, Filippo Buonaccorsi. Buonaccorsi, whose Latin pseudonym was Callimachus, had fled Rome because of an involvement in a conspiracy to assassinate the anti-humanist Pope Paul II and had been granted refuge by Gregorius Sanocensis, the bishop of Lwów, in 1470.[41] Buonaccorsi eventually became a foreign policy adviser to the kings Casimir Jagiellon and Jan Olbracht, and until his death in 1496 remained in Cracow, where he composed erotic poetry, historical biography, and political treatises.

The Polish magnates' and nobles' own travels and periods of study abroad strengthened their interest in Italian humanism, and also introduced them to the writings of Erasmus, an author who would expand their notions of neo-Latin literature. The Poles admired Erasmus's scholarship and began to collect his books and correspond with him.[42] Extant correspondence indicates that as many as twenty-two members of the social and political elite, including the king himself, exchanged letters with Erasmus from October 1523 until Erasmus's death in 1536, on topics ranging from politics and religion to personal news. At least eleven of these Polish dignitaries actually visited Erasmus,[43] and eight of them received from Erasmus the dedication of one or more of his books.[44]

The most influential of all the Cracow courtiers, Piotr Tomicki (1464–1535), the vice-chancellor of the kingdom,[45] had studied in Italy. Tomicki was, next to the royal couple, probably the most powerful person in the kingdom.[46] After receiving his MA degree from Cracow, he went to study at Bologna, where in 1500 he was awarded a doctorate in canon law. Tomicki entered the royal service in 1506, and was named vice-chancellor in 1515. He simultaneously rose up the church hierarchy, being appointed bishop of Przemyśl in 1514, of Poznań in 1520, and of Cracow in 1525. He was a vital supporter of humanist studies at Cracow and one of the patrons of Rudolf Agricola Junior and Leonard Cox. Tomicki was also a frequent correspondent of Erasmus, who dedicated to Tomicki his second edition of Seneca.

A second influential court figure, Krzysztof Szydłowiecki (1467–1532),[47] the grand-chancellor, travelled widely as an ambassador for the royal court, acted as the king's 'right-hand man,' and maintained his own splendid courts at Cracow and at Ćmielów. Szydłowiecki patronized the wandering young humanist writers of the region, among them Rudolf Agricola Junior and Leonard Cox. Like Tomicki, Szydłowiecki was in contact with Erasmus, who dedicated his treatise *Lingua* to him. Both Szydłowiecki and Tomicki amassed great libraries; both were patrons of Stanisław Samostrzelnik, the most outstanding miniaturist of the times and the initiator of the Renaissance style in Polish book illumination.[48]

The marriage of Sigismund to Bona Sforza in 1518 intensified the contact between the Polish nobles and Italy. When Bona arrived in Cracow, she brought a retinue of 287 Italians, of whom at least half remained in Poland. In the first half of the sixteenth century, such courtiers formed the largest group of Italian immigrants in Poland. Bona's chancellor, Ludovico Alifio (1499–1543), a lawyer, was active in humanist circles; he delivered a series of lectures on Roman law at the university during the academic year

1518–19, and oversaw the education of Bona and Sigismund's son and heir, Sigismund August. Bona's court thus became a focus for humanist learning. Andrzej Krzycki (1482–1537), the nephew of Bishop Tomicki, who had studied in Italy and who wrote humanist Latin poetry, served as her secretary until 1522. Rudolf Agricola Junior was hired to tutor her Italian pages. Bona herself became the subject of humanist panegyrics and received the dedication of religious works.[49]

From the royal and ecclesiastical courts, the patronage of Latin humanist literature spread quickly to the upper classes of Cracow. By the end of the fifteenth century, the patrician class of the city was made up mostly of German-immigrant merchants and bankers. These families were very influential in Polish society, and some of their members were ennobled by the king. They came to play an important part in promoting the new trends, through their support of the itinerant German poets and their fostering of the cult of Erasmus.[50]

Justus Ludovicus Decius (*c.* 1485–1545), the author of the aforementioned three-part history of the Jagiellonian family, was the foremost of these burgher-patrician literary patrons. He had come to Cracow from Alsace in 1508, became secretary to the Boner banking family, and, through the influence of Piotr Tomicki, was in 1520 named royal secretary and ennobled by the king.[51] From 1526 to 1535, he acted as monetary adviser to the king. Despite his lack of a university education, Decius was familiar with Italian humanism, as he had been sent on a number of missions to Italy on behalf of the Boners and of the king in the late 1510s and early 1520s. He and his sons built up an impressive library of theology, literature, history, and natural history.[52] Decius was the dedicatee of Erasmus's *Precatio Dominica*, printed at Basel in 1523, and he patronized the republication at Cracow of Erasmus's *De conscribendis epistolis* in 1523 and of his *Precatio* in 1525. (He had stopped in Basel to meet Erasmus on his return to Poland from Italy in 1520.) He took an interest in and promoted the educational writings of the Cracow humanists, such as the first edition of Valentin Eck's *De arte uersificandi opusculum* in 1515.

The Boner family had come from Alsace in the late fifteenth century, and the head of the family, Johann Boner (d. 1523), built up what was the biggest banking house in Poland up to that time. When Johann entered the ranks of the magnates, his nephew Severin (1466–1549) took over the business, part of which involved directing the renovation work on Wawel Hill for the king. Severin owned much property, including both a castle at Balice, just to the west of Cracow, and his town house on the main square in Cracow. Severin patronized a whole group of wandering humanists, many of whom were from Silesia, and had many religious and educational works dedicated to him. He sent his young son Jan to meet with Erasmus in Freiburg. Erasmus dedicated his edition of Terence's comedies in 1532 to Jan and his brother Stanisław. The Boners were associated commercially and socially with the Bethmanns and the Salomons, who also supported art and learning at Cracow.[53]

Cracow was not an island, but rather a link in the chain of commercial-cultural centres of east central Europe that included Vienna, Buda, and Prague, and the sub-centres of Olomouc and Wrocław.[54] These cities were instrumental in the proliferation of the new styles in art and literature because they communicated west and central European cultural innovations throughout the region, mainly through the personal contacts of the upper social classes.[55] Such contacts were exemplified by the Thurzó family, who were instrumental in promoting Renaissance art and humanist literature in Poland and Hungary.[56] Merchants and mining magnates and associates of the Fugger banking dynasty, the Thurzós had originated in Austria and migrated to the northern Hungarian kingdom, where they established their family seat in the region known as the Szepes, now the Spiš in eastern Slovakia.[57] In Cracow they maintained a residence in Szczepańska Street from the 1460s until the 1550s. The Thurzó town house in Lőcse and castle at Betlenfalva were both ornamented in the Renaissance style, and reflected the artistic communication between Cracow and Upper Hungary at the time.[58] Aside from the family's commercial interests, two Thurzó brothers held bishoprics in the early sixteenth century: Johann (1464–1520), bishop of Wrocław (from 1506), and Stanislaus (1471–1540), bishop of Olomouc (from 1497), both of whom fostered the arts in their cities. A younger brother, Alexius (*c.* 1490–1543), became a royal secretary at the Buda court and flourished there to become the chief justice of Hungary and vice-regent under the Habsburg reign after the battle of Mohács. He endowed a church and school at Lőcse and was the chief patron of Valentin Eck.

Humanism in literature could easily gain ground throughout east central Europe because the Latin language had long before crossed the borders of the multi-ethnic lands of the area and had unified those lands into a homogenized European regional culture.[59] If humanist literature was at first transmitted mainly by personal contacts, it rapidly came to be circulated through the medium of printing and publishing. The lack of a press in Buda in the first quarter of the sixteenth century reinforced the cultural triangle of Cracow–Buda–Vienna because the literature patronized by the magnates of Hungary normally had to be printed either at Cracow or at Vienna.[60] These three cities were connected by a trail of publications left either in Cracow or in Vienna by the itinerant German poets, such as Rudolf Agricola Junior, Caspar Ursinus Velius, Georg Werner, and Georg von Logau, who rubbed elbows as they passed through them, according to the circumstances of their residence in a given year. Such transience was reflected in the business of the Vietor press, a major publisher of humanist literature, which had an office in Vienna from 1510 to 1518, and in Cracow from 1518 until the 1540s.[61]

Through the writing of humanists active in the Cracow-Buda-Vienna triangle, the names of men already entwined in Jagiellon and Habsburg politics became connected in literature. Accordingly, we see the names of such dignitaries as György Szatmári (*c.* 1457–1524), the leading Hungarian statesman under the Jagiellon kings Vladislav II and Louis II, and Augustinus Moravus (1467–1513),[62] provost of Olomouc and Brno under Bishop Stanislaus Thurzó, appearing in print at Cracow.[63] Szatmári, bishop of Pécs and then archbishop of Esztergom, was one of Hungary's greatest patrons of arts and letters of the time,[64] as evidenced by his building projects at Kassa, his birthplace, and at Pécs and Esztergom, and by his support of humanist Latin literature. Moravus, formerly a secretary at the royal court in Buda, worked with Stanislaus Thurzó to promote humanistic studies and the arts in Moravia.

Just as Sigismund took no interest in the patronage of literature in his kingdom but left the Cracow elite to further that cause, so his brother Vladislav and his nephew Louis entrusted, by default, the patronage of literature to their magnates and nobles. Furthermore, at Buda (the seat from which the Jagiellonian kings governed both the Czech and the Hungarian kingdom) there was no university around which the wandering poets could congregate and teach the new trends in the composition of Latin literature as an accompaniment to their activity at court.[65] Many young men at the time therefore were sent by their families or patrons from the provinces of the Jagiellonian realms to be educated at the University of Cracow. Here these young scholars came into contact with humanist circles; when they returned to their places of origin, they spread humanist Latin literary norms via their places of work – in the service of the ecclesiarchs and lay nobles, and as town clerks and schoolteachers. As a result, Renaissance trends in Latin literature passed easily into the Czech and Hungarian provinces, where they were cultivated and permitted to mature.[66]

Aside from acting as patrons, certain members of the Cracow royal court wrote literature themselves, for their own patrons who were higher up in the hierarchy.[67] Decius, besides composing his three-part history in honour of the Jagiellons, wrote a diary of the wedding celebrations of Sigismund and Bona, *Diarii et earum quae memoratu digna in Sigismundi Poloniae regis et Bonae nuptiis gesta descriptio* (1518). In 1522, Decius, revealing certain philological interests, edited the Roman humanist Varino Camers's collection of ancient aphorisms, *Apophtegmata*.[68] In the 1520s and 1530s, he composed a series of political and economic treatises in Latin and German.[69] Johannes Dantiscus (1485–1548), a graduate of the University of Cracow, was a secretary at the royal court (1504–15) and then royal ambassador to the Habsburg court in the Netherlands and Spain (1518, 1522, 1524–32), and ended up as bishop of Warmia (1538). Dantiscus wrote throughout his career, starting with political panegyrics, epigrams, epitaphs, and love poetry and ending with religious verses.[70] Andrzej Krzycki,[71] the aforementioned nephew of Vice-Chancellor Bishop Tomicki, was an ecclesiastic who first served Bishop Jan Lubrański of Poznań and subsequently came to the Cracow court as a secretary to King Sigismund's first wife, Barbara. Krzycki was appointed a royal secretary in 1515. He went on to become bishop of Przemyśl (1523), then bishop of Płock (1527); finally, as archbishop of Gniezno (1535) he became primate of Poland. Krzycki essentially fulfilled the function of court poet during Sigismund's reign. Some of his early poetry was plainly obscene, but he went on to write epigrams, many of them quite satiric and providing a glimpse of court life, and political poetry. He also wrote standard panegyric verses in honour of Sigismund and Bona. Krzycki was a correspondent of Erasmus and was chastised by Erasmus for his liking for ribald, neo-pagan poetry.[72]

LITERARY PATRONAGE AT CRACOW II: THE WANDERING HUMANIST POETS

The writers who supplied the literature for these affluent patrons came from a new social element, the lay intellectuals who congregated around the University of Cracow.[73] Whereas in earlier times the teachers at the university had been connected to religious life and had been bound to celibacy, to sharing common quarters, and to wearing special garments, there was now a secular community springing up, composed of lay scholars occupying the academic residences of the university neighbourhood, and also of members of various circles of townsmen – administrators, notaries, doctors, and printers – all brought together by a common interest in the new learning of the Renaissance.[74]

Intellectual life, as if a complement to the culture of the royal court, was flourishing at the University of Cracow.[75] At the end of the fifteenth century, the university was enjoying an international reputation as a centre for the study of astronomy and the liberal arts;[76] moreover, certain scholars at the arts faculty were taking an interest, in their private study and writing at least, in the humanist approach to Latin letters.[77] At the same time, Italian neo-Latin literary trends were entering Cracow along German routes, spread by a group of wandering scholar-poets who had studied in Germany, and almost all of whom had never travelled to Italy. These scholars created, on the margins of the university, a literary culture based on a renewal of the study of the Latin classics and assisted to a certain extent by their familiarity with Italian humanist writing in Latin. The body of literature they composed was an amalgamation of Italian neo-Latin trends and their own, native literary norms, in much the same way that the body of visual art favoured at Cracow was a hybrid of German Gothic and Italian Renaissance idioms, reminding us once again that the Renaissance in Poland was a multi-ethnic, multinational phenomenon.

Yet three factors prevented the wandering scholar-poets from establishing themselves at the University of Cracow. First, although some of the masters at the arts faculty, such as Johannes Aesticampianus (the Elder), were dabbling in the new learning, humanism was penetrating university life only very gradually. Although senior academic officials began to admit lectures on classical grammar, rhetoric, and literature into the official curriculum towards the end of the fifteenth century, they were slow to drop the old scholastically biased instruction in Latin grammar and dialectics. This meant that the *poetae*[78] were not welcomed into the university fellowship with permanent lectureships, but were kept at a distance with the status *extraneus non de facultate.* Second, the university at Cracow, at the beginning of the sixteenth century, was far from undergoing the eventual process of laicization that would embrace lay scholars comfortably among its ranks. Most of the university's endowment came from ecclesiastical benefices, which gave the clergy the right to intervene in the university's affairs.[79] (The bishop of Cracow, for example, normally held the post of chancellor of the university.)[80] Powerful Cracow ecclesiarchs, such as Cardinal Fryderyk Jagiellończyk, Bishop Jan Konarski, and Bishop Piotr Tomicki, would naturally have an interest in taking on protégés who either were already ordained or would be willing to enter the clergy.[81] Unless a promising scholar-poet was prepared to take holy orders, he was unlikely to gain the wholehearted patronage of a church dignitary who would support him in a university post. Finally, during the second quarter of the sixteenth century, the university underwent a polonization of its student population, which occurred along with a polonization of the German patrician class of the city, and as a result German and Hungarian students were marginalized.[82] At that point, the ecclesiastical patrons, as ethnic Poles, may have lost interest in supporting foreigners at the university.

During the period 1433–1509, nearly half the students at the University of Cracow were of foreign extraction, having originated from Germany, Silesia, and Moravia and from the Czech lands and Hungary.[83] Foreign students were attracted to Cracow for two reasons: the strategic location of the city in east central Europe, and the renown of the university in the field of the liberal arts, especially astronomy.[84] Among these students were the late fifteenth-century wandering German scholar-poets (*Wanderpoeten*). At Cracow, none of these ever held an official, permanent post at the university, and their lectures on humanistic topics were not an integral part of the academic program.[85]

The best known of these was Conrad Celtis (1459–1508), who arrived in Cracow in 1489, presumably to study astrology under the Cracow lecturer Albert Blar, who was also the teacher of Copernicus. Before coming to Poland, Celtis had studied in Italy with Marcus Sabellicus, Battista Guarini, and Filippo Beroaldo. Celtis had also met Ficino and had come into contact with the Platonic academy of Pomponius Laetus in Rome. Celtis stayed in Cracow until 1491. Although he was granted the right to teach at the university, it was as *extraneus non de facultate*, and much of his instruction was given on an informal and extramural basis. In spite of such official restrictions, Celtis helped plant the seeds of the new learning through his lectures on rhetoric, the art of poetry, and epistolography.[86]

Celtis left a group of disciples, among whom was the Silesian Laurentius Corvinus (*c.* 1462–1527), who studied at Cracow from 1484 to 1489 and who continued to lecture there until he took up a teaching post in Silesia in 1494.[87] Corvinus wrote lyric and didactic poetry and was the author of a series of handbooks on Latin composition. Corvinus's pupil Heinrich Bebel (1472–1518), who originated from Ulm, studied at Cracow from 1492 to 1494, and went on to enrol at Basel before finally becoming professor of poetry and rhetoric at Tübingen. Aside from his pedagogical writings, Bebel was the author of the popular *Facetiae*, which underwent several printings into the middle of the sixteenth century.[88]

After Bebel and Corvinus left Cracow, there was a ten-year break until their work was resumed by another poet, also an ethnic German. Paulus Crosnensis (*c.* 1470–1517), who completed an MA degree at Cracow in 1506, was the first advocate of the new learning to obtain an official university post. The son of the mayor of a Ruthenian town, he had received his BA in 1500 at Greifswald. He was accepted into the Collegium Minus at Cracow in 1508 and worked towards the reform of the arts curriculum by lecturing on such authors as Terence, Cicero, Ovid, and Vergil. He based his university lectures on the work of the Italian commentators, such as Beroaldo, Politian, and Urceo Codro. Paulus also composed religious, occasional, and erotic poetry. He had contacts with Vienna, where he published an edition of the work of the Hungarian neo-Latin poet Janus Pannonius in 1512. Paulus was patronized early in his career by Stanislaus Thurzó, the future bishop of Olomouc, and then by the Hungarian nobleman Gábor Perényi (d. 1526).[89]

Two of Paulus's students, Rudolf Agricola Junior and Valentin Eck, together with a later arrival at Cracow, Leonard Cox, carried on the struggle to integrate the humanist curriculum into university and school education by their publishing of texts, handbooks, and treatises for teachers and students of classical Latin. Moreover, they composed occasional and religious poetry, panegyric orations, and didactic essays for their patrons. Having been educated in Germany and then operating mainly from within the German academic community at Cracow, these young scholars had to adapt their writing – in both form and content – to the perspective of their patrons, some of whom were attuned to the neopagan version of Italian humanism that had taken hold in court circles, and all of whom would expect their protégés to compose panegyrics in their honour and propaganda communicating their politics. Agricola Junior, Eck, and Cox did win over influential men to their pedagogical program and to their writing so that they were able to publish works of scholarship and their own compositions at Cracow amounting to some seventy books, but their effect on the curriculum of the University of Cracow was minimal. The patrons of the university, although they accepted the scholar-poets at their courts and supported their publications, were not willing, it seems, to support fully those lay humanists who were seeking an academic post. Agricola Junior was named to an official lectureship, but he died shortly afterwards, at the age of about thirty-one, in poverty, not encouraged in his endeavours by the university hierarchy and complaining that the bishops who were sponsoring him did not pay his stipend while at the same time putting pressure on him to take holy orders.

The achievement of Agricola Junior, Eck, and Cox would be their success in transmitting the norms of humanist Latin writing to the region of east central Europe. The three men drifted into Cracow from eastern and southern German regions. Agricola Junior, whose German name was most likely Baumann, arrived in Cracow in the summer of 1510, after spending 1507 and 1508 at the University of Leipzig and probably passing through Wrocław. Valentin Eck turned up in Cracow in 1511, having matriculated at Leipzig in 1508 and possibly having travelled to Poland through Moravia.[90] Agricola's and Eck's exit from Leipzig took place during a period of factionalism and animosity between the older and the younger members of the arts faculty, which was provoked by humanist-scholastic tension, and which peaked in the expulsion of Johannes Rhagius Aesticampianus, a former student at Cracow, from the University of Leipzig in 1511.[91] Finally, Leonard Cox reached Cracow in 1518, having journeyed from England through Paris and Tübingen and left Germany sometime after obtaining his BA degree in March 1516. Cox may have left Tübingen because of the departure of Philipp Melanchthon, his master there, who went on to teach at the University of Wittenberg in 1518.[92] By the time Cox appeared at Cracow, he had been crowned poet laureate.

Rudolf Agricola Junior remained a wandering scholar until his early death in 1521. After receiving his bachelor of arts degree at the end of 1511, he left Cracow around Easter 1514, passed through Buda, and spent the remainder of the year in Esztergom in charge of the cathedral school. He then spent the next two and a half years in Vienna, in the company of the humanists Joachim Vadian and Caspar Ursinus Velius, before returning to Poland at the end of 1517. Back in Cracow, Agricola took up the post of tutor to the pages of Queen Bona and also returned to his lectures at the university, finally being offered an official post through the financial backing of his patrons. Yet he complained in his letters to Vadian about the lack of support from his patrons and stated that he intended to return to his home region of Lake Constance.

Valentin Eck completed his BA degree in the summer of 1513 and stayed on in Cracow, teaching privately at the German students' hostel (Contubernium Germanorum), until sometime in 1517, when he took up the post of headmaster of the town school in Bártfa, now Bardejov in Slovakia, at that time part of the kingdom of Hungary. He came to assume positions of increasing responsibility in the town government, most remarkably those of town clerk (notary) and mayor. He revisited Cracow on several occasions, and nearly all his publications were printed there.

Leonard Cox, after matriculating at Cracow in September 1518, delivered a public lecture, *De laudibus celeberrimae Cracouiensis academiae*, in December of that year. He remained in Cracow, teaching as an *extraneus non de facultate* lecturer, for two years. In 1520 he, like Eck, travelled south across the mountains into the Hungarian kingdom, where he accepted a teaching post at the town school of Lőcse, not far from Bártfa. After a year he transferred to the nearby school of Kassa. He remained there for three years, with visits to Cracow for short periods, but in 1524 he returned to Poland and resumed his *extraneus non de facultate* lecturing. He also took up a position as a tutor in the household of Bishop Piotr Tomicki. In 1529 he returned to England, where he became headmaster at Reading School and supplicated for the MA degree at Oxford.

Agricola Junior, Eck, and Cox consciously transmitted neo-Latin literary norms to east central Europe, first of all through their republishing of classical texts and of the writings of Italian humanists at Cracow. In his preface to his edition of Maffeo Vegio's *Philalethes* (1512), Agricola stated that he had brought the work with him from Germany 'with a smile on his face.'[93] In fact, *Philalethes* had been printed at Leipzig in the 1490s.[94] Two other Italian neo-Latin titles edited by Agricola at Cracow at the same time, Francesco Ottavio Cleofilo's *De poetarum coetu libellus* (1511) and Antonio Mancinelli's *De componendis uersibus* (1513), had been published at Leipzig in *c.* 1500 and 1504 respectively,[95] so one can suppose that he became acquainted with them during his studies there. Agricola's importation of these Italian neo-Latin texts illustrates how the conventions of humanist Latin writing were introduced by the wandering scholar-poets into Cracow and the region served by its printing presses.

Second, Agricola Junior, Eck, and Cox spread humanist literary norms throughout east central Europe through their teaching and the example of their own writing, a product of their eclectic imitation of the classics and neo-Latin literature. They emulated the works of neo-Latin authors, especially the Italians, not only as a means of achieving the imitation of the classics, but as examples of beautiful and pure Latinity themselves. Leonard Cox, in his commentary to Adriano Castellesi's *Venatio*, a 427-line poem on hunting and banqueting, made it clear that a writer should not only imitate the Italians imitating the ancients, but also imitate the Italians themselves.[96] In his preface and notes to the text, Cox argued that Castellesi's work would open the way for beginning students to a felicitous imitation of the princes of Latin eloquence, and he also made it clear that he considered contemporary writers to be authorities as reliable as the ancients and declared that their style could be as refined. In his notes to *Venatio*, Cox referred both to classical writers and to the *recentiores:* Valla, Erasmus, Melanchthon, Beroaldo, Aldus Manutius, Wimpheling, Politian, Perotti, and Ermolao Barbaro. He echoed the old comparison of the poet to the bee, asserting that here, the learner had the honey produced from many flowers gathered from the fields of Latium.[97]

Valentin Eck (relying on Celtis's *Ars uersificandi*) expressed similar views on eclectic imitation when he wrote, in his handbook on versification, that in order to compose good poetry, it was worthwhile to read a variety of books by the best and most approved authors. Stating the importance of synonyms and epithets in the writing of good poetry, Eck acclaimed Vergil, Ovid, and Horace as models.[98] Moreover, as examples in the handbook, Eck employed citations from Baptista Mantuan (to whom he referred as 'Vergilius neotericus'), Ludovico Bigi, Faustus Andrelinus, and Filippo Beroaldo alongside those from the ancients.[99] Rudolf Agricola Junior also advocated an imitation of many authors, in his case by publishing *Institutiones uitae*, a collection of aphorisms excerpted from Cato and other early authorities.[100] In his prefaces to his editions of Cicero, Agricola Junior, moreover, did not argue for Ciceronianism as the exclusive imitation of Cicero, but simply recommended Cicero as a model of elegant Latin.[101]

The eclectic and academic *imitatio* that Agricola Junior, Eck, and Cox practised intermixed forms and themes taken from a wide range of the classics and of contemporary Latin authors. Classical influences materialized more as motifs and allusions than as emulation of genre. Rather, it was from the Italians that Agricola Junior, Eck, and Cox copied the neo-Latin genres of the elegy and the ode, and from Erasmus that they borrowed the *querimonia*. The works of Erasmus were also extremely influential in respect to the themes developed by the three *poetae* in their writing. Reminiscences of Erasmus's *Adagia* and of his educational and moralistic treatises figured in their works. In general, they favoured the Erasmian subjects of piety, marriage, and the family, and they took up Erasmus's interest in patristics and the education of youth. But the humanist theme of marriage in its physical or social aspects and interpretations of saints' lives as devised by the Italians appeared in their writing, too.

Although the poems of Agricola Junior, Eck, and Cox were filled with classical, pagan colouring, this was never erotic or lascivious, as in Italian neo-Latin poetry (or even in the works of Conrad Celtis, Heinrich Bebel, and Laurentius Corvinus). Rather, their writing shows the influence of the Italians as communicated through a pious German medium. Valentin Eck's *An prudenti uiro sit ducenda uxor*, composed at the very beginning of 1518,[102] is an example of such a conflagration of roots. Eck took a theme popular in humanist prose and turned it into verse, drawing on examples from the Old Testament, classical literature, and the Church Fathers to portray, first, insidious wives and, second, the virtues of married life. Since the theme of whether or not to take a wife had been so favoured by the Italian humanists from Petrarch on,[103] there were a number of sources that Eck could have had at his disposal, including Poggio's *An seni sit uxor ducenda*,[104]

Francesco Barbaro's *De re uxoria*,[105] and Antonio Bonfini's *Symposion de uirginitate et pudicitia coniugali*.[106] It is also possible that Eck was familiar with the work of Albrecht von Eyb, whose writings on women and marriage were influenced by Petrarch, Poggio, and Barbaro.[107] Still, Eck could have been inspired by Heinrich Rybisch's *Disceptatio an uxor sit ducenda*, a disputation relying on Urceo Codro's *An uxor sit ducenda* (*Sermo IV*), which Rybisch delivered at Leipzig in the autumn of 1509 while Eck was a student there.[108]

In the end, as northern humanists in the tradition of Paulus Crosnensis, Agricola Junior, Eck, and Cox viewed themselves as Christian scholar-poets.[109] Their writing was based on classical learning grounded in Christian morality, especially as taught by Erasmus, and was intended to be serious and pious, not lighthearted or jocular. As Rudolf Agricola Junior insinuated in a commendatory poem he wrote for Valentin Eck's *De mundi contemptu* in 1519, the poet should never turn his pen towards lascivious behaviour or describe the extravagant sumptuousness of a dissolute way of life.[110] For Agricola Junior, Eck, and Cox, the purpose of writing literature was to change the readers' lives for the better, whether it be ridding their Latin of barbarisms or leading them on the path of virtue. For the three poets, these two notions went together, for the chief goal of their educational program was the moulding of character.[111] So although Agricola, Eck, and Cox admired their predecessors Celtis, Bebel, and Corvinus, they did not imitate the amorous themes of their works.[112]

THE SEARCH FOR PATRONAGE

Artistic and literary patronage at Cracow in the early sixteenth century functioned in much the same way as in other parts of Europe during the Renaissance. An influential patron could arrange for a poet's employment as a tutor in a wealthy household, or help the poet obtain a post in a school. High-ranking ecclesiastics could even fund a post at the university. Patronage played a crucial role in the genesis of a work of art or literature, and the interaction of patron and artist produced a material result.[113] Thus, the humanist movement at Cracow was controlled by the prominent figures to whom Agricola Junior, Eck, and Cox turned for maintenance as a result of their need for advancement, of both a material and an immaterial nature.

In order to further their careers, Agricola, Eck, and Cox looked to the royal and ecclesiastical courts and to the patricians and burghers involved in commerce. Moreover, these three scholar-poets sought support from within the academic circles to strengthen their position at the university. Patrons were drawn from the Polish and German as well as the Germanic-Hungarian ethnic communities. The selection of patrons would not be restricted to within the city walls of Cracow because the scholars continued to require funding as they drifted in and out of the Hungarian kingdom and the Habsburg empire.

Yet, whether in Cracow, Vienna, or Buda, and whether seeking employment at court, at the university, or from a town council, the three scholar-poets needed to gain acceptance and to convert themselves from 'outsiders' to 'insiders.'[114] The methods they used to attract and cultivate patrons involved a considerable amount of self-promotion, including the creation of propaganda formed on the basis of membership in the transnational community of humanist scholars and of an ability to offer knowledge and skills superior to those already being taught – their expertise in the classics and in moral philosophy and their command of the Latin language. They embedded this propaganda in their panegyric writings and in the dedicatory letters they attached to the books they published. By composing panegyric poems and dedicating books to potential or actual patrons, not only did the poets flatter these patrons, they also reinforced the image of themselves as connected with and protected by erudite and powerful men and women. The dedication of a book to a famous man or woman would serve as a recommendation for the book and would help promote sales by winning over the literate public to the humanist cause.

Since there were no official lectureships open to the likes of Agricola Junior, Eck, and Cox within the university itself, they needed, if they were to succeed in their endeavours, the financial and political support of important people from outside the university environment who would be well disposed to the new learning. In this situation, they were no different from the scholar-poets wandering through the German lands, to the west, where it was normally a secular prince who supported the introduction of a poet and his educational program into the arts faculty, and who paid his salary.[115] Indeed, it was the assimilation of scholar-poets into the universities and subsequent university reforms that led to the laicization of the faculties of arts and theology and the resulting need for secular pay (not church benefices).[116]

Agricola Junior, Eck, and Cox were initially successful in attracting extremely powerful patrons at Cracow, the most highly placed being the king himself. Eck and Agricola both wrote verses for King Sigismund and Queen Bona. As early as 1514, for example, Eck managed to print a piece written for the king. His *Hymnus exhortatorius*, a poem in honour of Sigismund's victory over the Muscovites at Orsha,[117] appeared as an appendix to Johannes Dantiscus's poetic account of the battle, *Syluula de uictoria inclyti Sigismundi regis Poloniae contra Moschos*.[118] In 1516, Eck addressed to King Sigismund a short prefatory poem for Johannes Visliciensis's *Bellum Prutenum* (1516), a versified description of the Jagiellonian victory over the Teutonic Knights at the battle of Grunwald in 1410 and a work inspired by Sigismund's victory at Orsha.[119] Agricola composed a poem, *Illustrissimae reginae Bonae paraceleusis*, in honour of Bona's betrothal to Sigismund in 1518.[120] Agricola and Cox were clients of the grand-chancellor, Krzysztof Szydłowiecki, to whom each dedicated a book. Aside from Bishop Tomicki, Agricola, Eck, and Cox solicited support from the high-ranking ecclesiastics Jan Lubrański (bishop of Poznań, 1489–1520), Jan Konarski (bishop of Cracow, 1503–25), Jan Łaski Senior (grand-chancellor, 1503–10; archbishop of Gniezno, 1510–31), and Maciej Drzewicki (bishop of Przemyśl, 1503–13; bishop of Włocławek, 1513–31; archbishop of Gniezno, 1531–35), as evidenced from the prefatory letters and laudatory verses printed in nearly a dozen extant books.[121]

Agricola, Eck, and Cox relied for backing on the polonized Germans from the commercial sector. Early in their careers, Eck and Cox were patronized by Justus Ludovicus Decius. Eck dedicated the first edition of his *De arte uersificandi opusculum* to Decius in 1515, and Cox dedicated his oration *De laudibus celeberrimae Cracouiensis Academiae* to Decius in 1518. The Boner, Bethmann, and Salomon families assisted Agricola and Cox, as indicated by the dedications they received of editions of educational textbooks and of religious poetry from these two men. Upon Agricola's death in 1521, Ulrich Faber dedicated his funerary poem *Epicedion siue naenia funebris in obitum Rudolphi Agricolae poetae* to Nicolaus Salomon,[122] thereby revealing Agricola's close connections with the Salomon family.

A rapport with printers and booksellers could also advance a humanist's career. Rudolf Agricola had evidently become friendly with the bookseller Marcus Scharffenberg shortly after arriving at Cracow, and it is thought that he worked as an editor and proofreader for him. Marcus seems to have promoted Agricola, since Agricola first wrote to the Swiss humanist Joachim Vadian at Vienna at Marcus's urging.[123] In 1515, Agricola thanked Marcus for sending him, now in Vienna, a copy of Johannes Aesticampianus's *Modus epistolandi* so that he could reissue it there.[124] From 1515, Agricola collaborated with the printer Hieronymus Vietor, from whose press he issued a series of editions of classical and humanist authors.[125]

Within the university itself, Agricola, Eck, and Cox needed the support of the academic establishment for protection and promotion. Agricola and Eck received assistance from their teachers Paulus Crosnensis and Michael Wratislaviensis. Michael had completed his MA degree at Cracow in 1488 and was received into the Collegium Maius in 1501.[126] He entered the faculty of theology in 1512, just as Agricola and Eck were completing their BA degrees, and finished his doctorate in 1517. Before embarking on the study of theology, Michael specialized in astronomy, but he also lectured on the classical authors. Although immersed in the medieval philosophical tradition, he supported the new, humanist educational currents. Agricola particularly admired Michael and dedicated an edition of Maffeo Vegio's *Philalethes* to him in 1512, in which he thanked Michael for his kindness. In 1518, Agricola also wrote a commendatory verse for Michael's *Epitoma figurarum in libros physicorum et de anima Aristotelis.*[127]

A greater help to Agricola and Eck would be Paulus Crosnensis, the successor to the fifteenth-century German humanists at Cracow. In 1511, Rudolf Agricola Junior dedicated to Paulus his poem on St Casimir.[128] Paulus died in 1517, but Cox mentioned him the next year in his oration to the university, in which he stated that as a poet Paulus was not inferior to the ancients. The cultivation of Paulus paid off, for in 1512, only two years after arriving at Cracow, Agricola managed to contribute verses to the commentary on Ptolemy's *Cosmographia* written by Johannes de Stobnica,[129] an Aristotelian who lectured on both astronomy and grammar but who also understood the new cultural and intellectual currents.[130] Johannes de Stobnica had been accepted into the Collegium Maius in 1507 and had become an influential member of the college. *Cosmographia* was dedicated to the bishop of Poznań, Jan Lubrański (1456–1520), a pro-humanist cleric who had studied in Bologna and Rome and who founded an academy for humanistic studies at Poznań in 1518.[131] Agricola's contribution to *Cosmographia* must have been arranged by Paulus, since Paulus, known to be a friend of Stobnica, added a versified introduction to this book. Paulus probably also played a part in Eck's 1516 donation of his laudatory poem in honour of King Sigismund to the prefatory material accompanying the *Bellum Prutenum* of Johannes Visliciensis, mentioned above. Paulus, Johannes's teacher (as well as Eck's), wrote an introductory poem to the epic, and Johannes addressed his preface to Paulus.

Besides Johannes de Stobnica, Agricola and Cox had contact with two other astronomers. The first of these, Nicolaus de Toliszków (*c.* 1480–*c.* 1534), had obtained an MA degree in 1503 and was admitted to the Collegium Maius in 1515. From 1509 until the early 1520s, he published annual almanacs dedicated to elevated church officials.[132] Agricola wrote a prefatory letter to Piotr Konarski, a Cracow canon, for the almanac for 1518 and to Jan Konarski, bishop of Cracow, for the almanac for 1519. Nicolaus de Toliszków's role was taken over by the younger Nicolaus Schadkovius, who had matriculated at Cracow in 1504 and received his MA degree in 1512. Schadkovius became the author of the official Cracow calendars and astrological prognostics, which he published from 1517 to 1531, and it was he who formalized the genre of the Cracow almanac. His almanacs were embellished with the commendatory verses of Agricola and of Cox (for the years 1521 and 1527 respectively, with both almanacs dedicated to Piotr Tomicki). Nicolaus Schadkovius was of the same generation as Agricola and Eck, and, like them, was a pupil of Paulus Crosnensis. He was made professor of astrology in 1515; shortly after, he became curator of the university library, then housed in the Collegium Maius. Although he was a supporter of humanistic studies, he sustained the old scholastic order in his role as an academic administrator. The historian Henryk Barycz has suggested that Nicolaus assisted Cox when Cox arrived at Cracow, and that it was Nicolaus who supplied Cox with the information – on the history of the University of Cracow and the accomplishments of its members – that Cox needed to write his oration in praise of the University of Cracow, which he delivered in December 1518.[133]

PATRONAGE AND CAREER

Agricola Junior, Eck, and Cox saw themselves as lay educators: although they found employment occasionally as tutors at various courts, they did not become courtiers; because they were not ordained, the route to advancement in the Church was not open to them. In such a cultural climate as existed at the University of Cracow in the 1510s and 1520s, where the only possibility for promoting the introduction of humanist learning in the university would have had to come from external powers, but where it was the ecclesiastical dignitaries – not lay rulers – who had sway over the university, and also the ecclesiastical dignitaries – not lay rulers – who took an interest in curricular reform, a young lay scholar with humanist leanings had to be canny. The career strategies of Agricola Junior and Cox show that they placed too much trust in the Polish bishops, by relying on them for maintenance and at the same time not pursuing a career in the Church. Valentin Eck improved his career prospects immediately when he took a teaching post sponsored by the town government of Bártfa, from which he worked his way into prominence in the region of Upper Hungary, while receiving support from the Buda dignitary Alexius Thurzó, a layman whose family had Austrian roots. Cox, after two stays in Cracow, finally located a stable post when he returned to England and became headmaster at Reading School.

On the other hand, the three scholars, conscious of how to exploit the patronage system, managed to attract influential persons at Cracow who supported their aims. This they did through an active program of self-promotion that portrayed them as members of a cohesive transnational group of scholar-poets and that involved vigorous propaganda stressing the positive value of their new educational skills in contrast to the old, scholastic methods still found at the university. When these scholars found that support from a certain patron, or group of patrons, was slackening, they directed their efforts elsewhere. The actions of Agricola Junior, Eck, and Cox show that they were familiar with the conventions of patronage, that they had acquired a knowledge of the humanist strategies for advancing themselves and their pedagogical program, and that they believed they could fashion and direct their own careers.

Agricola, of the three men, enjoyed patronage of the highest rank, being associated with the royal family and participating in events of historical importance. But, having returned to Cracow after failing to find permanent work at Vienna, he became completely dissatisfied with his life there. By the time of his death in 1521, he was complaining that the city was unhealthy, that he did not like the people, and that he was not being paid for his teaching at the university; he intended to embark upon a low-level church career and desperately sought a benefice in Saint Gall, close to his home town of Wasserburg on Lake Constance.[134]

Although Agricola may have had contact with the Polish royal court before he left Cracow for Vienna,[135] his participation in an official capacity as poet and orator at the Congress of 1515, while he was in Vienna, unquestionably provided him with a connection to the elite of Cracow and Vienna. It was most likely Agricola's friendship with Joachim Vadian, who had been appointed vice-chancellor of the University of Vienna in 1514, that facilitated Agricola's inclusion in the ceremonies honouring the entourage of princes, nobles, and bishops attending the Congress, where the agreement between Vladislav II Jagiellon and Maximilian I, to arrange inter-dynastic marriages between their two families, was concluded.[136] Agricola Junior's verses appeared in *Odeporicon*, a record of the itinerary of Cardinal Matthäus Lang, the archbishop of Salzburg, composed by Riccardus Bartholinus, an Italian in the cardinal's service.[137] Agricola also wrote a poem, *Siluula*, in honour of Cardinal Lang, which was printed separately in February 1515 at Vienna by Vietor. Moreover, he composed an oration welcoming Bishop Tomicki to the University of Vienna, which was printed in a volume with more than twenty other speeches saluting Congress participants.[138] *Siluula* was reprinted, with minor amendments, in the book. Bishop Lang thanked Agricola and recommended him to Emperor Maximilian for the poet laureate's crown,[139] which Agricola received sometime before he returned to Cracow.

If the patronage at the imperial capital did not keep Agricola at Vienna, neither did the combination of lecturing and intensive publishing. At the university he taught only as a *freier Dozent*, lecturing mainly on Horace and Statius. Yet in two years (1515–16) the Vietor press published a sequence of eight classical and humanistic texts edited by Agricola and intended for school and university use: Anselm of Canterbury's *Elucidarius dialogicus theologiae tripertitus*, Cebes's *Tabula*, Aegidius Gallus Romanus's *Bophilaria*, Georg Peurbach's *Algorithmus*, Leonardo Bruni's *Isa-*

goge in philosophiam moralem, Johannes Harmonius Marsus's *Comoedia Stephanium*, Cicero's *De amicitia*, and Horace's *Epistolarum libri duo*. The poet Caspar Ursinus Velius remarked on Agricola's exhaustive scholarship in a versified epistle from these years addressed to the Wrocław canon Stanislaus Saur.[140]

When Agricola returned to Cracow at the end of 1517, his reputation as a poet and scholar, as well as his relationship with the royal court, was well established. Having the laureate's crown must have boosted his status.[141] By the spring of 1518, when the Polish king married the Milanese princess Bona Sforza, Agricola had already published a poem in honour of the betrothal. He subsequently prepared a prefatory verse for Decius's description of the royal marriage celebrations (*Diarii et earum quae memoratu digna in ... nuptiis gesta*).[142] In June 1518, Agricola dedicated his edition of Cicero's *Pro Archia* to the queen's secretary, Ludovico Alifio. In July 1518 he dedicated his edition of Johannes Glogoviensis's *Physionomia* to the queen's pages, whom he was tutoring. A further indication of Agricola's connection with the royal court was his *Hymnus de diuo Stanislao*, a poem about Poland's patron saint, published in 1519 and honouring Krzysztof Szydłowiecki, the grand-chancellor. Moreover, when the emperor's emissary to Moscow, Sigismund von Herberstein, returned to Cracow from the East in February 1518, Agricola and Dantiscus were solicited to write poems of congratulation on the success of his negotiations and on his safe return home.[143] Agricola was, at the same time, working as a tutor for the family of the bishop of Cracow, Jan Konarski. In 1518 he published an edition of the pseudo-Crates *Epistolae* for the bishop's nephews, and in 1519 he addressed to the bishop himself a prefatory letter to Nicolaus de Toliszków's *Iudicium Cracouiense*. Also in 1519, Agricola dedicated his edition of Johannes de Lapide's *Resolutorium dubiorum circa celebrationem missarum occurrentium* to the bishop.

Leonard Cox, like Agricola Junior, would end his stay in Cracow associated with the most powerful dignitaries of the Polish kingdom. When he arrived in Cracow in 1518, claiming the title *poeta laureatus*, Cox received support from the royal adviser Justus Ludovicus Decius and began teaching as *extraneus non de facultate* at the university, where he lectured on Livy and the letters of St Jerome. He may also have received assistance from the astronomer Nicolaus Schadkovius during his first year at the university.[144] Cox's contact with the commercial sphere at this time included acquaintance with the young patricians Andreas and Nicolaus Salomon, for whom he published Giovanni Pontano's *De laudibus diuinis opusculum* in 1520.[145] Cox continued to consider Decius a patron, even though he had been invited to teach in the town school of Lőcse, where his sponsor was Johannes Henckel, the parish priest.[146] Cox would follow Henckel to nearby Kassa at the end of 1521. In 1524, while he was teaching school in Kassa, Cox dedicated his edition of Adriano Castellesi's *Venatio*, a poem on hunting, to Decius. Upon Henckel's appointment as personal chaplain to Queen Maria of Hungary (the Habsburg wife of Louis II Jagiellon), Cox returned to Cracow.

During Cox's second stay in Cracow, dating from the middle of 1525, he fell into the sphere of Bishop Tomicki and contributed verses to three works that were addressed to him: the Cracow editions of Erasmus's *Hyperaspistes* (1526), of Erasmus's *Epistola ad inclytum Sigismundum regem* (1527), and of Nicolaus Schadkovius's *Iudicium astronomicum* (1527). Cox dedicated his own treatise on the education of youth (*Libellus de erudienda iuuentute*) to Tomicki in 1526. Tomicki's nephew, Andrzej Krzycki, was also a patron of Cox's, as Cox noted in his letter to Erasmus in March 1527.[147] In that same year, Tomicki's great-nephew Andrzej Zebrzydowski was being tutored by Cox. Also in 1527, Cox dedicated his edition of Martin Luther's letter to Henry VIII (*Epistola Martini Lutheri ad Henricum VIII*) to Krzysztof Szydłowiecki, the grand-chancellor and a political ally of Tomicki's.

As close as he had become to Tomicki and his circle, Cox managed also to be friendly towards Tomicki's political rivals, the Łaski family. In 1527 he dedicated his edition of Statius's *Siluae*[148] to Jan Łaski Junior, nephew of the primate of Poland, Jan Łaski Senior, whom Cox (in his letter to Erasmus) also listed among his patrons. During his second stay in Cracow, Cox continued lecturing at the university, where he commented on the classical authors Vergil, Cicero, and Quintilian. By 1529, Cox had departed from Poland, most likely because his pupil Andrzej Zebrzydowski had been sent to Erasmus in Basel, and Cox was thereby left without work.[149] Cox returned to England, took up the headmastership of Reading School, and, although buffeted by the waves of political danger, continued to publish on educational and religious matters.[150]

At Cracow, Cox stood at the centre of the Erasmian movement.[151] Although scholars at Cracow were familiar with the works of Erasmus in the early 1510s, Erasmianism did not become popular until after Cox's arrival in 1518, and it peaked with his departure. He and a group of younger scholars, most of them of Silesian origin,[152] played a role in publishing at least fifteen Erasmian titles from 1518 to 1528. Since Erasmianism was in vogue among the church dignitaries and wealthy Cracow burghers, the scholars had no difficulty obtaining support, and their patrons included Tomicki, Decius, and Severin Boner, who were all personal correspondents of Erasmus. Cox, as already mentioned, was close to the Erasmian Jan Łaski Junior, to whom Erasmus sold his private library, and who would become known internationally as the itinerant Reformer Johannes a Lasco.[153]

Like Cox, Valentin Eck first found patronage at Cracow with Justus Ludovicus Decius, and like Cox, he continued to have friendly relations with his early patron. But, unlike Agricola Junior and Cox, when Eck left Cracow in 1517 and accepted the post of headmaster at the town school of Bártfa, he used the position as a stepping stone to a political career. Eck would assume posts of increasing responsibility in the town government, most notably as town notary (1522–5) and mayor (1526–9, 1538–40, 1550–1). Eck may initially have been invited to Bártfa by students from the Szepes region who were studying at Cracow. In any case, his move to Hungary does not seem to have been provoked by dissatisfaction with the patronage of Decius, to whom Eck had, in 1515, dedicated the first edition of his handbook on versification. In his re-dedication of the book to Alexius with the second edition in 1521, Eck states clearly in his preface that the work had originally been dedicated to Decius, 'a man not deserving badly from me' ('sub Iodoci Decii uiri de me non male meriti nomine'), as he put it. Furthermore, Eck kept up contact with Cracow, where he reappeared at various times throughout his life, most likely to oversee the printing of his books or to arrange other personal affairs.

After the victory of the Turks at Mohács (1526), during the struggle between the count of Szepes, János Zápolya, and Louis II's brother-in-law, Ferdinand, for the throne of Hungary (which was finally settled in 1538), Eck's pro-Habsburg stance threw his life into turmoil. From the years 1531–7 no new literary compositions by Eck are extant; archival research attests to his having undertaken a variety of diplomatic missions for Bártfa and neighbouring towns at the time. He was in Cracow in 1537, but then returned to Bártfa. From 1539 to 1546, he held the post of tutor to the sons of the propalatine Ferenc Révai.[154]

According to tradition, Eck was, from 1517 to 1519, also tutor to the daughter of the nobleman Alexius Thurzó, a royal secretary at Buda, who would, in 1522, become the royal treasurer of the Hungarian kingdom.[155] Thurzó was a learned and refined man who had been tutored by Jacob Piso, a royal secretary and ambassador who had studied in Bologna and Rome, and who was a correspondent of Erasmus.[156] Once a protégé of Thurzó, Eck dedicated to him nearly all his works published between 1518 and 1543, the year of Thurzó's death. These included works of a religious, political, and purely panegyric nature.[157]

By 1530 the wave of humanism initiated at Cracow with the work of Rudolf Agricola Junior in 1511 would be spent. The primary reason for the disintegration of the group active at Cracow in the 1510s and 1520s was, as noted above, the inadaptability of the University of Cracow to new trends. The second obstacle to the establishment of a humanist movement at Cracow was the lack of support by an external lay dignitary who could fund an academic post for a poet. Any initiatives in curricular reform at Cracow remained in the hands of ecclesiarchs, the same people who regulated the university and kept it under the control of the Church. Third, tensions between the Polish and German populations at Cracow during the 1520s, exacerbated, undoubtedly, by the conflict with the Teutonic Knights in Prussia and the encroaching Reformation, and an ongoing polonization of the German community in the city, made it unlikely that a Polish patron would be enthusiastic about supporting an incoming German for a post at the university.

Rudolf Agricola Junior died in 1521, complaining that he was not being paid for his university teaching by the consortium of bishops that had awarded him his lectureship and charging that the Poles were antagonistic to the Germans. At the same time, the bishops were putting pressure on him to take holy orders. In any case, two of the bishops who were supposed to be supporting Agricola, Jan Lubrański and Jan Konarski, were both dead by 1525. The remaining ecclesiastical patron, Bishop Piotr Tomicki, who died in 1535, was evidently not constant enough in his devotion to the scholar-poets. With ethnic tensions being felt in Cracow and a polonization of the German members of the city's patrician class and of its university taking place during the second quarter of the sixteenth century, Tomicki may have lost interest in supporting foreigners at the university. And after his patronage slackened, no one else took on the responsibility of fostering the foreign scholar-poets.

Leonard Cox had departed from Poland by 1529, almost certainly because he found himself unemployed – he had neither a stable post at the university nor students to teach privately. The group of young Erasmians who had gathered around Cox had also dispersed: the Silesian students left, either to study in Italy or to return to Wrocław,[158] where they settled into positions at the bishop's court or in parish churches. This 'wave' can be considered to have peaked by 1527, the year by which most of the group had left Cracow in search of further education or work elsewhere.

Valentin Eck did well by leaving Cracow and securing his future in Hungary with the favour of the Thurzó family. Eck's student Georg Werner, who followed him, had an even more glorious career, in first teaching at Kassa and Eperjes and subsequently becoming a councillor and judge of the latter town, then castellan of Sóvár and Sáros, and finally royal vice-treasurer of Hungary.[159] Agricola and Cox, however, can be seen as naive for relying on the Polish bishops while not seeking careers in the Church. Stanislaus Hosius, a friend of Cox and a member of the Erasmian circle, for instance, fared extremely well with patronage at Cracow. He was sent by Bishop Tomicki in May 1530 to study in Italy. Hosius made a glorious ecclesiastical career for himself: he became bishop of Warmia in 1551 and, in 1561, was made a cardinal.

Yet, in spite of the restrictions under which they worked, Agricola Junior, Eck, and Cox proved themselves capable of attracting the most influential and wealthy patrons accessible at Cracow. Even if their 'movement' did not last beyond the 1520s at Cracow, these three men chronicled the major political and cultural events of the age in their writing and contributed to the formation of a Latin humanist literary culture not only at Cracow but also at Vienna and Buda, and even in the provinces of the Hungarian kingdom. They created a literature appreciated by a Polish court that was more attuned to Italian humanism than – with the exception of Erasmus's writings – to its northern version. Forced to operate on the margins of a university that had neither come to accept the new learning of humanistic study nor undergone a laicization of its professoriate, and originating in a milieu that was predominantly German, they managed to appeal to the Cracow elite and keep their pedagogical program afloat. Furthermore, by striking out into the intellectual communities farther afield in east central Europe, they helped to propagate west and central European cultural innovations – in philosophy, theology, and literature – throughout the region, despite the political and religious upheavals of the age.

TWO

Careerism at Cracow: Issues of Identity and Self-Promotion

In order to advance themselves both individually and collectively, that is, to find stable employment and to promote the acceptance of the transnational community of humanist scholars to which they belonged, the young poets needed to attract and retain patrons, and to win over the literate public. Humanism was still on the margins of intellectual life in northern and central Europe at the beginning of the sixteenth century, as it had been earlier south of the Alps. In central Europe, despite the efforts of the previous generation of the German *Wanderpoeten*, the young *poetae*, such as Rudolf Agricola Junior, Valentin Eck, and Leonard Cox, were outsiders in the social spheres in which they were employed – at universities, at courts, and in urban centres. To succeed – to gain approval and respect for themselves and their pedagogical program – these humanists, like those who had preceded them, deliberately strove to advance their cause through a self-portrayal as members of a cohesive transnational group, steeped in the classics and in moral philosophy, and possessing a thorough command of the Latin language that they were ready to impart to the sectors in need of this skill – printing businesses, court and town administration, and schools and universities.[1]

In the first decades of the sixteenth century, when the *poetae* were beginning to find employment at court and in town governments (hired as notaries and schoolmasters, but also named to posts on town councils), they still needed to maintain their relationships with their patrons by publishing panegyrics and dedicating books to them, and to solicit new patrons, especially when forced to move to another location to find work. Moreover, at the universities, where they met with significant obstacles to the inclusion of their pedagogical program in the curriculum, they had to portray themselves as offering knowledge and skills superior to those being taught. They had to stress their differences from the scholastics in order to distinguish themselves, even by ridiculing as 'barbaric' the Latin of those who had not been trained in the classics.

A large part of the humanists' success was due to their ability to form a collective identity and to create propaganda enhancing the reputation of their community. Young scholar-poets confirmed their membership in the new transnational intellectual elite through the cultivation of friendships with one another, reinforced by letter-writing and visits. By constructing networks of like-minded scholars, they fought off opposition in a hostile university environment. By prefacing their books with dedicatory letters to patrons, they reinforced the image that they were connected with and protected by erudite and powerful men and women. By writing commendatory verses for one another's work, they promoted themselves to the intellectual public.[2]

The humanists gained acceptance and converted themselves from 'outsiders' to 'insiders' in the intellectual and cultural life of early sixteenth-century central Europe using methods involving a considerable amount of self-fashioning and self-promotion. To operate successfully within the patronage system, the young poets were forced to act in accordance with the conventions of court life, in both its secular and its ecclesiastical versions, and so develop an acute sense of prudence that subordinated honesty to decorum.[3] When promoting themselves in writing, both in their personal correspondence and in print, they needed to disguise their inner feelings if their self-representation was to be astute. Especially when breaking into the new world of print culture, they had to acquire quickly the ability to create effective propaganda.

An examination of the methods of self-promotion used by Agricola Junior, Eck, and Cox shows that they were no strangers to the conventions of the patronage system and, moreover, that they had acquired a knowledge of the humanists' strategies for advancing themselves and their pedagogical program.[4] Along with the other humanist scholars of their generation, they believed that they could fashion and direct their careers, and they understood how to do so within the conventions of their social and cultural environments. By cultivating a friendship with Joachim Vadian, a senior, more prominent humanist scholar, Agricola Junior not only confirmed his membership in the Republic of Letters, but also made it possible for himself to exploit Vadian's influence so as to manipulate his way into the intellectual elite at Vienna. By means of the dedicatory letters with which they prefaced their books, Agricola Junior, Eck, and Cox linked themselves to the most powerful and celebrated members of the Polish and Hungarian courts; they observed the constraints of decorum in respect to their patrons while presenting an image of themselves as industrious and learned, and as pious Christian scholars. The commendatory poems they attached to their books served as advertisements not only for specific volumes, but also for the program of instruction in the newly revived Latin – based on the classics and a study of the Church Fathers – they were touting.

SELF-PROMOTION AND CAREER BUILDING: THE LETTERS OF RUDOLF AGRICOLA JUNIOR TO JOACHIM VADIAN

Letter-writing was the humanists' chief form of communication, not only in east central Europe but all over the continent. Because these scholars were geographically spread out, constant correspondence was necessary for building and maintaining networks. We may recall Erasmus's remark that he devoted half his day to the reading and writing of letters, and his claim that on some days he wrote sixty or ninety letters.[5] Letter-writing conveyed information about one's scholarly projects and career plans at the individual level, and disseminated the cult of antiquity and humanist pedagogical and literary norms at the collective level. Underlying all this epistolary activity, though, was the humanist notion that letter-writing was an exercise in persuasion.[6]

Humanist correspondence, furthermore, quickly became absorbed in the nurturing of friendships, since most lay intellectuals of this early period of the *respublica litteraria* lacked stable employment and were continually looking for jobs with the help of their friends. Letter-writing was part and parcel of the cultivation of friendship by aspiring young scholar-poets with persons of senior rank, and it involved a certain ritual. The process of winning the friendship of a respected and famous individual entailed, first of all, the showering of that person with praises. The type of panegyric that the young scholar included with his initial pleas for friendship expressed an image of the ideal humanist and thus constituted for the elite group of intellectuals a frame of reference for their concept of themselves. Just as in the Middle Ages the expression of patronage had been based on underlying feudal relations, so in the Renaissance (with patronal relations having changed to resemble more closely those of antiquity) the humanists found the Roman notion of *amicitia* a convenient expression with which to mask the pragmatism of their own patronal relations.[7] The rituals of friendship observed in the humanists' correspondence, as well as the catchphrases they used to refer to their philosophy of *humanitas* and *eloquentia* and their appreciation of *bonae litterae*, established a group identity for them. By taking part in exchanges of correspondence and cultivating friendships with other humanists, a young scholar-poet could demonstrate that he had assimilated the appropriate rules of behaviour and thereby was qualified to be admitted to the *nobilitas litteraria*.[8]

The extant letters of Rudolf Agricola Junior to the Swiss humanist and Reformer Joachim Vadian cover the whole of Agricola's professional life, from 1511, the year after his arrival at Cracow as a student, to February 1521, the month before his death (with the exception of the time he spent at Vienna in the company of Vadian and his colleagues, from 1515 to mid-1517).[9] The twenty-two letters from the young, aspiring Agricola to his mentor chronicle Agricola's search for stable and fulfilling employment from Cracow through the Hungarian kingdom to Vienna and back to Cracow.

That Agricola sought out Vadian indicates that Vadian's name was already known in the intellectual world outside Vienna at that early date.[10] A native of Saint Gall, Vadian (whose vernacular surname was von Watt) had received his master's degree at Vienna and was lecturing on classical texts. He had published editions of the pseudo-Homeric *Batrachomyomachia*, of Strabo's *Hortulus*, and of Sallust's *De coniuratione Catilinae et bello Iugurthino*, as well as having seen his own poems and orations printed.[11] During Agricola's stay in Vienna, from 1514 to 1517, Vadian would experience the high point of his academic career. In 1514 he became a member of the Collegium Ducale,[12] held the office of vice-chancellor, and was crowned poet laureate. Vadian was chosen as the university's chief representative at the Congress of 1515, where he headed the list of speakers at the reception held for visiting dignitaries. In 1516 he succeeded Angelus Cospus as professor of poetry and rhetoric, thereby becoming the third person after Conrad Celtis to hold the most celebrated humanist chair in the German lands. In the winter semester 1515–16, Vadian was elected rector of the university. He completed a degree in medicine in 1517, but continued to lecture on rhetoric and the art of poetry, while also applying his efforts to the study of geography. His academic publications culminated in 1518 with his book on the art of poetry, *De poetica et carminis ratione liber*, and his scholia to Pomponius Mela's *De orbis situ*. Vadian left Vienna in 1518 and returned to Saint Gall, where he married, set up a medical practice, and took a seat on the town council.

Agricola's letters to Vadian not only reveal facets of Agricola's relationship with Vadian, but also describe Agricola's interactions with his Polish and Hungarian patrons, most notably the royal secretary Johannes Dantiscus, the bishops Jan Konarski and Jan Lubrański, and the royal adviser Justus Ludovicus Decius. Agricola's critical tone in respect to some of his patrons gives the modern reader a view of the poet-patron relationship that departs from the panegyric adulations of the published literature and hints at not-so-cordial relations 'behind the scenes.'

The frank disapproval of certain Cracow dignitaries contained in Agricola's letters indicates that these missives were not intended for publication. Only one letter was printed during Agricola's lifetime, that of 25 August 1514, written from Esztergom, in which he stated his interest in geography and asked Vadian questions relating to Vadian's research on Persius, Pliny, and Pomponius Mela. This letter does not appear among those edited by Emil Arbenz as part of the collected correspondence of Vadian.[13] Bearing marks of polishing and revision, it is written in a more elegant style than the letters that remained in manuscript at Saint Gall, and it opens with a formal, extended panegyric of Vadian. Because of its lengthy praise of Vadian and because it contains phrases reminiscent of the extant letters written by Agricola to Vadian from Cracow in 1511,[14] one can only surmise that what started out as a 'private' letter, in which Agricola was still at the stage of ingratiating himself with Vadian by expressing an interest in the latter's research, gave Vadian an instrument for whetting the public's appetite by publishing a sort of advertisement for his forthcoming commentary on Pomponius Mela. Printed together, Agricola's letter and Vadian's response (in which he answers Agricola's queries and also offers a digest of contemporary notions of geography and of research methods in this field) formed a sort of treatise. This published exchange of letters – with its nod to the humanist convention of modesty – communicated scientific knowledge, whereas Agricola's other letters, which remained in manuscript, related events connected with the course of his career.

Although 'we have no adequate substitute for the words "public" and "private" when describing the tensions in humanist letter-writing,' simply because 'the humanists did not distinguish as insistently as we do between private and public letter-writing,'[15] it seems safe to regard Agricola's missives to Vadian as private reflections on his lot in life conveyed to a person who could help him improve his situation. The letters depicted his daily life, his relationship with his colleagues, and his work and leisure, and they referred to political and other newsworthy events at Cracow in which Vadian might have been interested.

Moreover, Agricola wrote his letters to Vadian in a casual style that suggests he was more interested in communicating a message than producing a polished piece of writing for publication. He begged Vadian to forgive his brevity and his mistakes, and he flattered Vadian by saying that when writing to him he could scarcely contain himself, and that in any case an elevated style would mask the truth he wished to communicate and therefore be displeasing to Vadian. On some occasions, Agricola claimed he was writing in haste, sending his letters with compatriots who were travelling and could serve as couriers. [16] But the excuse of 'haste in writing' was a topos used by the humanists to conceal the effort that went into their letters,[17] and Agricola's letters, in conformity with the requirements of humanist discourse, certainly displayed his erudition and wit, sprinkled as they were with proverbs and quotations from the classics, and clever jokes.[18]

By the time he started to write to Vadian, Agricola would have completed enough education to enable him to compose letters in accordance with the norms of humanist epistolography. Having learned the rudiments of writing Latin at school, Agricola would have mastered the art of Latin prose composition at Leipzig. It is not out of the question that he attended the lectures there on St Jerome's letters given by the wandering humanist Johannes Rhagius Aesticampianus.[19] Agricola most likely further refined his ability to write Latin prose during the time he spent with the Breslau teacher Laurentius Corvinus.[20] Agricola evidently gave extramural classes on epistolography at Cracow and Vienna, as evidenced by his connection with the printing of three handbooks on the subject – by Filippo Beroaldo (the Elder),[21] Johannes Aesticampianus (the Elder),[22] and Johannes Sacranus.[23]

In spite of the asserted sincerity of its author, therefore, Agricola's correspondence with Vadian served, for the most part, as a vehicle for his self-promotion. He portrays himself, first of all, as having a clear idea of his identity as a young poet and teacher: he is an exponent of humanist learning, eager for advancement. In fact, his participation in the ritual of letter-writing, as a younger scholar writing to a more established colleague, asking for a sign of friendship, demonstrates that he was seeking integration in the humanist elite.[24] As his relationship with Vadian developed and his own needs changed, the rhetoric he employed in the letters changed, thereby signalling an alteration in his posture towards Vadian in keeping not only with their maturing relationship but also with his own developing career strategies. In fact, Agricola's presentation of himself to Vadian is an exercise not in self-revelation or self-analysis, but in self-fashioning.[25] Although Agricola stressed that he and Vadian were bound by friendship and compatriotism, his letters contained no real sense that this was an egalitarian relationship, given that he revealed himself to be reliant on Vadian for advice and, in the end, to depend on Vadian, as a 'broker' in the patronage process, to secure a job for him.[26] Since Agricola was able to offer Vadian, either materially or through influence, very little in return for the latter's favours, the content of his letters to Vadian was taken up with his own project of self-promotion.

If it is correct that, at the end of the Middle Ages, finding one's identity had to do with 'the acquisition of a skill and its public recognition,'[27] then we can presume that Agricola, by virtue of his being trained in the tradition of the wandering poets, possessed a thorough notion of his identity as such a poet. By the time Agricola began his correspondence with Vadian in 1511, the occupational pattern of the wandering poet-scholar had been established for some sixty years in central Europe, having begun with Peter Luder (1415–72) and his generation, who went from university to university, serving as guest lecturers in poetry and rhetoric. The founding, in the second half of the fifteenth century, of new universities in the German-speaking lands by territorial princes and city councils – for example, Freiburg im Breisgau, Basel, Ingolstadt, Trier, Mainz, Tübingen, Greifswald – increased the number of 'resting places for the wandering humanists who continued the medieval *Studentenwanderung* with a *Professorenwanderung*.'[28] Cracow, although lying politically outside this area, fell within the region that attracted these poets, having been visited, for example, by Conrad Celtis at the high point of the early phase of central European humanism, at the end of the fifteenth century. Although Celtis's stay at Cracow took place twenty years before Agricola's arrival, a direct line can be traced from him to Agricola, through his disciple Laurentius Corvinus, whom Agricola claimed as a teacher.

These *Wanderpoeten* had not been ordained, and for Agricola ordination would have meant a change in career and the adoption of a new identity. So the dilemma in which Agricola found himself towards the end of his life – his indecision, in 1519 and 1520, over whether to remain in Cracow and take holy orders at the suggestion of his ecclesiastical patrons or to return to Lake Constance and be ordained there as a country priest – was a crisis of identity. His portrayal of his predicament to Vadian stands as the climax of his correspondence; here, more than in any other portion of the correspondence, the well-developed rhetorical strategies he employed reveal that the letters, as friendly and intimate as they may seem, served as a vehicle of self-promotion. They constituted, in fact, part of his attempt to convert himself from an 'outsider' to an 'insider.'

From the start and throughout his correspondence with Vadian, Agricola represented himself as a young and energetic scholar – referring to himself as *puer* or *adolescens*—willing to learn and eager for advancement.[29] He employed no modesty topos, as he would in his dedicatory letters (see the next section, 'Approaching the Patron'), but rather promoted himself overtly, stressing his own industriousness.[30] He praised his own works and sent Vadian copies of his books: his edition of Maffeo Vegio's *Philalethes* (which he termed 'not lacking refinement'),[31] his book of epigrams (which, he reported, his tutor Michael Wratislaviensis had called 'not ineffectual'),[32] his poem written for the wedding of King Sigismund and Bona,[33] his edition of the pseudo-Crates *Epistolae cynicae*, and his poem on St Stanislaus, *Hymnus de diuo Stanislao*.[34] He was quick to emphasize his credentials and his contacts, by naming the famous teachers under whom he had studied – Hemio Virotus Burgundus, Laurentius Corvinus, Constantius Italus, Johannes Amatus Siculus, and Michael Wratislaviensis[35] – and noting his connections with prominent contemporaries, such as Ulrich von Hutten (whom he had known by sight at Leipzig) and Henricus Glareanus (with whom he had been a pupil at Rottweil).[36]

Agricola thought of himself as a member of the Republic of Letters, of a network of scholars devoted to the revival of the classics and the renewal of the Latin language, as evidenced by his use of the term *respublica litteraria* and the phrases *bonae litterae* and *politiores litterae*.[37] In his very first letter, Agricola told Vadian that his (Vadian's) reputation had grown out of his devotion to the revival of authors who had been neglected. He praised Vadian as the restorer of good literature (*bonarum litterarum instaurator maximus*), at the same time complaining that he himself was tortured by the study of dialectic.[38] Agricola, furthermore, understood his role as a 'networker' in the transnational community of humanists; he exhibited a keenness to keep Vadian informed of scholarly activity at Cracow (and in Hungary, while he was there), at both the personal and the professional level, and he expressed an ongoing interest in being kept in touch with people at Vienna and Saint Gall. He introduced to Vadian the younger scholars from Cracow, his own student Sebastian Grübel (also a native of Saint Gall) and an unnamed graduate (*bonus ille homo titulo baccalaureatus insignitus*) from Ulm who had come to Cracow for the study of astronomy; and he commended scholars he met in Hungary, such as Michael de Unganartz.[39] He sent greetings from those whom Vadian knew at Cracow, such as Michael Wratislaviensis and Sebastian Steinhofer, and from those he knew at Esztergom, such as Stephanus Taurinus.[40] Agricola gave Vadian news of people visiting Cracow – from Vienna, for example, the humanist scholar and emissary Johannes Cuspinian and the poet Philipp Gundel.[41] He supplied Vadian with gossip, as when he wrote that the poet Johannes Hadelius was being touted at Cracow as the most learned of the Viennese scholars, much to his displeasure.[42] After his return from Vienna, Agricola asked to be remembered to those 'of our sort' back there, such as Georgius Collimitius; and after Vadian had moved back to Saint Gall, Agricola sent along his regards to friends in the Lake Constance region, such as Jacob Suter.[43] On a more professional level, Agricola kept Vadian informed of the work he and his colleagues were publishing at Cracow, such as the poetry composed for the wedding of King Sigismund and Bona Sforza in the spring of 1518 and his own poem on the life of St Stanislaus;[44] and he sent books to Vienna upon the request of the scholars there.[45] He related to Vadian what he had heard from Ludovicus Bovillus about Luther's activities in Wittenberg.[46] And, in an effort to keep up with publications by the German humanists, he inquired constantly of Vadian as to what people were doing. He expressed his admiration for Johannes Camers at Vienna, a man occupied with theology yet who was doing much to help the Republic of Letters.[47] Agricola praised Ulrich von Hutten's *De arte uersificandi*, stating that he would lecture on it.[48] He encouraged Vadian to keep publishing and to send him copies of his work, especially his commentary on Pomponius Mela.[49]

So, from the beginning, Agricola demonstrated that he had a concrete notion of his identity as a scholar-poet, formed in the tradition of the *Wanderpoeten*, and of his role as a member of the Republic of Letters. Yet the evidence that his correspondence with Vadian served as an instrument of his own self-promotion is found in the posture he adopted towards Vadian, which changed as his own needs changed. At each stage, Agricola constructed an image of himself designed to gain Vadian's approval. Even when he was not in need of Vadian's material help or influence, he hankered after a sign that he was accepted as a member of the international intellectual elite, which Vadian's friendship could offer. In his very first letters, Agricola heaped panegyrics on Vadian, by addressing him as the most learned professor of refined letters (i.e., literature) and admitting that he was apprehensive about writing to him.[50] He confessed that he admired Vadian as a model;[51] he let Vadian know that he was familiar with his work, and praised the quality of his scholarship; and he asked Vadian to produce more and to send him his books. Agricola also approached Vadian as an academic adviser, in asking him, for example, to criticize his work – his edition of Maffeo Vegio's *Philalethes*[52] and his own book of epigrams.[53] But after Agricola returned to Cracow from Vienna, his flattery of Vadian diminished: he no longer projected an image of himself as a poor young man wandering from town to town, but rather one of a successful poet busy attending to his many powerful patrons. At this point, he asked Vadian to recognize his success.[54] Agricola would turn to Vadian again for advice, especially in 1519 and 1520, when he became eager to leave Cracow.[55] During these last two years of his life, Agricola sought Vadian's influence in obtaining an ecclesiastical post for him. In every letter from February 1519 until his last in February 1521, he implored Vadian to intercede with the abbot of Saint Gall[56] to provide a benefice for him, and his pleading was intensified by images of his ill health and poverty, and the misery caused by the incessant wars being waged by the Poles.[57]

In his letters from 1511 to 1514, the years in which he completed his baccalaureate and began his career, Agricola fashioned himself as a struggling young man and, having made an attempt to ingratiate himself with Vadian, thrust himself upon Vadian for support at Vienna. Having left Cracow for Hungary in the second half of 1513, evidently in search of employment,[58] he ended up writing to Vadian from Esztergom a few months later, stating his intention to leave Hungary for Vienna. A crusade against the Turks called by Cardinal Tamás Bakócz, the archbishop of Esztergom, in the spring of 1514 had resulted in an uprising of the peasant recruits against the nobility, and forced the magnates of Hungary to gather their own armies to quell the rebellion. The uprising was put down in July of that year, but retaliations by the peasants took place for months afterwards. Beset by other worries, Agricola's patron at Esztergom apparently no longer felt concern for the intellectuals he had called to his courts.[59] In his letter of October 1514, Agricola depicted himself as taking up his cross, and wrote that he had no choice but to leave and find a quiet haven. Apparently destined by the stars to a life of poverty, he remarked, he would prefer to suffer in the midst of learned men than to continue as a poor courtier chasing after vain hope. Vadian had not invited him to Vienna, and it appears that Agricola informed him of his decision to leave Hungary and of the reasons for his departure only in this letter: he announced that he was setting out shortly for Vienna and did not have much money, and asked Vadian the favour of providing lodgings for him.[60]

After he returned to Cracow from Vienna towards the end of 1517, Agricola portrayed himself as a courtier flourishing in the company of aristocrats and ecclesiarchs. In his letters of 1517 and 1518, he referred in boasting tones to the dignitaries with whom he was now connected. In December 1517 he mentioned that he had been occupied because his patron, the bishop of Cracow (Jan Konarski), had come to town.[61] In January 1518 he wrote that he was busy because the king had returned to Cracow from Muscovy, and that 'those who needed to flatter him' were gathering at the court;[62] and in February he informed Vadian that Sigismund von Herberstein, the emperor's ambassador, had returned from the East and had asked Agricola and Johannes Dantiscus, then a royal secretary, to compose poems celebrating his mission to Muscovy as a gift for him.[63] In his letter of 30 April 1518, Agricola wrote that he was sending along the poem that Laurentius Corvinus had written for the widowed King Sigismund's wedding to the Italian princess Bona Sforza, and noted that his own epithalamium, as well as those of Caspar Ursinus Velius and Dantiscus, was in the press. Agricola ended this letter by promising Vadian that he would write more after the stipend money for his university teaching was settled by the bishops who were supporting him.[64]

The mood of his letters deteriorated when, after Vadian's visit to Cracow in February 1519,[65] Agricola began to plead with him to intercede with the abbot of Saint Gall for a benefice.[66] At this point, Agricola split his self-representation into two versions, one private and one public: to Vadian, he presented himself as in a state of crisis, and to the public, he presented himself as a successful poet and teacher. To Vadian, once again describing himself as *adolescens* and *pauper*, with an unstable career, he was critical of his patrons;[67] publicly he continued to lavish these same men with praises. Certainly he was at the peak of his career at this time. He had been crowned poet laureate in 1515 while in Vienna,[68] he could now claim the title *lector ordinarius* at the University of Cracow, and he had been appointed tutor to the Italian pages of Queen Bona.

Agricola's approach to Vadian during 1519 and 1520 consisted of two strategies. The first of these was to paint his situation at Cracow as being as miserable as possible. He called the Poles the proudest and most fickle of humans, and grumbled about the treatment received by the Germans in Cracow especially from the polonized German inhabitants.[69] Upon the death of Jan Lubrański, bishop of Poznań (23 May 1520), the attitude of the other bishops changed and they were not paying him in full.[70] By December 1520 Agricola was claiming real poverty. The Poles were promising great things, but Agricola scarcely had the means to dispel the cold. He did not like the climate or the people at Cracow.[71] All these complaints, whether true or not, reinforced Agricola's arguments for wishing to leave Cracow, but in reality he had not given up on soliciting the patronage of the dignitaries there.

Agricola's second strategy for persuading Vadian to seek out a benefice for him at Saint Gall was to represent himself to Vadian as a fellow countryman, even a sort of clansman. He reinforced his demands with sentimental, idyllic images of their common homeland, expressing his desire to be close to Vadian, to be 'at home,' to settle in the countryside and have a garden with vines, where Vadian, growing old, could enjoy himself with his children, of which Agricola hoped he would have many, who would resemble him, by his chaste wife. Agricola told Vadian to let the abbot know how much he wanted to return to *their* fatherland.[72] He had been quick to establish the regional (Lake Constance) connection at the outset of his correspondence, and his rhetorical tactics of 1519 and 1520 can be seen as the culmination of his appeal to Vadian as a clansman. In his very first letter, he stated that one of the reasons he had decided to write to Vadian was that he was a compatriot (*conterraneus*). He later addressed Vadian by the terms *confrater* (*confrère*) and *uernaculus* (belonging to one's country, with the implication of coming from the same language area). In encouraging Vadian to visit him at Cracow, Agricola mentioned that he and his colleagues had a jug of wine from Saint Gall.[73] After his return from Vienna, Agricola became friends with members of Vadian's family who were living at Cracow, and he reported on their well-being.[74] He wrote a poem to preface Vadian's *Elegia de insignibus familiae Vadianorum*.[75] In 1519, in the middle of his campaign to have Vadian obtain a benefice for him, Agricola asked Vadian to look after his father's affairs.[76]

In the representation of his identity to the public, Agricola showed himself to be a dedicated protégé, still actively seeking patronage. At the same time that he was writing scathing letters to Vadian about the treatment he was receiving, Agricola was showering the very patrons he criticized with panegyrics in the dedications of his books: in February 1519 he dedicated Johannes de Lapide's *Resolutorium dubiorum circa celebrationem missarum occurrentium* to Jan Konarski, the bishop of Cracow; in August 1519, his own *Hymnus de diuo Stanislao* to the grand-chancellor Krzysztof Szydłowiecki; also in 1519, Nicolaus de Toliszków's *Iudicium* to Jan Konarski, the archdeacon of Cracow (and a relation of the bishop), Robertus de Euremodio's *Institutiones uitae* to the royal banker Severin Boner, and Nicolaus de Błonie's *De sacramentis* to Piotr Tomicki, the bishop of Przemyśl; and in March 1520, his own *Passio dominica* to Johann Bethmann, a member of the powerful Cracow banking family.

Agricola's crisis seems to have been brought on by pressure placed on him by his patrons at Cracow to embark upon a church career. In his letter to Vadian of 13 June 1519, he told Vadian that he had never demanded anything from his patrons at Cracow other than a stipend for his teaching at the university, but now the bishop of Poznań, Jan Lubrański, was promising a canonry.[77] He also mentioned that Maciej Drzewicki, the bishop of Włocławek, was keeping him in Cracow with promises, which most likely also had to do with an ecclesiastical post.[78] In his letter to Vadian of 25 August 1519, Agricola admitted that he understood taking holy orders at Cracow would help him establish a stable career there, but that he had rejected the idea of an ecclesiastical career in Poland.[79] In August 1520 he stated that he had been offered a benefice with a salary of twenty florins, but that he had turned it down because he wanted to leave Cracow. By December 1520 the offered salary at Cracow had been increased to fifty florins, but again he had rejected it. He had, of course, previously complained that the climate at Cracow was unhealthy, and that the Poles were antagonistic towards the Germans there.[80]

Agricola's crisis peaked in the summer of 1520, and the letters from the last six months of his life were full of dithering over whether or not to leave Cracow. By September 1520, not having had a satisfactory response from Vadian to his request for a benefice, Agricola stated that he would go to Leipzig or Wittenberg – that is, unless the Cracow bishops started paying him. In December he wrote that he was determined to go home and to take holy orders there. Two months later, in February 1521, he wrote that the climate at Cracow was unhealthy and that he was ill. Having mentioned again the possibility of his going to Wittenberg, he confirmed that he wanted to leave Cracow, but indicated that he was still held back by the promises of the bishops. He was prepared to go to Basel in the meanwhile, even without a stipend.[81]

The favour that Agricola asked of Vadian was never granted, and Vadian's biographer, Werner Näf, remarks that after Vadian returned to Saint Gall, he quickly loosened his ties with Vienna and Cracow and turned his sights to the west, towards Basel and Paris, as he became more adjusted to his new, family-oriented life in a small Swiss town.[82] Agricola's constant complaints that his correspondent did not write, therefore, seem to have been more than a literary topos. Rudolf Agricola Junior died at Cracow on 4

March 1521. Sebastian Steinhofer wrote to Vadian shortly after, informing him of the poet's death and describing his final days. From Steinhofer's letter it would seem that Agricola's description of his poverty had not been an exaggeration: in Steinhofer's opinion, it was Agricola's indigence and adverse fortune that had led to his death. In the end, his books and his household goods were estimated to be worth scarcely ten florins.[83]

Throughout the correspondence, Agricola addressed Vadian as a friend and supporter (*amicus, fautor*). In a characteristic manoeuvre for gaining acceptance into the intellectual elite, Agricola asked to be counted among Vadian's friends; he stated that he wished to live and die with Vadian; and he continually implored Vadian to return his affection.[84] When complaining that Vadian's letters were becoming scarce, Agricola stressed the tight personal bond of friendship between them, one based on their common place of origin and their common interest in humanist scholarship, so as to induce a feeling of guilt in him.[85] In spite of these assertions of friendship, Vadian remained as Agricola's mentor and his broker in the patronage system, and Agricola was aware of how little he could do in return for his favours: he could try to spread Vadian's fame; he could give him hospitality at Cracow; he could send small gifts, such as wild fowl.[86]

As 'personal' as Agricola's letters to Vadian may appear, they were a means of self-promotion on Agricola's part, and they involved considerable self-fashioning. To be able to manipulate his identity as he did, Agricola must have started with an awareness of himself as a *poeta.* His crisis – over whether to choose to keep the patronage of the Polish bishops (and hence to enter the priesthood at Cracow) or to look elsewhere for employment – resulted in a significant discrepancy between the identity he was presenting to Vadian and the one he was displaying publicly. The crisis had been provoked by the suggestion of a change in career – and thus a change in identity – when the bishops advised him to take holy orders. Agricola's resistance to entering the priesthood at Cracow certainly involved his desire to maintain his independence from the 'fickle' Poles, but it affirmed even more his desire to remain teaching poetry and rhetoric at the university, and his reluctance to forsake his identity as a lay *poeta.* If he were going to change careers, then he would do so only back in his homeland, by retiring to the countryside as a rural parish priest.[87]

APPROACHING THE PATRON: THE DEDICATORY LETTERS OF RUDOLF AGRICOLA JUNIOR, VALENTIN ECK, AND LEONARD COX[88]

Renaissance dedicatory letters, which reshaped a classical genre to suit the needs of the early modern patronage system, represent a form of 'metaliterature' that allows us to study methods of self-promotion and career building in the sixteenth century. The images of the writer and his relationship to his work, his patrons, and his public that were projected in these letters were shaped by rhetorical strategies[89] that were complex yet familiar to the intellectual community of the time. The dedication of a book as a monument to a patron conferred fame on the patron, and simultaneously, the public contact of its author with a well-known and respected person assisted the author by boosting his reputation[90] and conferring on his book an importance that would help promote sales. Furthermore, in the dedicatory letter the writer could bring a political, pedagogical, or religious agenda to the attention of both influential persons and the general public.[91]

Rudolf Agricola Junior, Valentin Eck, and Leonard Cox were well aware of the advantages of dedicating a book to a famous person.[92] In their dedicatory letters, they employed the complex strategies of this genre to attract and retain patrons, thereby demonstrating that they were versed in the rules of decorum and that they could observe the boundaries of modesty while directly promoting their books, their own scholarship, and their pedagogical program and political views. Surely they had taken note of the methods of book dedications employed by central European humanist poets of the 1490s.[93] In their own dedicatory letters, Agricola Junior, Eck, and Cox projected an image of themselves as competent scholars of pious Christian character, eager to advance their careers and conscious of how to work within the patronage system, just as did other poets of their generation, such as Caspar Ursinus Velius.[94]

Agricola, Eck, and Cox were familiar with the aims of dedicatory letters. In his dedication of Ptolemy's *Cosmographia*, to which Agricola contributed prefatory verses, the Cracow astronomer Johannes de Stobnica explained that scholars dedicated their books to a good leader in order to show gratitude for benefits accepted from him and to add his approval to the book.[95] Eck stated more than once that books dedicated to a 'literate and wise' man were widely read.[96] Agricola noted that those who wanted their works to appeal to posterity formally dedicated them to deserving patrons.[97] In his handbook on versification, Eck told Justus Ludovicus Decius explicitly that he was dedicating the book to him to make it more marketable.[98]

In spite of this apparent self-consciousness on the part of the authors, the dedicatory letters themselves are extremely formulaic. They are full of florid, sycophantic language designed to flatter the patron. The writers humble themselves and speak modestly of their work before the patron, although they take care to present themselves as industrious and their writing as useful for students. The language employed by Agricola, Eck, and Cox in their dedicatory letters was, quite simply, the manifestation of an effort to conform to the requirements of an ostentatious rhetoric.[99] Every dedicatory letter was a variation of a literary pattern conditioned by the ceremony of offering a work to a person connected with the author either by friendship or by the possibility that he would provide support.[100] So, although modern readers might perceive in the scholars' approach to their patrons a conspicuous absence of originality or inventiveness, the hackneyedness of the formulas employed bothered neither the scholars, nor, one can presume, their patrons. Valentin Eck recycled catchphrases from one dedication to another and still managed to attract patrons.[101] Rudolf Agricola took his letter to Jan Łaski, the archbishop of Gniezno, from *Statuta prouinciae Gnesnensis* and reprinted it in its entirety the following year in Nicolaus de Błonie's *Tractatus de sacramentis*, where he addressed it to Piotr Tomicki, at that time bishop of Przemyśl and vice-chancellor of Poland, and the political rival of Łaski.[102]

To be successful in their dedications, Agricola, Eck, and Cox needed to be able to manipulate rhetorical conventions effectively, so as to communicate their message in an elegant and refined manner and to create an image of themselves as learned, pious, and sincere men. The dedicatory letter appears as an oratorical monologue, in which the author states why he is dedicating his work to the patron and describes its genesis.[103] This speech, of course, is addressed to the dedicatee, but because the letter is written for publication, it is also addressed to readers.[104] So Agricola, Eck, and Cox were faced with the task of representing themselves and their books to a double audience.

Agricola, Eck, and Cox conformed with the most important

requirement for the author's presentation of himself in the dedicatory letter: emphasis on his modesty.[105] The most direct way of showing modesty was by using a vocabulary of submission and inferiority. Agricola, Eck, and Cox displayed humility before their dedicatees by using such expressions as *rogo, praecor, obsequium,* and *humiliter subicio* when asking the dedicatee to accept the gift.[106] A greater degree of submission was shown by the use of such verbs as *parere* and *cogere,* as in a letter from Agricola to Carolus Antonius Moncinereus, the secretary of the bishop of Płock,[107] emphasizing Agricola's relinquishing of responsibility in the publishing of his work and his surrender to authority.

Modesty could also be expressed by stressing devotion to the patron. Justus Ludovicus Decius, the secretary to the Boner banking family, described Eck's eagerness to have Bishop Maciej Drzewicki's patronage when he recommended Eck's poem *Threni neglectae religionis* to Drzewicki.[108] Likewise, Agricola, in his preface to Eck's poem *De antiquissima nominis et familiae Thurzonum origine,* informed Alexius Thurzó that Eck was eager for his patronage.[109] In 1524, Cox wrote to Decius, then royal secretary, that he owed everything to Decius's country, Poland.[110] Eck told Alexius Thurzó that he was 'completely his' and owed everything he had to him.[111] When writing to Thurzó, Eck put his surname in a diminutive form, 'Ecchiolus,' referred to himself as *clientulus,* and recorded his residence as *ex nostra domuncula.*[112]

Another strategy for expressing modesty was for the author to underplay his own responsibility for the work and to place emphasis on the contribution of the dedicatee or others associated with him.[113] The writer could deflect attention from himself by stating that he had been requested by the dedicatee or others to write, or even that he had been forced into publishing the work. Leonard Cox, for example, stated that he had produced his oration in praise of the University of Cracow at the request of many people.[114] In the prefaces to both editions of his handbook on versification, Valentin Eck wrote that he was publishing his notes on the composition of poetry in the first instance at the insistence of students (whom Eck wished to save from further tedious lectures) and in the second at the request of friends.[115] In 1524, Cox noted in his dedication to Justus Ludovicus Decius of *Venatio,* a lengthy poem on hunting and banqueting by Adriano Castellesi, that it was Decius who had originally recommended the poem to him.[116] Rudolf Agricola mentioned in the preface to his *Hymnus de beatis-*

simae uirginis conceptu passiuo, that the dedicatee, Johannes Salomon, scholastic of Gniezno and canon of Cracow, had frequently encouraged him to write on the Immaculate Conception.[117] Furthermore, in his preface to *Illustrissimae reginae Bonae paraceleusis*, Agricola claimed that Carolus Antonius Moncinereus, the secretary of Bishop Erazm Ciołek (the bishop was the actual dedicatee of the poem), had forced him to print a poem that he felt was not yet ready for publication.[118] Probably the most extreme example of the avoiding of responsibility is found in the two letters by Eck's patron Decius that precede Eck's poem *Threni neglectae religionis*. In the first, Decius recommends Eck as a client to Bishop Drzewicki, and in the second, he urges Eck to publish the poem. Eck evidently still felt it necessary to have some say in the presentation of his work because he also included a short prefatory poem praising the bishop.

Although the writer of the dedicatory letter exhibited severe modesty in regard to himself,[119] he did not condemn himself. The humanist scholars may have diminished their own talent,[120] but they never hesitated to point out their diligence and to place emphasis on their industriousness. The diligence of the writer was often linked to the prompting of the patrons, and the relationship of the writer to the dedicatee was thereby reinforced. Agricola, for example, told Jan Konarski, the bishop of Cracow, that he was so inspired by the support of the bishop and his family for students, that he, Agricola, let no hour pass that he did not devote to commenting on texts or reading the celebrated authors.[121] Agricola also told members of the Salomon banking family that he was grateful to them for having assisted him for the past ten years in his services to the university, to philosophy, and to the rest of the liberal arts.[122] Valentin Eck worried lest he fall into idleness when he was not teaching.[123]

The writer's diligence could also be expressed as a concern for scholarship – especially for accuracy in scholarship and elegance in the writing of Latin. Rudolf Agricola stated that he had taken the trouble to rescue from oblivion 'a brilliant work,' Maffeo Vegio's dialogue *Philalethes* (while not wishing, of course, to seem envious of another author's praise).[124] Agricola worried about letting his work be published before it was polished and corrected, and referred to Horace's precept to keep a work for nine years.[125] And Leonard Cox informed Decius that he had put his effort into his commentary on Castellesi's *Venatio* so that the students could learn from the book how to imitate elegant classical Latin. Moreover, Cox stated that he was submitting his work to Decius for scrutiny by him so that his published scholia would be worthy of him.[126] By using the word *lucubrationes* here to describe his work, Cox hinted at his diligence. This term, meaning 'works produced by lamplight,' was a topos in use since Cicero, tied to the popular image of a learned man sitting up and reading by candlelight when the rest of the world was asleep.[127]

The rhetorical rules calling for a display of modesty on the part of the writer of the dedication were also applied to the representation of the book, as the book was seen as an extension of its author or publisher.[128] Agricola's claim, in his dedication of Beroaldo's *Modus epistolandi* to the Franciscans Jacob Wirtenberger and Otto Vinerius,[129] that the book he was publishing was 'small but useful' was typical of the tone of the presentation of the work to the patron. Accordingly, Valentin Eck excused himself to Alexius Thurzó in the dedication of his poem *An prudenti uiro sit ducenda uxor* by asking Thurzó not to consider the smallness of the book, but rather the attitude of the giver.[130] The writers might also say that the book was unequal to the favours or benefits they had received from the patron, as did Rudolf Agricola to his teacher Michael Wratislaviensis in 1512.[131]

The book, no matter what its size, was always referred to in the diminutive, *libellus*, *opusculum*, or *munusculum*, and was termed *paruum*, *gracile*, *tenue*, *minutulum*, or *pusillum*. Even references to the dedicatory letter itself were in the diminutive, *epistolium*.[132] Yet the scholar had to take care not to undermine the value of the book, especially if he was editing someone else's work. For example, when Leonard Cox presented his edition of Henry VIII's letter to Martin Luther to the royal chancellor Krzysztof Szydłowiecki,[133] Cox was faced with the delicate need to maintain modesty in regard to his own work while not detracting from the work of a great king. He struck a balance by retaining the use of the diminutive but adding a laudatory adjective, terming the book *aureus libellus*.

So, while keeping within the bounds of modesty, the writer had to emphasize the value of the book. The book functioned as a gift to the dedicatee, not just as an extension of the writer, and was tied in with expressions of friendship and the offering of thanks for benefits received from the patron. Rudolf Agricola told the Swiss student Sebastian Grübel that his edition of Octavius Cleophilus Phanensis's *De poetarum coetu* stood as a monument to their friendship.[134] And Valentin Eck felt that the publication of his panegyric poem in honour of Augustinus Moravus, provost of Olomouc, would stand as a monument and token of his respect for the dedicatee, Sigismund Glotzer, canon (*canonicus*) of Olomouc (of whom Augustinus was also a patron), and would bind their friendship.[135] Valentin Eck remarked to Alexius Thurzó that he had no great gift or money with which to honour Thurzó, but offered him a small poem.[136] Agricola believed that his gift of Johannes de Nova Domo's *De constitutionibus humani corporis* to Jodocus Glatz, a Cracow city councillor, would let people see that a patron should be thanked (even if only a little bit).[137]

Furthermore, the writer of the dedicatory letter could arouse the interest of readers by highlighting the seriousness of the book's subject and its usefulness to an audience that needed it.[138] Of course, the rules of decorum required that the scholar could not be seen to be giving advice to a superior, so the author had to state clearly that the patron did not need the knowledge contained in the book because he himself was already so learned. The most effective way to stress the importance of the book's subject matter was to connect it with classical literature or history, thereby not only displaying the erudition of the writer but also providing a point of departure for discussion of the subject matter.[139] Accordingly, Valentin Eck began his introduction to *An prudenti uiro sit ducenda uxor* with a résumé of the treatment of this topic by the Greeks and Romans; his first sentence signalled its importance: 'Socrates ille Atheniensis grauissimus philosophus qui primus relicta naturalium rerum indagatione Ethicen adinuenit ...' Likewise, in his dedicatory letter for the edition of Prudentius's *Cathemerinon* published at Vienna by Vietor in 1515, Agricola gave an account of the history of the relationship between poetry and music. Noting that many Old Testament books were composed in verse, Agricola went on to quote from Plato, to mention Origen, to touch on Pythagorean theory, and to refer to the musical theorist Aristoxenes and the literary historian Dicaearchus. The list of authorities reinforced the importance of the book, a first edition of Prudentius's hymns with a musical score provided by Wolfgang Grafinger (whose works, the reader was informed on the title-page, included the music for Horace's *Carmina*).

Since the writer of a dedicatory letter had chosen precisely this form of preface for his book, his manner of approaching the dedicatee was crucial for the letter's success. The two points of direct address to the patron were in the opening and closing of the letter. The opening direct address to the dedicatee appeared immediately following both the title-page and any preliminary verses, in the form of a header in which the name of the dedicatee was printed together with his titles,[140] whether he was *episcopus, comes, magister, contionator, consul,* and so on.[141] The name of the patron was also usually prefaced by a laudatory adjective such as *reuerendissimus, illustris, magnificus, eruditissimus, uenerabilis, clarissimus, spectabilis,* or *praestantissimus,* the degree of which was adjusted to the occupation and rank of the dedicatee.[142] It was usual for the name of the patron to appear in the opening of the letter, as in the dedication of Caspar Ursinus Velius's *Epistolarum et epigrammatum liber* by Rudolf Agricola to Ladislaus de Boskovice, the chamberlain of the marquis of Moravia, which addressed Ladislaus, *magnifice Ladislae,* immediately, in the first sentence.[143] In the body of the letter the patron was normally addressed by such terms as *fautor, fauentissimus studiosorum maecenas, dominus/patronus colendissimus,* and *generosus et magnificus dominus.* In the closing, the client usually made mention of how generous or helpful the patron had been to him in the past, asked the patron to receive the book with a smile on his face, and wished him well.[144] Typical was Valentin Eck's closing to the dedication of his poem *De diuo Alexio,* which informed Alexius Thurzó that the work was a small attempt to repay Thurzó for his kindness towards him, entreated Thurzó to receive the gift with a peaceful expression on his face, and wished Thurzó a long and happy life.[145]

In the body of the letter the writer could compliment the patron by praising him for his virtue, his learning, and his benevolence; the patron would be associated with the quality of *humanitas, mansuetudo, liberalitas, eruditio, beneuolentia,* or *munificentia.* He could be described as having the charm of Isocrates (*iucunditas Isocratis*), the fairness of Trajan (*Traiani iustitia*), or the prudence of Nestor (*Nestoris prudentia*). Here, again, a model figure from Greek or Roman history was used. Linking the dedicatee to an ancient hero not only flattered him, but also anchored him in history and suggested that his fame would be handed down to posterity. The comparison of the patron with an ancient hero also served to make the patron an example, as when Eck compared Alexius Thurzó to Nestor as a ruler who could throw off barbarism and stated that he wished the kingdom of Hungary would have more leaders similar to Thurzó.[146]

Here the decorum, that is, the degree of modesty expressed on the part of the writer and the degree of glorification of the patron, was determined precisely by the rank of the dedicatee.[147] A change in tone from that of a letter written to a highly placed patron is easily observed in dedicatory letters where the dedicatee is not a superior, as in Rudolf Agricola's second edition of the letters of pseudo-Crates,[148] in which he prefaces the text with a dedication to Nicolaus Salomon, a young member of the Cracow banking family.[149] The glorifying adjectives used for high-ranking officials are missing; the young Salomon is addressed in the heading as *ingenuus praeclaraeque indolis adolescens*, and in the body of the letter simply as *charissime Nicolae*. The tone is clearly that of a teacher to his pupil, as Agricola advises Salomon to scorn idleness, giving the example of the Indian gymnosophists who would throw a pupil out the door if he did not learn well. Agricola states politely, however, that Salomon is not wanting in his studies, nor does he spend his time unwisely.

Although is difficult to know to what extent the praises found in the dedicatory letters were exaggerations, it seems that Agricola, Eck, and Cox had a concern for sincerity and were aware of the risk of flattery. For example, on the one hand, Valentin Eck declared that words could not express the virtues of the Thurzó family,[150] and even compared the relationship between patron and client to that between gods and mortals.[151] On the other hand, he wrote to Decius in the letter prefacing his handbook on versification that he would celebrate Decius's praises, except that he feared destructive critics might accuse him of flattery.[152] And Rudolf Agricola remarked to Johannes Salomon that he wished he could find acceptance with Johannes and the other Salomons honourably, without recourse to flattery.[153]

Since a dedicatory letter was written to appear in printed form along with the book dedicated, its writer had to be conscious of the public. A dedication promoted the book commercially, but it could also bring a pedagogical or political message to the attention of the public, as well as communicate it to the dedicatee.[154] The writer of the dedication normally promoted the book by describing its content, as did Valentin Eck in the dedicatory letter accompanying his handbook on versification, *De arte uersificandi opusculum*, when he outlined the material it covered. In the second edition, he indicated what he had changed in the book and what new material he had added. But the writer could also give guidelines on how the book should be read.[155] Rudolf Agricola, in his prefaces to both printings of his edition of pseudo-Crates, stated that the philosopher should be read with a view to active imitation of his philosophy.[156] In his introduction to Giovanni Pontano's *De laudibus diuinis*, Cox told the young Salomon brothers that he had chosen for them some inspirational reading for Lent.[157]

The scholars often took the opportunity, however, to use dedicatory letters to advance their own views on education or culture. In the prefaces to his editions of Cicero's *Pro Archia* and *Pro rege Deiotaro*, Agricola expressed his complaint that because people had not been taught the classical authors at a young age, there was a want of elegant Latin at Cracow.[158] Eck, in the letters to Alexius Thurzó prefacing his dialogues *De mundi contemptu* and *De reipublicae administratione*, held up Thurzó and King Louis II as models of virtue and learning, while stating a hope that Latin letters and culture would start to flourish in Hungary.[159] In his dedicatory letter prefacing the letters and epigrams of the Silesian poet (and Viennese courtier) Caspar Ursinus Velius, Agricola expressed his views on the quality of German scholarship by comparing the Germans to the Italians and claiming that the Germans were no less erudite or elegant in their Latin composition. Moreover, his listing of two dozen prominent German humanists not only linked his own name to their accomplishments, but, in an echo of Ulrich von Hutten's 1510 poem *Ad poetas Germanos*, also projected an image of the humanists as a powerful, respectable, and cohesive group.[160]

A political or religious message could be reinforced, as well, in a dedicatory letter. For example, Decius wrote to Bishop Drzewicki in 1518 asking for Drzewicki's patronage of Eck's *Threni neglectae religionis*, a poem urging the Polish king to defend the faith against the Muscovites and the Turks; apparently he believed that having Drzewicki's name attached to the poem would help surmount opposition to this policy.[161] Also, Eck himself wrote in the dedication to Thurzó of his life of St Paul the Hermit that Paul could be invoked against the Mohammedan rage.[162] In 1524, Eck told Thurzó in the dedication of his poem *Ad Ludouicum regem* that King Louis II was worthy of praise for instituting an expedition against the Turks, and that he hoped the other Christian leaders would follow his example.[163] And in 1527, after the defeat of Louis at Mohács, Eck wrote to Thurzó that he hoped the new leader, Ferdinand, would be able to repair the damage done to the country.[164] Leonard Cox, when dedicating the exchange of letters between Martin Luther and Henry VIII to the Polish royal chancellor Krzysztof Szydłowiecki, praised both Szydłowiecki and King Sigismund for their efforts in defending the holy faith and in eradicating heresy.[165]

In their dedicatory letters, Rudolf Agricola Junior, Valentin Eck, and Leonard Cox revealed themselves to their dedicatees and to their public as competent scholars of pious Christian character. An examination of their dedicatory letters shows that the genre demanded complex strategies to keep the balance between the expression of the writer's modesty and the promotion of his book. The dedicatory letters of the three humanist scholars are filled with examples of the writer's observation of the boundaries of modesty combined with the direct promotion of his books, his own scholarship, and his pedagogical and political views. Agricola, Eck, and Cox demonstrated that the rules of decorum required in the verbalization of the client-patron relationship were a matter of knowing how to address properly dedicatees of different political and social ranks and occupations. Lack of historical evidence makes it difficult to say to what degree each of their dedicatory letters fulfilled the expectations of the patrons.[166] In any case, the three humanists come across to a modern reader as representative of their time and place: scholar-poets of some talent, eager to advance their careers, and conscious of how to behave within the patronage system.

APPROACHING THE PUBLIC: COMMENDATORY POEMS ACCOMPANYING THE WORKS OF RUDOLF AGRICOLA JUNIOR, VALENTIN ECK, AND LEONARD COX

Commendatory poems, which contained testimonies as to the merits of the author and his work, constituted another principal method of self-promotion and career building for humanist scholars. Although these short poems functioned as advertisements, they also allowed humanists to project to the public an image of intellectual exclusivity and superiority and to sell to aspiring students a pedagogical program that would impart their skills – a knowledge of the newly revived Latin and the ability to write and speak effectively.

Commendatory poems had come into being soon after the invention of printing, as an innovation of the fifteenth-century Italian humanists, and by the 1520s they constituted an established genre. They regularly appeared alongside prefaces, dedicatory letters, and other preliminary or finial material.[167] These short poems had a sole purpose – to sell the book – and thus were advertisements. With the invention of printing, knowledge could be 'captured, packaged, and sold,' but before this could happen, the public needed to be informed of the importance of such knowledge, and much prefatory material in the sixteenth century 'marketed the expertise' of authors and editors as a commodity.[168] The importance of prefatory material in the marketing of books can be illustrated by the example of Erasmus, who, concerned about the printer's abilities to write Latin, composed Johann Froben's preface to the reader for him, emphasizing the editorial superiority of Froben's edition of *Lectiones* by the Italian wandering scholar Lodovico Ricchieri to the rival edition of Jodocus Badius Ascensius.[169]

The situation for booksellers in east central Europe was no different than in other parts of the continent. Hieronymus Vietor, the printer with whom Agricola Junior, Eck, and Cox most frequently published their books, was not without rivals. If, in coming from Vienna and setting up his press at Cracow in 1518, he aimed to capture the Cracow market, he needed to interest the academic sector (the university population made up a large portion of the potential book-buyers in the city) and win this group away from Johannes Haller and Florian Ungler, who had established their printing houses in 1505 and 1510 respectively.[170] Vietor, then, needed to engage the members of the intellectual circles, and one way to do so was to hire scholars to work as editors and correctors. A mark of his success was that he attracted Rudolf Agricola Junior as a collaborator, presumably having lured him away from Ungler's workshop.[171]

In advertising a book, commendatory poems had to assume various tasks: accounting for the text and justifying its publication; providing information about the book, its author, and its printer; and recommending the title to potential buyers, even going so far as appealing directly to customers to buy the book. Yet these verses were more than sixteenth-century equivalents of today's dust-jacket blurbs; working hand in hand with dedicatory prefaces, commendatory poems were designed to control the kind of interpretation the book would be given.[172] In the case of the commendatory verses accompanying the books that Agricola Junior, Eck, and Cox authored or edited, these poems indicated that their work, which abounded in classical knowledge and biblical wisdom, was to be taken seriously, and not as light and entertaining reading matter. Like epistolary dedications, the commendatory verses served to give these books intellectual and moral authority.

In fact, commendatory verses worked in tandem with epistolary dedications to win the support of the reading public by portraying the humanist author/editor as skilled and knowledgable, and as belonging to an elite group of scholars. The role of commendatory poems as support to epistolary dedications, especially in connecting the humanist scholar-poet with a public figure, was made clear whenever the association between the author of the book and his patron was depicted in a commendatory poem. So Valentin Eck's relationship with his patron Alexius Thurzó, then royal secretary under King Louis Jagiellon at Buda, was glorified by Valentin Carbo, the town clerk (*grammateus*)[173] of Kassa, in Carbo's commendatory verse for Eck's panegyric on Thurzó and his family.[174] Carbo termed Eck 'the trumpet of Thurzó's house' for having acclaimed Alexius's nobility and the glory of the Thurzó family. Carbo closed by noting that Eck sought out Thurzó as a patron and felt safe under his protection. Eck's relationship with Thurzó was further magnified by Nicolaus Salomon, a young member of the prominent Cracow merchant family, when he stated in his commendatory poem for the same work that Eck alone had taken on the burden of writing a poem about such an illustrious family. Similarly, Leonard Cox was linked to the highest-ranking dignitaries of the Polish kingdom by Stanislaus Hosius, then a member of Bishop Piotr Tomicki's court at Cracow, in his commendatory poem for Cox's edition of Martin Luther's apology to Henry VIII.[175] Hosius praised Krzysztof Szydłowiecki, the grand-chancellor of Poland and the dedicatee of the book, for his virtue and his upholding of the true religion, and remarked that his fame had reached to farthest Britain and that Erasmus had immortalized him by dedicating his *Lingua* to him. The poem also praised King Sigismund and King Henry for their concern for the preservation of the true religion, as well as

Bishop Tomicki's nephew, Bishop Andrzej Krzycki, for initiating publication of the work. Hosius praised Cox as the primary hope of Polish education (Cox had already published his treatise on the education of youth) and ended the poem by entreating Szydłowiecki to accept Cox's gift.

Besides publicizing the relationship of the author or editor of a book with a high-ranking patron, the author of a commendatory poem could hint at his own relationship with the dedicatee of the book, thus advertising an expanding circle of humanists connected with the dignitary. In his poems for Cox's works, as well as his poem for Eck's *Exhortatio* to King Louis, which urged the king to defend Hungary against the Turks,[176] Stanislaus Hosius referred to himself as 'most devoted' (*deditissimus*) to the dedicatees of these books. In his poem to Krzysztof Szydłowiecki for Cox's publication of Martin Luther's apology, Hosius begged the grand-chancellor to deem him worthy of his favour.

So, like dedicatory letters, these short poems should not be overlooked. They played a significant role in representing the book, as well as its author or editor, to the public. They not only promoted the book for sale, but also projected an image of the author or editor that was designed to advance the humanist and his cause. Through the medium of commendatory verses, the scholar-poets sold not only their books but also themselves. The commendatory poems made the statement that Agricola, Eck, and Cox were offering both a new, superior pedagogy, based on Christian morality, and also the ability to communicate in a pure Latin based on a thorough study of the classics, the Church Fathers, and Italian Renaissance writers. The command of the new humanist Latin that Agricola, Eck, and Cox possessed was their 'selling point.'[177]

The commendatory verses attached to the publications of Agricola, Eck, and Cox number some ninety. They appear in books dating from 1511 to 1527, all of which were printed at Cracow, except for a dozen titles edited by Agricola during his stay at Vienna and published with Hieronymus Vietor or Johannes Singrenius there. The commendatory poems turn up at highly visible points: on the title-page or the verso of the title-page, either before or following the dedicatory letter (if there was one), or even at the end of the book. If two works were being printed together, verses could appear at the end of one or the beginning of the other. The poems were brief, for the most part no more than twenty lines long.[178] Obviously, a large number of commendatory poems could call attention to the book being promoted, but the number of commendatory poems included in a volume does not seem to have been correlated with the rank of the dignitary to whom the book was dedicated. For example, whereas the first edition of Valentin Eck's handbook on versification, dedicated to the Polish economist and royal adviser Justus Ludovicus Decius, had six commendatory poems, Leonard Cox's edition of Martin Luther's letter to Henry VIII, dedicated to the Polish grand-chancellor, had only one.[179]

The poems were composed by colleagues and students of Agricola, Eck, and Cox, and reflected the circles with which they were involved at the time of the book's publication, whether at the university, at a court, or in a town. Although it was common for Agricola, Eck, and Cox to write their own commendatory verses for the works they edited, they normally did not write them for the works they authored.[180] A commendatory poem could occasionally be printed without the name of an author, but usually the author was identified in the header to the poem at least by his name and place of origin: Johannes Castor Lipcensis, Sebastianus Grubel de Sancto Gallo, and so on. The latinization of his name in the headers to these poems proclaimed the writer's affiliation to the humanist community.[181] The expertise of the author of the commendatory poem could be stressed by his providing his academic rank or honours, or his occupation. Rudolf Agricola appended *poeta a Caesare laureatus* to his name after having been crowned poet laureate. Johannes Benedictus Solfa, the Cracow astrologer and future medical doctor, included his title *magister*, Fabian Eysenberger gave his occupation as 'town clerk at Bártfa' (*grammateus Bartphensis*), and Valentin Carbo styled himself 'a most distinguished man, town clerk of Kassa' (*praestantissimus uirus, grammateus Cassouiensis*) – all when commending Valentin Eck's various works.

Eck's young students applied epithets to themselves that may seem amusing today, but that were concocted so as to stress their status as scholars at Cracow and their attachment to humanist studies. Georg Werner called himself 'a vigorous soldier of the Muses' (*strenuus musarum miles*), Johannes Sagittarius described himself as 'the most vigilant pupil of Apollo's lyre' (*uigilantissimus Phoebeae lyrae alumnus*), and Ludovicus Bovillus titled himself 'an outstanding pupil of the Muses' (*praeclarus musarum alumnus*).

The relation of the writer to the author or editor of a book could be indicated. For example, Ludovicus Bovillus and Bernardus Dantiscus Flachsbinder mentioned in their commendatory poems for Agricola's edition of Robertus de Euremodio that they were writing to commend their teacher's book.[182] The affectionate testimonies of these students could only confirm Agricola's reputation as a teacher. Moreover, the recommendation provided by Fabian Eysenberger, the town clerk of Bártfa, 'for the little book of his friend' (*pro amici sui libello*), that is, for the first printing of Eck's versified treatise on whether or not to take a wife, would have been a boost to Eck, who was just settling into his teaching post at Bártfa and acquiring a new patron, the Hungarian nobleman Alexius Thurzó.[183] Agricola's use of his title of poet laureate and his terming Eck 'dear to him' in the heading of the poem ('In Ecchii sui libellum') he composed for the second edition of Eck's handbook on versification surely added credibility to Eck's work.[184]

The tediously formulaic character of the commendatory verses in the books of Agricola Junior, Eck, and Cox attests that the poems belonged to a recognized genre and that the humanists of east central Europe were familiar with their composition. They had a common structure, involving a conditional proposition, with the protasis designed to capture the attention of potential buyers by characterizing the audience for whom the book was written, and the apodosis boasting the benefits of reading the book. This format not only introduced the content of the book to potential customers, but specified what the book could do for them. For example, Eck began the commendatory poem for his edition of the Roman historian Florus with 'Whoever desires to learn about the battles of the Romans, and the famous deeds and glorious triumphs of their leaders,' and concluded with 'Let him read this succinct tract of Florus and regard himself as having grasped Livy's [hefty] tome.'[185] Fabian Eysenberger introduced Valentin Eck's poem on whether or not to take a wife with the consideration 'Should you get married or lead a chaste life with your bed empty,' and ended with the advice 'Read these writings of the learned poet so that later you do not regret your deeds.'[186] And, according to Mattheus Holnstein, Cox's edition of St Jerome's *Epistola ad rusticum monachum* offered its readers the way to a happy life on earth and heaven afterwards: 'If you wish to lead a prosperous life now and to enjoy the eternal delights of the soul, read [this book]!'[187] The conditional structure could also be simplified, to omit a characterization of potential readers and to state merely the benefits of the book: to make readers more learned, to polish their Latin, to help them lead a better (that is, a more Christian and moral) life. This format placed emphasis on the purpose of the book, as exemplified by Rudolf Agricola's verses for his publication of Georg Peurbach's algorithms: 'If, dear reader, you do not scorn this brief work of learned George, you will know many things in a short time.'[188]

The commendatory verses were saturated with aphorisms, which lent them a moralizing tone and an air of superiority, and communicated that the book they were representing treated a weighty subject and was to be taken seriously. Agricola, when recommending his edition of Anselm of Canterbury's *Elucidarius*, stated that the prudent person knows he has been born for the practice of virtue and the knowledge of God. [189] Leonard Cox introduced Valentin Eck's dialogue *De mundi contemptu* with a poem considering the right path in life: the path that leads to eternal peace and heaven is strewn with rocks, but the soft path is full of vices and causes the traveller to fall into an abyss; the person who wishes to walk with Herculean steps should follow Eck's lead, which he has indicated in his book.[190] Johannes Rullus's verses for Leonard Cox's treatise on the education of youth painted a portrait of bad pupils – the one who despises learning Latin grammar, the other who follows the crowd without discrimination, still others who spend their days in idle chatter. Rullus went on to point out that the future of the Republic depended on its youth, who needed to be taught correctly, and ended by recommending the teaching methods of Cox.[191]

In spite of their formulaic character and moralistic tone, these poems could be artistic, and certainly the more skilful the commendation, the more likely it was to impress potential buyers. The generic constraints of commendatory poems, with their required short length, would have been a challenge to a poet, yet Agricola, in the poem for his 1515 edition of Cebes, injected vividness into a brief eighteen lines of iambic trimeter by claiming that Cebes painted the lot of human life just as vividly as Zeuxis and Apelles, and then offering a description of the paintings of the Greek masters.[192] Agricola, moreover, in his prefatory poem for Eck's *De mundi contemptu*, through the repetition of *si* (if) in the first half of the poem, built up suspense in order to lead into his central argument, that virtue alone raises men to the heavens. Then he balanced the first twelve lines of the poem, containing the premise that riches and luxuries of the body all decay, with the final eight lines, arguing that men should dedicate their lives to virtue and noting that Eck's book taught the appropriate, unsophisticated way of life. Stanislaus Hosius similarly effected a sense of rhythm and balance in his poem for Cox's *De erudienda iuuentute* by constructing it around the alliteration of 'qu' and 'cu,' with the first seven lines praising Bishop Tomicki and the following seven lines praising Cox and his work. The vocative *antistes* (bishop) at the beginning of the first line is repeated at the beginning of the seventh line, with the repetition signalling the closing of the tributes to the bishop. Such poems as these displayed the virtuosity of which the more experienced humanist poets at Cracow were capable.

The commendatory verses attached to the books of Agricola, Eck, and Cox were, as would be expected, peppered with figures from classical history and mythology, both Roman and Greek. Thus, a man could be as wealthy as Midas, his riches coming from Arabia or India; a person could live as long as Nestor, or suffer the evils and disease that Pandora had let into the world; and an ambitious boy would want to become Marcus Crassus or Phocion. More often than not an attribute rather than the actual name of a god or hero was given; historical figures, too, were referred to by their birthplace or their attributes. Hercules appeared as 'Amphitryoniades,' Achilles as 'Aeacides,' Apelles as 'Macedo.' When Rudolf Agricola warned students not to waste time reading lascivious poets, he referred to the works of the 'Rhodian poet' (Apollonius and his epic, *Argonautica*), of 'Battiades' (Callimachus), and of the 'Mytilenean man' (Alcaeus).[193] In accordance with humanist practice, moreover, the poems intermixed Christianity with paganism, and contemporaneity with the classics. Christian authors were compared with their ancient predecessors: St Jerome with Demosthenes, Vergil, and Thucydides,[194] and the fifteenth-century French monk Robertus de Euremodio with Plato and Xenocrates.[195] A book on a Christian topic could be praised in mythical terms, as in Matthias Pyrser's invocation of Calliope, the muse of epic poetry, when recommending Valentin Eck's poem on St Paul the Hermit.[196] A current event could be matched with one from ancient history, as when Stanislaus Hosius stated that Eck's urging of King Louis II of Hungary to fight the Turks echoed the verses of Tyrtaeus, the elegist of the seventh century BCE who exhorted the Spartans to fight for their city against the Messenians.[197]

By sprinkling their verses with mythological imagery, the authors of these poems were not merely adding colour to their writing but displaying their erudition. A familiarity with classical history was one of the elements of humanist pedagogy that set it off from scholasticism. Comprehending these poems required a knowledge of ancient history and mythology on the part of readers, that is, a classically based education of the type the humanists had to offer, not only because of the wide range of classical figures and events presented, but also because of the allusive method of their presentation. The display of erudition was here both a matter of snobbery, designed to emphasize the classical education of this group of scholar-poets as distinguished from the 'barbarism' of the scholastics, and a matter of promoting the humanist method, showing what the scholar-poets had to offer.[198]

When proposing to potential customers that they buy the volume, the author of a commendatory poem praised it using a variety of adjectives, such as 'polished' (*tersus, politus, emunctus*), 'gleaming' (*candidus*), 'elegant' (*nitidus, lepidus, concinnus, decorus*), 'charming' (*uenustus*), 'eloquent' (*disertus*), 'distinguished' (*conspicuus*), and 'useful' (*utilis*).[199] But more often than not a book was described as *paruus, pusillus, breuis, succinctus*, or *exiguus* – all adjectives connoting smallness, brevity, or succinctness. An adjective indicating a small size was not, unless connected with the presentation of the book to the patron, used to satisfy the requirement of modesty, but was to be taken literally, indicating that the book was a digest or compendium and not a full treatise. With such digests, students could quickly acquire knowledge of a subject, as when Valentin Eck suggested that having read Florus's *Bellorum Romanorum libri quattuor*, a succinct tract, buyers could consider themselves to have grasped all of Livy.[200] Agricola commended Eck on his brevity when writing for the second edition of Eck's handbook on versification, stating that potential buyers would read nothing briefer or better; and Leonard Cox praised him for his conciseness in composing the treatise *De mundi contemptu*, saying that no one had depicted shorter routes to virtue more briefly.[201] Cox promoted his own edition of Johannes Murmellius's *Oratiunculae* by claiming that it would give buyers the advantages they were seeking – although it was short, readers would learn much from its brevity[202] – and Agricola endorsed his own edition of Johannes Harmonius's *Comoedia Stephanium* by noting that it would teach many things in little time.[203] Most pointedly, Agricola's edition of Robertus de Euremodio was to be preferred to Plato's wordy volumes, for, from Robertus's short book on the rules of eloquence and virtuous conduct, boys could learn enough.[204]

Occasionally the work was highlighted as being 'new' – an attribute that once again differentiated the literary and educational program of the humanists from that of the scholastics. In the earlier works of Agricola and Eck, novelty could be a cause for apology, as in 1511 when Eck introduced Octavius Cleophilus Phanensis's *De poetarum coetu* by explaining that although the poet was not known in Cracow, his work was still refined,[205] or as in 1512 when Agricola apologized for both the brevity and the novelty of Beroaldo's *Modus epistolandi*, but defended the work, by stating that boys would have many benefits from reading it.[206] After 1515, *nouus* seems to have had only a positive connotation. For example, Johannes Rullus and Leonard Cox included novelty as a benefit of the book in their verses for Valentin Eck's life of St Paul.[207]

The author of a book was represented, above all, as learned (*doctus*), with 'learned' defined as the ability to write humanist Latin; this ability was central to the identity of this group of scholar-poets and was their status symbol, as it was throughout the *respublica litteraria*.[208] Cox was extolled as the most learned man in Cracow for his treatise on the education of youth. Eck was described as a most skilled poet by Cox in his commendation of Eck's life of St Paul, and as inspired and talented by Stanislaus Hosius in his poem for Eck's *Ad Ludouicum Hungariae et Bohemiae regem pro bello Turcis inferendo exhortatio*. Hosius, in a particularly humanist turn of phrase, stated that Eck 'wetted his mouth with water from the sacred fountain of the Muses and poured forth ambrosian song from his mouth.'[209] An author could also be termed 'industrious,' as when Eck was described by Georg Werner as spending both night and day polishing his splendid books.[210]

If an editor of a book was mentioned in a commendatory poem, he was also acclaimed for his accuracy or diligence. Thus, Erasmus was praised for returning St Jerome's letters to their proper splendour,[211] and the translators of Aristotle's *Libri de anima* were congratulated for producing an elegant version of the text, free of barbarisms.[212] Moreover, a printer could be extolled as learned and renowned (*doctus, clarus*) or as 'having foresight' (*prouidus*), as Florian Ungler was by Agricola for producing his editions of Proclus and Maffeo Vegio's *Philalethes*. Hieronymus Vietor was described as 'the best' (*optimus*) and his type 'the most beautiful' (*bellissimi*) by Agricola, who asserted that Vietor wanted the reader to know Christ better and come to imitate him through this printing of St Jerome's letters.[213]

Possible critics of the book were dealt with mercilessly in commendatory verses, whose authors warned them to keep their distance. Critics were termed 'envious' ('ne te liuor agat,' 'liuidulas repone uoces'), 'bitter' (*acerbus*), or even 'stupid' ('procul stultas reprimas loquelas'). They were called 'haters' (*osor*), depicted with dogs' mouths ('canina uerte ora,' 'ne laceres idyllion ore canino') or as vomiting poison ('tu qui gelidum uomis uenenum,' 'qui pestiferum spuis uenenum'). They could be characterized as classical figures: Momus, the evil spirit of fault-finding from ancient Greek literature; Zoylus, the censurer of Plato, Isocrates, and Homer; and Codrus, the miserable poet hostile to Vergil. In introducing his long poem *Threni neglectae religionis*, Valentin Eck told his muse to bare her buttocks to the critics.[214] In spite of the vividness with which the critics were portrayed in the commendatory verses, such characterizations were probably rhetorical and without actual basis.[215] References to critics in these commendatory verses most likely represented an attempt by the humanist scholars at Cracow to give themselves a collective identity by creating a common enemy – consisting here of the old-guard scholastics, that is, the clerics trained in pre-humanist Latin. It was common for groups of humanists operating on the fringes of universities around central Europe to create myths enhancing the size and solidarity of their communities in order to influence public opinion.[216] Moreover, references to critics, especially fictitious ones, could have been included in commendatory verses to augment a book's importance – a book that had critics was a book that was being noticed.

Above all, though, the commendatory verses stressed piety: the ethical value of the humanist method lay in the imparting of virtue. Knowledge was of no use if it was not revealed to the world through one's behaviour.[217] The authors of the books, their subjects, the patrons, and even the potential readers were all described at one point or another in the commendatory poems as *pius*. Additionally, the commendatory poems signalled that the publications of Agricola, Eck, and Cox were serious works. This point was particularly made if the material of the book might have been regarded as lascivious or joking, such as when Georg von Logau stated that although Caspar Ursinus Velius wrote love poetry, his epigrams were free of moral turpitude.[218] Similarly, Johannes Antoninus made it clear in his poem for Eck's *An prudenti uiro sit ducenda uxor* that Eck's work was about marriage and not about the amorous adventures of Jove or Venus. [219] Even where the title of the book indicated a religious topic, the writers of commendatory verses emphasized the moral principles found therein. So potential buyers were informed that St Jerome's letters were suitable for young boys in their first years of schooling and contained mystical thoughts, not erotic jokes;[220] and that Valentin Eck's life of St Paul the Hermit had nothing to do with jokes, but was about a saint whose bones rested in Hungary.[221]

Overall, the commendatory verses stressed that the book would change potential readers' lives for the better, whether by ridding their Latin of barbarisms[222] or leading them on the path of virtue.[223] In fact, these two notions went hand in hand, for the chief goal of the humanist educational program was the moulding of character.[224] Accordingly, the commendatory verses attached to Agricola's edition of Robertus de Euremodio's *Institutiones uitae* stressed that the book gave the precepts for instruction in Latin *and* for living a blessed life;[225] and Agricola, in publishing St Jerome's letters, stated that the book could be beneficial *both* for a direction in life and for improving one's Latin style.[226]

If all else failed, commendatory verses could encourage buyers by arguing that the book was cheap. The commendatory poems for Agricola's edition of Proclus's *Sphaera* told customers not only that by buying the book for a brass farthing they were giving thought to both intellect and eloquence, but also that by buying the book at such a low price they were being clever.[227] When recommending Horace's epistles, Agricola noted that because Horace had composed the work, Angelus Cospus had lectured on it, and Hieronymus Vietor had printed it, a customer was buying great things for a small price. At the end of the poem Agricola asked potential buyers whether he had said enough to persuade them to buy the book.[228] Finally, the author of a commendatory poem could simply order a customer to buy the book ('Hunc emito librum'), as Leonard Cox did when introducing his publication of Johannes Murmellius's *Oratiunculae.*

Despite being formulaic and short, these commendatory poems not only advertised a body of work produced at Cracow and Vienna during the first quarter of the sixteenth century, but also fashioned an elite identity for the circle of scholars responsible for that body of work, an identity that would set them off from the less learned, especially those who lacked a classical education. The commendatory verses attached to the works authored or edited by Agricola Junior, Eck, and Cox communicated to the public that they and their associates formed a group offering a distinguished pedagogy, based on Christian morality and classical learning, which, although perhaps new, was serious and pious, succinct and effective. The snobbery inherent in the poems was part of a strategy employed generally by the humanists of central Europe to create an identity for themselves.[229] In the commendatory verses attached to their work, Agricola Junior, Eck, and Cox were presumed to be well-educated men with valuable knowledge to impart to a less learned population, and those without a command of the revived, classically based Latin could be ridiculed, as the person who 'suffered from a stammering pen or tongue' was scorned by Agricola Junior.[230] The commendatory verses thus did more than serve as advertisements for the books of these scholar-poets. They served as part of the program of propaganda aimed at promoting the humanist poets themselves and easing their acceptance into the spheres of the university, the court, and town government.

It should be no surprise to find Agricola Junior, Eck, and Cox projecting an image of themselves as poets-teachers-clients identical to that established by the earlier *Wanderpoeten*, some of them former Cracow residents, such as Conrad Celtis and Johannes Rhagius Aesticampianus. By the time Agricola, Eck, and Cox began their professional lives, the occupation of the humanist poet-scholar had become recognized in central Europe, and these three men had been trained not only in the craft of Latin composition, but also in the behaviour appropriate for members of their profession – behaviour that consisted of working to advance their own careers by seeking patronage and finding stable employment, and making efforts to promote and win acceptance for the international community of humanist scholars. In the 1510s, the courtly patrons of literature, the town councils, and the universities of central Europe were in the process of accepting humanist trends in the writing and teaching of poetry, and the laicization of their educational system with the attendant humanist curriculum reform. Agricola Junior, Eck, and Cox were prominent members of a regional group of scholar-poets who worked towards that acceptance.

The analysis of the three methods of humanist self-promotion examined in this chapter – correspondence, dedicatory letters, and commendatory poems – provides a portrait of humanist activity specific (though not unique) to Cracow and its sphere of cultural influence in the first quarter of the sixteenth century. The picture shows a substantial group of humanist scholar-poets operating on the margins of the university: Agricola, Eck, and Cox are depicted in the commendatory poems attached to their works as surrounded by their admiring students, Sebastian Grübel, Georg Werner, Ludovicus Bovillus, Johannes Rullus, and others. Agricola names whole clusters of students and associates in his correspondence. Furthermore, the commendatory poems demonstrate that humanism had spread throughout the region embraced by the Polish and Hungarian kingdoms, and that it had adherents even in the far-flung towns east of the Tatra mountains – with Fabian Eysenberger, the town clerk of Bártfa, and Valentin Carbo, the town clerk of Kassa, both writing in support of Eck's poetry. Agricola's correspondence with Vadian not only confirms that Buda was a centre of humanist activity, home to learned poets and influential patrons, but attests to the open lines of cultural communication between Cracow and Vienna.

Most important, however, an examination of these three genres of humanist self-promotion reveals that even though the humanist writing style and pedagogical methods were being accepted at Cracow, lay scholars were not being promoted by the patrons who held sway over university education. Although their dedicatory letters and commendatory verses portray Agricola, Eck, and Cox as enjoying the patronage of the Cracow courts, Agricola's letters to Vadian affirm a lack of enthusiasm not just for the integration of the humanist method at the university but also for lay scholars as a social group. Admittedly, the royal court at Cracow employed such as men as Johannes Dantiscus and Andrzej Krzycki, who wrote Latin poetry in the humanist style; Queen Bona had her own retinue of Italian courtiers educated in the new learning; and Bishop Tomicki employed local humanists such as Stanislaus Hosius to teach in his court school. But the secular patrons who took an interest in humanist pedagogy, such as Krzysztof Szydłowiecki and Justus Ludovicus Decius, did not have the same grip on university education as had the consortium of bishops who supported Agricola Junior in his post as lecturer in poetry. In his letters to Vadian, Agricola expressed his anguish over being pressured to forsake his professional identity as a scholar-poet and the frustrations of trying to establish his career in a university that was not prepared to accept lay intellectuals, and it is tempting to view Agricola as a martyr for the cause. Eck's move to Bártfa, where he found acceptance as a schoolmaster and member of the town government (as evidenced by locals, such as Eysenberger and Carbo, who were willing to endorse him), and where he benefited from the protection of Alexius Thurzó (as evidenced by Eck's continuing book dedications to him), illustrates that the scholar-poets came to be accepted as 'insiders' more easily in the courts and towns of east central Europe outside Cracow.

THREE

Hero-Making: The Image of the Great Man

STRATEGIES FOR THE PORTRAYAL OF THE HERO

The patrons of the lay intellectuals were, in a sense, repaid for their patronage by the intellectuals' glorification of them in their works. The patron supported the poets with the expectation of being honoured in their writings, and the poets cultivated patrons by flattering them in print. Panegyric poetry, therefore, is an unadulterated manifestation of the client-patron relationship. But, in praising their patrons, the humanist poets of central Europe went beyond a skilful use of the traditional formulas for the laudation of a person with the view to evoking admiration for that person on the part of the audience, and created a hero that conformed with their own values. Through the grafting of traditional aristocratic virtues onto their own, specific humanist ideals, they formed a sort of propaganda to advance their own goals.[1] The panegyric poetry of Rudolf Agricola Junior, Valentin Eck, and Leonard Cox reveals not only their dependence on rich and influential persons, but also their attempt to create a cultural environment that would foster their own activities.

In glorifying a hero they had created to their own specifications, the scholar-poets were promoting a scheme of behaviour, and, through the identification of such behaviour with a highly placed public figure, they expected to secure approval for themselves. The representation and glorification of virtuous behaviour in print was part of the humanists' ongoing attempt to gain the approval of the general public and to convert themselves from 'outsiders' to 'insiders.'[2] Hero-making helped establish a collective identity with a positive connotation for the *poetae* who composed the poems. But not every subject of a panegyric poem was an aristocratic patron; the poems could praise associates and friends (often respected citizens in the milieu where the scholar-poets were working) who supported or adhered to the program of humanist learning that Agricola Junior, Eck, and Cox were promoting. By praising these associates, the poets established their position in the spheres of learning and literature; they established their reputation as scholars.[3] Altogether, the panegyric poems of Agricola, Eck, and Cox created a fictional world in which noble patrons, town officials, and humanist scholars played a role, a world in which the renewal of the Latin language and classically based learning, as well as the sponsorship of the *poetae*, was highly esteemed.

That poets were the custodians of fame was an idea handed down from classical literature to the Renaissance. From the time of the Greeks, poetry had been considered a branch of moral philosophy of which the goals were teaching and exhorting the audience to good actions. The function of panegyric poetry, in particular, was to encourage reverence and patriotism, and its efficacy depended on its ability to stimulate the audience to the emulation of a great man. Panegyric poetry revolved around one human emotion – the hunger for fame – but, ideally, it was to use this emotion to strengthen society by inculcating virtue. The linking of moral philosophy with rhetoric had been one of the founding principles of the *studia humanitatis*, and humanist poets strove, through their eloquence, towards the moral perfection of humans.[4] Furthermore, the Renaissance continued the classical association of the rhetoric of praise (epideictic) with ceremony in its occasional poetry, which treated contemporary events and people, and which aroused patriotism, stimulated interest in current events, promoted admiration for ecclesiastical and political leaders, and attempted to 'demonstrate the existence of virtue in the society in which the reader actually lived.'[5] Through its imitation of classical poetry, the Renaissance revived the ancient cult of glory, and so a person praised in an oration or a poem, exalted as a model of behaviour, was transformed into a hero.[6]

In the Renaissance, then, the 'truest' poetry was the poetry of praise, but a fine line developed between 'exaggeration for the sake of moral edification and for servile flattery.'[7] Moreover, Renaissance panegyric poetry shared with chronicles and histories the presentation of the hero, a presentation that had originated in rhetorical praise and the model for which had been formed on the groundwork of the heroic epic.[8] The panegyric poems of Agricola Junior, Eck, and Cox show that they were familiar with the Renaissance norms of the rhetoric of praise. In the poems considered in this chapter (all of which, with the exception of Eck's *Panegyricus in laudem doctoris Augustini Moraui* and *De antiquissima nominis et familiae Thurzonum origine,* were short verses attached to larger works), one finds an ostentatious style and hackneyed motifs throughout, with images often repeated from one poem to another. Such a treatment of the hero was required by the genre, which was regarded as literature, and a contemporary audience would have been receptive to it; indeed, it was society, spurred on by the phenomenon of patronage, that demanded such panegyrics.[9] In this genre, any biographical facts concerning the subject of the poem tended to 'disappear behind a cloud of idealized vignettes.'[10]

In the address to the subject of a panegyric poem, the poet humbled himself before the person in order to elevate the person (the subject of the poem) in the eyes of readers. The address also linked the poet to the great person in a way that portrayed the poet as belonging to the great person's society. In the main body of the poem the writer glorified the subject of the poem by describing his life and character using traditional rhetorical devices. Through his characterization of his subject and the methods he used to 'argue' his virtues, the poet created a hero who was not only praiseworthy in the eyes of readers but also supported the poet's own activities and goals. For example, he could fashion an image of a nobleman who was not only valiant in war but also intelligent and generous to the arts and learning, or of a bishop who was not only the virtuous leader of his flock but also a scholar and a poet. Moreover, the poet could honour figures in his own social or political milieu and thus raise the standing of his own circle. In praising such a hero and in stimulating his readers to admire and emulate the hero – indeed, in shaping the public image of his patron – the poet was advancing his own cause.

From the start, the poet had to establish his subject as a person worthy of admiration. This was normally done in the address to the person. Since the subjects of panegyric poems varied in social class and profession, the poet had to identify at once the rank of the subject as well as describe his own relationship to him. Furthermore, in a direct address to the subject of the poem the poet could communicate publicly his feelings towards the person – for example, by showing concern for him or by making a request of him. A display of concern would not only win readers' affection for the subject of the poem, but also link the poet to the great person in an immediate way.

The most significant element used in evoking admiration for a person was the topos of the poet's modesty, usually expressed at the beginning of the poem together with the poet's statement of intent. The modesty topos was designed to exalt the hero while disposing the audience favourably towards the author of the poem. For example, when introducing his poem on the history of the Thurzó family, which contained an extended panegyric to his patron, Alexius Thurzó, Eck used a specific vocabulary of humility in referring to himself and his writing. He put his latinized name, 'Eckius,' in a diminutive form, 'Eckiolus,' and described his poem as 'modest' (*modicum opus*).[11] Agricola Junior, when addressing Bishop Maciej Drzewicki of Przemyśl, and Eck, when addressing Provost Augustinus Moravus of Olomouc, explained that they had no riches or jewels to offer their patrons, but only a simple poem.[12]

As in the dedicatory letters, the poet's modesty could be expressed in terms of a relinquished or diminished responsibility for writing the poem, so that more honour would be transferred to the subject of the poem.[13] When addressing King Sigismund in his preface to *Threni neglectae religionis*, Eck stated that he was forced to write because the king's glory was so great.[14] In his poem to Nicolaus Goldberger (the parish priest, or *protomysta*, at Korpona), Eck said that the god Apollo persuaded him to write.[15] In line with this topos was the statement that nothing could keep the poet from singing the subject's fame, as Agricola Junior wrote to the priest Nicolaus de Czebinio,[16] or that the possession of knowledge made it a duty to impart it, as when Eck declared that because no one alive remembered clearly the history of the Thurzó family, he felt he must record it so that there would be no doubt as to the family's noble origins.[17]

Overwhelmingly, though, the poet formulated his modesty in these panegyric poems in terms of a lack of inspiration or ability. Panegyric poetry was considered a matter more of art than of scholarship, so the poet's inspiration was personified by Apollo and the Muses, and his ability was expressed in terms of his age or experience. The lack of ability could be stated simply, with the poet claiming insufficient talent to sing the subject's praises. Valentin Eck stated a number of times that his want of talent would defile the glory of the subject – in his short poems to Sigismund Glotzer, the canon (*canonicus*) of Olomouc; to Johannes Tulner, the vicar (*uicarius*) of Olomouc; to Justus Ludovicus Decius, the adviser to the Polish king; and to Lukács Pálóczy, the castellan (*castellanus*) of Makovica castle.[18] Early on in a poet's career, the lack of ability was blamed on youth and insufficient experience. In 1513 the young Agricola began a poem to the bishop of Poznań, Jan Lubrański, by saying that his youthful muse was stupefied at the prospect of singing the bishop's praises.[19] And in 1515, Eck, writing to the bishop of Zagreb, Ferenc Csaholyi (*c.* 1496–1526), described his muse as not yet worthy of praising him because it was still drinking from the tender streams of Pimpla (the fountain in Pieria sacred to the Muses) and so was able to produce only uncultured sounds.[20] An exaggerated version of the lack-of-experience topos was the expression of shame or fear when composing panegyrics. Eck wrote to Goldberger that shame struck his mouth whenever he attempted to utter Goldberger's name, a venerable name that bristled at the infantile verses Eck was scarcely able to bring forth from his stammering mouth.[21] And Eck cited trepidation at the sight of Bishop Maciej Drzewicki as the cause of his difficulty in writing.[22]

A lack of inspiration could be blamed simply on fate. For example, Eck told his friend and student Sebastian Steinhofer that he had no muse because he was ill.[23] And, in a particularly idyllic passage, where he employed Vergilian and Horatian images of the constellation Leo raging with fire-vomiting roars, the harvester cutting grain in the fields, and the Greek shepherd Corydon collecting bundles of wood to last him through the winter, Eck explained to Augustinus Moravus that he could not write during the summer months because of the heat.[24]

In panegyric poetry the poet tempered his expressions of modesty by stating his willingness to make an effort despite his lack of ability or experience. This topos is comparable to that of the poet's industriousness, used in dedicatory letters to qualify expressions of the writer's own modesty and in commendatory poems to glorify the author of the book. Implicit here is the classical topos that idleness is to be shunned.[25] Valentin Eck especially favoured the topos of making an effort, and it appears cloaked in various images in his work. At the start of his lengthy panegyric to

Augustinus Moravus, he compared his attempting to write with the launching of a boat. Having stated that until now he had been satisfied with composing short, light verse, he affirmed that he was ready to 'rise up' with more daring poetry, to push his trembling boat out from the 'wave-breaking coast,' and to strengthen his trireme with sail-yards.[26] When addressing Bishop Csaholyi, Eck used the boat metaphor again, saying that if he 'tried to part turgid waves, his skiff would be overturned by the billowy water,' but that he could attempt a smaller work, as a sort of preface to a longer, serious poem.[27] He continued by drawing a comparison between his attempt to write lofty verses and the flight of Icarus. Eck noted that he would be very fearful of praising Csaholyi with his puerile verse, that he would be forced to remain at the beginning stage since the boy Icarus had travelled too close to the sun and had ended up giving his name to the sea below.[28] He used the motifs of Icarus and the boat yet again three years later, in 1518, when writing in praise of Bishop Drzewicki, this time adding to the example of Icarus that of Phaethon driving the sun's chariot too close to earth. Eck claimed that if he should dare to 'sweep the waves, [his] alder-wood boat would overturn in the sea,' but that in the meantime, as an inexperienced poet, he could take on a shorter work in honour of the bishop rather than a longer one.[29] In closing his lengthy poem on the history of the Thurzó family, Eck used no mythological imagery, but when declaring that his poetic ability was no match for the glory of Alexius Thurzó, he stated – rather dramatically – that as long as he lived he would continue to attempt to write verses worthy of the merits of Alexius.[30]

Similar to the topos of making an effort to write in spite of one's lack of talent was the topos of asking the addressee to accept a small gift now and the promise of a future gift, a topos that Agricola Junior, Eck, and Cox frequently used in their dedicatory letters. When employed in panegyric poetry this topos normally was placed at the very end of the poem, although it could appear at the end of the introduction to a long poem. In the preface to his panegyric to Augustinus Moravus, Valentin Eck twice asked Moravus to accept the poem now, and promised a better gift soon. Eck likened his poem to the wilted flowers of summer, saying that in the autumn he would give sweet wine.[31] At the end of his extended panegyric to Alexius Thurzó, he asked Thurzó to accept his poem with pleasure – he would receive greater things in the future.[32] When writing to the bishop of Pécs, György Szatmári, Eck ended his short poem by promising to celebrate the bishop's fame and that of Alexius Thurzó.[33] Even when writing to his friend Steinhofer, Eck asked him to be content with a short poem, for soon he would receive a longer one.[34] Agricola Junior also made use of this topos when telling Bishop Drzewicki that he would write many verses in his honour in a short time.[35]

Not all the panegyric poems authored by Agricola Junior, Eck, and Cox were written to honour a magnate or nobleman. Some were directed to colleagues or even students. In such cases, the poet modified the modesty topos to fit the rank of the person and his own relationship to him. Indeed, in many such examples there is a remarkable absence of a modesty topos expressing the inexperience of the poet or his inability to do honour to his subject. For example, Agricola's poems to the young patrician and student Nicolaus Salomon skip a modesty topos and proceed directly to a description of the qualities that made Salomon admirable – he is both naturally gifted and studious – and to words encouraging him to continue to seek virtue and to study.[36] Eck's poem to the young man György Soós, protégé of Bishop László Szalkai of Eger, similarly lacks the modesty topos.[37] Instead, Eck notes that many people wonder why Bishop Szalkai is offering Soós so many favours. He himself is not astonished, because Soós is endowed with virtue and wisdom; Eck encourages him to stay on the path of virtue so that the bishop will continue to favour him.

But the absence of a modesty topos does not necessarily indicate that the subject of a panegyric is inferior to the writer. A case in point are the poems addressed by Eck to his colleagues at Bártfa – Andreas Räuber, the mayor; Fabian Eysenberger, the town clerk (*grammateus*); and Peter Zipser, the parish priest (*parochianus*) and archdeacon (*archidiaconus*) – that were printed together with Eck's *An prudenti uiro sit ducenda uxor* (1518). The poems to Räuber and Eysenberger are both missing a modesty topos, whereas at the end of the poem to Zipser, Eck declares himself an ineffective thunderer of the priest's praises. Certainly, Eck needed to show reverence for a pastor. Yet Räuber and Eysenberger were two figures to whom Eck must have needed to pay public tribute in order to ingratiate himself, as the new schoolmaster, with Bártfa's establishment. Most likely, the political character of the poems to Räuber (concerning his election and re-election as mayor) and the occasional nature of the poem to

Eysenberger (it was a New Year's gift) precluded the use of a modesty topos.[38]

Moreover, the degree of glorification of a poem's dedicatee was expressed not only by means of the modesty topos, or its absence, but by the use of vocabulary adjusted to the subject's rank. Descriptors were normally part of the header of the poem and/or the salutation to the patron at the beginning of the poem. Typical epithets included *uenerabilis, reuerendissimus, amplissimus, christianissimus, praestantissimus* (outstanding), *ornatissimus, humanissimus, uigilantissimus, egregius* (excellent), *eminentissimus, nobilis, eximius* (distinguished), and *doctus*. The title of the addressee was usually given, whether *episcopus, cancellarius, uicarius, magister, archidiaconus, canonicus, grammateus*, and so on. A patron could be addressed simply as *fautor singularis* (extraordinary patron), but if he was a royal, a noble, or a high-ranking ecclesiastic, the poem would begin with an elaborate greeting, such as 'greatest king, born of the noble blood of the gods,' as in Eck's address to King Sigismund;[39] or 'most dignified protector, the greatest glory of Hungary and manifest splendour of bishops'[40] or 'illustrious light of bishops, and most famous glory of the Hungarian people,'[41] as in Eck's salutations to Bishops Csaholyi and Szatmári; or 'bishop, the renown of a mighty people and the splendour of the fatherland,'[42] as in Agricola's address to Bishop Jan Lubrański. Lesser-ranking persons could be given a plainer address, such as *pastor dignissime*,[43] but in their case a glorifying address was often left out entirely.

The approach to the patron in a panegyric poem could exhibit concern for the person, and the panegyric poetry of Agricola Junior, Eck, and Cox is filled with phrases wishing their supporters a long and healthy life and praying that they will spend eternity in paradise. These expressions of concern were designed to persuade the readers of the poems that the subject of the poem was worth caring about and that the author of the poem was accepted as a protégé by the great man. Eck ended his poem to Csaholyi with a wish for his patron's longevity, and his poem to Augustinus Moravus not only with a desire that his patron's glory grow and endure but with a prayer that Moravus see eternal joy in heaven. (Moreover, he had prefaced his poem to Augustinus Moravus with the claim that no poem could equal his affection for the great man.)[44] Eck concluded his poem to Maciej Drzewicki with a desire that Drzewicki reach a happy old age, and his verses to Nicolaus Goldberger with a wish for a long life for him and paradise in eternity.[45] In 1530, Eck wrote to Alexius Thurzó that he hoped Alexius would always experience happiness and never be oppressed by fate.[46] In his poem for Jan Konarski, bishop of Cracow, Leonard Cox glorified the life of John the Baptist, but the narrative led up to a prayer for Konarski and ended with his praises and an acknowledgment by Cox of Konarski's patronage.[47] In an elaborate expression of concern for Justus Ludovicus Decius, one sure to win over the readers, Eck painted a touching picture of the wife as helpmate and, in closing, expressed his prayer for Decius's happiness with his new wife and future children.[48]

Finally, the address to the subject of a panegyric poem could also contain a request by the poet. In *Ad dominum Franciscum Chahol episcopum Zagrauiensem*, a poem printed in 1515 (but obviously composed a few years earlier, during Eck's time as a student), Eck, after an extended expression of modesty and praises of Bishop Csaholyi, begged the bishop for money so that he could continue his studies. Eck naturally stressed the bishop's well-known generosity. [49] In a brief poem attached to his *Ad Ferdinandum epistola*, printed at Vienna in 1530, Eck asked Alexius Thurzó to facilitate the payment of a stipend that King Ferdinand of Hungary had promised him. Eck's plea illustrated Thurzó's favour and influence with the king, and one can only imagine that Thurzó was flattered to have an acknowledgment of his power at court expressed in print in this way.[50]

After addressing the subject of the poem, and thus both capturing the attention of readers and establishing the subject of the poem as a person worthy of admiration, the poet had to demonstrate, in his description of the person, why he was laudable and deserving of emulation. Five rhetorical strategies were commonly used in this process: a simple listing of the patron's attributes (*enumeratio*), a comparison of the patron's qualities with those of the ancients (*comparatio*), telling by not telling (*praeteritio*), hesitation (*dubitatio*), and narrative (*narratio*).[51]

Enumeration (*enumeratio*) was the most straightforward strategy, and the most frequently used, especially in shorter poems. This simple compilation of the merits of the person in a brief space was intended to appeal to the readers' emotions. The goal was to augment or, if the enumeration was placed at the end of the poem, to sum up the qualities of the subject of the poem. Rudolf Agricola told Bishop Lubrański that he would be remembered for his virtues, and then named them – his clemency, piety, kindness, and erudition, and his caring and generosity.[52] At the end of his poem to Goldberger, Eck recapitulated the virtues of the pastor by noting that he protected his sheep with decency, reverence, faith, justice, and impassioned preaching.[53]

Comparisons (*comparatio*) to the ancients, a type of *exemplum*[54] in which the subject of the panegyric poem was said either to equal or to surpass a venerable figure from the classical tradition, could be used to expand and enhance the glorification of the patron. The subject of the poem could be as just as Trajan; as learned as Camillus; as religious or honest as Numa; as eloquent as Vergil; as skilful in speaking as Cicero, Pericles, or Isaeus; as upright as Titus; as rich as Croesus; as modest as Spurinna; as virtuous as Cato; or as simple or severe as Crassus, Curius, or Brutus.[55] He could be wished a life as long as that of Nestor. The antique figure of comparison need not have been historical (or pseudo-historical); mythological gods and heroes were also employed. In his poem on the art of printing addressed to Maciej Drzewicki, Agricola (most likely inspired by Celtis's *Carm.* 3.9) compared the German invention of printing to Hermes's (Thoth) devising characters for the Egyptians, Cadmus's inventing the alphabet for the Greeks, and Carmenta's teaching the Italian tribes to write.[56] Eck claimed that Augustinus Moravus surpassed Apollo and Orpheus in poetry.[57]

Preterition (*praeteritio*), or telling by not telling, was a slightly more complicated embellishment. The poet stated that his talent was not great enough, or that he did not have enough space in the poem, to describe all the patron's virtues, but then went on to list them anyway (*percursio*). The ironic effect, of course, was to call attention to the qualities of the subject of the poem. Eck wrote to Bishop Csaholyi that, owing to his lack of experience, he could compose only a brief poem and would omit the genealogy of Csaholyi's famous family, their nobility, Csaholyi's many gifts of soul and body, his intelligence, his riches, and the fame he had acquired by virtue.[58] To Bishop Drzewicki, likewise, Eck said that his youth confined him to writing a short poem and that he could say nothing about the bishop's great family, or the honours he had obtained through study, or his gifts of mind and body, or his intelligence, his riches, and his titles.[59]

The use of hesitation (*dubitatio*) was similar to that of preterition. The poet called attention to the patron's qualities by appearing to hesitate over or feel doubt about presenting them in the poem. Valentin Eck began his poems to Johannes Tulner, Justus Ludovicus Decius, and Lukács Pálóczy by remarking that the custom when writing poetry about a great man was to describe that man's handsome body, the virtues of his family, his wealth, his natural ability, and so on. He went on to say that he thought it not worthwhile to proceed with this sort of description because the subject of his poem possessed all these qualities; in the case of Tulner and Decius, he did not want to defile the subject's virtues with his simple voice,[60] and in the case of Pálóczy, he did not know which quality to begin with.[61] Eck ended the poem to Tulner by saying that he would not write until he gained more knowledge. To Pálóczy, he said that his inexperience prevented him from writing more. And in the poem to Decius he changed the topic and proceeded to wish Decius a long and happy marriage.

Narrative (*narratio*), another type of *exemplum*,[62] involved an extended scene designed to enhance through illustration the poem's argument for the subject's virtues, and so add interest and emotion to the poem. For example, Eck demonstrated that Augustinus Moravus's intellect and desire for learning had developed early in his childhood by telling how the baby Augustinus spurned boys' games and instead would draw letters with a stick in the sand and open books, pretending to read them aloud.[63] Eck also used narration to portray the virtues of the auditor general Johannes Baptista Bonzagnus, canon and vicar of Eger, with a scene (reminiscent of Erasmus's *Querela pacis*) in which Erigone, the figure of Justice, comes down from heaven to search for a religious and just man.[64] At first she finds no one, but later she comes across a happy crowd shouting the praises of Bonzagnus.[65]

In characterizing the subjects of their panegyric poems, the *poetae* created images of their heroes by drawing upon qualities from a standard, traditional repertoire of virtues that had been handed down from antiquity. The characteristics of the ideal human had been formulated by ancient writers on rhetoric such as Quintilian, Cicero, and the author of the *Rhetorica ad Herennium*. They were part of the progymnasmata designed by the late-antique second sophists, Hermogenes and Aphthonius, and were found in such medieval authors as Matthew of Vendôme and Geoffrey of Vinsauf. In the early Renaissance, with the discovery of the complete text of Quintilian and of Cicero's *De oratore*, and with the revival of the study of Horace, the classical concepts of goodness and their personifications were once again stressed in the literature of praise.[66] The humanists of central Europe, even though they worked within a standard format, shaped the characters of their heroes by the choice of qualities they included in their panegyrics and by the emphasis they gave to each. They submitted the traditional virtues to their own ideas, thereby producing a hybrid set of values that would further their acceptance into powerful spheres.[67] In praising a patron's nobility, virtues, physical handsomeness, intelligence and learning, and wealth, the scholar-poets were praising qualities that they themselves admired and that would promote their own activities.

If the subject of a panegyric poem was a nobleman, his nobility was normally cited before any of his other qualities, and was treated as bound up with his bloodline, in accordance with the classical tradition that panegyrics should deal with the hero's forebears.[68] The importance of the family line in verifying nobility was indicated by Eck in his poem on the Thurzó family, *De antiquissima nominis et familiae Thurzonum origine*, one-third of which is devoted to establishing the divine origin of the family and praising Alexius Thurzó's ancestors and siblings.[69] Agricola Junior composed a preliminary poem for Joachim Vadian's elegy on his own family, *De insignibus familiae Vadianorum*, in which he praised Vadian's nobility.[70] The Latin word *stemma* or *stirps* signalled family origins; it could appear anywhere the poet wished to stress the nobility of the patron. The glorification of the family was an essential element of the praise of the hero, and a noble patron was often addressed as the 'glory' or 'honour' (*gloria, decus*) of his family. Agricola told Jan Lubrański, 'You, Bishop, are the very glory of the powerful Lubrański family.'[71] Or the patron could be identified as the 'progeny' or 'offspring' (*soboles*) of a certain noble family, as György Szatmári, *soboles Zottmara*, and Lukács Pálóczy, *soboles Palocyna*, were addressed by Eck.

The ideal, though, according to Agricola and Eck, was to be both noble and virtuous. Agricola stated that if a man both is descended from a good family and has virtue he is at once lucky and blessed.[72] And on the relationship between nobility and virtue, Eck remarked that true nobility was perfected by the double gift of outstanding virtue and outstanding blood.[73] *Virtus*, which implied both being virtuous and avoiding vice, was probably the most important quality stressed in the panegyrics of Agricola, Eck, and Cox.

The other virtues stressed were the four cardinal virtues handed down from archaic Greek times – prudence, justice, fortitude, and temperance – to which were added the Roman and patristic virtues of clemency, piety, modesty, liberality, magnanimity, honesty, religiosity, and so on.[74] Not only were these classical virtues commonly cited in the humanist Latin literature of the time, they were brilliantly displayed in the visual arts of northern and central Europe, especially as part of the Habsburg dynastic ethic, for example in Albrecht Dürer's woodcuts *Triumphal Arch* (*Ehrenpforte*, 1515) and *Large Triumphal Chariot* (*Grosse Triumphwagen*, 1522) and in the tapestry series *Honores*, created in the early 1520s by Pieter van Aelst at Brussels for Charles V.[75] The virtues referred to in the poems of Agricola Junior, Eck, and Cox were thus not only widely recognizable but belonged to a repertoire specifically designated for the aggrandizement of royal and noble patrons.

Normally, the virtues mentioned in the poems were tailored to the specific profession of the patron in question. For bishops, canons, and other churchmen, we find *pietas*, *fides*, *pudor*, *iustus*, *uerecundus*, and *religio*; for persons in positions of power, *clemens*, *prudens*, *aequus*, and *benignus*. The virtues that Eck ascribed to his noble patron Alexius Thurzó in the text of *De antiquissima nominis et familiae Thurzonum origine* were printed in the margin for the convenience of readers: *fortitudo*, *temperantia*, *comitas* (kindness), *mansuetudo* (gentleness), *magnificentia*, *ueritas*, *iustitia*, *liberalitas*, *amicitia*, *modestia*, *magnanimitas*. Virtues were also adjusted to fit a particular situation, as when Valentin Eck, addressing King Sigismund concerning the defence of the Christian faith, stressed that the king was *pius* and *clemens* and fostered *pietas* and *fides*.[76]

Although the patron's physical beauty was praised in these panegyrics, his physical appearance was never actually described, that is, no details were ever given as to his height, the colour of his hair or eyes, and so on. Physical beauty instead was idealized: the youthful Alexius Thurzó was told that he would develop like a calf and grow like an oak, and was compared to the athlete Milo.[77] Preferably, physical beauty should be coupled with virtue: Eck described Augustinus Moravus as a person in whom virtue and a handsome body were combined – a rarity to be admired.[78] Eck addressed only one poem to a woman, a short poem to Alexius Thurzó's second wife, Magdolna (Magdalena), printed in 1530,[79] which he developed around the famous mythological beauty contest on Mount Ida judged by Paris. If Magdolna had been present, she would have been awarded the prize over Juno, Minerva, and Venus.[80] In the title of the poem, *De formosissima atque pudicissima domina Magdalena*, Eck made sure to refer to his subject's virtue as well as her beauty, thus paying tribute to his patron's wife as the ideal woman.

Classical rhetoric had mentioned the praises of the subject's mind and spirit as among those to be included in an encomium, and the humanists especially stressed the intellectual abilities and learnedness of the patron. For them, study was associated with virtue and good morals, and they remarked on the intellectual ability and learning of their patrons in the course of enumerating their virtues wherever appropriate. Agricola lauded Nicolaus Salomon for his continual study; Eck cited Bishop Csaholyi for his intelligence and Bishop Drzewicki for his education, and extolled the priest Goldberger for his study of law and, especially, of the Old Testament. In *Panegyricus in laudem doctoris Augustini Moraui* and *De antiquissima nominis et familiae Thurzonum origine*, Eck devoted long passages to an exposition of his patrons' studies and their devotion to learning.

As a feature of his learnedness, the patron could also be praised for his industrious cultivation of the Muses, that is, for his own Latin compositions. Mastery of Latin was, of course, central to the educational program of the humanists, and it was through such mastery that the scholar-poets set themselves off from the *profanum uulgus* of the scholastics. Eck lauded Augustinus Moravus for his learning and his ability to write a pure Latin, and claimed that Moravus, having studied thoroughly the works of Tibullus, Ovid, Vergil, and Cicero, could surpass the ancients.[81] Eck centred his poem to Peter Zipser, the parish priest at Bártfa, on Zipser's eloquence in Latin; he admired Zipser's exhaustive studies, and compared him with Vergil, Cicero, and Pericles.[82]

An extension of the praises of learning were the praises given to a particular vocation – normally the Church or law – and to the patron's excellence in his profession. Agricola admired Nicolaus de Czebinio's preaching because it brought people to the faith.[83] Eck cited Nicolaus Goldberger for his pastoral care of his church, noting that he watched over his parish with prudence and removed any anxieties from the inhabitants of the town of Korpona.[84] Eck demonstrated his respect for law-giving and good government when he honoured Andreas Räuber, the mayor of Bártfa, with three poems (1517, 1518, and 1519), in which he commented on Räuber's willingness to assume the weight of government and his ability to win support from the townspeople. In the first of the poems, Eck credited Räuber with having a bachelor of arts degree and asserted that his application of justice surpassed that of the ancient law-givers.[85] Also, Eck informed the inhabitants of Eger that if they were looking for a fair judge, they should seek out the canon and vicar Johannes Baptista Bonzagnus.[86]

Wealth could be esteemed, if it came from virtue and was wisely used. Traditionally, *philanthropia* was revered as the most comprehensive virtue.[87] Eck, in describing the splendour of Augustinus Moravus's house, stated that his riches were obtained through the exercise of virtue.[88] He marvelled at Moravus's art collection (just as wonderful as the works of the ancient Greek painters and sculptors) and his book collection (full of the Greek and Latin classics). At the end of the poem, he remarked that Moravus gave money to the poor.[89] In his poem in honour of the Thurzó family, Eck described how Alexius Thurzó's father had gained riches through industry – mining and trading – and how he had used wealth to foster economic growth throughout Hungary.[90]

But wealth was most approved of by these humanist poets, of course, when the patron used it in support of the revival of classical art and learning. When Eck lauded Augustinus Moravus as a patron of poets, he emphasized that it was his aid to the humanists that brought him glory.[91] Agricola alluded to the naturalness of a learned man's wishing to be surrounded by other learned men and thus patronizing intellectuals when (describing Nicolaus de Czebinio and praising him as *doctus*) he wrote that Nicolaus associated himself with learned men in such a way that he could justly be called their patron.[92] Agricola extolled Bishop Lubrański for establishing monasteries to shelter priests and commended him for his concern for young students.[93] Eck portrayed Bishop Csaholyi as a wealthy man who helped poor students.[94] He also asserted that Alexius Thurzó should be honoured for his support of the arts.[95]

Even though their writing of panegyric poetry was prompted by the humanist poets' dependency on rich and influential people, they used the genre to their own advantage. By creating an admirable figure whose qualities coincided with their own interests, they promoted their own goals. First of all, the very act of putting the praises of a nobleman or other public figure in print gave the poets a public link to the nobility of east central Europe. The association created a positive identity for the poets and aided their effort to become accepted members of society. The humanists' esteem for nobility and their desire for acceptance into society is demonstrated by the complete latinizing of their names by those, such as Agricola Junior, who sought to mask their poor backgrounds.[96] The humanists' praise of virtue, even though it was expressed in worn-out topoi handed down from classical times, was slanted to suit their own program. Virtue and learning were connected because the moulding of character was a principal goal of the humanist program of study; learning had no value if it had no effect on behaviour. Physical beauty could also be admired in relation to nobility and virtue, since the body itself was seen as a medium of social distinction and an expression of inner virtue. The humanists, an exceptional group in a mainly agricultural and crafts-oriented world of labour, had developed their own work ethic as part of their identity and so would want to create respect for industriousness and the successful practising of an occupation.[97] Connected with this was wealth, which, when obtained through industry and virtue, marked a person with distinction and honour. The proper use of wealth was to help others, especially the disadvantaged, and to cultivate and support the arts and learning. Through the expression of all of these ideas in their praises of their patrons and important associates in print, they created an environment in which their values were esteemed. By praising their patrons, they were praising themselves.

THE IMAGE OF THE PATRON IN VALENTIN ECK'S *PANEGYRICUS IN LAUDEM AUGUSTINI MORAUI* AND *DE ANTIQUISSIMA NOMINIS ET FAMILIAE THURZONUM ORIGINE*

Valentin Eck wrote two extended panegyric poems, one while he was still a student and seeking patrons, the other as he was approaching creative maturity and enjoying the support of the statesman Alexius Thurzó. The first was dedicated to a scholarly churchman retired from the royal Buda court, the second to a lay magnate bent on accumulating political power and wealth. Although Eck possessed much greater expertise as a poet when he wrote the second work, and although the two dedicatees differed in age, occupation, social background, and education, in both poems Eck created a hero to suit his own needs, one who fostered humanist learning and who created a cultural or political ambience in which the arts could flourish. He praised Moravus, whose heroic virtue rested in his learning, as the ideal humanist ecclesiarch, who used the wealth he had gained through his benefices to support poor poets. He depicted Thurzó, whose virtue was bound up with his nobility, as the ideal ruler, industrious, just, magnanimous, but also steeped in the classics, who through his influential position promoted the arts and the humanist cause.

Eck composed his *Panegyricus in laudem praestantissimi uiri doctoris Augustini Moraui praepositi Olomunczensis et Brunnensis, nec non Pragensis atque utriusque ecclesiae Vratislauiensis canonici aeditus* at Cracow in either 1512 or 1513, just as he was finishing his baccalaureate.[98] Eck had apparently spent some time in the Moravian city of Olomouc in 1511 and had enjoyed the hospitality of its provost, Augustinus Moravus (1467–1513),[99] who had received his MA degree at Cracow in 1487 and who then studied canon law at Padua (1492–5). Moravus had worked from 1496 until 1511 as a secretary in the chancellery of King Vladislav II at Buda, where he was a member of the Sodalitas Litteraria Ungarorum and where he met Conrad Celtis, with whom he subsequently entered into correspondence. After returning to his birthplace, Olomouc, Moravus strove, under the auspices of Bishop Stanislaus Thurzó, to promote humanist studies and the arts in Moravia. A learned man, he authored, among other works, *Dialogus in defensionem poetices* (Venice, 1493), *De modo epistolandi* (Venice, 1495), and *Catalogus episcoporum Olomucensium* (Vienna, 1511).[100]

From a biographical point of view, Eck's *Panegyricus* is important because it demonstrates that Eck's connections with the Thurzó family had been established more than half a decade before he became the protégé of Alexius. Alexius's half-brother Stanislaus had been invested as bishop of Olomouc in 1497, after studies at Cracow, and Eck certainly would have made his personal acquaintance during his stay in Moravia.[101]

Stanislaus had instituted a centre of humanist learning at his court, and, although not a scholar himself, he had fostered ties with the new intellectual circles emerging in east central Europe, especially with Wrocław, where the eldest Thurzó brother, Johann, was installed as bishop in 1506 after having studied at Cracow and in Italy. Johann was a correspondent of Erasmus (from 1518) and the patron of the humanists Caspar Ursinus Velius (who held the chair of rhetoric at Vienna and who entered the imperial service there) and Georg von Logau (who became secretary to King Ferdinand and canon of the Wrocław cathedral). At Olomouc, Stanislaus oversaw a chapter library rich in both manuscripts and printed books, and he encouraged the establishment of printing. He had contact with Beatus Rhenanus, and, after the death of his brother Johann, he continued both the communication with Erasmus (who dedicated to him his edition of Pliny's *Naturalis historia* and his commentary on Psalm 38) and the support of Ursinus Velius (who honoured him with a collection of his poems). During Stanislaus's tenure as bishop, Olomouc received visits from Conrad Celtis, Johannes Cuspinian, Ulrich von Hutten, Rudolf Agricola Junior, and Joachim Vadian.[102]

Valentin Eck's lengthy poem of 285 lines, a gift of thanks for support during his stay in Moravia, is a tribute to the urbanity and learning of Augustinus Moravus and to the civility of Olomouc. Besides the panegyric to Moravus, the book contains a group of writings addressed to the high-ranking ecclesiastics of Olomouc.[103] Eck prefaced the main work with a dedicatory letter to Sigismund Glotzer – the canon of Olomouc, executor of Moravus's last will and testament, and a humanist patron in his own right – and inserted a brief panegyric verse to him following the main work. He ended the book with a short poem in honour of Johannes Tulner, the vicar of Olomouc.

Henryk Barycz dismissed Eck's *Panegyricus* as 'simple,' and Gustav Bauch criticized it for its 'youthful, in places almost unbearable bombast.' But Peter Wörster, although conceding that Eck's biographical sketch of the hero was not realistic, has credited Eck with producing a lively description of Olomouc and the way of life of a celebrated sixteenth-century humanist, citing as high points Eck's details concerning Moravus's house and his collection of books and artwork.[104] Admittedly, we must take into account that this was in all probability Eck's first publication, and that he was only about eighteen years old when he wrote it, having not yet obtained his BA degree. Yet the *Panegyricus* deserves consideration as a landmark in the history of the literature of east central Europe.

Although encomiums of cities had been popular in the humanist Latin poetry of central Europe since Konrad Wimpina's praise of the university and city of Leipzig in 1488,[105] Eck's poem in honour of Moravus was the first to be written on the city of Olomouc and would be followed by four others by the end of the sixteenth century.[106] Eck most likely took inspiration from Celtis's praise of the German towns. Certainly, the humanist centre of Olomouc as depicted by Eck in his *Panegyricus* reflects Celtis's intellectual world.[107] Eck would have known the encomiastic poems of Laurentius Corvinus (*c.* 1462–1527), the Wrocław schoolmaster and notary, on Cracow and on the Silesian towns of Wrocław and Nowy Targ.[108] As for his portrait of Moravus, Eck may have taken his cue from Janus Pannonius's panegyric on Guarinus Veronensis, a poem that appeared in the edition of his works printed by Eck's teacher Paulus Crosnensis at Vienna in 1512. Like Pannonius, Eck adapted a standard genre – a genre in which a hero is defined as one who on the strength of his *sapientia* and *uirtus* deserves heaven – to include scholarship as a heroic virtue.[109] Moreover, Paulus Crosnensis's *Carmen elegiacum in uitam, mores, fatum clarissimi doctoris Adalberti de Szamotuli conditum*, which praised the learning of Adalbertus de Szamotuły (?–1507), the Cracow professor and medical doctor who served as physician to King Alexander of Poland (Sigismund's elder brother), may also have provided a model. The ingenuity in Eck's work, though, lies in his blending of the praise of a humanist scholar and the praise of a city.

In 1519, some seven years after the appearance of his *Panegyricus* in honour of Moravus, Eck published *De antiquissima nominis et familiae Thurzonum origine et singulari praestantissimi domini Alexii Thurzonis panegyris* with the Vietor press in Cracow. At the time *De antiquissima nominis et familiae Thurzonum origine* was printed, Eck had held the post of headmaster at Bártfa school and had been a protégé of Alexius Thurzó for at least a year and a half.[110] The first work that Eck dedicated to Thurzó, *An prudenti uiro sit ducenda uxor*, appeared in Cracow in 1518, with the dedicatory letter dated January 1518. It was followed in February 1519 by the prose dialogue *De mundi contemptu*, printed together with *Supellectilium fasciculus*, an elegy on the outfitting of a house. Eck had completed his panegyric on the Thurzó family by October of that year (according to the date given by Rudolf Agricola Junior to his dedicatory letter to Alexius). The details of Eck's move from

Cracow to Bártfa are not known, nor are the circumstances of his introduction to Alexius Thurzó.[111] At any rate, Eck's move to Hungary in 1517 coincided with Thurzó's being named controller of the mining revenues at Körmöcbánya (*camerarius Cremnicensis*), now Kremnica in central Slovakia.[112] He had been royal secretary since 1515 and, with the support of Bishop György Szatmári, whose niece Anna he had married in 1510, he was fast becoming influential at the Buda court. In 1519, Alexius became the officer of the central administration, and at the same time he served King Louis II directly as chamberlain (*cubicularius*).[113] By 1521 he had been promoted to chief chamberlain (*supremus cubicularius*), and in 1522 he was appointed royal treasurer (*thesaurarius regius*), positions that gained him admission to the highest echelon of the Hungarian government. While tending to his political career he also oversaw his family's business interests in Hungary, acting as Jakob Fugger's agent and managing the Thurzó mining and minting concerns. The Thurzós' business association with the Fuggers had begun in 1495, and Alexius's elder half-brother Georg was married to the daughter of Ulrich Fugger. A man of refinement and culture, Alexius patronized the humanist movement in Hungary, and Erasmus dedicated his translation of Plutarch (1525) to him. He had been tutored by Jacob Piso (d. 1527), the neo-Latin poet, ambassador, and correspondent of Erasmus, who had studied in Bologna and Rome, and who would also teach the young King Louis II and become provost of Pécs. Alexius Thurzó conformed with the ideals of his age, which saw no hypocrisy in pursuing one's own prosperity while ostensibly dedicating oneself to public affairs.[114] Over the course of his life, he accumulated great wealth along with his important government posts.

It is probably no coincidence that *De antiquissima nominis et familiae Thurzonum origine* appeared just as Valentin Eck and Alexius Thurzó both were on the point of being transformed from 'outsiders' into 'insiders.' Evidently, Eck composed his panegyric on the Thurzó family in order to affirm his position as Alexius Thurzó's protégé. It is no less remarkable that he published this poem just as Alexius was beginning to rise up the court hierarchy, so that *De antiquissima nominis et familiae Thurzonum origine* served as a propaganda piece testifying to the ancient and noble origins of Alexius's family and claiming for Alexius the virtues that qualified him for civic leadership. The poem was designed to bolster

Thurzó's status at court just as it was designed to establish Eck's tenure at Bártfa with Thurzó as his protector.

Eck's notions of the panegyric genre may have had their roots in the poetry of his teacher Paulus Crosnensis, most of which was written for his patron Gábor Perényi, master of the royal chamberlains and one of the most powerful Hungarian nobles of the time. Certainly Eck's comparison of Alexius Thurzó with Hercules in *De antiquissima ... origine* is reminiscent of Paulus's comparison of the Hungarian king Ladislaus (1077–95) with that same antique hero in his *Panegyricus in laudem diui Ladislai regis et patroni Hungariae,*[115] which was dedicated to Perényi.[116] Moreover, Eck was surely familiar with the poetry produced by Celtis and his followers at Vienna, who, since the beginning of the century, had been busy glorifying Maximilian and his circle by combining the traditional medieval themes associated with nobility – heraldry, mottoes, genealogy – with the classical tradition, using Latin hexameters and Roman motifs. Celtis, for example, compared Maximilian with Hercules in his *Ludus Dianae.* This group of poets also cloaked praises of the emperor in bucolic or epic garb, examples being Heinrich Bebel's *Egloga triumphalis ... de uictoria Caesaris Maximiliani contra Boiemos* (1509) and Joachim Vadian's *Aegloga, cui titulus Faustus* (1517).[117] Finally, Caspar Ursinus Velius was evidently composing the preface to his planned epic *Thurzeis* while he was a guest of Stanislaus Thurzó at Olomouc at the end of 1517,[118] that is, at the same time that Eck could conceivably have been starting to write his *De antiquissima ... origine.* Like Eck, these poets were seeking to commit their patrons to the discipline of the humanities; in the expectation of rank and influence for themselves, they shaped the image of their patrons in their own image.[119]

Panegyricus in laudem Augustini Moraui and *De antiquissima nominis et familiae Thurzonum origine* have a similar printed format. Both are prefaced by a dedicatory letter and accompanied by commendatory verses that outline the contents of the book and advertise it to potential readers. In his letter to Sigismund Glotzer, Eck praises the canon for his learning and his virtues and asks him to accept the gift of his poem written in honour of their common patron, Moravus. Eck's brief panegyric poems to Glotzer and to Tulner and Johannes Benedictus Solfa's commendatory poem for Eck's work complement the dedicatory letter by their praises of Moravus and the members of his court, and enhance the image of this scholarly and honourable circle of men with which Eck has been connected. Rudolf Agricola Junior's dedicatory letter for *De antiquissima ... origine* stresses that Alexius and his family are so virtuous they deserve to be praised in writing for posterity. Just as other famous families had a poet to celebrate them, so the Thurzós have Valentin Eck, and Agricola wishes that more patrons would have regard for fostering better Latin literature. The commendatory poems of Ludovicus Bovillus and Nicolaus Salomon reiterate Agricola's remark that Eck has taken on the responsibility for putting the praises of the Thurzó family into poetry; and Eck himself stresses his role as the 'trumpet' of the house of Thurzó, also claiming that Alexius, alone in his time, has made it his duty to renew poetry, which had been deteriorating. The prefatory and finial material of both books thereby sums up Eck's purpose in writing them – to guarantee eternal fame for these two heroes, the patrons of the revival of Latin letters.

Eck's *Panegyricus* and *De antiquissima ... origine* also have a similar structure. In both poems Eck has followed a pattern for the praising of a person that was originally sketched out by Quintilian and then elaborated by Hermogenes in the second century and Aphthonius in the fourth in their progymnasmata, or school exercises. Although Hermogenes was rediscovered as an individual author during the Renaissance and was studied in the universities, his formula, transmitted to the Middle Ages by Priscian in his sixth-century *De pre-exercitamentis rhetorices*, was taught in Priscian's version into the sixteenth century.[120] Priscian was revitalized in the Renaissance in new, printed versions as well as through the very popular works of the late fifteenth- and early sixteenth-century humanist grammarians Niccolò Perotti and Johannes Despauterius.[121]

Eck was clearly familiar with the work of Perotti and Despauterius, both of whom he quoted in his own handbook on versification, *De arte uersificandi opusculum* (first edition, Cracow, 1515). Furthermore, Priscian was the ancient grammarian on whom Eck relied most frequently in producing his handbook.[122] Priscian's outline requires listing the praises of the honoured person throughout his life, beginning with birth and following with his childhood and education. The nature of his soul and of his body should be described, as should his pursuits and deeds. Finally, his 'external resources,' including his possessions, household, and fortune, should be noted. The poetic encomium could come closer to biography than to oratory.[123]

An analysis of Valentin Eck's two poems on the basis of Priscian's instructions for the praise of a person reveals that, although Eck has created two heroes – one whose virtue resides in his scholarship, the other whose virtue is connected to his leadership – the two characters are actually the same: an admirable person who supports the revived disciplines of classical learning, and who not only makes possible an existence for a poet like Eck, but also converts him from an 'outsider' to an 'insider.' The differences in *Panegyricus* and *De antiquissima ... origine* lie, rather, in the intermixing of genres specific to each poem. In *Panegyricus* (written in dactylic hexameter), Eck admits pastoral elements, with which he paints Olomouc as an idyllic town and digresses into a description of Moravus's house, whereas in *De antiquissima ... origine* (written in elegiac distich), he introduces epic features, evident in his genealogy of the Thurzó family and his narration of Alexius's temptation by Voluptas.

One can see from the start of the two poems their similarity of aim in respect to the characterization of the hero. Beginning with praises of ancestry, Eck slants his panegyric of Moravus towards *ciuitas* (Moravus having been born into a cultured society), whereas for Thurzó he must prove that his bloodline is of the highest rank. Eck gives little detail to illustrate the background of Moravus, noting only that the Moravian fields engendered Augustinus under a lucky star; he came forth from the womb of a chaste mother (ll. 16–17). No further mention is made of Augustinus's parents other than that his mother is termed 'lovely' (*bellula*) (l. 26). Instead of inventing a noble lineage for Augustinus (he was, in reality, the son of an Olomouc burgher),[124] Eck uses an idyllic description of *felix Olomuncia*, inhabited by the Muses, as a setting for Augustinus's birth. For Thurzó, on the other hand, the establishment of a noble pedigree is paramount, and Eck has concocted even a divine origin for Alexius's family. By connecting the name Thurzó with *t(h)ursio*, the Latin word for 'porpoise,' he arrives at an origin from Neptune. He provides a complete genealogy, listing the Thurzó family among the sea god's most famous descendants (ll. 25–54).[125] Moreover, since part of Eck's purpose in writing, as indicated by the title of his poem, *De antiquissima nominis et familiae Thurzonum origine*, was to narrate the history of the Thurzó family, he has devoted the next fifty-six lines to sketching the lives and deeds of Alexius's grandfather, father, and brothers. Although Alexius's grandfather Georg is only briefly, and blandly, characterized as having the piety of Titus, the religious fervour of Numa, the military ability of Peleus, and the eloquence of Cicero, Alexius's father Johann is described in lines giving lively details of his industriousness, his building up of the family's mining and smelting business, and his creation of a thriving commerce for the Hungarian kingdom.[126] Indeed, Eck claimed, whatever sort of divine gift the Hungarians had received, they owed it to Johann Thurzó.[127] The sons of Johann, the bishops Johann of Wrocław and Stanislaus of Olomouc, are singled out as 'great heroes, two stars of the world, in whose holy hearts every virtue resides,'[128] and the other three brothers, Georg, Alexius, and Johann, are mentioned as 'three noble leaders famous for their great name.'[129]

It was a prescription of the progymnatists that praises of a hero include some miraculous event at his birth, and Eck depicts both his heroes as being attended by the Muses at their births. Augustinus, 'the Apollinean boy,' has his arms and legs bound with ribbons by the Muses, and has flowers strewn around his cradle by the Graces.[130] After stressing once again that Alexius has sprung from the most noble of lines and stating that he possesses even a 'double nobility,' both through exceptional virtue and through distinguished blood (ll. 129–30), Eck recounts that soon after Alexius's birth the dryads (wood nymphs) wove a laurel crown for him that was placed on his head by Calliope, the chief of the Muses.[131]

The references to the Muses signify, of course, that neither Moravus nor Thurzó is an enemy of poetry and the *litterae politiores*, and dispel any suggestion of barbarism in the upbringing of the two men. On the contrary, they are both steeped in the *artes*. From the start Eck relates his hero to the spreading of learned culture. Although the figure of an erudite leader had existed in the Latin literature of the Middle Ages, for the humanist poets of early sixteenth-century central Europe such a connection between leadership and learning was essential, as a means of linking the leader not simply to general precepts of learning but also to a whole educational program.[132]

Both Moravus and Thurzó are shown in childhood to be eager learners. Moravus shuns children's games and toys; he does not like to ride his wooden horse or to go fishing.[133] He is already drawn to acquiring knowledge: he attempts to write by tracing letters with a stick in the sand and to read by lisping out the sounds of letters he sees in books.[134] Here, Eck's portrait of the child Augustinus is similar to Janus Pannonius's depiction of the toddler Guarinus, who was fond of 'lisping out the sounds of letters, following their outlines marked on a slate or a scrap of paper.'[135] Thurzó as an infant is nourished with water from the fountain Aganippe, sacred to the Muses; it is offered to him in cups by Pallas Athene, an image signifying that the young Thurzó was infused with inspiration and wisdom. Eck characterizes him as 'a reckless little kid' (*incautus tirunculus*), but *incautus* is used in a positive sense since Thurzó is quick and zealous of new learning.[136]

Eck portrays Moravus as an articulate adolescent, who shines with talent and grace, whose voice is full of seriousness and beauty, and who loves virtue and wisdom (ll. 56–70). Moravus begins to write poetry at a young age, and Eck compares him with the mythological musicians Amphion and Orpheus, the first whose playing moved stones to build the walls of Thebes, the second whose singing calmed wild tigers and uprooted the mountain ash of Thrace (ll. 73–6); Eck claims that Moravus could surpass not just the ancient Roman poets, but even the Greeks, including Homer himself (ll. 77–82).

Eck completes his description of Thurzó's youth with an extended digression of eighty-five lines in which the figure of the young Alexius is approached by two maidens, Voluptas (Vice) and Virtus (Virtue). This is, of course, the allegory of Hercules at the Crossroads, one of the best-known Hercules stories, which harked back to the fable of the fifth-century BCE sophist Prodicus. By equating Thurzó with Hercules, Eck represents his patron as a virtuous man, not only intellectually but physically, morally, and spiritually, for by the end of the fifteenth century Hercules was seen not only as a moral force but as a symbol of the active life, a man strong in both mind and body, full of fortitude, who could subdue horrendous wild beasts, tame savage monsters, and overcome cruel tyrants.[137] The motif of Hercules at the Crossroads was current in central European literature in the first quarter of the sixteenth century, having been revived by Sebastian Brant in his *Narrenschiff* (1494). The Ingolstadt humanist Jakob Locher, who produced the Latin version of Brant's work (*Stultifera nauis*, 1497), expanded the motif into his *Concertatio uirtutis cum uoluptate*.[138] From there the fable passed quickly onto the stage: in November 1497, Joseph Grünpeck's *Comedia*, produced at Augsburg, replaced Hercules with Emperor Maximilian, who was faced with the choice between Virtus and Fallacicaptrix.[139] In 1509, Johannes Pinicianus inserted the young Prince Charles, later Charles V, in the hero's role in his dialogue-drama *Virtus et Voluptas*.[140] In 1515 the Viennese abbot Benedictus Chelidonius composed a play, *Voluptatis cum uirtute disceptatio*, performed by young aristocrats attending the Congress of Vienna for Maria, the queen-designate of Hungary. Although the Chelidonius piece diverges from the Hercules at the Crossroads motif (by having Prince Charles appear as a judge in the classic 'Venus versus Athena' debate while Hercules appears as a witness for Athena), it still contains the theme of a judgment between Virtue and Vice.[141]

So Alexius is put to the hero's test. The temptation of Voluptas is to follow an easy path in life, to enjoy his father's riches, to take delight in leisure and amorous pleasures. Virtus presents the alternatives: pleasure does not last long; the way of virtue may be more difficult, but it leads to rewards in heaven. Virtus encourages Thurzó to bear what Hercules bore and recites a list of the hero's labours, ending with the statement that 'all eminent deeds require hard labour.'[142] Thurzó is instructed to make good use of his time; by abiding by virtue, he will avoid sloth. Virtus, moreover, tells Thurzó to develop his physical strength so that no task will become difficult. The end of Eck's digression is easy to predict – the adolescent Alexius, captured by love of Virtus, chooses her lofty path rather than the ignoble way of Voluptas.

Eck next praises the studies of his two heroes, stressing the effort that each man has put into learning the classics. Moravus, for example, spent sleepless days and nights before he reached the end of his course of study. He learned poetry, rhetoric, mathematics, and philosophy. Eck paints Moravus's enjoyment of the classics in pastoral terms, comparing his enthusiasm with that of the bee collecting honey.[143] Moravus's studies culminated in his writing of poetry, and Eck mentions the various Roman poets whom Moravus imitated and surpassed – Vergil, Tibullus, and Melissus.[144] Likewise, Eck emphasizes Thurzó's industriousness: Thurzó put his heart and soul into his studies; he read the poets, historians, and other monuments of classical wisdom. When elaborating on Thurzó's efforts, Eck inserts the comparison with the bee, lifted almost verbatim from the poem on Moravus.[145] Like

Moravus, Thurzó, having completed his course of study, is now prepared to harvest the fruits of his labour.

Before proceeding to discuss Moravus's and Thurzó's pursuits and deeds, Eck pauses to recount their virtues. Those of Moravus clearly are those of a scholar, and of Thurzó, those of a civic leader. Though not omitting to mention Moravus's uprightness, gravity, piety, justice, and prudence, Eck compares his eloquence with that of Cicero and even the god Mercury. He comments that Moravus possesses not only every virtue, but also a handsome body, remarking that the combination of the two in one person is 'rarer than a white raven' (l. 135). It is such talent and virtue found together in a beautiful body that makes Moravus even more pleasing as a person, as when a lily has been mixed in with purple roses, or Massican wine is served in golden cups (ll. 144–9).

When listing Thurzó's virtues, however, Eck makes no mention of his physical beauty, other than to state that in taking up the way of virtue the young Alexius would develop like a calf and grow like an oak, with strength comparable with that of the athlete Milo. Rather, Eck links Thurzó's virtue to his nobility: Thurzó shines with manifold nobility since virtue, industry, honour, and fame are joined in him.[146] A list of Thurzó's virtues, most of which are discussed in the text, is printed in the margin: *Fortitudo, Temperantia, Comitas* (kindness), *Mansuetudo* (clemency), *Magnificentia, Veritas, Amicitia, Modestia, Magnanimitas*. These are all classical qualities of an ideal ruler. Eck predicts, once again linking virtue to nobility, that on the strength of his outstanding virtue Thurzó is even nobler than his ancestors.[147] Eck ends his praises of Thurzó's virtue by recommending him as an example to the leaders of the world (*mundi proceres*).

When Eck finally arrives at the present lives of his two heroes, that is, at their pursuits, deeds, and 'external resources' (possessions, house, furniture, etc.),[148] Moravus receives a far more extensive treatment than does Thurzó. Having depicted Thurzó as the ideal ruler – industrious, and kind and just to his people – Eck celebrates him as a dedicated patron of the arts and humanist learning, before closing the poem by asking Thurzó to accept the small gift of his poem. On the other hand, in order to emphasize Moravus's collection of art and books, Eck dedicates 110 lines, that is, 40 per cent of *Panegyricus*, to a digression that continues until the poem ends with the closing praises of the provost.

Eck's profile of Moravus's wealth, surroundings, and daily

pursuits is extended so that Eck can showcase the way of life of the ideal humanist. In lines 154–263 of *Panegyricus*, Eck has produced a humanist idyll, a *locus amoenus* in the heart of east central Europe, where the humanist scholar-poet, living in an urban (that is, urbane) centre surrounded by rich, fertile countryside, can peacefully cultivate classical learning and appreciate the arts, as well as share out his wealth in the support and encouragement of younger poets. Moravus has gained riches through virtue; he has the resources of his benefices (the fertile grain fields of Silesia and the sweet wine of Moravia). He lives in a beautiful house, painted in lively colours in splendid Olomouc, whose rooftops are made of Phrygian marble and whose towers reach to the stars. Moravus's collection of paintings and sculpture rivals the accomplishments of the ancient Greeks – Apelles, Lysippus, Praxiteles, Zeuxis, Myron. Eck comments that the characters depicted in the works of art displayed in Moravus's house seem to be alive, as if they could speak or move (ll. 177–9), and he remarks specifically on a representation of Hercules and his labours (ll. 183–97). Moravus's library brims with works of classical learning, both Greek and Latin; Eck mentions Homer, the Greek philosophers, Lucan, Vergil, Statius, Ovid, the Roman historians, the Greek and Roman rhetoricians, and books on law (ll. 201–39). Moreover, Moravus is to be praised for his own writings, which have been inspired by the classic authors, such as Tibullus, Ovid, Vergil, and Cicero (ll. 240–6). He has built up a book collection richer than the famous libraries of antiquity, and so has become more learned than his ancestors.[149] Eck completes his applause of Moravus by congratulating the flourishing city of Olomouc for having produced such a wise and learned son, and he lauds Moravus for using his wealth to support poor poets so that, with their minds relieved of care, they can live a happier life.[150]

The 'truth' of panegyric poetry lies not in its adherence to fact but in the overall portrait of the person being praised and the poet's ability to evoke admiration for him or her.[151] Peter Wörster, in his book on humanism at Olomouc, has remarked that in his *Panegyricus* Eck tells us little about the real hero of his poem.[152] Certainly, Eck makes no mention of Moravus's time in Italy or his career at the Buda court. Neither does he paint a true picture of Alexius Thurzó, the virtuous young man who turns away Voluptas for the rocky path to virtue. Gustav Bauch has reported that Thurzó had a reputation as a womanizer among his contemporaries.[153] But with the figure of Moravus, Eck evokes admiration for a linguistically talented young man who puts such enthusiasm and effort into his study of the classics and his amassing of a collection of ancient texts that he is able to write poetry that not only imitates but surpasses that of the most skilful of the Latin poets. Likewise, with the character of Thurzó, Eck prompts in his readers a respect for an industrious young nobleman who refuses to live off the riches of his father but instead takes on the labours of an active life, completes his studies, and becomes a leader of his people. Unlike in the realms of lazy and cruel rulers, in Thurzó's land there is justice, and his country thrives.

Yet to say that Eck has been successful in creating two admirable heroes is to stop short of explaining the full motivation of these two poems. Eck has included the support of humanism as a prominent component of their heroes' virtue. Both heroes – although the virtue of the one lies in his learning and of the other in his nobility – are responsible for generating conditions under which the arts and humanistic study can flourish, Moravus in his urbane court and Thurzó in his kingdom where justice and magnanimity prevail. Furthermore, in his concluding praises of each hero Eck stresses that each personally patronizes the humanist *artes*. In this way, Eck has transformed his thanks for his patrons' personal gifts to him into generalized propaganda for the humanist program by demonstrating that this program has been accepted and is supported by two admirable men, members of the uppermost echelon of Hungarian society.

FOUR

The Need for the Immediate Production of Poetry: Political Propaganda and Occasional Verse

Maximilian I exploited the medium of print to create a program, in German and in Latin, of *Gedechtnus* (public relations propaganda) designed to spread and perpetuate his fame. He was the proverbial patron of literature and art, in prompting such poets as Conrad Celtis (recipient of his support as professor of poetry and rhetoric at the University of Vienna) and Riccardus Bartholinus (chaplain to his adviser, Cardinal Matthäus Lang) to celebrate his deeds in classically inspired verses, with the latter creating a national epic in his honour (*Austriados*, 1516). Maximilian even composed his own texts, such as the chivalric *White King* (*Weisskunig*), a loosely disguised autobiography, and he commissioned artists and writers, at whose fore were Albrecht Dürer and Willibald Pirckheimer, to work under his close supervision. They produced monumental woodcuts such as the *Large Triumphal Chariot* (*Grosse Triumphwagen*), which depicted Maximilian in a 'personal apotheosis,' decorated by his personal virtues, and books printed in Maximilian's own Fraktur script, designed for him by the Augsburg calligrapher Leonhard Wagner, and cut by that city's printer, Johannes Schoensperger. By insisting on a certain level of luxury – a profusion of illustrations and ornamentation, and the use of parchment instead of paper – Maximilian ensured that although these works of art were reproducible, they would never appear as a cheap and disposable mass medium. Maximilian's printed propaganda was intended to be distributed over a wide geographical region without the loss of artistry or grandeur. Through the use of visual and poetic allegory, Maximilian projected his glory across his empire, not only for the present, but for future time.[1]

King Sigismund of Poland was not as energetic as the emperor in conducting a public relations campaign in print. The architectural and sculptural monuments he commissioned on Wawel Hill show him as more concerned with promoting the glory of his reign in future time than in the here and now; the task of creating propaganda to spread the image of the Jagiellons as a powerful element in contemporary European politics was left to Sigismund's magnates at Cracow, such as his grand-chancellor, Krzysztof Szydłowiecki, and vice-chancellor, Piotr Tomicki, and to the magnates of his brother Vladislav II and of Vladislav's son Louis II at Buda, such as György Szatmári, László Szalkai, and Alexius Thurzó. These court dignitaries took on the responsibility for promoting the splendour and majesty of the Jagiellonians and their courts through patronage of the local poets, who were charged with composing the poetry needed to publicize and glorify the roles of the monarchy and magnates in contemporary events.

Rudolf Agricola Junior and Valentin Eck, along with other poets of Germanic and Polish origin (such as Johannes Dantiscus, Caspar Ursinus Velius, Christopher Suchten, Bernard Wapowski, Johannes Hadelius, and Bishop Andrzej Krzycki), contributed to the corpus of Latin political poetry published at Cracow and Vienna in the first quarter of the sixteenth century that propagandized the achievements of the Jagiellons in maintaining their influence in east central Europe and in keeping the heretics and infidels – the Muscovites and Turks – at bay. Their poetry reflected the role of the Jagiellonian realm as the 'bulwark of Christendom' (a concept promulgated by the Roman Curia in the mid-fifteenth century in the face of an expanding Turkish empire), the interpretation of which formed the focal point of Polish politics in the early sixteenth century.[2] Besides chronicling the political negotiations and military manoeuvres of the times, the poets also recorded celebrations and other formal occasions, such as weddings and the arrival of visiting dignitaries.

The political and occasional poetry of the sixteenth century is no longer interpreted as a source of historical fact, as it was by the Polish literary critic Juliusz Nowak-Dłużewski in the 1960s.[3] Indeed, Renaissance political and occasional poetry is no longer interpreted as a source even of the poet's personal opinions about the events appearing in the poems. John Martin's 1977 study of prudence during the Renaissance demonstrates that the conventions of court life demanded the development of an acute sense of prudence on the part of a poet, and thus subordinated honesty to decorum.[4] But Renaissance political and occasional poetry could represent specific philosophical ideas and did contain opinions of which the poet wished to persuade his audience, so much so that the historical events presented in this poetry can be seen as of secondary importance, even as merely a pretext for the poetic composition.[5] The political and occasional poetry of Rudolf Agricola Junior and Valentin Eck was rooted in classical rhetoric and employed poetic images in order to build up an argument. Their political poetry reinforced, naturally, the policies of the ruling parties, and their occasional poetry, of course, flattered their patrons. Yet in both genres Agricola Junior and Eck shaped the poetic heroes they created from the historical persons they were flattering in accordance with their own, humanist norms; they argued for their own, humanist concepts of heroism, virtue, and nobility. While understanding that the value of panegyric poetry in their society resided in its ability to legitimize the power of a ruler,[6] they drew attention to their own role in conferring fame and immortality on the subjects of their poems. In advancing the interests of the Jagiellonian rulers and their magnates, Agricola Junior and Eck also magnified their own importance as *poetae*. The propaganda written for the Jagiellons and their magnates acted, as well, as propaganda for the scholar-poets and the humanist movement.

DYNASTIC PRETENSIONS: POLITICAL NEGOTIATIONS AND WAR

The Congress of 1515

The Congress of 1515 was called at Vienna to celebrate the marriage of Anna, the daughter of King Vladislav II Jagiellon of Bohemia and Hungary, to Emperor Maximilian's grandson Ferdinand, and of Vladislav's son Louis to Maximilian's granddaughter (and Ferdinand's sister) Maria. The issues that prompted the meeting of Sigismund I of Poland and his brother Vladislav II with Maximilian were the resolution of the fight against germanization by Hungarian nationalist elements, which threatened Vladislav's hold on the throne, and of the Habsburg-Jagiellon rivalry in the central Danube basin, which exacerbated Sigismund's conflicts with Prussia and Muscovy. The outcome of the Congress would be positive for neither the Austrians nor the Poles. Although after the Congress Maximilian would become an intermediary in ending the hostilities of the Muscovites towards the Poles, the Jagiellons, by negotiating with Maximilian and surrendering their interests in the west, would lose their influence in that region. Similarly, although the agreements reached at the Congress facilitated Maximilian's expansion beyond the Danube, they did not guarantee the Habsburg succession to the Hungarian throne.[7]

At the time of the Congress, Rudolf Agricola Junior was resident in Vienna. As a member of the university and a friend of Joachim Vadian, who had been chosen as the university's chief speaker for the reception of the official guests at the university, Agricola was involved in the celebrations surrounding the meeting and wrote three pieces: a poem in praise of the emperor's chief negotiator, Matthäus Lang; a commendatory poem for Riccardus Bartholinus's mixed-genre epic *Odeporicon*, which chronicled the journey of Cardinal Lang through the preparatory meetings; and an oration welcoming Piotr Tomicki to Vienna. These works were part of the literature panegyrizing the leaders of the negotiations and celebrating the eased relations between the Jagiellons and the House of Austria.

The Congress was conducted with a huge amount of festivity.[8] Although most of the political meetings were held in Pozsony (Bratislava) in the months leading up to the actual congress, the final formalities were hosted by Maximilian in Vienna in July 1515. There was an imposing public display on 17 July, as the three monarchs with their retinues officially entered the city. The sight of the soldiers and horsemen, and of the nobles, in their colourful national costumes and armour, waving banners (especially those in Sigismund's entourage who had come from the east), would have made quite an impression on the residents of the city. In the following days, banquets and balls were held for the Congress officials, and games and acrobatics were organized for the public. The university hosted a reception at which Joachim Vadian welcomed the emperor; other scholars gave orations saluting the chief dignitaries upon their arrival. The double wedding, the high point of the festivities, took place in the cathedral on 22 July.

The roots of the Congress of 1515 lay in the contest between the Jagiellons and the Habsburgs for governance of the middle

Danube region. The Jagiellons had managed to wrest control of the Czech and Hungarian lands from the Habsburgs at the end of the fifteenth century through the marriage of Sigismund's father, the Polish King Casimir, to Elizabeth Habsburg. Sigismund's brother, Vladislav, who came to the Czech throne in 1471 and to the Hungarian throne in 1490, was not able to effect a dynastic consolidation of these kingdoms with Poland-Lithuania because of lack of enthusiasm on the part of the Hungarian and Czech nobility, who were not keen for a closer relationship with Poland, even though they did not wish to see a Habsburg on their thrones. This absence of support for the Jagiellons, in spite of Sigismund's anti-Habsburg stance, meant that the region would remain an object of the political rivalry between Cracow and Vienna.[9]

In the years 1505–7, the situation in Hungary came to a crisis as the Habsburgs took advantage of the weakness of Sigismund's predecessor Alexander to expand their influence at the Buda court. The birth in 1503 of Vladislav II's daughter, Anna, sparked a rivalry for her hand, and thus for rights to succession, between the patriotic Zápolya magnates and pro-Maximilian courtiers. Vladislav himself was in favour of arranging a marriage with one of Maximilian's grandsons, but opposition from the Hungarian national faction was so strong that he risked being dethroned if he pursued it. At the beginning of 1505, the national faction demanded that Vladislav publicly declare that Anna's hand would be given to János Zápolya (Szapolyai). As the Hungarian nobles gathered arms, Maximilian swiftly decided to take military action in defence of the king. It was left to Sigismund, then still prince, to sort out the matter.

The rival factions met at Rákos in October 1505 and resolved that henceforth any foreigner would be excluded from declaring himself a candidate for the Hungarian throne. Maximilian, seeing vanish the possibility of regaining Hungary, was even more bent on military intervention. Finally, in December 1505 and March 1506, secret talks conducted by Vladislav's emissaries reached an agreement with the Habsburgs: Anna would be married to Maximilian's grandson, Ferdinand; if Vladislav should produce a son, he would have Maximilian's granddaughter Maria as his wife. In order to defend his new rights against the decisions of the previous October, Maximilian moved his troops onto Hungarian soil. Happily, the whole situation was resolved in July with the birth of Louis, son of Vladislav and heir to the throne. The two opposing factions came to a compromise, not renouncing the terms of October 1505, but adding a clause that ensured Maximilian's family could keep the rights of succession to the Hungarian throne that they had won.

During the Hungarian crisis of 1505–7, the Jagiellons did little to ensure their right of succession after the death of Vladislav. This passive attitude would change with Sigismund's ascent to the Polish throne. Although the new king at first showed little interest in the Hungarian problem, after a meeting with Maximilian's representatives in 1510 in Poznań, where, in discussions concerning the Polish conflict with the Teutonic Knights in Prussia (which had been continuing since the beginning of the fourteenth century),[10] the Viennese emissaries took an uncompromising position in favour of the Knights, Sigismund understood that the only solution to the Baltic question lay in confronting the Habsburgs in the Danubian lands.[11]

In the face of a mounting anti-Polish coalition led by the Habsburgs, who were not only taking the side of Sigismund's adversaries in Prussia but also negotiating with his aggressors in the east, the Muscovites and Walachians (Moldavians) (with whom Poland had come into open conflict in 1507–8 and 1509 respectively), Sigismund, in 1511, chose Barbara, the sister of János Zápolya, the voivode (governor) of Transylvania and leader of the Hungarian anti-Habsburg faction, to be his wife, much to the irritation of the emperor. In the winter of 1512–13, the Muscovite army, assisted by Maximilian, laid siege to Smolensk, Polotsk, and Vitebsk, along the Lithuanian border. In the meantime the Teutonic Knights, also with assistance from Maximilian, were preparing an uprising. While Sigismund sent his representatives to negotiate with the Knights and while he attempted to use his victory over the Muscovites at Orsha in 1514 to break down the friendship between them and Maximilian, the tensions between the Hungarian national faction and the pro-Habsburg courtiers continued to fester, complicated now by the Turks, who, under their new ruler Selim I, were threatening Hungary's border lands. Finally, Sigismund, having suffered losses on the Lithuanian-Muscovite front, understood that he was surrounded by enemies and that the cause of his misfortune was the intrigue provoked by Maximilian. He realized that he had to make a choice: either withdraw from military action in the east and go to war with Maximilian over Hungary and Prussia or try to come to an agreement with the emperor and intensify his battle with Muscovy. He chose the latter path and modified his attitude towards the Habsburgs.[12]

The Congress of 1515 was promoted by many pamphlets and leaflets announcing and describing the event.[13] The ephemeral literature appearing in German for the local population doubtlessly had been influenced by the Latin literature that grew out of the political side of the Congress.[14] Riccardus Bartholinus, the secretary and chaplain of Maximilian's chief negotiator Cardinal Lang, wrote a report of the travels of the cardinal from Augsburg to Pozsony in preparation for the Congress. The report, in prose and poetry, was entitled *Odeporicon idest itinerarium ... Domini Mathei Sancti Angeli cardinalis Gurcensis*, and was published by Vietor at Vienna in 1515.[15] Attached to Bartholinus's work were poems by Johannes Dantiscus (a member of the Polish delegation),[16] Caspar Ursinus Velius (secretary of Johann Thurzó, bishop of Wrocław), and Rudolf Agricola Junior. Another imperial diplomat, Johannes Cuspinian, wrote an account of the Congress proceedings, *Diarium de congressu Maximiliani Aug. et trium regum Hungariae Boemiae et Poloniae, Vladislai, Ludouici, ac Sigismundi, in urbe Viennensi facto xvii Iulii, anno Christi MDXV*.[17] Cuspinian's task was to assist in the preliminary negotiations for the Congress, in connection with which he travelled back and forth from Vienna to Buda and Innsbruck, and participated, as a member of Cardinal Lang's delegation, in welcoming Vladislav and Sigismund to Pozsony.[18] As Cuspinian was the person most intimately occupied with the preparation for and the staging of the Congress, his *Diarium* is considered to be the most important contemporary account of the proceedings.[19] The collection of orations given by members of the university was printed the following year, 1516, by Vietor's press at Vienna. Paulus Crosnensis also wrote *Carmina ... de felicissimo redito ex Vienna ... regis et domini Sigismundi regis Poloniae* (Cracow: Florian Ungler, 1515), which, despite the title suggesting that it might give details of the Congress, related more to Sigismund's victory over the Muscovites.[20]

Agricola's poem to Cardinal Lang was written specifically in connection with the preparations for the Congress of 1515. Matthäus Lang was the bishop of Gurk, coadjutor to the archbishop of Salzburg, and the emissary of the emperor. Lang (1468–1540), from an Augsburg burgher family, had studied at Ingolstadt, Vienna, and Tübingen before entering the service of Frederick III. He became one of Maximilian's closest advisers and was rewarded for his work with benefices and distinctions, those of provost of Augsburg (1500) and bishop of Gurk, in southern Austria (1505). He was raised to nobility in 1508 and awarded the cardinal's hat in 1512. In 1515 he was made coadjutor to the archbishop of Salzburg.[21] On 23 February, Lang came to Vienna, called by Maximilian to carry out negotiations with Sigismund and Vladislav. He stayed only three days before setting out to meet the Jagiellons at Pozsony, but the university community paid its respects to Lang in the form of a reception, at which the rector, Sebastian Winderl, gave an oration.[22] To this oration Rudolf Agricola Junior contributed his elegy, *Pro reuerendissimo domino Matheo Langio episcopo Gurcensi, Romanae Ecclesiae cardinale siluula,* which was printed by Vietor on 26 February.[23]

Agricola's *Siluula,*[24] a poem of 122 lines written in elegiac couplets, celebrates Lang's rise to ecclesiastical honours and favour with the emperor. The poem's style is straightforward and oratorical, and the series of rhetorical questions that introduces the poem suggests the likelihood that it was read aloud during the reception for Cardinal Lang (although neither Cuspinian nor Bartholinus makes mention of it). On the other hand, the simplicity of style may have been the result of Agricola's being given only a short period of time in which to compose the work.

In *Siluula,* Agricola projects the image of a man who is truly worthy of the rank to which he has risen and the honours showered on him. Lang has attained glory through virtue, especially probity, through the hard work of his studies, and through his talent. In describing Lang's talents as 'gifts of the Muses' (*nouem dona deae,* l. 36), Agricola signals that Lang was no stranger to the *artes.* Agricola highlights the cardinal's relationship with the emperor, noting the trust that Maximilian has placed in Lang in making him his chief aide and, now, in commending to him, as an ecclesiarch, his flock, and compares the relationship of the two men to that between Aeneas and his armour-bearer and friend Achates. Agricola lauds Maximilian for his wisdom in promoting the virtuous Lang and for having conferred eternal glory on Lang by ennobling him and seeing him raised him to the rank of cardinal.[25] In closing his encomium of Lang, Agricola cites the example of Lang's service as a courtier, noting once again his upright morals,[26] and remarks how fortunate the country and the city of Vienna are in having Lang as a leader.

Agricola's *Siluula* is a refined piece of propaganda for Cardinal

Lang. An inventive work, in which the praises of the hero are couched in vivid images and not tediously compiled in a crude listing of qualities, the poem has a contemporary tone brought about by references to recent events, as well as by a subtle use of mythology, contained in metaphors rather than in a constant, dull repetition of comparisons between modern figures and classical models, of the sort that is prevalent, for example, in Eck's panegyric poems. Agricola infuses colour into this poem by using the vivid symbols of the bishop and cardinal to allude to Lang's rank: the two-peaked diadem (*cidaris bicornis*), the red cap (*rubeus galerus*), the staff decorated with an ivory hook (*baculus libyco distinctus dente*), the cope woven with gold (*attalicus amictus*). He adds dramatic interest (and perhaps alludes to Lang's reputed ostentatiousness) with his depiction of Lang performing his episcopal duties: his face gleaming as brightly as the stars; his fingers covered with the jewelled, golden rings of his office; his shins protected by greaves.

Yet *Siluula* served also as propaganda for Agricola Junior as a *poeta*. The role of the poet in the promotion of the good fortune of the poem's subject and in the conferring of eternal fame on him are signalled both in the middle of the poem and at its end. Agricola, in recording his prayers, as poet, for Lang's good fortune (ll. 67–88), claims that the gods favour poets and that poetry can reach the heavens. Using the metaphor of the ship, Agricola has begged the gods, the stars, and the winds to guarantee 'smooth sailing' for Lang. As a result, Lang secures the approval of the people and of the religious authorities and receives a cardinalship. At the very end of *Siluula*, Agricola states that his poem is a gift that will not decay, his paper resistant to the teeth of the bookworm.[27] By voicing these claims for the power of poetry Agricola is arguing for the indispensability of the poet to the courtier pursuing his career. So *Siluula* should be considered not only as a glorification of the achievements of Lang but also as an advertisement for the services that a poet could provide at court. For his services in writing this poem, it should be noted, Agricola was thanked by Cardinal Lang, who recommended him to Emperor Maximilian for the poet laureate's crown.[28]

During the Congress, the highest-ranking dignitaries – the emperor, the Jagiellonian kings, Anna and Louis (the children of Vladislav), Maria (the granddaughter of Maximilian), the Hungarian primate (Tamás Bakócz), the German princes, and the various Polish, Hungarian, Moravian, Croatian, and Bavarian bishops – were saluted in a series of orations given by representatives of the University of Vienna. The oration was the genre traditionally chosen by humanists for such court festivals, which were significant in the development of literary activity in early modern Europe and provided an opportunity for the *poetae* to establish themselves. Moreover, the speeches given by Agricola Junior and other scholars of the university formed an important element of the festivities surrounding the Congress and contributed towards legitimizing the power of the dignitaries involved in the negotiations and proceedings taking place.[29] Although a few of the speeches were published separately, a collection of twenty-two was printed by Vietor in January 1516.[30] According to bibliographical tradition, Agricola Junior's oration delivered to welcome Bishop Tomicki on 18 July was printed separately by Johannes Singrenius, but no copy has come to light since its listing as part of Count Załuski's library in the eighteenth century.[31]

Piotr Tomicki was the bishop of Przemyśl, and during the Congress of 1515 he was named vice-chancellor of Poland. Together with the grand-chancellor, Krzysztof Szydłowiecki, who also was promoted to his post during the Congress, Tomicki formulated the Polish political platform to be presented at the meetings and took part in the negotiations with Cardinal Lang at Pozsony. Tomicki entered Vienna as part of the royal retinue on 18 July.[32] There is no indication that Rudolf Agricola Junior had ever met Tomicki before then; his welcoming oration, therefore, was most likely the first opportunity he had to impress the powerful man who would become his patron upon his return to Cracow.

Rudolf Agricola Junior's elegant oration in praise of Tomicki revolves around notions of modesty, both the poet's and the bishop's. The speech opens with the topos of the poet's modesty, and consists of hesitation and preterition (see chapter 3). Agricola is in awe at having been chosen to greet Tomicki on behalf of the university and to honour him with a speech. The bishop possesses so many qualities that he hesitates as to how to begin. After naming Tomicki's virtues, Agricola continues the modesty topos by claiming that 'when a matter seems more divine than human, it is more modest to remain silent about it than to speak inadequately.'[33] In this case, Agricola asserts, he will omit speaking about the nobility of Tomicki's family, will pass over what a perfect orator could express: the family's famous deeds, as well as

Tomicki's 'divine' virtues, in particular his gravity in mediating, his swiftness in completing agreements, and his justice in transacting affairs and governing. Agricola will also omit Tomicki's sanctity, his devotion to the Catholic faith, his veneration of God, the refined elegance of his behaviour, and his admirable kindliness (*humanitas*). Having used preterition to lead into a discussion of Tomicki's virtues, Agricola notes that the honours showered upon him by King Sigismund are a reward for his knowledge and virtues: his intelligence, his education, his eloquence, his religiosity, and his kinglike eminence and grandeur (*magnificentia*). Tomicki is like Cyrus in purity, like Augustus in clemency. Agricola returns to the theme of modesty in closing his speech, by comparing Tomicki with Scipio and Cato, who did not seek out rewards. He stresses that in Tomicki one perceives no self-exaltation, no arrogance, no puffed-up words. Tomicki has come to the reception at the university not to hear Agricola trumpet his praises, but rather because he understands the extent to which Agricola, his client, is sincerely partial to his praise and glory. Here Agricola mentions his own role as a 'trumpeter' (*buccinator*) of fame; even though Tomicki, as a modest man, does not exploit this function, Agricola is speaking in order to broadcast the praises of the great man.

Within this frame of *modestia*, Agricola portrays Tomicki as the ideal humanist ecclesiarch and magnate. He acknowledges the bishop's diplomatic skills ('... in deliberando grauitatem, in conficiendo celeritatem, in agendo gubernandoque iustitiam ...'), which obviously account for Tomicki's being part of the Polish negotiating team. Agricola praises Tomicki's knowledge (*scientia*) as much as his virtue. He asserts that Tomicki believes that nothing is better than to be equipped with knowledge. Agricola, naturally, attributes Tomicki's knowledge to his study of the humanities. Tomicki acquired a foundation in literature at Cracow and then spent many years in Italy. Industrious in his study, like Nasica, the member of the Scipio family who was declared the most virtuous man in the country, he scorned leisure.

After summarizing Tomicki's education, Agricola mentions his studies twice more during the oration. Tomicki's studies of the most noble *artes* (*pulcherrimarum artium studia*) justify his being elevated to a high government rank by King Sigismund. Furthermore, Agricola asserts, it is precisely the study of the humanities and sacred literature (*optimarum artium et sacrarum litterarum stu-*

dia) that have instilled in Tomicki the virtue of modesty: these studies taught him to disdain all human cravings ('humana omnia despicienda docuere').

So the figure of Bishop Tomicki emerges from Agricola's speech as endowed with the qualities the humanists admired in a governor (*magnificentia, grauitas, iustitia, nobilitas*) and in an ecclesiarch (*sanctimonia, religio*), all enhanced by his overriding *modestia*, the rejection of worldly values being perhaps the virtue most esteemed by humanists at this time.[34] In Agricola's speech, though, Tomicki's qualities not only are complemented by his knowledge (*scientia*), but also are the result of this knowledge, which he has acquired through the study of the *artes*. To complete his encomium, Agricola alludes to Tomicki's support of humanist scholars and links himself to the great bishop by referring to Tomicki specifically as his patron. In both his elegy to Cardinal Lang and his speech to Bishop Tomicki, therefore, Agricola not only creates a vivid image of a humanist hero but also touts his own role as *poeta* in spreading the fame of the patron and ensuring his immortality.

Agricola's third printed contribution to the Congress of 1515 was a brief commendatory verse for Bartholinus's *Odeporicon*. Coming at the very end of the book, the poem vouches for the veracity of Bartholinus's report on the Congress proceedings. Agricola's poem, printed on the same page as commendatory verses by Caspar Ursinus Velius and Joachim Vadian, put him, for the first time, publicly in the company of both these important Viennese poets. Moreover, Agricola's appearance in *Odeporicon* linked him also for the first time to Johannes Dantiscus, the Polish royal secretary, who supplied a prefatory poem, and who (along with Ursinus Velius) made poetic contributions to Bartholinus's text. Furthermore, Agricola's endorsement of Bartholinus's work places him in the Habsburg camp, if one assumes that he indeed approved of the peacekeeping politics of the emperor and of the demand for war with the Turks that Bartholinus expressed in his book.[35] Agricola's participation in the Congress of 1515, then, not only elevated him to the ranks of established humanist poets but also thrust him into the forefront of regional politics. His pieces in honour of Lang and Tomicki have a content more panegyric than political; their politics lie in Agricola's having written generally in support of the aims of the Congress. When he returned to Cracow,

Agricola would be called upon to comment more directly on politics in his poetry.

The War with Muscovy

The Congress of 1515 had its roots partially in the Polish-Muscovite conflict. In the 1490s, Ivan III had begun to express his pretension to the Russian lands under Lithuanian control in a series of military attacks.[36] Although a treaty was signed in 1494, a second Lithuanian-Muscovite war broke out five years later. This time Ivan III was joined in his attacks, which continued into the late 1490s, by Lithuania's southern neighbours, the Crimean Tartars and the Walachians. The Polish king Jan Olbracht managed to subdue the Walachians in 1497. After Ivan's death in 1505, the friendship between the Muscovites and the Tartars disintegrated, and the Lithuanian leader Michał Gliński defeated the Tartars at Kletsk (now Klyetsk in Belarus) in August 1506. However, in the meantime, war with the Muscovites had broken out again, in 1500–3. When, in 1507, the conflict started up yet again, under Ivan's successor, Vasily III, the situation was complicated by Gliński's having staged an uprising against Poland-Lithuania and his now siding with the Muscovites. The Tartars in the meantime took advantage of the situation by attacking the Polish border areas around Podole (southeastern Poland), Volyn (Ukraine), and Slutsk (Belarus). A peace treaty with the Muscovites was drawn up in 1508. Skirmishes with the Walachians and Tartars continued until the former were defeated in 1509 and the latter in 1512.

The peace treaty with the Muscovites of 1508 settled matters on Poland-Lithuania's southeast borderlands, but consequently intensified Jagiellonian-Habsburg tensions in the Hungarian lands. In February 1512, King Sigismund married Barbara, the sister of János Zápolya, the Hungarian magnate and leader of the Hungarian anti-Habsburg faction. Maximilian was anxious to temper the Jagiellons' control of the Czech lands and Hungary; at the same time, Vasily was uncomfortable with the Poles' new friendly relations with the Crimeans. With the support of the Habsburgs, Vasily launched an attack on Lithuania at the end of 1512. In 1513 and 1514, the Muscovites attacked Polotsk and Vitebsk (both now in Belarus) and managed to lay siege to Smolensk (Russia). The turning point in the war came in the autumn of 1514. On 8 September the Polish-Lithuanian forces smashed the Muscovites at Orsha (Belarus). The victory was remarkable, not only for its psychological value in overturning the advantage of Muscovy, but also because Sigismund's forces won it against all odds: 80,000 Muscovites against 34,000 Lithuanian and Polish troops, according to contemporary chronicles.[37]

In spite of this victory, though, Sigismund's second war with the Muscovites would go on until 1522, and he needed to take full advantage of his momentary military success in order to fracture the relationship between Moscow and Vienna. He sent ambassadors to Buda, to the Italian states, and especially to Rome to notify the west as to the cause of the attacks on Poland's eastern front, precisely at the time of a great threat to Europe by the Turks. It was especially important for Sigismund to gain the support of Pope Leo X, who had been partial to Maximilian and the Teutonic Knights. Sigismund especially feared an alliance of Austria, Prussia, and Muscovy, which could feasibly annihilate the Polish-Lithuanian union. Already in 1513, Jan Łaski, the primate of Poland and former grand-chancellor, had gone to Rome on the pretext of taking part in the Lateran Council, but his mission as leader of the Polish anti-Habsburg party was to sway papal opinion. After the battle of Orsha, the pope changed sides and supported the Poles as the defenders of Christian Europe.

Valentin Eck first published his *Hymnus exhortatorius* as an appendix to Johannes Dantiscus's *Syluula de uictoria inclyti Sigismundi regis Poloniae contra Moschos* (for which he also wrote a preliminary commendatory poem). It was published by the Ungler press at Cracow on 23 September 1514 (according to the colophon) – thus, only fifteen days after the battle with the Muscovites at Orsha.[38] The pamphlet (the title-page of which reads at the top *Ioannis Dantisci Carmen extemporarium de uictoria insigni ex Moschis illustrissimi principis Sigismundi Dei gratia Regis Poloniae, Russiae, Prussiae, magnique ducis Lithuaniae domini et heredis,* and which displays at the bottom Eck's commendatory poem urging prospective buyers to read the details of the victory and features in the centre a crude woodcut of the king's crest borne by two putti) was the first piece of literary propaganda published in response to Sigismund's victory. In November 1514, Christophorus Suchten, the Gdańsk humanist and former pupil of Paulus Crosnensis, printed his *De nobili et gloriosa uictoria per ... Sigismundum a Moscis reportata,* and early in 1515, Andrzej Krzycki, then secretary to

Queen Barbara, printed his *Ad Sigismundum Poloniae regem post partam de Moschis uictoriam carmen*, both with the Haller press.[39]

All these poems were republished together in a pamphlet under the title *Carmina de memorabili caede scismaticorum Moscouiorum* the following year at Rome, where Primate Jan Łaski was still residing. Suchten was at Rome as well, as a member of the entourage of the papal secretary, Johannes Coricius of Luxembourg. Along with the works of Dantiscus, Eck, Krzycki, and Suchten, there were printed poems by Bernard Wapowski (the Cracow geographer, historian, and lawyer, and friend of Copernicus), who was in Rome as part of the entourage of Erazm Ciołek, the bishop of Płock, on the service of King Sigismund;[40] Jacob Piso, then the papal legate to Poland; and Tranquillus Andronicus, the wandering Dalmatian humanist, probably in Rome as a member of Łaski's staff. Primate Łaski prefaced the collection of poems with a letter to King Sigismund and was most likely responsible for its publication as part of his program of propaganda at Rome.[41]

The printing of Eck's poem together with that of Dantiscus and the inclusion of his poem in the Rome pamphlet indicate that Eck, at the time still teaching on the margins of the University of Cracow, not yet even having published his handbook on versification – *Hymnus* was only his second published work, following his poem in honour of Augustinus Moravus – was already accepted as eligible to write a panegyric for the king. Perhaps the absence of Agricola Junior, then in Vienna, pushed Eck into the role of court poet, a function that Agricola would assume upon his return to Cracow three years later. In any case, it seems that Eck, through some channel, had personal contact with Dantiscus in 1514 related to the production of the Cracow pamphlet.

Juliusz Nowak-Dłużewski, in his book on political poetry in sixteenth-century Poland, in slighting Eck's *Hymnus exhortatorius*, admits that Eck's lack of time in which to compose the poem may explain its mediocrity.[42] Eck did make reference to the little time he had, in a modesty topos at the end of the work, where he states that he was pressured by many tasks at the moment. Dantiscus also, and more directly, expressed the circumstances of his having to respond quickly to the announcement of the victory by entitling his work *Carmen extemporarium* (a timely poem – in the sense of a poem resulting from the event). Furthermore, in the header to the poem on the following page, the title is given as *Syluula de uictoria*

... *Sigismundi Regis Poloniae.*[43] In Latin literature *siluua* denoted the 'raw material' of a literary work and could refer to a draft. Here, Dantiscus is, of course, alluding to the *Siluae* of Statius, a collection of occasional poems. And evidence of haste in printing is certainly given by the numerous errors in the text (later corrected in the 1515 publication).

Besides the haste with which these poems were written, we must take into account that Eck's poem was intended not as a major work, but as a complement to Dantiscus's *Sylua*. Dantiscus's name appears at the top of the title-page as the author of *Carmen extemporarium*, and Eck's appears at the bottom as the author of the commendatory poem of four lines. No mention is made of his *Hymnus exhortatorius* until it turns up tacked onto the end of Dantiscus's work.

Furthermore, the subject matter of Eck's poem echoes that of Dantiscus's *Silua* and reinforces Dantiscus's argument that Vasily was such a threat that King Sigismund was justified in assuming the offensive and attacking the Muscovites. Dantiscus's poem does not describe the battle itself, nor does it deal particularly with the horrors of war. It concentrates on the events leading up to Orsha (the terror that Vasily kindled in the Dnieper River region, his capture of Smolensk) and the aftermath of the battle (the people's joy at Sigismund's miraculous victory against overwhelming odds, their response to being liberated from the fear of invasion and siege). The poem details, on the one hand, the flight of the routed Muscovites, and on the other, the victory festivals of the Poles and Lithuanians. The importance of Sigismund's victory is thus affirmed by the release of his people from the intimidation of Vasily. As Danticus writes, 'He who recently had to be feared now himself is afraid.'[44] Eck's shorter poem (68 lines to Dantiscus's 108) likewise leaves out a description of the actual battle. As in Dantiscus's poem, the horrors of war are alluded to when the poem addresses the Polish-Lithuanian slaughter of the Muscovites. Whereas Dantiscus refers in a more graphic way to the bodies of the slain Muscovite soldiers lying decaying on the fields or twisting in the waters of the Dnieper River,[45] Eck makes mention of the scattering of the Muscovite battle lines and of the cutting through the raging crowds of the enemy.[46]

Addressed to the people of Cracow, Eck's poem announces the Polish-Lithuanian victory and calls for celebrations in the city. With some artifice, Eck paints the lead-up to the battle, comparing the Muscovite to a wild animal, a tiger (*fera, tigris*) roving through the forests. But this beast (*bestia*) would be caught, just like a Hercynian boar.[47] It is when handling the aftermath of Orsha that Eck especially replicates the images contained in Dantiscus's poem. Eck, like Dantiscus, portrays the fleeing Muscovites running in vain for safety. Dantiscus shows them hiding like stunned deer or birds in thick forests and swamps.[48] Eck describes them as terrified, wandering through the fields, where they will be torn to pieces by wild dogs and have their eyes plucked out by birds.[49]

Eck also takes up Dantiscus's theme of the release of the people from fear. As Dantiscus announces that Vasily need no longer be feared, Eck urges the city of Cracow to put aside its fear.[50] Eck's words encouraging the Cracovians to return to a calm state of mind echo those of Dantiscus,[51] and Eck's scene of the victory celebrations, which follows, is strikingly similar to that of Dantiscus in its description of the victory congratulations shouted and sung in the streets, of boys jumping around fires, and of jubilant dancing.[52]

A comparison of Eck's *Hymnus* with Dantiscus's *Sylua* therefore demonstrates that Eck's poem was written as secondary to Dantiscus's, and that it was included in the pamphlet as a reiteration of Dantiscus's justification for and glorification of Sigismund's victory. The comparison of the two poems also reveals that Eck's poem is not, on the whole, any less vivid than Dantiscus's in its classically inspired depiction of the background to the conflict at Orsha and of the celebrations that should rightly follow the Polish-Lithuanian victory. As propaganda for Sigismund, Eck's poem should be considered to be as successful as Dantiscus's.

There is, however, a significant difference between the two poems, and this lies in the author's voice. Dantiscus was a notary rising within the ranks of the royal chancellery, the recipient of church benefices (he was named coadjutor canon of Warmia and canon of Chełmno in 1514), and a recognized poet (he debuted in 1510 with *De uirtutis et fortunae differentia somnium*, a long elegy on the theme of the battle between good and evil; and in 1512 he published an epithalamium in honour of Sigismund's marriage to his first wife, Barbara).[53] In *Silua*, Dantiscus includes no modesty topos. He ends his poem with a call to toast King Sigismund, and makes only brief mention of the haste in which he composed his work, saying that he has published the verses written in the heat of the moment as a testimony to the king's great triumph.[54] Eck's seven-line modesty topos at the conclusion of his *Hymnus*, however, reveals him to be making an effort to establish himself as a poet at court. He apologizes for not having written a longer or loftier poem and claims to have been distracted by his work. He promises to write, when a quiet moment will permit, something more substantial in praise of Sigismund and his military commanders. It is noteworthy that Eck refers to himself as intending to 'raise the king and the leaders above the heavens'[55] in this future work, and thus reminds the court and the public of his importance, as a poet, in the creation of fame and immortality for his patrons.

Relations between Sigismund and Emperor Maximilian were greatly modified as a result of the battle of Orsha. Having now gained military ground over the Muscovites and won the favour of Pope Leo X, who acknowledged the Poles as the bulwark of Christianity,[56] Sigismund realized that he could neutralize the coalition that Maximilian had been building with the Muscovites against him through diplomacy and negotiation. After the Congress of 1515, the emperor, seeing that (with Sigismund's consent to the marriage of the Jagiellonian prince and princess into the House of Austria and thus the integration of the Jagiellonian realms into the network of Habsburg alliances) it was no longer necessary to promote the Russian war with Lithuania, backed down from his compact with the Muscovites and undertook to elaborate an agreement between them and the Poles. Yet Vasily, taken aback by Poland's change in its relations with the emperor, refused to receive the ambassadors that were sent to him from Vienna, and preferred instead to deal with the Lithuanians directly, against Sigismund's wishes. Finally, in 1517, a new envoy, Baron Sigismund von Herberstein, succeeded in reaching Moscow through Vilnius.[57]

Herberstein (1486–1566), a nobleman from Vipava in Carniola (now in Slovenia),[58] equipped with a bachelor of arts degree (1502) and further juridical studies from the University of Vienna, had entered the military service of the emperor and fought with the imperial army in a number of battles against the Hungarians and the Venetians. After being knighted by Maximilian, Herberstein became a member of the court in 1514 and was sent on his first foreign mission, to Denmark, in 1516. After this, he set out on his first trip to Russia. In February 1517 he entered Poland and stopped in Cracow, where he conferred with Sigismund's administrator (and banker) Johann Boner. From there Herberstein travelled to Lublin and into Lithuania, and reached Vilnius in March, where he met with King Sigismund, Vice-Chancellor Tomicki, and the Lithuanian leaders. Finally, he made his way to Polotsk and into Russia. Early in 1518, Herberstein was back in Cracow to report on his negotiations, and although a treaty with the Muscovites would not be signed until 1522, his breakthrough was celebrated by the composition of two poems that can be considered the final elements in the Orsha cycle.[59]

Sigismund von Herberstein passed through Cracow on his way back from Muscovy at the beginning of 1518. At this time Johannes Dantiscus, now a royal secretary, had returned to Poland from his travels as an emissary to Austria and the Netherlands, and to the Teutonic Knights in Prussia, and was at court.[60] Dantiscus had previously met Herberstein at a gathering in Augsburg in December 1516.[61] Herberstein now requested from him and from Rudolf Agricola Junior, back in Cracow from his sojourn in Vienna and eager to gain favour at the Polish court, the gift of a congratulatory poem.[62]

Dantiscus titled his work *Soteria*, after the Roman poet Statius (*c.* 45–*c.* 96), who dedicated a poem with this title (*Siluae* I.4) to the convalescence of Rutilius Gallicus, the proconsul of Asia. Here, *soteria*, meaning gifts given upon the recovery from illness, is evidently intended to congratulate Herberstein, 'recovering from' the difficulties of his mission.[63] Agricola called his work *Ad magnificum dominum Sigismundum de Erberstain, ad uictoriosissimum Sigismundum Poloniae Regem etc. et magnum Moschorum ducem congratulatio*, and to this he added a brief poem, *Patria domini Sigismundi.* In 1518 these two were printed together, along with Dantiscus's *Soteria* and *Ad Grineam* (an amatory elegy with Ovidian echoes seemingly composed a couple of years earlier)[64] and the anonymous *Ioannes Samboczki ad taxum equum suum morientem* (concerning a duel between two Cracow courtiers, Jan Zambocki and Andrzej Zakrzewski, in which only Zambocki's horse was killed) at Cracow by the Haller press. Dantiscus's and Agricola's poems in praise of Herberstein would be reprinted among the tributes to the ambassador in the volume of his memoirs, *Gratae posteritati*, published at Vienna in 1558.[65] In the 1518 Cracow pamphlet, Dantiscus supplied a dedicatory epistle to Jakob Spiegel, secretary to the emperor, dated 4 February 1518.

As with the printing of Eck's *Hymnus*, nowhere on the title-page is mention made of Agricola's contributions, intended to be read, obviously, as an appendage to Dantiscus's *Soteria*. In fact, Agricola makes it clear in *Congratulatio* that his poem has been written as an appendix to Dantiscus's, as he states that Dantiscus has enumerated the great deeds of Herberstein and broadcast his fame in *Soteria*. Certainly, Dantiscus does take up in detail the adventures of Herberstein in the service of the emperor, by relating the ambassador's triumphant battle together with the Graf of Salm against the Venetians, and his missions to Denmark and Switzerland. Furthermore, Dantiscus discusses the conflict between the Muscovites and the Poles (placing the blame squarely on Muscovy) and recalls the battle of Orsha, while recounting Herberstein's trip to Lithuania to meet Sigismund and the dangerous continuation of his journey into Muscovy. Dantiscus congratulates Herberstein on his happy return to Cracow from the east, praises him for his bravery, and compares him with Ulysses, but does not refer specifically to Herberstein's mission to Muscovy; and Agricola praises Sigismund and his brother Georg for their success in putting down the farmers' uprising that had spread across Styria, Carinthia, and Carniola.

Even though Agricola's ninety-two-line poem is meant as a complement to Dantiscus's 155 lines, the two works can be compared on the basis of their praises of Herberstein. Both Dantiscus and Agricola create a noble and virtuous hero, one who has been honoured by the emperor for his skills and his bravery. Both Dantiscus and Agricola refer to Herberstein as 'the glory of knights' (*equitum decus*), both play on the name 'Herberstein' to make claims for Sigismund's character as 'a rock of honest virtue' (*Soteria*, ll. 25–6), a stone that stands up against violent waves, 'a noble stone,' and 'the stone of a ruler' (*Congratulatio*, ll. 66–73). Both poems mention that Maximilian has rewarded Herberstein for his efforts with titles and honours. Dantiscus notes particularly that Herberstein was ennobled after his success in the Italian campaign,[66] and Agricola devotes fourteen lines to describing the enhanced coat of arms that the emperor has, subsequent to the Farmer's War, given him (ll. 74–87). Dantiscus and Agricola both cite Herberstein's bravery in carrying out his missions. Dantiscus writes that God gave Sigismund an unconquerable spirit and as a result he has borne all sorts of dangers with a strong heart,[67] and Agricola notes that the anxiety produced by adverse fortune never robs Herberstein of his strong spirit.[68] Finally, both Dantiscus and Agricola compare Herberstein to a variety of ancient heroes, both mythical and historical. Dantiscus likens his qualities to those of Hercules (ll. 19–23), who chose virtue over vice and was led to the height of virtue,[69] and his deeds to those of Ulysses, since Herberstein, also having passed through numerous kingdoms and cities, has seen many things and has come to know the diverse customs of men. Agricola equates Herberstein to the Spartan and Roman generals Lysander and Cincinnatus and to the members of the patrician Roman families the Pisones and the Fabii, families that produced many celebrated military and political leaders.

The essential difference between Dantiscus's *Soteria* and Agricola's *Congratulatio* lies, once again – as in the difference between Dantiscus's *Silua* and Eck's *Hymnus* – in the poet's extended argument for the power of poetry to confer the immortality of fame on its subjects. Whereas Dantiscus only indirectly makes this claim for poetry, in stating that if any poet of the time would be a Homer then Herberstein would become better known than Ulysses (ll. 146–7), Agricola devotes the first third of his poem to the theme of the power of poetry. Beginning by proclaiming that only fools belittle the perpetual fame of virtue, illustrious deeds, and everlasting name, or the genuine honours of a herald, Agricola uses the example of Homer's praises of Achilles to illustrate how a poet can immortalize a man and his deeds: Alexander paused at Troy to give offerings in honour of the fallen heroes.[70] Agricola's point, summed up in lines 31 to 36, is that poets are devoted to and skilled in writing about the great deeds of men and in communicating everlasting glory and praise in an aesthetically pleasing medium (i.e., metre).[71] Agricola adds that Dantiscus has just done this for Herberstein in *Soteria*.

So, in his *Congratulatio*, Agricola not only accomplishes his goal of praising Herberstein but also manages to splice on a piece of propaganda for his own profession, implying that men of Herberstein's calibre cannot do without the poet's services if they want their actions to be recorded and their names to be spread. There is no modesty topos, as such, in this poem. Agricola's concluding remarks that his poem remains 'half-baked' owing to his lack of time have more of a realistic than a rhetorical ring here.[72] *Congratulatio* is as much a panegyric to the *poetae* as it is to the knight Herberstein.

At the same time as Agricola Junior was composing his poem

in honour of Herberstein, Valentin Eck was writing a long political poem (228 lines), which he published with the support of Justus Ludovicus Decius (at the time still a secretary in Johann Boner's employment but becoming increasingly involved in royal affairs) and dedicated to Maciej Drzewicki, bishop of Włocław and former chancellor (1511–15). The poem was published in February 1518 with the Haller press. Eck's *Threni neglectae religionis*, although calling for an alliance with Maximilian against the Turks, sums up Poland's political situation during the efforts to draw up a lasting peace treaty with the Muscovites (the conflict with whom was not to see a resolution until the 1520s) and gives a picture of the dangers facing Poland on its eastern borders at the beginning of 1518. The poem, therefore, should be considered together with the Muscovy poems, and its anticipation of the anti-Turkish poetry of the 1520s kept in mind.

Both the dedicatory letter written by Decius to Drzewicki and the brief letter addressed to Eck from Decius are dated February 1518. No address is given for Eck in the header of Decius's letter, but from the dedicatory letter to Alexius Thurzó with which Eck prefaced his poem *An prudenti uiro sit ducenda uxor* (dated at the end of January 1518), it is known that Eck was in Cracow at the time, although he had already taken up his teaching post at Bártfa. Gustav Bauch suggests that Eck might still have been trying to establish himself at Cracow,[73] and indeed, Decius's dedicatory letter states that Eck is eager to acquire Drzewicki's patronage.[74] In any case, Eck would be back in Bártfa as a schoolmaster that same year.

In his book on political poetry in early modern Poland, Nowak-Dłużewski speaks dismissively of Eck's poem, arguing that it was not based totally on political reality – there were no events in 1517 necessitating a call to war with the Turks – and that (since Eck's poem calls for an attack on the Turks coordinated with Maximilian) it had most likely been written at the command of the emperor and certainly in his interests.[75] But, in saying so, Nowak-Dłużewski overlooks that Maciej Drzewicki was one of the chief architects of the Polish pro-Habsburg policy. Drzewicki had advanced from vice-chancellor to chancellor in 1511, upon the resignation of Jan Łaski Senior, who had been named primate of Poland, and as soon as Łaski, the leader of the anti-Habsburg faction at court, went to Rome to participate in the Lateran Council, Drzewicki took the opportunity of the absence of the powerful man's influence to direct Polish politics in favour of negotiating with the Habsburgs. Drzewicki could not have effected such a significant change in policy without the approval of the king. In 1515, Drzewicki would be replaced as chancellor by the more powerful Krzysztof Szydłowiecki, with Szydłowiecki's ally Piotr Tomicki taking the vice-chancellorship. Both these men were supporters of pro-Habsburg policies.[76]

As for there not being a political basis for a call to war with the Turks in 1517, it should be remembered that after the Congress of 1515, Bishop Drzewicki was entrusted, along with Johannes Dantiscus, with a mission to Venice to encourage the Venetians to negotiate with the Habsburgs over disputed territories along the Adriatic and to drum up support for a crusade. Furthermore, in March 1517 the final sitting of the Lateran Council passed a resolution for the defence of Christianity in the face of threats from the Turks. In November the pope issued a memorandum proposing a land and sea attack on Constantinople. In late December, Maximilian wrote his own memorandum in response to the pope's, which formulated a strategy for destroying the power of the Turks, not only in Europe but in North Africa and Asia Minor as well, and which would magnify the role of the Germans in the operations but keep France, Maximilian's rival, at a distance. In order to create public support for his policies, the pope sent out emissaries to all the major Christian powers ordering bishops to preach the crusade and to organize processions. The emperor sent emissaries to Hungary, Poland, and Muscovy in support of his own plan. There is a record that in mid-January 1518 he instructed his representatives to go to Poland.[77]

So it is most likely that Eck wrote his *Threni* not at the command of Maximilian but in response to his memorandum and/or to the arrival of imperial ambassadors promoting the idea of a crusade against the Turks, and also with the papal orders in mind. In spite of Decius's statement in his dedication to Drzewicki that he (Decius) had read Eck's poem (as if by chance) the day before and had encouraged Eck to publish the poem under Drzewicki's auspices,[78] one can suspect that Decius, and perhaps Drzewicki too, played a role in prompting the composition of this poem. Decius remarks that if Eck's text is published with Drzewicki as the patron, Eck will prevail over any rivals.[79] Whether anything significant lies behind this statement is difficult to ascertain – does it indicate that several poets had written on the same topic and were vying for chances at publication? Decius's statement may only have been part of a topos to call attention to Eck's work and to stress his modesty in respect to the bishop. There is also the question of whether by publishing his *Threni* Eck ran the risk of angering the anti-Habsburg faction at Cracow and therefore needed Drzewicki's protection. In his letter to Eck, printed immediately after his dedicatory letter to Drzewicki, Decius, in encouraging Eck to publish his poem, refers to the rivalry between Quintus Fabius Maximus Verrucosus and Publius Cornelius Scipio Africanus, the former who was against taking Rome's war against Carthage into Africa and the latter who was determined to invade Africa and who then defeated Hannibal at Zama in 202 BCE. Decius, citing Livy, Book 28, compares Eck's publishing of his poem to Scipio's speaking out against Fabius in the Senate. Fabius held a narrow patriotic view, desiring simply to get rid of Hannibal, but Scipio's wider-reaching and more penetrating vision was that Rome should become a Mediterranean power and that Rome would never be safe until Carthage was destroyed.[80] So Decius may be referring to simple envy at the growing prestige of an upstart or he may be alluding to political realities.

Eck's poem is not the dirge its title, *Threni*, would suggest, but is rather a complaint, a *querela* (or *querimonia*), a genre originating in Roman literature but popular in the Renaissance, and its format may have been inspired by Erasmus's *Querela pacis*, which was printed by Froben at Basel at the end of 1517.[81] Although *Querela pacis* was not issued in Cracow until April 1518, a copy could have been brought to Cracow shortly after its appearance in Basel. In any case, *Querela pacis* had a significant impact on Polish Renaissance writing in both Latin and the vernacular, as the Erasmian scholar Maria Cytowska states; and Eck's poem would be followed shortly, in 1522, by Andrzej Krzycki's *Religionis et reipublicae querimonia*, in which both 'Religio' and 'Respublica' are personified. As Cytowska notes, though, the writers at Cracow adapted Erasmus's ideas to suit the conditions affecting the Polish-Lithuanian Commonwealth at the time, imposing upon them their own specific political outlook, which was steeped in local patriotism. So although the figure of 'Pax' in Erasmus's treatise argues for peace, the 'Religio' of Eck's poem urges the country to war. Erasmus addressed two letters to King Sigismund in 1527, in which he congratulated the king for placing peace above ambition: for his piety, tolerance, and prudence in preserving peace and order in his own country, in keeping Christianity safe in the East, in shepherding Protestant Prussia back into the Catholic fold, and in maintaining a peaceful balance of power in the Baltic region and the Hungarian provinces.[82]

Although in Eck's *Threni* the figure of Religio speaks to the king, urging him to go to war against the enemies of Roman Christianity, the poem is not actually an address to the king but rather a propaganda piece portraying Sigismund as a humanist hero and encouraging the acceptance of Maximilian as an ally against the Turks. Religio describes the political situation of the times in stereotypical, anti-Eastern images that associate the Turks and peoples of the East with idolatry and cults of carnal pleasure, and that are designed to inflame the poem's audience.[83] Religio claims she is tormented by enemies – the Turks, the Tartars, the Walachians, and the Muscovites. Of the five seats where she was traditionally revered, she has only Rome left, and even Rome is covered in mud (a likely reference here to the Reformation).[84] Antioch laughs at the dogma of St Peter;[85] the church at Constantinople houses sows;[86] the churches at Jerusalem and Alexandria are also used as animal coops.[87] Meanwhile, the situation has worsened because the Ottomans occupy Thrace, the Muscovites hold the northern Polish borders, the wicked Walachians fatten themselves on the shore of the Black Sea, and the Tartars feel cold in the Scythian fields.[88] The Jews, although dispersed, covet wealth and live in Jerusalem. The horde trembles at the commands of the tyrant Sultan, who represses the kingdoms consecrated to the Christian God.[89] Yet, having set the scene for conflict in the first quarter of the poem (44 of 228 lines), Religio moves quickly to the presentation of her hero, Sigismund, who is her only hope for halting the attacks on her.

The encomium of Sigismund takes up nearly half of *Threni* and forms the core of the poem. Asking the king for assistance, Religio harks back to the deeds of his father, Casimir, who gave just laws and holy dogma to his people and who, through his own great piety, taught them to live civilly.[90] In this, Casimir is compared with Orpheus taming the Armenian tigers. Moreover, he has received intelligence from Minerva and eloquence from Apollo. Venus has given him handsomeness, Mars strength in battle, and Jupiter the toga of victory. Casimir is to be congratulated for having pushed the peoples hostile to Christ back to the nether worlds.

The poem then turns to Sigismund himself, endowing him with the qualities that humanist writers of central Europe normally admired in a king: he is a conqueror of the temptations of Venus, superior in wisdom and likewise in military strength, and exemplary in *clementia* and *pietas*.[91] Humanists presumed that monarchs aimed to acquire honour, glory, and fame; they believed that true fame was achieved by the man who, exemplifying individual virtues, would come to typify the whole of virtue itself. So Eck claims that Sigismund is handsome because his body reflects virtue and nobility, and compares his physical beauty with that of Paris and Alexander the Great.

Eck, like other humanists of the times, conceived of the ideal monarch as a just king, and in *Threni* he emphasizes this virtue as Sigismund's chief quality, by referring to Sigismund as 'the most just judge' (*iudex iustissimus*) and remarking that Sigismund is more just than the Athenian hero Aristides or the Roman emperor Trajan. Eck explains that Sigismund's justice is not severe; the king is also generous, in helping the unfortunate, the downhearted, and the destitute (ll. 101–2), and he continually gives gifts to demonstrate his gratitude (ll. 121–4). But kingly justice needs to be accompanied by prudence, a humanist conviction that Eck would defend two years later in his dialogue *De reipublicae administratione*,[92] and that he illustrates here in the character of Sigismund, whose prudence and providence enable him to consider matters of pressing moment and also to think through those of the future. For this reason, Sigismund has been victorious against the Tartars, Walachians, and Muscovites. Moreover, Eck here exploits the humanist notion of kingly justice as enhanced by prudence and wisdom to insert publicity for the *poetae*, by noting that the humanists at Cracow, in return for the favours given them by the king, sing out his deeds in lively poetry.[93]

So when Nowak-Dłużewski attacks Eck's poem for having no basis in reality, he misses the point. Eck's praise of Sigismund's temperance and chastity (ll. 115–20) is an element in his representation of Sigismund as a virtuous, strong man, one who can face up to the threats of the unholy peoples from the East. The irony that in his private life the king had extra-marital relationships may seem amusing today, but it does not mean that Eck was ignorant of what was going on 'behind the scenes' at Wawel castle, nor does it necessarily indicate that Eck was attempting to counteract gossip about the king. The king here is glorified for propaganda purposes; the political propaganda of Sigismund's court strove to present the king's virtues in a way that would justify his claim to be a true *uir uirtutis*, that is, a true leader of his people.[94] Eck mentions Sigismund's temperance and chastity because he, as a humanist scholar and poet, considers them essential virtues for the ideal monarch, and he expects their mention to produce a positive response in his audience.[95] Logically, Eck must build up his panegyric of the king as a just ruler if he wishes his call for an attack on the heretics and infidels to evoke agreement from his readers.

If Eck's first goal in *Threni* is to portray the king as a hero in conformity with the humanist notions of the ideal ruler, then his second is to argue for the acceptance of plans for an attack on the enemies from the East with Maximilian as an ally. In lines 135–228 (the end of the poem), Eck presents the political realities affecting the Poles: Sigismund, in consequence of his virtue, has been the just victor over the Tartars, Walachians, and Muscovites, but the threat of attack still exists, especially by the Turks. Sigismund must be mindful of the well-being of his people. Furthermore, Sigismund is so powerful that he does not need help from the Italians, or the French, or the Teutonic peoples, but should he wish neighbouring troops to join in, Maximilian stands ready to send auxiliaries.[96] Eck sums up the post-Congress change in attitude towards Maximilian in line 200, where he describes him as the 'emperor joined to you (Sigismund) by happy affection' ('Caesar felici iunctus amore tibi'), spelling out the message of the poem in the clearest of expressions.

Eck could not have published *Threni neglectae religionis* at Cracow without the tacit approval of the court. Maciej Drzewicki was no longer grand-chancellor of the kingdom when the poem went to print, but he continued to exert a significant influence in public affairs. Justus Ludovicus Decius, although still technically in the employ of the Boner banking family, was insinuating himself into court business and obviously wished to gain favour with the king. Moreover, the new chancellor, Krzysztof Szydłowiecki, and vice-chancellor, Piotr Tomicki, were representatives of the pro-Habsburg faction, their appointment confirming the policies of the Congress of 1515. The themes that Eck presents in *Threni* – Sigismund as a strong ruler who is able to tackle the danger threatening Europe from Moscow and Turkey, and the need for the unification of Christian rulers against that danger – were common in the Polish-Latin anti-Turkish poetry of the sixteenth century and functioned simply as a political argument for the pro-Habsburg elements of the Polish government.[97]

So Eck's *Threni* served as propaganda for Sigismund, the son of a great father who gave Christian law to this people, and himself a just but benign king, who has waged war in the defence of his people and their religion, and who, with Emperor Maximilian as a friend, will continue to repel the unholy enemies of the East. Yet it is easy to find elements of self-interest in this poem. As in the other poems of this period written by himself and Agricola Junior, Eck blended political propaganda with propaganda for the *poetae* and the humanist movement. In *Threni* he depicts Sigismund not only as a Christian warrior and as politically astute, but also as a humanist hero, endowed with the qualities the humanists admired most in a ruler: nobility, justice, generosity, integrity, temperance, prudence, providence, bravery, and overall virtue. Moreover, Eck has managed to insert in the poem a couplet (ll. 125–6) promoting the *poetae*, who sing out the accomplishments of the king in their role as the broadcasters of great deeds – scholars who can confer immortal fame.

Admittedly, Eck's poem reads as blatant propaganda, but the poet has put some effort into artistry, as evidenced by the vivid (if somewhat stereotypical) images of Religio and her enemies, and of the various ethnic groups of Poland-Lithuania ready to go into battle against the infidel and the heretic, and as demonstrated by Eck's use of *reduplicatio* (or *anadiplosis*,[98] in which the second half of one line is repeated at the beginning of the next line) in the last quarter of the poem. The weakness of the poem – the lack of *inuentio* in the inflammatory stereotypes of the Eastern peoples and the repetition of hackneyed comparisons with the ancients – can be attributed to Eck's shortage of time in which to prepare the poem, especially if it was written for the visit of Maximilian's emissaries. The speedy production of the pamphlet is evidenced by the primitive woodcuts (one a full-page depiction of Religio tormented by her enemies), which are without refinement or craftsmanship. The poverty in the design of this pamphlet can be compared to the richness of the propaganda efforts produced at Vienna, and point once again to the want of financial backing by the Cracow court for graphic artists and humanist scholars.

Hagiographic Poetry

The three hagiographic poems – on St Stanislaus, St Alexius, and St Paul the Hermit – written by Rudolf Agricola Junior and Valentin Eck between 1519 and 1522 are not religious poems in the strict sense but rather secular poems with a religious theme that serve political aims. These three pieces reflect the unease caused by the continuing conflict with the Teutonic Knights in Prussia and by the Turkish expansion into Europe at the end of the 1510s and beginning of the 1520s. They have the same format (the story of the life of the saint with a prayer for the safety of the country tacked on at the end), and they demonstrate how, in the Jagiellonian world, religious icons could be employed to promote the image of a political figure or to propagandize a political point of view.[99]

The earliest in this series of political-hagiographic poems, Rudolf Agricola's *Hymnus de diuo, praesule et martyre Stanislao, tutelari Poloniae patrono,* was printed at Cracow by Vietor in 1519. In his dedicatory letter to Chancellor Krzysztof Szydłowiecki, dated 28 July of that year, Agricola states that he has written the poem on the occasion of his recovery from an intestinal illness, the cure of which he attributes to St Stanislaus. He is dedicating the work to Szydłowiecki because he knows the chancellor is a reverent devotee of the saint. He hopes that Szydłowiecki will accept the poem, however small it might be, and that, when he has time free from his preoccupation with the weighty affairs of government, he will read the work without hesitation.

It is significant that Agricola chose to write on St Stanislaus (*c.* 1030–79), whose life and cult had traditionally been seen as intimately connected with the fate of the Polish kingdom. This bishop of Cracow was martyred in 1079 by King Boleslaus II (ruled 1058–79), who, according to legend, had been irritated by Stanislaus's constant public criticism of his wicked way of life. The king finally challenged Stanislaus over his possible confiscation of village property for the Church. The bishop, to the king's fury, managed to resurrect the dead nobleman Petrus (Piotr), from whom the land had been legally purchased, as a witness to his innocence. The king ordered his soldiers to hunt Stanislaus down. But the king himself killed Stanislaus with a sword while he was saying mass at Skałka (just outside the city walls of Cracow). The soldiers hacked his body to pieces, but the corpse, shining with a heavenly light, was guarded by eagles and was put back together by attending priests, and the pieces miraculously resewn together. The priests buried the body in the basilica of St Michael at Skałka, until it was moved to the Wawel cathedral after the saint's canonization.

The bishop's body was traditionally viewed as a symbol of the unity and vitality of the Polish kingdom, which had deteriorated in the eleventh century (Boleslaus fled Poland after Stanislaus's murder) and was then regenerated in the fourteenth. The fifteenth-century historian and hagiographer Jan Długosz, for example, viewed the assassination of the bishop as a crime for which the Piast dynasty would pay with its own extinction, and as a result of which the Polish nation would be subjected to the ascendancy of a foreign dynasty – the Jagiellons, whom Długosz reproached for having more concern for the welfare of Lithuania than for that of Poland.[100] Stanislaus was canonized in 1253 and came to be regarded as the patron and protector of the Polish monarchy.[101] Stanislaus appeared in the chronicles of Gallus Anonymus in the early twelfth century and of Vincentius Kadłubek in the early thirteenth century, but his story did not fully enter Polish literature until the middle of the thirteenth century (*c.* 1253–61) with the works of Vincentius de Kielcza, *Legenda sancti Stanislai* (also known as *Vita minor*) and *Vita sancti Stanislai* (also known as *Vita maior*). Stanislaus's biography passed from the Middle Ages into the Renaissance in the hagiographical writings of Długosz.[102]

The Jagiellonian family and their magnates promoted the cult of Stanislaus as a symbol of their own authority. Although when they first ascended the Polish throne the Jagiellonians only half-heartedly embraced the cult, in the late fifteenth century Cardinal Fryderyk Jagiellon, Sigismund's younger brother, revived devotion to the saint by commissioning artwork bearing Stanislaus's image and by launching new rituals connected with him. After Sigismund took the throne in 1506, he heightened the court's identification with the cult by funding new silver panels for Stanislaus's tomb and by ordering, in 1512, statues for the church at Skałka. When Piotr Tomicki became bishop of Cracow in 1525, he too would exhibit solidarity with the royal family in their preference for the cult of Stanislaus by donating a silver statue of the saint to the Wawel cathedral and by having himself depicted, in miniatures painted in manuscripts ordered for his personal use, kneeling at the feet of St Stanislaus.

The royal family's exploitation of the cult of St Stanislaus was intended to stress the Polish identity of the Jagiellons while subtly distancing them from their Lithuanian origins, to create the impression of an intimate relationship between the Jagiellonian family and Poland's elective throne, and to make a public statement of personal piety with a view to legitimizing and augmenting their authority and raising their social prestige. The story of a villain who was the antitype of a virtuous Catholic king and the image of the murdered Stanislaus could serve as a reminder of notions of royal power and good kingship.[103]

Agricola claimed, in his dedicatory letter, that Chancellor Szydłowiecki was a devotee of St Stanislaus, and this claim is backed up by historical evidence. In the illuminated manuscript of Jan Długosz's *Catalogus archiepiscoporum Gnesnensium* and *Vitae episcoporum Cracouiensium* that Tomicki had executed by Stanisław Samostrzelnik and his workshop during the years 1530–5, there appears a miniature portrait of Tomicki and King Sigismund kneeling at the feet of St Stanislaus, and next to the king the figure of Szydłowiecki is clearly visible. Obviously, Szydłowiecki joined with Tomicki in supporting the royal cult of the saint and thus the propaganda that furthered the prestige and authority of the Jagiellonian family.[104] By printing a poem on St Stanislaus dedicated to Szydłowiecki, Agricola won himself a place as agent for the most elite and personal form of royal propaganda.

Agricola may also have had his own reasons for selecting Stanislaus as a topic for his poem and Szydłowiecki as a dedicatee. These may have had less to do with his belief that he had recovered his health owing to the intervention of the saint than to his waning economic prospects and precarious political situation as a German in Cracow, which demanded that he bolster the faltering patronage he was receiving at Cracow and project a public image as a follower of the Polish royal religious cult. In a letter to Joachim Vadian dated 25 August 1519 (just a month after the dedication to Szydłowiecki), Agricola stated that he had been ill twice recently. The climate of the city was unhealthy and he really would like to leave. In the same letter he told Vadian that the group of bishops patronizing him were great 'promisers' but were 'growing cold' towards him. So his seeking out Szydłowiecki may have been a tactic aimed at diversifying his patronage base, especially given that he was approaching a layman as opposed to a cleric.

To make matters worse, Poland was again at war: the grand master of the Teutonic Knights was instigating skirmishes in Prussia; some citizens and businessmen at Elbląg had been killed; four thousand Tartars had plundered a great portion of Lithuania and Poland. The Poles at Cracow were becoming antagonistic towards residents of German origin (most likely because of the violence flaring up again in Prussia).[105] Since Agricola mentioned in this letter that he was sending along a copy of his 'hastily written' (*subito scriptum*) poem to Vadian, it is easy to imagine that these matters were on his mind.[106] So the choice of St Stanislaus as the subject of his poem and the statement in his dedicatory letter that he believed he had recovered from his illness thanks to the saint's intervention may well have been intended to associate Agricola personally with the cult of St Stanislaus and to reinforce his own image as one loyal to the country and crown. The topic of Stanislaus was a timely one, not only because of King Sigismund's increased participation in the cult in the 1510s but also because the cult of the saint had been highlighted during the marriage ceremony of Sigismund to the Italian princess Bona the year before.[107]

For his material on St Stanislaus, Agricola followed the tradition of humanist hagiographic writing in Poland. This tradition had its roots in the work of Jan Długosz (1415–80), the secretary of the Cracow humanist Cardinal Oleśnicki, who wrote his *Vita beatissimi Stanislai Cracouiensis episcopi* about 1460–5. It would be printed at Cracow by the Haller press in 1511 in a volume along with Długosz's lives of the other Polish patron saints.[108] His life of St Stanislaus would provide inspiration for Callimachus, that is, Filippo Buonaccorsi (the Italian who had fled Rome and settled in Poland in 1470 to become a foreign policy adviser to Sigismund's father, King Casimir, and his elder brother, King Jan Olbracht),[109] when Buonaccorsi composed his *Carmen sapphicum in uitam gloriosissimi martyris sancti Stanislai episcopi Cracouiensis Polonorum gentis patroni*.[110] Agricola's immediate model was Paulus Crosnensis, who, drawing on both Długosz and Callimachus, published *Panegyricus ad diuum Stanislaum, praesulem sanctissimum et martyrem uictoriosissimum ac patronum regni Poloniae beneficientissimum* at Vienna in 1509.[111] The part of the original legend in which Stanislaus cursed Boleslaus was omitted by the humanist writers Callimachus, Crosnensis, and Agricola because their relationship to the king differed from that projected in the medieval text – the conflict between the Church and the royal authority was no longer an issue for them; and in fact (in opposition to Długosz's political views) they wished to enhance the king's public expression of his interest in Polish, as opposed to purely Lithuanian, affairs.[112]

Agricola's *Hymnus de diuo Stanislao* has received criticism from Polish scholars for its lack of inventiveness. Albert Gorzkowski notes that Agricola plagiarized from his teacher Paulus[113] and criticizes Agricola's poem for lack of balance by paying much attention to the circumstances of the saint's birth but treating the further events of his life only superficially.[114] Krystyna Stawecka hypothesizes that Agricola planned to write a longer poem describing in detail the life of the saint, but was forced by time pressure to summarize the saint's life.[115] Certainly, Agricola mentioned, both in his dedicatory letter to Szydłowiecki and in his personal letter to Vadian, that he wrote the poem in haste. Yet notwithstanding criticism by both Gorzkowski and Stawecka for want of imagination, Agricola's poem exhibits some inventiveness, at both the beginning and the end. These two sections contain the specific ideas the poem most likely was designed to advance.

First of all, Agricola does not conform with the statement he makes in the introductory lines to his poem – that it is better to write in honour of the Trinity, of the Mother of God, and of Christ's martyrs and virgins, the true divinity and the saints, than to follow the ancient poets who praised false gods and mythological beings – throughout his poem.[116] Instead, he goes on to refer to God as *tonans* and Bishop Stanislaus as *praesul* (instead of *episcopus*, as Długosz did), to praise Stanislaus for his study of ancient doctrine ('septem ueterum per annos dogmata discas'), to describe King Boleslaus's anger as 'his heart being disturbed by the Furies' ('cui pectus Furiae inquietant'), to express his desire that the Fates favour King Sigismund's military actions ('Fata Sismundi faueant triumphis prospera regis'), and to depict Phoebus Apollo warming the Polish fields with his light ('Quos suo Phoebus moderetur igne'). Agricola had included mythological figures and antique colouring in his writings previous to his poem on St Stanislaus and would continue to do so.

So Agricola's opening lines to *Hymnus de diuo Stanislao* cannot be considered a policy statement – that he was choosing to abandon classicizing, humanist norms for writing poetry – especially since the dedicatee of this poem, Chancellor Szydłowiecki, along with Agricola's other patron, Bishop Tomicki, were champions of the new Italianate style in art at the royal court. Rather, these verses compare sources of poetic inspiration – the pagan poet, inspired by false gods, rages with tainted poems, while the saints rejoice in the Christian poet's lyre and inspire him to sing better songs – and refer to Agricola's choice in seeking Christian inspiration for this poem with a religious theme.[117] Moreover, and more important, by devoting the first forty-eight lines of his poem to the topic of poetic inspiration, Agricola calls attention to the creative power of the poet and the importance of his role in society.

Second, at the end of the poem Agricola couches his concern for the country's welfare in his prayer to St Stanislaus, and it seems here that he is referring both to the skirmishes with the Teutonic Knights in Prussia that would turn into outright war by the end of 1519 and to the attacks by the Tartars in the southeast. The Knights were being provoked into violence against the Poles by the Muscovites, who in 1519 were again threatening the Lithuanian border, and who had recruited the Tartar khan into their alliance. In July 1519 the Tartars invaded Polish-Lithuanian territory and attacked the area of Lublin and Lvov.[118] In his poem Agricola asks St Stanislaus to repair the country, which has been injured by the bloodthirsty enemies of faith; he recalls the repair made to Stanislaus's body by God, with *repares* in line 234 reiterating the *reparent* of line 223. And Agricola prays that the king will win military victories, that the Polish fields will be fertile, and that the population will not be threatened with disease.[119]

In *Hymnus de diuo Stanislao*, then, Agricola Junior used St Stanislaus as a symbol of the ideal chaplain-pastor, representative of the whole nation, and an image of the supernatural protection of both the kingdom and the nation, with the publication of the poem coinciding with the royal court's enthusiastic adoption of the cult of the saint as an expression of its official politics. Through his treatment of St Stanislaus, Agricola not only contributed to the propaganda of the royal cult, but also linked his own name with those of Chancellor Szydłowiecki and the court elite. Moreover, just as the Jagiellonian kings wished to dissociate themselves from their image as Lithuanians interested more in the affairs of their native land than in those of Poland, so Agricola may well, during this time of conflict in Prussia and growing prejudice against the ethnic German population in Cracow, have wished to dissociate himself from his German background and show his solidarity with the Polish nation. Agricola not only advances the causes of his patrons in this poem, in praying for Sigismund's military success, but also promotes himself, by calling attention to the role of the poet as one inspired by God and suggesting the poet's ability to create charming and effective prayers (much as he did in his poem in honour of Cardinal Lang, where he proclaimed his prayers for Lang's good fortune, and claimed that the gods favoured poets and that poetry could reach the heavens).

Valentin Eck's *De diuo Alexio patricio Romano hymnus sapphicus*, the second poem in this political-hagiographic series, was printed in Cracow in the spring of 1521. Eck signed his dedicatory letter to Alexius Thurzó on 11 May at Buda. In it, Eck writes that he composed the poem in consequence of having some free time and thinking that the story of St Alexius would offer a good example for students. He is dedicating the poem to Thurzó not only because it is the story of the life of his patron and he knows Thurzó to be a devotee of the saint, but also because it is fitting for him to return the kindness Thurzó has shown him with the gift of a literary work. Although Eck does not hint at the poem's political nature in his dedicatory letter, his remarks at the end of the poem refer to the Turkish attacks of that season. The poem can be regarded both as promoting the image of Alexius Thurzó as the ideal humanist Christian leader (Thurzó was at this time a rising figure at the Buda court, holding the post of *cubicularius*, or chamberlain) and as publicizing the anti-Turkish politics of the Hungarian government.

Selim I (ruled 1512–20) had posed a threat to the Europeans by extending Turkish rule into Syria, Mesopotamia, and Egypt, but he seemed inclined to refrain from engaging in open conflict with Hungary – and with Poland – so as to be free to operate on these other fronts. In March 1519 he signed a three-year treaty with King Louis II of Hungary, who had come to the throne after the death of his father, Vladislav II, in 1516. But Selim's successor, Suleyman, showed no interest in long-term treaties and attempted, by attacking the Hungarian kingdom, to fortify his position on the Black Sea. Hungary should have wanted at all costs to preserve peace with the Turks, but managed only to sign a one-year treaty with Suleyman. King Sigismund needed a strong Hungarian kingdom and peace with the Turks, and he took an anti-war stance. But Hungary, unable to count on outside support and suffering from weak internal government, adopted an aggressive policy. The Turks marched into Hungarian territory in the spring of 1521 and attacked Transylvania and Nándorfehérvár (Belgrade). But Hungary was slow to react, and its army was rife with insubordination and corruption. Nándorfehérvár, the gateway to southern Hungary, fell to the Turks on 28 August 1521.[120]

The subject of Eck's poem, the story of St Alexius of Rome (most likely an invented figure and/or the product of a confusion of one figure with a certain Eastern holy man called Mar Riscia), had its origins in fifth-century Syria. The legend of Alexius came to the West in the tenth century, when Greek monks were given the abbey of St Boniface on the Aventine and thereafter rededicated it to Sts Boniface and Alexius. Devotion to St Alexius quickly spread throughout central and western Europe and was especially influential as a source of the religious ideals of chastity and denial of the world. Besides its transmission in Latin, the Alexius legend was translated into the vernacular languages. It existed, for example, in Old French in the early eleventh century, and it reached England in the twelfth. A version in *mittelhochdeutsch* is known from the thirteenth century, and a Polish manuscript dating from the middle of the fifteenth century is thought to contain a text that actually dates from the fourteenth. By the sixteenth century, the legend had been translated into Hungarian. Churches were already being dedicated to St Alexius in central Europe in the eleventh century.[121]

So common was the legend of St Alexius that Valentin Eck would have known it from childhood. Indeed, his poem adheres to the version of the story that was popular in Germany, in which Alexius's wife agreed to an unconsummated marriage in preference to being abandoned by her husband.[122] Alexius was born the only son of wealthy parents. The boy studied religion and, despising the joys of the world, made a vow of chastity. His father, fearing that the family line would die out, found a fiancée for him. Alexius agreed to the wedding, but when it came time to consummate the marriage, he talked his bride into a vow of chastity. He then went on a pilgrimage to Syria, where he lived at Edessa (now Şanliurfa in Turkey) as a pauper, performing charitable works. Alexius shunned the popularity he had gained at Edessa and returned to Rome, where he lived for seventeen years, unrecognized by his family, as a pauper under the stairs of his father's house. When he saw that the end of his life was near, he wrote a book, inspired by the Holy Spirit, about his life. After his death, a voice was heard from heaven, and many people gathered at Alexius's father's house. His father found the paper on which Alexius had written, but when he tried to take it into his hands, it became harder than stone. The pope, however, was able to take the paper and read the text, and thereby identify the body as that of Alexius. The crowds approached to touch Alexius's body, and through his intercession many miracles began to be worked.

Eck's long poem (228 lines in sapphic metre) is an unembellished retelling of the Alexius story, but one that retains the dramatic elements of the traditional narrative. For example, when Alexius does not return from Syria, his father misses him and sends his servants out to search the whole world to find his son and bring him back. But the servants, when they do come across Alexius in Syria, fail to recognize their former master, now a beggar on the street, and simply give him a donation.[123] At the climax of the story, when the pope is reading out Alexius's memoirs and his identity becomes known, Eck takes care to sketch the sentiments of Alexius's family: his mother throws herself on the corpse, and his father and his abandoned widow weep copious tears day and night.[124]

Valentin Eck's *De diuo Alexio patricio Romano hymnus sapphicus* can be considered propaganda for Eck's patron Alexius Thurzó, with St Alexius, the symbol of chastity and rejection of worldly values, as a stand-in for the real Alexius. The issues of chastity and of contempt for the world figured prominently in Eck's writings, especially in his descriptions of rulers. In humanist thinking, contempt for the world did not necessarily mean withdrawal into a monastery, but simply the rejection of evil, as Erasmus argued in his *Epistola de contemptu mundi*.[125] Eck therefore could imply that Alexius Thurzó, without withdrawing from the world, was emulating the qualities of his patron saint, as he hints in his dedicatory letter to Thurzó. In 1519, in *De antiquissima nominis et familiae Thurzonum origine*, Eck had portrayed his subject as choosing virtue over voluptuousness, and had highlighted the temperance and modesty of Thurzó, who, in refusing to live off the riches of his father, had rejected leisure and amorous pleasures. In 1518, in his poem *Threni neglectae religionis*, Eck had stressed chastity as one of King Sigismund's virtues (ll. 115–20), and had characterized Sigismund as a strong and virtuous man who could face up to the threats of the unholy peoples from the East. Moreover, Eck had dealt with the theme of the rejection of worldly values in his prose essays, *De mundi contemptu et uirtute amplectenda dialogus* (Cracow, 1519) and *De reipublicae administratione dialogus* (Cracow, 1520), where he asserted that the virtuous man despises voluptuousness, luxury, and leisure, and espouses modesty, moderation, and temperance, especially the reigning in of sexual and material desire. Although in his poem of 1518, *An prudenti uiro sit ducenda uxor*, Eck had argued in favour of Christian marriage (and not for a 'chaste,' or unconsummated, marriage) in preference to celibacy, in *De diuo Alexio patricio Romano* he was asserting that chastity and the rejection of worldly values were qualities desirable in the nobility (the hero of the poem is, after all, a patrician), and was attributing more importance to them than to the preservation of the noble line.

The final twenty-eight lines of *De diuo Alexio patricio Romano* constitute a prayer to St Alexius, imagined now 'in residence' at Rome, to look after the welfare of Hungary and to force the Turks out of the region. Eck refers to recent events, stating that the Turks have entered Hungarian territory not to rule, but to slaughter Christians.[126] He asks Alexius to have mercy on the Hungarian people and to grant them peace, by eliminating vice and crime from their lives and removing the 'sad pyre of the hellish tyrant' (*Stygii tyranni triste sepulchrum*). Finally, he asks Alexius, as the patron of a happy death, to accompany the souls of the Hungarians to heaven when they die.

In 1522 the advance of the Turks into Hungary was stalled by Suleyman's southward move in July to take siege of Rhodes, which would capitulate on 18 December.[127] At the end of November, Valentin Eck published, with the Vietor press at Cracow, his *Vita diui Pauli primi eremitae*, a poem recounting the life of a patron saint of the Hungarian nation and the third in this series of political-hagiographic poems. In his dedicatory letter to Alexius Thurzó, written from Bártfa, Eck congratulated Thurzó on his appointment as royal treasurer (*regius thesaurarius*) and stated his conviction that Thurzó, a diligent administrator, would not fail in his duties. He characterized Thurzó as a leader who put the interest of the nation before his own private concerns, a leader on whom the Hungarian people could depend to keep them safe at this dangerous time, when the country, if fractured by discord, could become the plunder of the enemies of the Christian religion. He compared Thurzó to Nestor, an experienced statesman whose advice was sought out, even by the commander of the Greek army. Thurzó upheld all the old virtues: he cared for freedom, security, the family, and fatherland. Eck ended his dedication by saying that the only way the country could be safe from the attack of the Turks was through the exercise of virtue, religion, and devotion to the national patron saints, among whom St Paul the Hermit did not occupy the last position. Eck composed *Vita diui Pauli primi eremitae*, therefore, both to advertise Thurzó's promotion to treasurer of the kingdom and to call for national unity against the Turks in the form of a prayer to St Paul.

The life of Paul the Hermit (also known as Paul of Thebes, d. *c.* 345) was transmitted to the West from the Greek tradition via St Jerome's *Vita Sancti Pauli primi eremitae*, composed in the late fourth century (although it has also been argued that Jerome may have been the original written source). The story takes place during the persecution of the Christians by Emperor Decius, when Paul is a young man. He flees and takes up a hermit's life in the Egyptian desert. When he is very old, St Anthony, a younger but still elderly hermit, comes to look for his predecessor. Upon their meeting, a raven comes down from heaven and feeds them with bread. Paul knows that he will soon die and asks Anthony to bring to him the cloak that had once been given to Anthony by St Athanasius so that his body may be wrapped in it. When Anthony returns, he finds that Paul has died. Anthony realizes that he has no implements with which to dig a grave for Paul, but miraculously two lions approach and claw a grave out of the sand.[128]

The legend of St Paul became popular throughout medieval Europe, and St Jerome's text was not only spread in the original Latin, but also translated into many vernacular languages, as attested by countless manuscripts. The saint's life was printed, in both Latin and German, from the 1470s to the 1510s by the major German presses (Cologne, Strassburg, and Augsburg).[129] Erasmus included it in his *opera omnia* edition of St Jerome's works printed at Basel in 1516. Moreover, a monastic order of St Paul was founded at the beginning of the thirteenth century in Hungary and quickly branched out, its religious houses flourishing throughout central Europe – in Hungary, Austria, Germany, and Poland.[130]

Like St Stanislaus in Poland, St Paul the Hermit was one of a group of 'national' saints in Hungary who during the Middle Ages had come to be commonly represented in art and literature in connection with the promotion of royal authority. The 'most spectacular cultic coup' of the era had been the acquisition from Venice of the relics of St Paul by the Angevin King Louis I (Nagy Lajos, ruled 1342–82), upon his signing a peace treaty with the city-state in 1381.[131] The king and his queen, Elizabeth, had favoured the Pauline monks, the only religious order to be founded in Hungary, by supporting the establishment of their monastic houses. The Hermit's relics rested in the Pauline cloister of St Lawrence near Buda;[132] he came to be identified with royal power and was invoked for protection against the Turks. As late as the eighteenth century, for example, he was shown in an engraving assisting King Matthias Corvinus's (ruled 1458–90) triumph in a battle with the Ottomans.[133]

As with the life of St Alexius, Eck most likely knew the legend of St Paul the Hermit from his youth in Germany. Although the life of Paul was normally accompanied by a life of Anthony as the agent who put into practice and propagated Paul's ideals by setting up monasteries, Eck, obviously wishing to concentrate on Paul as the patron and protector of Hungary, ended his story with Paul's death and burial. Eck's life of St Paul is longer (300 lines of dactylic hexameter) than his poem on St Alexius and shows more inventiveness. Eck introduces the historical background and creates a sense of fear with motifs of instruments of torture (whips, wheels, swords, and fire) and a list of early martyrdoms (Agnes, Agatha, Apollonia, Concordia, Lawrence). He provides some drama in the scenes of Paul's flight from persecution with the images of a ship tossed at sea and of a sheep, its heart pounding, escaping from the open jaws of wolves, and in the scene of Paul's decision to reject the world and lead the life of a hermit with the image of a snake shedding its skin.[134] The longest section of the poem (ll. 64–109) is taken up with Paul's decision to leave the world and his meditations in the desert, and points to Eck's concern, as in his other works, with the contempt of worldly values and the commitment to a life of virtue.

Eck connects the life of Paul to the subsequent role of the saint as a patron of the Hungarian nation. His tomb was hidden by holy guards for many years, until Emperor Emanuel removed his body to Constantinople and erected over it a church to the Virgin Mary. Later, St Paul's body was taken to Venice, and finally King Louis I brought it to Buda, where it rested next to the royal walls. Eck concludes his poem with a prayer to St Paul to have mercy on

Hungary and to give the Hungarian leaders the manly courage to expel the enemies of the faith from the kingdom so that the Hungarian people might enjoy peace. Finally, Eck asks St Paul to protect his patron, Thurzó, to grant him many years and many grandchildren, and, at the end of his life, to accompany him to heaven.

Eck's emphasis on Paul's rejection of the world in *Vita diui Pauli eremitae* – a digression of forty-five lines, taking up nearly a sixth of the poem – echoes his admonishment to the Hungarians to return to the pristine virtues named in his dedication to Thurzó. As he did in his life of St Alexius, Eck creates, in Paul, a hero who shows 'contempt for the world' to promote his own, humanist values. In the former work Eck was attempting to enhance the public image of his patron, whereas here he is endeavouring to advance Thurzó's political views. Yet Eck's life of St Paul also portrays Thurzó as Hungary's ideal leader, not only on the occasion of his appointment as royal treasurer, but also during a time of national crisis. In this poem, furthermore, Eck promotes himself, by linking himself publicly to Thurzó in referring to him as *noster patronus* (l. 292) and thereby formalizing the relationship between himself, the client-poet, and the great man Thurzó.

The Battle of Mohács and Its Aftermath

In early January 1524, Valentin Eck published, with the Vietor press in Cracow, a poem of sixty-four lines in dactylic hexameter, *Ad inuictissimum Ludouicum Hungariae et Bohemiae regem pro bello Turcis inferendo exhortatio.* Eck accompanied this exhortation to King Louis II to wage war against the Turks with a longer, eighty-six-line poem addressed to the Hungarian leaders, *Ad proceres Hungariae.* In his dedicatory letter to Alexius Thurzó, Eck congratulates the king on his recent, successful military action against the Turks. He expresses his hope that the other European kings will be inspired by Louis II's courage and come to the aid of the Hungarians, since the brutality of the Turks is so fierce everywhere that the Hungarians will be unable to survive without military assistance. Eck praises the king for taking action to check the advance of the Turks and reminds the people, advising them to move quickly to stop the invasion, that God helps those who show themselves worthy of his protection. Eck makes no mention in his dedication of Thurzó's appointment in 1523 to *magister tauernicorum*, a prefect responsible for the affairs and jurisdiction of a group of Hungarian free royal towns, but he titles him thus in the header to the letter and includes a congratulatory poem.

In his dedicatory letter, Eck was referring to the rout of the Turks under the command of Ferhad, the pasha of Bosnia, at Mitróvicza the previous August by Hungarian troops led by Pál Tomori, the archbishop of Kalocsa. After the fall of Nándorfehérvár (Belgrade) in the summer of 1521, Hungary's southern border was exposed, and though Tomori did his utmost to secure the southern frontier, its defence was on the brink of collapse. Moreover, the Hungarian treasury was virtually bankrupt, and Tomori's only source of financial support was the papal nuncio. Even though it was clear that Hungary could not defend itself alone, no one wished to come to its aid. King Sigismund was about to sign a peace treaty with the Turks, and he counselled Louis II to do the same. Charles V was preoccupied with the Lutherans and with the French. Louis II's brother-in-law, Ferdinand, the archduke of Austria, despite later being willing to send troops into Croatia to defend the Austrian provinces against the onslaught of the Ottomans from that direction, made only empty promises for the military support of Hungary. Louis's meeting with him and with the Polish grand-chancellor, Krzysztof Szydłowiecki, at Wiener Neustadt in October 1523 would produce no results.

Moreover, the power struggle between the Hungarian magnates (led by the palatine István Báthori) and the lower nobility (headed by István Werbőczy) was pushing the country towards an internal breakdown. The nobility, although opposed to any peace treaty with the Turks, was hampered by its national zeal for ridding the government of foreigners and the country, in general, of Lutherans. The pro-Habsburg faction in Hungary, in which Alexius Thurzó played a central role, was at the same time the pro-war faction, and Valentin Eck, as Thurzó's client, supplied it with anti-Turk, pro-war propaganda. Looking in vain for support from the Habsburg empire, this faction pushed Hungary into the path of conflict. With an empty treasury, an unstable government, and no support from the outside, Hungary should have wanted to keep peace with the Turks, but a mood for war prevailed, and the atmosphere was right for the Habsburgs to let Hungary slide into a disastrous battle with the Ottomans.[135]

Ad Ludouicum Hungariae et Bohemiae regem exhortatio imitates Eck's earlier poem *Threni neglectae religionis*[136] in both format and theme, with 'Ecclesia' speaking here, urging King Louis II to go to war with the Turks.[137] In fact, lines 17 to 29 of *Exhortatio* are a recapitulation of lines 17 to 44 of *Threni*, with Ecclesia complaining that she is mocked and tormented as she wanders through the world searching for a place that will revere her. Her lament that of her five former seats only Rome remains, the others (such as Antioch and Jerusalem) having been defiled by the enemies of the faith, is borrowed from Eck's earlier poem, even down to the image of the female figure with her hair being torn out. Ecclesia, like the earlier Religio, is referred to as a mother or parent.

In *Exhortatio*, though, Eck has shortened the praises of the king. Louis II is addressed as 'the most famous king of kings' (*clarissime regum rex Lodouice*) and termed 'the glory of his country' (*decus patriae*), the constant protector of the ancestral faith (*fidei paternae assertor constans*), and the lover of piety and justice (*pietatis amator et aequi*). In *Exhortatio*, Eck does not embark upon an extended panegyric of the monarch, as he did in *Threni* in glorifying the deeds of Sigismund's father, Casimir, and in listing Sigismund's virtues. Rather, when commending Louis for his military strength, Eck turns to the figure of the people whom Louis governs – the Hungarians, whom he characterizes as taking pleasure in slaughtering the Turks.[138] As an example, Eck cites the victory of János Hunyadi and Giovanni da Capestrano over the Ottomans at Nándorfehérvár (Belgrade) in July 1456.[139] Employing a vocabulary of violence, with such commands as *irrue* (rush headlong), *scinde* (cut to pieces), *feri* (strike), and *trucidare* (slaughter), he fills his poem with inflammatory language as Ecclesia encourages Louis to gather his powerful forces for war and set out to kill the Turks, even without the help of other nations. Only at the end of the poem does Eck return to expressing admiration for the king, by saying that God will favour his brave deeds and that after death he will be celebrated as a victor in heaven.[140]

In *Ad proceres Hungariae*, which accompanies *Exhortatio*, the poet speaks directly to the Hungarian magnates and higher nobility – *proceres* being the term used to refer to the dignitaries who made up the royal council[141] – without the intermediary of a personification. Eck has no praise for this group of lazy men, who should be ashamed of their lack of concern for their faith and for the safety of their country. While they have been idle, the Mohammedan enemy has been coming closer and is now poised to slaughter the whole Hungarian nation. The poet urges the leaders of Hungary to recover their ancient powers, to rise up and take up arms against the Turks. Providing classical examples to reinforce his argument, Eck compares the shameful inactivity of the Hungarian leaders with the effeminacy to which certain mythical heroes were reduced: Hercules, who as a slave of the Lydian queen Omphale was dressed as a woman, and Achilles, who was dressed in girl's clothes at the court of Lycomedes, king of Skyros, where he was hidden while the Greeks were deciding to go to war against Troy.[142] Moreover, in order to create a climax that will demonstrate how powerful the Turks have become and how close they are to conquering the Hungarians, Eck uses his usual technique of *enumeratio*. He takes up nearly thirty lines with a list of the names of the regions and nations that have been subdued by the Turks, including not only Egypt, Africa, India, and Greece, but also the Thracians, Assyrians, Persians, Arabians, Euboeans, Boeotians, Cappadocians, Phrygians, Carians, and so on. These examples should have warned the Hungarians. If they do not take action, the Hungarian nation will become prey for the bloody jaws of the doglike Turks.[143]

The Polish neo-Latin scholar Barbara Milewska-Waźbińska states that the criticism found in the Polish-Latin anti-Turkish poems of European rulers for their failure of responsibility regarding the fate of Christian Europe, and of citizens for their failure regarding the fate of the nation, stemmed from these poems' being addressed to Polish nobles, who participated in a parliamentary system and had responsibility for their nation's destiny.[144] The same could be said of Hungarian nobles, and hence the critical tone of Eck's poem. Finding fault with one's own people in the context of anti-Turkish poetry had its roots in the writings of the early Italian humanists and was linked to religious interpretations of the Western confrontation with the Turks, in which humanists criticized Christian society for its failure to live up to its own religious standards.[145] So Eck's concern for the fate of the Hungarian kingdom in *Ad proceres Hungariae* not only gave voice to the particular political situation in which the Hungarian nobles found themselves, but also expressed an opposition to the Turks based in religion.

In *Ad proceres Hungariae* and *Exhortatio*, Eck makes it clear that King Louis II is to be admired for his leadership and that the Hungarian nobles are to be censured for their inactivity. The Hungarians are justified in rising up to battle the Turks because they are being threatened with captivity by a people hostile to the Christian religion. In *Exhortatio*, praises of King Louis have been reduced in favour of violent imagery of the Church being attacked and torn to pieces, imagery that advances Eck's argument for war against the Turks. In *Ad proceres Hungariae*, Eck's censure of the Hungarians by means of classical examples of unmanly weakness and his attempt to arouse to fear with an extended list of nations conquered by the Turks are bolstered by images of the valour exercised in defending one's country and religion. In both these poems the epithets applied to the Turks are designed to evoke not just antipathy but abhorrence and loathing of the enemy. The Turks are portrayed as a dreadful or savage enemy (*dirus hostis, hostis atrox, Ad proceres Hungariae*, ll. 4, 30), as wicked people (*saeua gens, Exhortatio*, l. 51; *Ad proceres Hungariae*, l. 78), as barbarians (*barbaricus, Exhortatio*, l. 9), as a schismatic or foreign tyrant (*schismaticus tyrannus, Exhortatio*, l. 50; *externus tyrannus, Ad proceres Hungariae*, l. 9), as enemies of Christ (*inimica cruci Christi Selima propago, Ad proceres Hungariae*, l. 12), and even as animals (*rictus caninus, Ad proceres Hungariae*, l. 52).

In using these violent and inflammatory images, Eck was conforming to the characterization of the Turks common in the humanist poetry of his time and place. According to József Jankovics, in the poetry of the sixteenth-century Hungarian humanists the Turks were typically portrayed by means of such harsh stereotypes, especially in the *querela Hungariae*, which 'reiterated Hungary's role as the shield and bulwark of Christendom.'[146] Mihály Imre states that the theme of Hungary as the defender of Christianity against the Turks, a topic that often emphasized military virtue, recurred in the literary and political rhetoric of central Europe throughout the sixteenth century.[147] Barbara Milewska-Waźbińska, furthermore, notes that the use of such inflammatory imagery and epithets in the anti-Turkish poetry of the sixteenth century reveals the influence of classical literature on the authors, in that the poets' attitude to the Turks was similar to the ancient Romans' attitude to the barbarians. She states, 'The image of the Turk in Latin poetry created in Poland is quite schematic; elements of topics created in ancient times to present the constantly threatening danger to Rome on the part of barbarians from the East are obligatory in it.'[148] Yet the use of stereotypes borrowed from classical literature to express a conception of the Turks as a barbarous people threatening Christian Europe was not invented in the 1510s and 1520s by the humanists of east central Europe; it can be found in Petrarch, Coluccio Salutati, and Leonardo Bruni, who asserted the cultural superiority of West over East and feared for the loss of the Christian faith and European learning at the hands of the Ottomans. Like the early Italian humanists, the central European humanists of the sixteenth century stretched the ancient notions of barbarity to fit the contemporary military advances of the Turks.[149]

In both *Exhortatio* and *Ad proceres Hungariae*, Valentin Eck, as a poet, speaks with authority and projects an image of himself as one to whom people should listen. The aggressive voice he adopts in these poems, by using stark and brutal imagery and making a harsh statement of what the Hungarians stood to lose if they did not face the Turks immediately, would have presented him as an 'insider' at court. Moreover, his mention of Alexius Thurzó as his patron (*patronus obseruandissimus*) and as a benefactor of literature (*sua propensa humanitate, litterarium fouente otium*) in the header of the dedicatory letter of the booklet and in the header to the poem *Ad proceres Hungariae* would have signalled his status as a court poet. The inclusion of his own title as a town official of Bártfa (*Bartphanae Reipublicae a consiliis atque libellis*) on the title-page of the booklet would certainly have lent his voice credibility and also have revealed his political links to the court (Bártfa being a royal free town and therefore pro-crown). In this way, Eck associated himself publicly, and as a poet, with the highest ranks of the Hungarian government.

In November 1525, through the instigation of Queen Maria, a royal league was formed to strengthen the authority of the king. Although much of the opposition was won over and Maria succeeded in having laws passed that would reinforce royal power and form a more effective government, her efforts came too late. In April 1526, Suleyman left Istanbul to march on Hungary. By the end of July he had captured Pétervárad, in the very south of the country. King Louis II came rushing in from Buda, but with a force of only 4,000 men. The Hungarian army would be joined by new contingents by the time it reached the south, but even at 40,000 strong it was no match for Suleyman's 80,000 regular troops plus auxiliaries. On 29 August they battled near the town of Mohács; the Hungarians were defeated in less than two hours. The king, both archbishops (Tomori and Szalkai), five bishops, and nearly two dozen magnates were killed. Suleyman proceeded to sack Buda, but his aim was to seize Vienna, and he would not conquer Hungary as such until 1541.[150]

Alexius Thurzó, along with Tamás Szalaházi (bishop of Veszprém), had stayed in Buda to protect Queen Maria, and after Mohács he fled with her and other dignitaries to Vienna. With the death of Louis, Ferdinand could claim the Hungarian throne, and only the Czech and Hungarian national movements could block his access to it. But on 23 October 1526 the Czechs elected Ferdinand, who was unopposed, as king. King Sigismund advised the Hungarians to elect their own king immediately. The Hungarian national faction elected the magnate János Zápolya as its king (King János I) on 10 November 1526. But the country had broken into two camps, and on 16 December 1526 the Habsburgs saw to it that Ferdinand was also elected to the Hungarian throne. He was officially crowned on 4 November 1527.

Civil war broke out as the two kings battled for control of the country. Poland decided to remain officially neutral. On 7 July 1527, Ferdinand declared war on Zápolya; he entered Buda on 10 August, and went on to defeat Zápolya at Tokaj on 27 September 1527 and then again at Kassa on 3 March 1528. After the first battle, some of Zápolya's supporters went over to the Habsburg side, but later, many Poles supported the Hungarian national cause and joined Zápolya's army. After the second defeat Zápolya slipped into Poland and took refuge there; he decided to seek help from the Turks.

Meanwhile, the Habsburg faction had taken control of northeast Hungary (Szepes) and had even crossed over into Poland. In the summer of 1529 the Turks, welcomed by Zápolya, marched through Hungary. They took Buda and attacked Vienna. Though everyone feared the Turks, their support did not guarantee Zápolya the throne. Indeed, the involvement of the Turks provoked the opposite reaction, and the pope publicly cursed Zápolya. In 1530, King Sigismund tried to neutralize the situation by arranging the marriage of his son Sigismund August to Ferdinand's daughter, Elizabeth. Although Sigismund did what he could to bring about a rapprochement between Ferdinand and Zápolya, he continued to sympathize with Zápolya. Until Zápolya's death in July 1540, there remained two kings on the Hungarian throne, with Ferdinand in control of Slavonia, Croatia, and part of Hungary proper, and Zápolya in possession of Transylvania and the remainder of Hungary. Afterwards, Ferdinand kept his kingdom, while Zápolya's son, János Zsigmond, ruled over Transylvania and Partium as a vassal of the Turks.

Valentin Eck's patron, Alexius Thurzó, worked towards Ferdinand's confirmation as king of Hungary.[151] In reality, aside from Thurzó only a small group of magnates supported Ferdinand against Zápolya: István Báthori, palatine of Hungary (1526–30); Pál Várdai, archbishop of Esztergom (1526–49); Tamás Nádasdy, castellan of Buda (1527) and future palatine of Hungary (1554–62); Ferenc Batthyány, ban of Croatia and Slavonia (1525–7); and Tamás Szalaházi, bishop of Veszprém (1526–7). Eck supported Thurzó by seeking endorsement for Ferdinand from the free royal towns inhabited by Germans in Upper Hungary, among which was Bártfa, where Eck was living. Certainly Thurzó's Austrian origins may have prejudiced him towards the Habsburgs, but Ferdinand's campaign promised the Hungarians protection against the Turks. Thurzó assessed the odds in the rivalry between Zápolya and Ferdinand and 'joined the candidate he thought was strong enough to triumph over his rival and thereby secure the future of the country and his followers.'[152] Thurzó's early commitment to Ferdinand after the battle of Mohács won him rewards. In November 1527 he was elevated to the rank of *judex curiae* (justice royal), the second-highest dignitary after the palatine. From 1527 on, Thurzó made use of his connections with the Fugger family to secure large loans, which he then passed on to Ferdinand to prop up his government. Thurzó used his own estates, which had been given to him by the crown, as collateral for these loans from the Fuggers. In 1532, Thurzó would be appointed, finally, *locumtenens* (governor) – meaning that, in the absence of Ferdinand, he was the head of the country's central administration.

Valentin Eck, as a client of Thurzó and as mayor of Bártfa during the years 1526–9,[153] used versified propaganda to support Ferdinand's effort to gain control of Hungary. He wrote three poems during the period of the civil war: *Ad proceres Hungariae exhortatio*, printed in 1527[154] (with a reprint in 1528), *Ad regem Ferdinandum epistola*, and *Epistola ad Alexium Thurzonem* (the final two published together in 1530). *Ad proceres Hungariae exhortatio* is thought to have been printed by Hieronymus Vietor at Cracow.[155] Neither printing of the poem gives the place or name of the printer, and only the second gives a date. If *Ad proceres Hungariae exhortatio* was printed at Cracow, it may well have been a clandestine printing, given the pro-Habsburg nature of the topic and the anti-Habsburg sentiment of the Polish court at the time. The poem seems to have been written for Ferdinand's entry into Buda in August 1527; the second printing may have taken place after his coronation or after his expulsion of Zápolya from Hungary early in 1528. The pamphlet in which *Ad regem Ferdinandum epistola* and *Epistola ad Alexium Thurzonem* are printed does not contain a dedicatory preface; the publication information on the title-page gives Hieronymus Vietor as the printer, at Vienna, with the date 1530.[156] Eck prefaces his poem to Ferdinand with the date 13 November 1529, and his poem to Thurzó with the date 2 December 1528 (*sic*).

Ad proceres Hungariae quo serenissimum principem et dominum, dominum Ferdinandum, Hungariae et Bohemiae etc. ... dominum suum uerum et naturalem etc. plausibiliter excipiant ... exhortatio, 127 lines in dactylic hexameter, is a plea for the acceptance of Ferdinand as king of Hungary by the Hungarian nobility and for a celebration of the king's arrival at Buda. In it, Eck expresses a desire for the protection of his country from the Turks and for peace within the country itself, the creation of a strong government, and a return to the old laws and customs. The poem portrays Ferdinand as a new hero for Hungary who will create a cohesive government along with those Hungarian leaders who have survived Mohács and who support a strong monarchy.

Eck bases his poem on the opposition of Ferdinand, the great man and saviour of Hungary, to Zápolya, the illegal usurper of the throne. He devotes twenty lines to Zápolya's unwarranted seizure of the Hungarian throne and his downfall, but centres his *exhortatio* around thirty lines of praises of King Ferdinand. Eck cites the new king's intellectual and corporeal gifts – his mental powers and physical strength. Ferdinand is full of virtue; he equals the ancients and surpasses his contemporaries in his natural gifts. He resembles Achilles in his strong spirit, Cato in his gravity, Fabius in his exercise of judgment, Pompey in his prudence, Titus in his benevolence, and Trajan in his moral rectitude.[157]

Eck makes the point that Ferdinand has royal blood and a legitimate claim to the Hungarian throne. Not only does he have the serene face of a prince (*ora serena principis*), but he is a prince by birth (*natus princeps*), the true heir to the throne (*regni certissimus heres*), the flower of the House of Austria, the heir to the Holy Roman Empire (*inclytus Austriacae stirpis flos, inclytus heres Romani Imperii*). Ferdinand places the public good before his private life;

he will work tirelessly in his office. Eck contrasts Ferdinand's background with Zápolya's, which is distinguished neither by virtue nor by family line (*nec uirtute nec alto stemmate praesignis*). Zápolya, therefore, has no real claim to the throne. Eck terms him a plague (*lues*) who is pushing the country into danger, and a monster (*belua*) who has not only made a pact with the Sultan but also encouraged groups of conspirators – neither of whom could prevent Zápolya from being ejected from the royal palace.[158] Eck finishes the poem with a scene in which a lion (Ferdinand) chases a wolf (Zápolya)[159] out of the sheep pen (Hungary) (ll. 103–11).

In *Ad proceres Hungariae exhortatio*, Eck highlights his own role as a *poeta*. He calls attention to himself in the poem by using first-person verbs, such as 'I think' (*reor*) and 'what am I doing?' (*quid ago*), and a modesty topos, insisting that his verse is too rough to express Ferdinand's qualities.[160] Moreover, his use of a refrain in the imperative mood – ordering the Hungarian *proceres* to applaud the new king – to introduce each section of the poem reinforces his identity as an authoritative speaker.[161] Other details reinforce Eck's authority: his name is printed with his position as mayor of Bártfa (*praefectus Bartphensis Reipublicae*) both on the title-page and in the header to the poem, and he addresses Thurzó as his very respected patron (*patronus suus obseruandissimus*) in his dedicatory letter.

Furthermore, in this poem Eck promotes humanist norms by portraying the men surrounding Ferdinand as heroes with humanist qualities. When describing Ferdinand being led to the throne by the 'old' Hungarian dignitaries (the palatine István Báthori [d. 1530], Alexius Thurzó, and Tamás Szalaházi, bishop of Veszprém [d. 1537], who would become bishop of Eger and chancellor of Hungary at the end of 1527), Eck attributes to these men the virtues typically admired by the humanists. Báthori is renowned for his ancestors; Thurzó for his piety, probity, and faith; and Szalaházi for his upright heart, his eloquent counsel, and his admirable gravity. Notably, Eck remarks on Szalaházi's humanist education – he was reared in fields sacred to the Muses and among bards, where Apollo kept watch.[162]

In March 1528, János Zápolya had been defeated by Ferdinand's troops at Kassa, just to the south of Valentin Eck's town, Bártfa. Zápolya was forced to flee to Poland, where he hid out in the Carpathian mountains for the remainder of the year. Zápolya had already appealed to the Turks for help in 1528, and when

Suleyman decided to launch a second campaign against Hungary early in 1529, he supported Zápolya in his war with Ferdinand. In September of that year, the Turks occupied Buda and installed Zápolya as king of Hungary. They marched on to Vienna also in September, but they failed to take the city and withdrew, leaving the kingdom of Hungary to Zápolya, who was, by the autumn of 1529, gaining power. In October, for example, he had taken control of the mining region of Upper Hungary (what is now central Slovakia), to the southwest of the area where Valentin Eck resided. It remained to Ferdinand to reconquer Buda and the lands in Upper Hungary that he had lost to Zápolya. Zápolya's raids and the ensuing counter-attacks by Ferdinand's forces led not only to loss of life, but also to the destruction of churches, of the grand residences of ecclesiastical and lay dignitaries, and of cultural objects such as books and works of art. The intellectual and cultural life of the Szepes province, into which such educators as Valentin Eck and Leonard Cox had inculcated their humanist values, was shattered.[163]

Eck's second civil-war poem, *Ad inclytum Hungariae et Bohemiae regem etc. archiducem Austriae etc. dominum Ferdinandum ... epistola*, seventy-six lines in elegiac metre, was a call to Ferdinand to chase the Turks, now withdrawing from Hungary, and push them back across the Aegean Sea, and to defend Upper Hungary from the attacks perpetrated by Zápolya and his pack. The poem is a *querimonia* in which Upper Hungary ('Hungaria Superior') addresses King Ferdinand, and is thus similar to Eck's *Threni neglectae religionis* and *Ad Ludouicum Hungariae et Bohemiae regem exhortatio.* The poem's title lists the towns that Eck, as author of the work and also mayor (*iudex Bartphensis*)[164] of Bártfa, is representing in the poem: Kassa, Lőcse (the home of the Thurzó family), Bártfa, Eperjes, Kisszeben, and Késmárk.

In *Ad regem Ferdinandum epistola*, Eck is concerned with painting a bleak portrait of the blighted Szepes region rather than creating propaganda for the king. So the comparison of the great man with the heroes of antiquity, for example, is missing, as is a modesty topos. Allusion to the role of the poet as the bestower of immortal fame is also absent. Eck's credibility here rests not on his role as a poet, but on his authority as mayor of Bártfa.

Eck praises Ferdinand in his address to him throughout the poem as 'renowned king' (*rex inclytus*), 'great king' (*rex magnus*), and 'generous king' (*rex generosus*) but omits any extended panegyric to him. Rather, he characterizes Ferdinand as the monarch in whom rests the responsibility for saving Christianity from the onslaught of the Turks. Even though Upper Hungary has been ravaged by Zápolya's gang,[165] the region does not dare to complain to the king because a more important burden, the defence of Christianity, rests on his shoulders. Eck devotes the remainder of the first half of the poem to the damage done by the Turks, through force, fire, and sword, as they cut their way through Hungary on the road to Vienna. The Turks attacked Vienna, but since God was listening to the appeals of the people, the city was saved, and the Turks were expelled from Austria in a deserved slaughter, with Ferdinand as the leader of the rout.[166] The first half of the poem ends with Hungaria Superior urging the king to complete the task – to go after the retreating Turks and drive them out.

In spite of Upper Hungary's opening lines, that she does not dare to grieve to the king, the poem continues as a complaint of the Szepes region: she is open to the attacks of Zápolya, the domestic monster allied with the Turks; she is worn out by war; both the public treasury and the private coffers are empty.[167] Hungaria Superior reminds the king of her constant fidelity to him and begs him to deliver her from danger.[168]

In *Ad magnificum dominum Alexium Thurzonem Regiae Curiae iudicem etc. epistola*, the third of his civil-war era poems, Eck addresses Alexius Thurzó, without any intermediating personification, in eighty-six lines of elegiac poetry and asks his patron, now the justice royal, to intercede with Ferdinand on behalf of Upper Hungary. In this poem Eck returns to his usual motifs of modesty before his patron and concern for his patron's welfare, once again highlighting his role as poet. He begins with a modesty topos – the region is suffering many troubles, but he will list only a few since he does not wish to take up Thurzó's time with an unpolished poem – and states that there is no peace for the people either at home or out of doors: outside, a war is raging, and inside their homes, people are dying from an incurable plague.[169] In the first half of the poem, Eck describes the symptoms of this plague in vivid imagery (the delirium, the vomiting, the heart palpitations, the trembling bones) and employs a classical motif (the fire of Mount Etna) to illustrate the intensity of the fever.[170]

Eck devotes the second half of the poem to the civil war raging in the area. Zápolya, whom Eck likens to a wolf, crossed the border from Poland on 27 October and made his way to Homonna, a town in the highlands to the southeast of Bártfa. Throughout the poem Eck makes clear how much of an enemy Zápolya is: he refers to him twice as a wolf (*lupus*, ll. 36, 54), twice as a beast (*ferus*, ll. 47, 56), and once as an impious man (*impius*, l. 60). He builds up to the climax of the poem by stating that, as he writes, a messenger has come in crying that Zápolya has arrived and is setting up camps in the area – at the towns of Varannó and Tőketerebes, to the southeast of Bártfa.[171] Eck begs Thurzó to obtain, from the king, military help for the people of his region.[172] He then wishes Thurzó good fortune and, referring to Thurzó's recent marriage, hopes that his new wife will bear him offspring who will resemble him and inherit his goods.[173]

The pamphlet containing *Ad regem Ferdinandum epistola* and *Ad Alexium Thurzonem* was published as propaganda to gain support at Vienna for the cause of the royal free towns of Upper Hungary still loyal to Ferdinand. Both these poems stressed the plight of the region, devastated by war and plague, having few remaining resources with which to fight the enemy, and now depending on the intercession of the king to rescue them with his troops. In this pamphlet Eck also cultivated his relationship with his patron, Thurzó, and publicized himself, both by mentioning the official posts he was holding at Bártfa and by alluding to the importance of his role as a poet.

Although Eck did not include an extended panegyric of his addressee in *Ad Ferdinandum epistola* and did not refer to his own role as a poet in that poem, in *Ad Alexium Thurzonem* he both described the desperate situation of plague and war in Upper Hungary and promoted his patron while calling attention to his own function as poet. Moreover, at the end of the pamphlet, he added the short poem *Marti militans musas ablegat Ecchius*, in which he glorified his role as a poet. Mentioning his fatigue caused by the ongoing struggle against Zápolya, he stated that he could not write. It was not enough that he was working for the public good on the domestic scene as a town official; he was forced into war, where he had to remain at a post keeping watch and then join in the battle. In poetic language, he sends his muse away, since he must go and fight.

These poems demonstrate that although Eck became an insider in Bártfa, having risen through the ranks of the town government, he still needed to cultivate his patron and garner support from his own humanist friends in order to have influence at the Buda court. This need is also attested by his brief poem *Ad eundem dominum Thurzonem Ecchius*, which appears just before *Marti militans musas ablegat Ecchius*, in which Eck asks Thurzó to intercede so that he might receive the stipend the king has promised him, but that has not yet been paid. In May 1529, Georg von Logau, a Silesian who had studied with Eck at Cracow and was working as a secretary to King Ferdinand at Vienna, published a poem expressing solidarity with Eck and praising him and his former student Georg Werner, the town clerk of Eperjes, for their fidelity to King Ferdinand and their efforts to rid their region of the 'wolf' Zápolya.[174]

HUNGARY UNDER LOUIS II JAGIELLON

After the splendour of the reign of Matthias Corvinus, the rule of the Jagiellons in Hungary can be seen as entering a decline. Matthias's court had become an international centre of culture, and during his reign Buda was the residence of such celebrated humanists as Johannes Vitéz (*c.* 1408–72), Antonio Bonfini (1427 or 1434–1502 or 1503), Janus Pannonius (1434–72), and Jacob Piso (d. 1527). Matthias constructed his palace in the Italianate style and filled it with sculpture, paintings, and an important collection of manuscripts.[175] However, Matthias also built up his power and expanded his territory through the ruthless exploitation of his country's resources, in the course of which he developed a huge army of mercenary soldiers. By the time of his death the drain on the country's resources could no longer be maintained; the army had to be disbanded, and the national defence system therefore collapsed.[176]

Vladislav II (ruled 1490–1516) accordingly inherited an empty treasury from Matthias, and he was never able to recover from his financial difficulties. Indeed, the Jagiellonian king spent his first year on the throne trying to consolidate his power, as revolts erupted on the fringes of the country and the empire that Matthias had built quickly broke apart. Moreover, the country's centralized authority disintegrated as the magnates, who made up the royal council, and the nobles, who populated the parliament, demanded more power. Vladislav II proved to be an apathetic king, who allowed the Hungarian chancellor to preside over the government's decision-making. The peasant revolt of 1514 nearly destroyed the country, and the Turkish expansion of the early

1520s presented a threat with which the government could not even begin to cope.[177]

By the time Vladislav's son Louis came to the throne in 1516, the situation had become chaotic. György Szatmári was returned to the office of chancellor but lost his political influence to László Szalkai. A struggle for power between the magnates and the nobles was fought out in the parliament, which was convened no fewer than sixteen times during Louis II's ten-year reign. István Báthori and János Zápolya operated together as strongmen against the other magnates. The treasury was in shambles: in 1521 the currency was devalued in an attempt to increase revenues, and the silver content of the penny was reduced. This action ruined the treasury and subsequently forced the government constantly to devalue the currency; ultimately, in 1525, it stopped minting money altogether.[178]

In spite of these political and financial difficulties, Louis was considered a kindly king, cultured and interested in the arts. Vincenzo Guidotti, a Venetian envoy to Buda in the 1520s, remarked on how humble the court of Louis II was, but reported that the king was cheerful and generous, that he was a physically well built man who excelled in hunting and jousting, that he enjoyed listening to music, and that he practised a variety of crafts, among them wood carving. Guidotti also commented that Louis was talented at languages, in that he spoke Hungarian, Polish, Latin, and German well, and understood some Italian.[179]

The poverty of the Jagiellonian court reduced its ability to foster art and culture at the same level as had Matthias Corvinus. But the gap in royal patronage was filled at this time by the high-ranking dignitaries of the Bohemian-Hungarian realm, who played a major role in sponsoring artists and writers. Magnates such as Tamás Bakócz (1442–1521), György Szatmári (*c.* 1457–1524), László Szalkai (1475–1526), Gábor Perényi (d. 1526), and Alexius Thurzó (*c.* 1490–1543) at Buda, and Zdeněk Lev (1470–1535) and Stefan Schlick (d. 1526) at Prague ensured that the Jagiellonian age in Hungary and Bohemia bloomed as a productive period for art and culture.[180]

At Buda, the tradition of humanist Latin was carried on by such poets as Stephanus Taurinus (d. 1519), Stephanus Brodericus (*c.* 1471–1539), and Nicolaus Olahus (1493–1568). Moreover, the Viennese poets Caspar Ursinus Velius (1493–1539) and Johannes Alexander Brassicanus (*c.* 1500–39) had Buda connections and were agents of the transmission of humanist values across the region of east central Europe, as was Paulus Crosnensis (d. 1517), from Cracow, who was patronized by Perényi and who published an edition of Janus Pannonius's poetry at Vienna in 1512. An interest in the works of Erasmus at Buda was promoted both by Jacob Piso and by Queen Maria's chaplain, Johannes Henckel (d. 1539), who had been responsible for inviting Leonard Cox to teach at Lőcse and Kassa. Valentin Eck, patronized by Thurzó, should be counted among the humanists of this generation who were associated with the Buda court.[181]

Three occasional poems written by Eck typify the flowering of culture in Hungary and characterize the cultural and political activities of the country's magnates during the pre-Mohács period. These poems, composed to celebrate events involving the highest-ranking dignitaries of the kingdom, contributed to the legitimization and glorification of the Jagiellonian rule. The first, *Iubilus heroicus Cassouiae habitus ob aduentum reuerendissimi antistitis domini Georgii Quinqueecclesiensis episcopi*, marked the visit of György Szatmári to his home town of Kassa, to the south of Bártfa. Szatmári was, at the time, bishop of Pécs and chancellor. He was a supporter of the Jagiellonian monarchs, pro-Habsburg, and the chief engineer of Hungary's foreign policy, and he had played a leading role as a Hungarian negotiator at the Congress of 1515. During the civil strife of 1514, Szatmári had lost his chancellorship, but he was reinstated when Louis ascended the throne. After that, his political clout was unshaken until the last year of his life, when he was overshadowed by the greedy and corrupt bishop of Eger, László Szalkai. Szatmári's family was connected to the Fuggers and the Thurzós through business, and György promoted Alexius Thurzó's career at the Buda court. Alexius's marriage to György's niece Anna came about a result of their contact.[182]

Szatmári was, along with Cardinal Tamás Bakócz (who preceded him in the archbishopric of Esztergom), the greatest patron of art and humanist literature in Jagiellonian Hungary. Although it has not been proved that Szatmári studied in Italy, he did have contact with the humanists at Bologna, especially Giovanni Battista Pio, to whom he sent for study his protégés Sebestyén Magyi, Bálint Hagymási, and Lőrinc Besztercei. It was at Bologna that Szatmári and Magyi (who had been taught by Paulus Crosnensis at Cracow) had the panegyric poem of Janus Pannonius to Guarinus published in 1512. As a patron of architecture, Szatmári financed the building of a new side-chapel in the St Michael chapel near St Elizabeth's church at Kassa, his family's home town. He also donated ecclesiastical garments and sacred vessels to the St Elizabeth church. At Pécs (Quinque Ecclesiae), Szatmári commissioned a tabernacle for the cathedral. He went on to remodel the episcopal palace and to rebuild the chapter house in the Renaissance style. On a hill above the city, Szatmári built his summer villa, an outstanding example of early Hungarian Renaissance villa architecture. It is presumed that the reconstructions of buildings in the Renaissance style at Esztergom were carried out by Szatmári in his capacity as chancellor and while Bakócz was still alive. The Esztergom Breviary (Breuiarium Strigoniense), a magnificent illuminated manuscript of 529 leaves, which Szatmári commissioned from the Florentine artist Boccardino il Vecchio, represents one of the pinnacles of Szatmári's art patronage. The book was perhaps ordered when Szatmári's rise to the archiepiscopal chair seemed possible during Bakócz's leave at Rome (1511–14), but Bakócz returned and Szatmári would not be made archbishop until Bakócz's death in 1521.[183]

Valentin Eck's poem in honour of Szatmári, *Iubilus heroicus* (seventy-two lines in dactylic hexameter), was printed together with his *Apophoreticum carmen de Christi natiuitate* and *Epithalamium pro nuptiis domini Ioannis Sayslich* by Vietor at Cracow in 1520.[184] The whole book was dedicated to Alexius Thurzó. Eck preceded his *Iubilus heroicus* with a short dedicatory letter to Thurzó; he went on to introduce *Iubilus heroicus* with a brief panegyric poem to Szatmári and ended it with a *corollarium* of three elegiac couplets in praise of Thurzó. It is unlikely that Eck's poem was read out during Szatmári's visit. Eck stated in his prefatory letter that he had already finished the *Apophoreticum carmen de Christi natiuitate* for Christmas of 1519, when a friend asked him to compose a poem in honour of Szatmári. The request may have been prompted by Szatmári's visit to Kassa in September 1519, when the bishop and chancellor set up a foundation for masses and other religious services to be held at St Elizabeth's church there.[185] In his dedicatory letter, Eck hoped that his effort would find favour with both Thurzó and Szatmári and asked Thurzó to commend him to the reverend bishop.

The dedicatory letter preceding *Iubilus heroicus* is addressed to Thurzó, but to introduce *Iubilus,* Eck inserted a thirty-three-line poem, *Ad reuerendissimum ... dominum Georgium episcopum ecclesiae*

Quinqueecclesiensis ... et secretarium et cancellarium Regiae Maiestatis ... carmen, in which he speaks to Szatmári and asks him to look approvingly upon his efforts in writing *Iubilus*. At the beginning, *Ad dominum Georgium episcopum ecclesiae Quinqueecclesiensis* appears to consist solely of a modesty topos. Eck, addressing Szatmári as the most renowned splendour of bishops (*inclyta pontificum lux*) and the most shining glory of the Hungarian people (*clarissima gentis gloria Pannonicae*), states that, putting his fear of Szatmári aside, he was inspired by the brilliance of Szatmári's virtue to write *Iubilus*. At the end of the poem, Eck refers to *Iubilus* as a poem of moderate proportions, composed under time restraints for the occasion on which he will pay homage to Szatmári and his patron, the great Thurzó, with due honour.[186] *Ad dominum Georgium episcopum ecclesiae Quinqueecclesiensis* also includes the 'promise of future gifts' topos.[187] Here Eck writes that he is in the midst of preparing an epic poem in honour of the Thurzó family, one that will be so great he cannot rush it into publication but must spend ten years polishing it.[188]

The core of *Ad dominum Georgium episcopum ecclesiae Quinqueecclesiensis*, however, is simply a blatant advertisement for Eck as a poet. After telling Szatmári that he has written a poem, *Iubilus*, for him, he boasts that he learned to write serious poetry some time ago and lists his successes – his poems glorifying the deeds of the Polish king and against the treachery of Muscovy (*Hymnus exhortatorius* and *Threni neglectae religionis*) and in tribute to the Thurzó family (*De antiquissima nominis et familiae Thurzonum origine*). In announcing the epic that he has in preparation, he claims that if the poem does not surpass the poems of Vergil, it will still place the Thurzó family among the stars. Moreover, two or three poets together, even poets laureate, could not compose a poem equal to Eck's new composition, in which Szatmári's family will also be celebrated.[189] Eck ends *Ad dominum Georgium episcopum ecclesiae Quinqueecclesiensis* with a return to the traditional modesty topos, but he endorses himself by linking himself with Thurzó, who is specifically mentioned as his patron, and once again with Szatmári.

The main poem, *Iubilus heroicus*, combines a humanist panegyric with elements of festival poetry. In its description of the festivities taking place at Kassa, it is reminiscent of Eck's poem in praise of King Sigismund's victory at Orsha, *Hymnus exhortatorius*. Eck praises the administration of Chancellor Szatmári and the rule of King Louis II, under which security and prosperity have returned to Kassa. He addresses the town of Kassa, and opens the poem in the same manner as Agricola did in his poem in honour of Cardinal Lang, with a series of rhetorical questions, here asking what the town's applause is all about and who is being celebrated. Eck reminds Kassa that Szatmári had his origins there and that the town owes as much to him as Rome did to the powerful Quintus Fabius Maximus Verrucosus, whose policy of delaying battle enabled Rome to win the war against Carthage.

Iubilus heroicus is centred around the image of Szatmári as the hundred-eyed mythological Argus watching over the town (ll. 32–44). The figure of the town guardian is one that suited an ecclesiarch, as an extension of the figure of the shepherd watching over his flock; Eck would use it to describe Nicolaus Goldberger, the parish priest at Korpona, in the short poem to him that he published the next year, in which he remarked that Goldberger watched over his parish with prudence and removed any anxieties from the inhabitants of his town.[190] Szatmári, the guardian of Kassa, is also the chancellor of Hungary, and Eck states that he has been greatly honoured by the magnanimous King Louis II. Eck continues by praising Szatmári for his virtue, his clemency, his generosity, his faith, and his just government of Hungary, and compares him with Trajan and Cato. If the King is the sun, then Szatmári is the moon; he surpasses all the bishops in the world in virtue, and it is right for the citizens of Kassa to render him the greatest honour.

The enumeration of virtues, so typical of Eck's poems, is here broken up by a geographical description that, in its detail, gives the poem some local colour and variety. Szatmári watches over the Hungarian kingdom, whose borders the Danube washes; the Danube and its tributaries the Sava and the Drava form the three great rivers of the region. (These rivers, together with the Tisa, were represented from the Middle Ages on the coats of arms of the town of Kassa by four silver stripes. In 1502, King Vladislav added the Jagiellonian eagle to the town's crest as a symbol of his favour.)[191] The poem is also given colour through an enumeration of classical festivities in which the citizens of Kassa are supposedly taking part – the tossing of Tyrian (crimson) flowers at the crossroads, the sprinkling of the streets with balsam, the decorating of the town with Phrygian (embroidered) hangings, the adorning of the city walls with Attalic (woven with gold) coverlets, the burning of triumphal fires in the towers, the shooting of solid bombs into the air (firing of cannon in salute), and the sounding of loud tymbals (ll. 13–20).

Eck ends the poem with a traditional expression of modesty, stating that he will endeavour to write an adequate verse for such a solemn occasion. He finishes by wishing a long life for Szatmári and praying that his soul will be taken to heaven at the end of his days. The *corollarium* that Eck tacks onto the very end of *Iubilus heroicus* brings Alexius Thurzó, who has not been mentioned since the prefatory poem to Szatmári, back into the picture. Eck returns to his simile likening King Louis to the sun and Szatmári to the moon. Thurzó is then *lucifer*, the morning star who follows the moon and precedes the rising of the sun. There is no greater glory in Hungary than he.

The final poem printed with *Apophoreticum carmen de Christi natiuitate* was *Epithalamium pro nuptiis domini Ioannis Sayslich*, an epithalamium for Johannes Saytzlich,[192] the former mayor, now senator and *comes camerae regalis* (*Kammergraf*)[193] from Kassa, who was marrying Helen, the niece of László Szalkai, then the bishop of Vác and royal chancellor. (Upon Szatmári's death in 1524, he would become the archbishop of Esztergom until his own death in the battle of Mohács in 1526.) In the brief dedicatory letter to Saytzlich, Eck reveals that he had met Saytzlich at Valentin Carbo's wedding nearly four years earlier. Carbo was the town clerk (*grammateus*) of Kassa and had written a commendatory verse for Eck's panegyric to Thurzó and his family, *De antiquissima nominis et familiae Thurzonum origine*, published in 1519. It is possible that Eck had met Carbo while still a student at Cracow, and that it was Carbo who persuaded Eck to settle in Upper Hungary.[194]

In the dedicatory letter to Saytzlich, Eck excuses himself for his delay in printing the poem, which he composed to be read at Saytzlich's wedding ceremony and which Saytzlich had asked him to publish, but says he simply had no opportunity until now.[195] In any case, Eck writes, it does not seem inappropriate to print the nuptial poem along with his New Year's poem for his patron Alexius Thurzó. In closing, Eck trusts not only that he is not offending Saytzlich, but, even more, that he is fulfilling his promise by publishing the nuptial poem, and he asks Saytzlich to accept his little gift gladly.

The poem, written in elegiac couplets, is divided into two parts, a *prooemium* of twenty-two lines and an *epithalamium* of ninety lines. The *prooemium* is an extended modesty topos. Eck begins by declaring that others may write of war, specifically the Hungarian peasant uprising of 1514 and King Sigismund's victory at Orsha, also in 1514, but that he prefers to celebrate Johannes's marriage. Using the metaphor of the sailor in a boat, Eck explains that he normally avoids grandiose forms of poetry and has a fondness for humbler forms. But now his small boat, daring, has wandered from its course and has come to rest at Johannes's house.[196] Eck does not neglect to mention the importance of the poet in the conferring of immortality. He is anxious to celebrate the marriage of Saytzlich in a report, even though it may not be a worthy one, and to transmit the account of the wedding ceremony to the remote future; perhaps future centuries will read it. He admits that this is just a pious wish; all poets predict fame and a great future on the basis of their poems.[197] Eck concludes the *prooemium* by begging Saytzlich to accept his little gift and the effort he has made, and wishes him a long life and much prosperity.

Eck's epithalamium for Saytzlich is a typical humanist marriage poem, in mixing classical imagery of the gods Hymen, Cupid, and Venus, inspired by such poets as Catullus, Ovid, Propertius, and/or Vergil, with humanist reflections on the sanctity of the sacrament of marriage. Although classical images appear throughout the poem, Eck alternates between depicting a pagan celebration and declaring the Christian notions of marriage, all the while singing the praises of the groom and his bride. Mieczysław Brożek remarks that the neo-Latin epithalamiums of sixteenth-century Poland were written with a great degree of 'independence' of their classical models.[198] Eck's poem for Saytzlich conforms with this assessment; the classical motifs provide the composition with an antique flavour but do not hinder Eck from communicating his humanist message.

Having begun with an invitation to the marriage festivities addressed to Venus (whom the dancing maidens and young men call) and her son Cupid,[199] Eck launches into a consideration of the holiness of marriage, claiming as benefits of marriage the producing of children and the tempering of passion. Marriage, says Eck, restrains the human senses and guides the sentiments of men, right up to pious affection. He condemns the sin of promiscuity, citing the lack of marriage law among the Parthians as leading to polygamy and even incest, and employing the Persian *magus*, born illegitimately, as a symbol of decadence.[200] He then returns to the subject of Saytzlich's wedding by invoking the Muses, begging them to come and deliver Saytzlich quickly to his marriage bed, while he is still burning with love.[201] He urges Saytzlich to submit to the marriage yoke, with Juno giving her blessing. He ends with a wish that timid propriety be present in Saytzlich's bed, for illicit love is wicked, whereas the marriage bed is sacred.[202] Eck prays for obedience in Saytzlich's new spouse, and for a long and happy marriage with handsome and noble offspring; may Saytzlich, like King Arganthonius, live to see his brilliant grandchildren.

Chastity and the sanctity of marriage were recurring themes in Eck's writing. In 1518 he had published a lengthy poem on the topic, *An prudenti uiro sit ducenda uxor*, which would be reprinted in 1524,[203] in which he presented much the same argument as in the epithalamium for Saytzlich. Eck had also authored, in 1519, a poem on the setting up of a married household, *Supellectilium fasciculus* (a little bag of furniture), that went through three printings.[204] Moreover, he considered the notions of temperance and chastity in his two prose works *De mundi contemptu et uirtute amplectenda dialogus* (1519, 1528) and *De reipublicae administratione dialogus* (1520). In the former work, he argued for leading a temperate life, which included modesty (*modestia*), abstinence (*abstinentia*), and chastity (*castitas, pudicitia*). These virtues should be present in the ideal home, along with moderation and sobriety (*parcitas, sobrietas*) and moral rectitude and self-control (*honestas, moderatio*). In the latter work, he alleged that extravagant living (*luxus*) and unrestrained lust (*cupiditas*) were destructive to the state (*respublica*). Eck was not alone in advocating the virtues of chastity and piety in his poetry. The majority of the sixteenth-century neo-Latin poets of central Europe considered as fit for poetry only the type of love that was connected with wedlock and children, and understood that the subject of family, next to that of religion, evoked the strongest emotions in their audience.[205]

The neo-Latin epithalamium not only served as a vehicle for encouraging the Christian idea of marriage, but also, following the model of the fourth-century poet Claudian, provided a platform for the praise of one's patron. Panegyric elements were an essential part of the genre of the epithalamium in early sixteenth-century central Europe.[206] Eck takes advantage of this feature of the genre in *Epithalamium pro nuptiis domini Ioannis Sayslich* to portray Saytzlich as a humanist hero. In the dedication and header to the poem, he immediately terms his patron 'prudent' (*prudens*) and 'outstanding' (*egregius, praestans*), his bride 'most chaste' (*pudicissima, castissima*), and his bride's uncle, the bishop of Vác, 'most magnificent' (*amplissimus*). In the text of the poem, Eck praises Saytzlich for patronizing poets while noting that Saytzlich himself is to be congratulated for his humanist education.[207] An intelligent and industrious man, Saytzlich so excelled in his studies of poetry and oratory that he can speak on the same level as Cicero.[208] At the very end of the poem, Eck compliments Saytzlich and his new wife on their physical beauty and their nobility by trusting that they will produce handsome children who will inherit the nobility of both parents.[209]

The political life of the magnates during the reign of Louis is reflected in Eck's *De electione illustris atque magnifici domini, domini Alexii Thurzonis de Bethlemfalua etc. in regalium tauernicorum magistrum plausus heroicus*. This poem, 121 lines of dactylic hexameter printed in 1524 along with Eck's *Ad inuictissimum Ludouicum* and *Ad proceres Hungariae*, portrays Alexius Thurzó as a hard-working, energetic, and virtuous man devoted to his country and truly deserving of his titles. Alexius had become royal secretary (*secretarius*) in 1515, chamberlain (*cubicularius*) in 1519, and chief chamberlain (*supremus cubicularius*) in the middle of 1521. He had been appointed royal treasurer (*thesaurarius regius*) in 1522.[210] Then, in 1523, Thurzó was named *magister tauernicorum* (*Kellermeister*), a prefect responsible for the affairs and jurisdiction of a group of free royal towns of Hungary and the fifth in rank among the five national high dignitaries of Hungary. Eck's poem may not have been pure panegyric, for at the time Thurzó received his appointment, Sigismund von Herberstein, the envoy from Vienna, remarked in a report on Thurzó's 'unflagging energy' (*indefesso*) in attending to royal affairs.[211]

In any case, Eck had reason to celebrate his patron's glory. In a very few years, Thurzó had risen from the ranks of the lower nobility to the aristocracy. Alexius's career at court had begun in 1508, when, upon the death of his father, Johann Thurzó Senior, Jakob Fugger made him the firm's representative at the Buda court. The Thurzó family, involved in banking and mining concerns, had been connected in business with the powerful Fugger banking clan since 1495. In 1510, with his marriage to Anna, the niece of György Szatmári, chancellor and bishop of Pécs, Alexius's career was promoted through the growing influence of Szatmári, who became royal chancellor in 1503, and chief chancellor and archbishop of Esztergom in 1521.

Although Thurzó's rise was not without troubles, he managed to recover from his difficulties and remained, throughout his life, one of the closest advisers to the royal couple, first to Louis and Anna, then to Ferdinand and Maria. After the peasant uprising of 1514, the national party of Zápolya gained power, and Thurzó was criticized for his role, as a Fugger agent, in attempting to stabilize government finances. Thurzó remained in the office of royal treasurer until 1525, when, blamed for the financial crisis that spread throughout the country, he was replaced by János Dóczy. (With the death of Szatmári in 1524, Thurzó had lost his protector.) The new archbishop of Esztergom and chancellor, László Szalkai, was aligned with business groups in Nuremberg who wanted to replace the Fuggers in Hungary. In the same year that Thurzó lost the post of royal treasurer, Szalkai saw to it that the Fugger mining concerns in Hungary were confiscated. Thurzó himself was imprisoned on a charge of corrupt management of state revenues. Alexius and his younger brother resigned from all their shares in the Fugger business. In 1526, following the formation of an alliance among the magnates to strengthen the power of the king, Thurzó was reinstated as royal treasurer. Now rehabilitated, Thurzó continued on course with his court career, while securing large loans from the Fuggers to prop up first the Jagiellonian and then the Habsburg government. Yet, having gained the confidence of King Ferdinand after the battle of Mohács, Thurzó would go on to amass a personal fortune and ascend to the posts of justice royal and governor of the kingdom of Hungary.

In *De electione,* Valentin Eck praises his patron Thurzó for his administrative abilities, but he also glorifies himself as a poet. The poem is constructed around the opposition of virtue and vice, with Eck making good use of an accumulation of examples in both categories, by which he displays his profound knowledge of Greek mythology and Roman history. *De electione* is similar to *Ad inuictissimum Ludouicum* and *Ad proceres Hungariae,* with which it was printed: to the latter in that Eck's use of *exempla* to illustrate his arguments forms the basis of the poem, and to the former in that the examples used overshadow the panegyric elements. Moreover, the opening line and a half, informing the audience that Thurzó has received new honours that are well deserved ('Plaudite, Thurzo nouos iterum suscepit honores et dignos meritis titulos'), turns into a refrain with which Eck signals a change in the subject matter of the poem, a technique that he first used in *Threni neglectae religionis* (1518) and would use again in *Ad proceres Hungariae exhortatio* (1527?).

Beginning with the aphorism that virtue elevates her adherents and neglects wrongdoers, Eck embarks on an extended comparison of the after-effects of vice and virtue that takes up more than half the poem (ll. 11–78), and in which he mixes images from the Bible, Greek mythology, Roman history, and antique pagan religion with Christian ideals. Calling first upon the example of the Assyrian king Sardanapalus, a lazy, effeminate man and a coward who ran away from war, Eck contrasts the notion of decadence with that of glory, which comes from virtue and lasts forever. Eck cites the lives of the glorious Roman statesmen: Pompey the Great, a military commander who led a blameless personal life; Pompilius Numa, the legendary early king of Rome celebrated for his legal, religious, and economic reforms; Quintius Fabius, whose cautious military strategy won victory for the Romans; Marcus Aurelius, the philosopher-ruler; and Cato the Censor, the brilliant orator and writer. Eck maintains that history has shown that while virtue brings reward, vice can bring destruction and ruin to civilizations. He lists figures from antiquity whose debauchery and evil brought them ruin, including Phaethon, who, borrowing the sun-chariot of his father, Phoebus, and unable to control it, drove the sun off its course and so was hurled to earth by Zeus; Gehazi, the servant of Elisha, whose desire for wealth was punished by leprosy; the apostle Judas, who, having betrayed Jesus, hanged himself; the Thessalian king Ixion, who, having attempted to rape Hera, was condemned by Zeus to be turned on a wheel in hell; the Syrian princess Myrrha, who was changed into a tree to escape the wrath of her father, whom she had tricked into committing incest; Zoïlus, the envious poet and censurer of Homer, who was hanged from an oak tree for his criticism of the king Ptolemy Philadelphus; Hannibal the conqueror, who took poison rather than be captured by the Romans; and Hercules, who murdered his children in a fit of madness and ended his life on a funeral pyre. Eck counters these examples of ignoble downfall with a definition of virtue, which remains constant and is never conquered. Virtue is accompanied by religion and reverence for God (expressed by Eck as the pagan *reuerentia diuum*), and by glory, the majesty of law, probity, faith, peace, honour, triumph, rule, victory, and fame, which wage war against evil and repel her enemies. The pupils of virtue are ushered, at the end of their lives, to the threshold of 'Olympic joys.' Eck mentions a few examples from antiquity – Elijah, Abraham, Moses, Jacob, Joseph, and the 'other holy fathers' – but claims that he can scarcely list them all in a short poem.

From the comparison of virtue and vice, Eck proceeds to the aim of the poem, the praises of Thurzó. Using the refrain 'Plaudite, Thurzo ...,' Eck divides the panegyric portion of the poem (ll. 79–121) into three sections: on the qualities of Thurzó that make him suitable for the post; on Thurzó's administration as the return of the golden age; and on Thurzó as a protégé of King Louis II. Eck claims that no one more worthy has been found who can administer the treasury laws with justice, and that no one is quicker to care about the public good and put his own affairs second.[212] He compares Thurzó's *grauitas* with that of Solon, the great Athenian legislator of the early sixth century BCE, and Thurzó's prudence with that of Lycurgus, the mythological king who prohibited the worship of Bacchus and ordered the destruction of all the Greek vines. Thurzó keeps in mind the precepts of Draco, the severe Athenian lawgiver, and the decisions of Numa, the legendary Roman king. Alluding to the economic crisis and corruption plaguing the Hungarian government, Eck states that under Thurzó's administration the citizens of the free royal towns will have their worries removed. Under Thurzó, all good things will return: solemn laws will preserve their ancient vitality; flowery rhetoric will cease.[213] Thurzó has been raised to his well-deserved titles not only by 'Virtus' but also by King Louis II, neither of whom has any greater honour with which to decorate him.[214] There remains now only the gift of eternal life, which God (*Iuppiter*) will bestow once Thurzó's spirit has left his tired body.

Although Eck glorified Thurzó in the final third of *De electione*, two-thirds of the poem consists of Eck's argument that vice brings only shame and ignominy whereas virtue leads to glory and everlasting fame. In his presentation of this argument, Eck displays the wide-ranging erudition characteristic of a humanist scholar-poet. Moreover, the allusive method by which Eck refers to the qualities he wished to represent in the poem would have demanded a certain level of education on the part of his audience. When he lists the ancient heroes who gained glory as a result of their virtue (ll. 28–9), he does not cite their deeds, but leaves it to readers to make the connection as to why these men should be named as examples. Eck's reference to the punishment of Korah, Dathan, and Abiram (l. 38) would have required the audience to be acquainted with the story of the rebellion against Moses in the Book of Numbers, chapter 16, and his mention of Gehazi's desire as meriting leprosy, Ptolemy's drinking wolf-bane, and Hannibal's being overcome by Campanian Bacchus (ll. 39–60) would have entailed a familiarity not only with the Old Testament but with ancient history as well.[215] His allusions to notorious characters from the Bible and from classical history and legend were not just literary ornament, but a display of his erudition – a matter of snobbery, which emphasized the humanist education he possessed and promoted him as a poet in the service of the renowned Thurzó and of the town of Bártfa.

Patronage connected the creative lives of Rudolf Agricola Junior and Valentin Eck with the key political events of their times. But just as they wrote orations and poems to glorify the deeds of their patrons and to advance the politics they espoused, so Agricola and Eck exploited these occasions to promote themselves. The propaganda they produced for the dignitaries of the Jagiellonian realm also promoted their own cause, both on the personal level, in enhancing their own careers, and on the collective level, in bolstering the cause of the humanist educational program and stating the need for support of humanist writers by courts and town councils.

Agricola Junior and Eck advanced their careers by writing propagandist prose and verse for all the major political events of their time. Their names turned up on the title-pages of pamphlets published in association with Emperor Maximilian's meeting with the Jagiellonian kings at Vienna in 1515, King Sigismund's victory over the Muscovites at Orsha in 1514, the Hungarian economic and political crisis of the 1520s, the Turkish invasion of Hungary, and the disaster of Mohács and the civil war that ensued. The works of Agricola and Eck published during this time were either addressed or dedicated to the highest-ranking dignitaries of the Habsburg empire and the Jagiellonian realm, to cardinals and courtiers, even to the kings themselves, and they chronicled the Jagiellonian family's eventual loss to the Habsburgs in the power struggle in east central Europe.

In Agricola's and Eck's political and occasional works, the author's voice played a significant role in the poem – that of the humanist scholar-poet, drawing attention to himself either in a modesty topos, or in a reference to himself as the conferrer of eternal fame, or in a display of erudition. The modesty topos could announce the author of the poem and publicly establish his association with a person of high rank, as at the end of Eck's *Hymnus exhortatorius*, where the poet revealed his effort to establish himself at the Cracow court. The role of the poet as the conferrer of glory could be stated quite explicitly, as by Agricola in his poem *Siluula* in honour of Cardinal Lang, the emperor's negotiator at the Congress of 1515, where he wrote that poetry was a gift that would not decay and even asserted that poets had a special relationship with the gods. Flaunting one's knowledge of the classics, as in Eck's display of Greek mythology, Roman history, and the Bible in his poem *De electione*, written on Alexius Thurzó's nomination as *magister tauernicorum*, signalled the poet's affiliation with the humanist program of study.

Even when glorifying their patrons, Agricola and Eck managed to endorse humanist ideals. In their portrayals of a hero, the person portrayed was endowed with qualities according to the humanist canon and compared with classical heroes typically evoked by humanist writers. In his writings for the Congress of 1515, Agricola praised both Cardinal Lang and Bishop Tomicki for their humanist education, extolling them as steeped in the *artes*. In *Threni neglectae religionis*, Eck attributed to King Sigismund of Poland the virtues of faith, prudence, justice, and temperance – all qualities esteemed by humanists in an ideal ruler – and compared him with Alexander the Great, the Greek hero Aristides, and the Roman emperor Trajan. When praising his patron Alexius Thurzó, Eck characterized him as a wise, temperate, and just administrator, and compared him with such legendary and historic statesmen as Nestor, Numa, Trajan, and Cato. In enhancing the public image of their patrons, Agricola and Eck were also advancing their own humanist beliefs. Their formation, by combining traditional aristocratic virtues with humanist ideals, of an image of the hero that would be agreeable to the highest echelon of society was a means by which the *poetae* of east central Europe won acceptance for themselves and their pedagogical program.[216]

Conclusion

By the time they reached the height of their careers, Rudolf Agricola Junior, Valentin Eck, and Leonard Cox had managed to connect themselves with the most powerful dignitaries in the Jagiellonian realms. Observing the constraints of decorum in respect to their patrons, they had presented an image of themselves as industrious and learned, and as pious Christian scholars. They had created an identity for themselves as members of an elite group offering a distinguished pedagogy, based on Christian morality and classical learning, that, although perhaps new, was succinct and effective. In their panegyric writings, they had, in expressing praise of their patrons, created heroes who conformed with their own values: who possessed nobility and virtue, were industrious and mindful of their public duties, were steeped in classical learning, and supported the arts. Finally, these poets created a *persona* for themselves by calling attention in their writing to their own role as poets in legitimizing the power of their patrons and in creating eternal fame for them.

Rudolf Agricola Junior's poem in honour of Princess Bona Sforza (1518) and Leonard Cox's edition of a portion of a polemic exchange between Martin Luther and Henry VIII (1527) demonstrate the methods by which, nearly a decade apart, these two poets used their writings as self-promotion to raise their status at court. Both works revolve around critical moments in the political life of Poland: King Sigismund's engagement to the Italian princess Bona Sforza and Sigismund's defence of Christianity in the face of the Turkish invasion of eastern Europe and the expanding Reformation. In each work, the poet, by observing the decorum of the patronage system regarding flattery and modesty, not only publicizes the issues of the moment and glorifies the Polish dignitaries involved in them, but also draws attention to his own role as a spokesperson for these topics and people. In both works, the poet thus ingratiates himself with these same dignitaries, who could offer support, moral as well as monetary, for the humanist pedagogical program. Although these publications appeared nearly a decade apart and are of two different genres – one an elegy, the other a prose dedicatory letter – the strategies used in them are remarkably similar, and testify to the continuing success of the wandering poets of east central Europe in the 1510s and 1520s in exploiting the patronage system in their writings.

Bona Sforza (1494–1557, the daughter of the duke of Milan, Gian Galeazzo Sforza, and Isabel of Aragon) married the widowed King Sigismund in April 1518.[1] The search for a new queen of Poland had taken place through the mediation of Emperor Maximilian, who after the Congress of 1515 was eager to keep the Polish king within his political sphere. (Sigismund's first wife, Barbara, had been a Hungarian noblewoman and the sister of János Zápolya, the voivode, or governor, of Transylvania and leader of the Hungarian anti-Habsburg faction.) Sigismund gave notice of his agreement to take Bona as his wife to the emperor in the spring of 1517. At the end of the year, after all the prenuptial agreements had been completed, Sigismund sent his representatives, the bishop of Poznań, Jan Lubrański, the grand-chancellor, Krzysztof Szydłowiecki, and the castellan of Poznań, Łukasz Górka, to Vienna to meet Bona and to accompany her back to Cracow. Sigismund expected that Bona would arrive in Vienna at the beginning of January 1518, but she did not leave Italy until the beginning of February. During this time Sigismund became anxious for news, and sent a messenger to Bari with a letter to her mother. But Bona was already on her way, and she and her retinue reached Vienna on 19 March. Sigismund wanted Bona to spend Easter in Olomouc and arranged for his representatives, Lubrański, Szydłowiecki, and Górka, as well as Erazm Ciołek, the bishop of Płock, to welcome her officially there, in the capital of Moravia, on 29 March, and to conduct her safely and comfortably to Cracow.

In honour of the betrothal, Rudolf Agricola Junior, in the spring of 1518,[2] composed *Illustrissimae reginae Bonae paraceleusis*,[3] an eighty-five-line elegy welcoming Princess Bona to Poland. The praises of Bona form a minor element of the poem, and Agricola instead focuses on the missions of the Polish delegates to negotiate the betrothal and to meet Bona and accompany her to Cracow. He fills the second half of the poem with publicity for these men, so that *Paraceleusis* is dedicated more to the promotion and legitimization of their status at Cracow than it is to the celebration of the forthcoming marriage, or even to the glorification of Bona.[4] Moreover, by means of his references to himself in the poem, Agricola Junior presents himself as a spokesperson for these dignitaries, and creates an image of himself as an 'insider' at the Cracow court.

The praises of Bona are found in lines 23 to 40, only after the poet opens the piece with a plea to Bona to come to Cracow, expresses the longing of the king and his people for the day of her arrival, and depicts her journey from Italy to Vienna. The king and his country are waiting for the happy day when Bona will arrive in Cracow. They know that she has left Italy and has reached the German empire; the winds and the gods have favoured her journey. The expression of the country's pleasure in having such a noble woman coming to be their queen, since there is no equal in virtue to the Sforza family, leads into the glorification of Bona. Agricola insists that his poetry is no match for her. She is beautiful and elegant. Nature has endowed her with every type of beauty and grace. She has all the dignity befitting the ancient and famous origins of her family. Finally, she is filled with virtue and brilliance and will play a great part in Polish history. The subject of Bona takes up very little of the poem, and the praises of Sigismund are even more sparse: he is congratulated only in line 5 for 'having deserved the honours of the gods' ('qui superum meruit honores').

In line 43, Agricola begins the panegyric of the Cracow dignitaries, Jan Lubrański, Erazm Ciołek, Krzysztof Szydłowiecki, and Łukasz Górka. The emphasis in Agricola's poem is on these dignitaries, whom Agricola praises not only as leaders of their country but also as humanist heroes, endowed with the qualities championed by the *poetae:* nobility, learning, oratorical ability, industriousness. This section of *Paraceleusis* is similar to Eck's *Ad proceres Hungariae exhortatio*, written nearly ten years later, where Eck portrays the new King Ferdinand being led to the throne by the Hungarian dignitaries, whom he extols for possessing, among other qualities, noble origins, piety, probity, faith, eloquent counsel, admirable gravity, and, notably, humanist education. Perhaps Eck had *Paraceleusis* in mind when he composed his own poem.

Agricola lists first Jan Lubrański (1456–1520), the bishop of

Poznań (1489–1520). After receiving his master of arts degree at Cracow, Lubrański had studied law in Bologna and Rome, and he would later (in 1518) found an academy for humanistic studies at Poznań.[5] Agricola had already written a panegyric to him, printed in 1512 with the commentary on Ptolemy's *Cosmographia* written by the Cracow astronomer Johannes de Stobnica. In *Paraceleusis*, Agricola Junior notes Lubrański's position as bishop of Poznań and refers to him as the leader of the expedition to meet Bona. He calls him 'a most honourable bishop' (*optimus antistes*) and a 'supporter of learned men' (*doctorum fautor*), compares him with Pompilius Numa (the legendary early king of Rome supposed to have enacted legal, religious, and economic reforms), and proclaims him a patron of humanist writers.[6]

Paraceleusis was actually dedicated to the next man on Agricola's list, Erazm Ciołek (*c.* 1474–1522), the bishop of Płock (1503–22) and royal ambassador to Rome and the Viennese court, known as a brilliant orator. Not only was Ciołek a member of the group welcoming Bona at Olomouc, he also had played a major role in negotiating the betrothal arrangements for Sigismund. Although Ciołek never studied in Italy (he had received an MA from Cracow), he had close contacts with the country and was a supporter of humanism. He became a patron of the arts, in which role he accumulated an impressive collection of illuminated manuscripts and commissioned architectural works, notably the enlarging of his episcopal palace in Płock and his house in Cracow, where he carried out renovations in the Renaissance style.[7] Agricola refers to Ciołek's two missions to Rome and terms him an 'orator with great gravity' (*orator magna cum grauitate*).[8] He claims that Ciołek surpasses Titus (the Roman emperor remembered for his goodness to his people) in kindness and Metellus (a great Roman military commander and politician) in gravity, and, a learned man, recalls Nestor (the Trojan hero renowned for his eloquence) in his sweet voice. Agricola includes a mention of Ciołek's architectural projects, stating that he zealously constructs lofty buildings and repairs ancient abodes at great expense.[9]

Next, Agricola writes that King Sigismund ordered Palatine Szydłowiecki to go and welcome Bona.[10] Agricola describes the grand-chancellor as possessing virtue and nobility, and as having won the king's affection by his virtue, so that the king loves him as Aeneas did Achates. Here Agricola borrows lines from his poem *Pro reuerendissimo domino Matheo Langio siluula*, in which he compares the relationship between the emperor and his adviser Cardinal Lang with that between Aeneas and his armour-bearer and friend Achates.[11]

Finally, Agricola mentions Łukasz Górka (1482–1542),[12] the castellan of Poznań, an active politician and parliamentarian, an in-law and friend of the vice-chancellor, Piotr Tomicki, who frequently took part in meetings in which he represented the interests of the province of Poznań and in foreign missions for his king, one of which was the journey to meet Bona at Olomouc. Agricola states that Górka is distinguished by wealth and also by his wisdom and intelligence. He is destined to manage public affairs (*rebus natus agendis*) and is also known for his faithfulness to the king (*regi sincera cognitus usque fide*).

As well as a panegyric to Sigismund's ambassadors sent to meet Bona, *Paraceleusis* should be considered a piece of self-promotion by Agricola Junior, who by means of references to himself connects himself with the most powerful men in the Polish kingdom. He calls attention to himself, first of all, in the modesty topos. In his dedicatory preface to Bishop Erazm Ciołek's secretary, Carolus Antonius Moncinereus, the canon of Płock, he states that he wrote *Paraceleusis* at the request of the canon, in a hurry, and gave it to the printer, in an unpolished condition, as soon as he had finished it. It is certainly plausible that Agricola felt pressure owing to the date of Bona's travel to Poland, but his declaration that Ciołek's secretary has personally requested the poem from him indicates his importance as a court poet. Agricola completes his expression of modesty in the dedicatory letter by saying that he has written more poetry for Bona, but will publish it only when it has been corrected by his friends and finally polished.[13] In the text of the poem itself, he includes a modesty topos at lines 28 and 29, where he claims that his verses are unable to praise Bona because they are stunned.[14]

Whereas Agricola's expressions of modesty call attention to himself, his use of direct address to Bona gives authority to his voice. No one, naturally, would speak publicly to the future queen without having a rank that would permit him to do so. Agricola ties the poem together with a refrain containing a verb in the imperative mood ('Exoptata ueni tandem uotisque tuorum / Et precibus regis sponsa beata tui'), which he inserts whenever he intends to change the subject (e.g., to Bona's journey from Italy, to a list of her praises). The repetition of *ueni* (come!) throughout the poem adds force to the voice of the poet because it reminds the reader that it is the poet who is speaking to Bona and calling out to her to come to Cracow. Agricola refers to himself at the very end of the first half of the poem when he states in line 39 that he will summarize Bona's qualities in a majestic manner: she will play a very great part in the history of Poland.[15]

When Agricola writes, in the first person plural, '*we* know' (*scimus*) at the beginning of the poem (ll. 10–11), in explaining that the people of Cracow know that Bona has left Italy and has arrived in Vienna, he acts as a representative of the king and the leaders of Poland. In line 40, when he claims that Bona will play a great part in the history of the country, his exact phrase is '*our* history' (*nostrae historiae*). Whether or not Agricola wished to portray himself as a citizen of Poland is beside the point. What is central here is that he shows himself to be an 'insider,' an accepted Cracow court poet.

The image of Agricola as the Cracow poet laureate, fulfilling an official duty as part of court society, is reinforced at the end of the poem, where he writes that the king's envoys, these bishops and leaders, commend themselves to Bona wholeheartedly and seek her favour, and where he goes on to ask Bona to ascend the throne with happiness, and to hope that God will make her the mother of royal children (ll. 75–82). Agricola is making these requests on behalf of the Polish leaders, and therefore presenting himself as their agent.

We can see Agricola's self-fashioning in *Paraceleusis* as part of a whole strategy of self-promotion at Cracow at this time, which included, for example, his printing of his poem of congratulation to Sigismund von Herberstein along with Johannes Dantiscus's *Soteria* (early in 1518). It seems that Agricola's strategy was successful, in that during these few months he advanced quickly at Cracow.[16] Shortly after the wedding of Sigismund and Bona, he mentioned in a letter to Joachim Vadian that he was to be granted a stipend from the bishops.[17] In July 1518 he dedicated the *Physionomia* of the late Cracow professor Johannes Glogoviensis to the pages of Queen Bona, referring to them as his pupils.[18]

Nine years later, Leonard Cox would be in a position similar to that of Agricola Junior. Having returned from teaching school in Upper Hungary, he would resume his lecturing at the university and would seek to ingratiate himself with court circles. In February 1527, Cox printed the final two pieces of a five-part polemical exchange between Henry VIII and Martin Luther, a debate that also involved Henry's councillor, Thomas More. Cox dedicated his publication to the grand-chancellor of Poland, Krzysztof Szydłowiecki, and he prefaced the text with a dedicatory epistle to the grand-chancellor from himself. Cox, moreover, added a panegyric poem to Szydłowiecki written by the Cracow courtier Stanislaus Hosius. Cox's prefatory material, which not only compared the king of Poland, Sigismund I, with the English King Henry in his defence of the faith but also touted Chancellor Szydłowiecki's connections with Erasmus, was designed as propaganda to glorify the image of the Polish ruling family as one of the most powerful dynasties in Europe. Yet his publication also served as a means of self-promotion for the poet laureate Cox, intended to raise his status at the Cracow court.

Cox's initial advancement at court seems to have come in April 1526 with the publication of *Libellus de erudienda iuuentute*, a treatise on the education of youth modelled on Erasmus's *De ratione studii*, which Cox dedicated to the vice-chancellor, Piotr Tomicki. From this time until he left Poland in 1529, Cox was employed as a tutor at Tomicki's court, where one of his pupils was Tomicki's great-nephew, Andrzej Zebrzydowski.[19] He had close contact both with the grand-chancellor, Szydłowiecki, upon whose encouragement he wrote a letter to Erasmus in March 1527, and with Tomicki's nephew, Andrzej Krzycki, who would play a major role in Cox's publication of the final two pieces of the polemical exchange.

Cox's publication of *Epistola Martini Lutheri ad Henricum VIII* and *Responsio dicti inuictissimi Angliae ac Franciae regis* in February 1527 was significant because of its timeliness in conveying the most recent developments in the crucial issues of the Reformation to the intelligentsia of east central Europe. The controversy between the Reformer and the English monarch had begun back in 1521, when Henry VIII, hoping to receive an honorary title, such as *rex Christianissimus*, from the Pope, wrote a book condemning Luther's errors, the *Assertio septem sacramentorum*, which was printed by Pynson at London in July of that year. Luther responded with his *Contra Henricum regem Angliae*, published in September 1522, an abusive diatribe attacking the king in extremely rude language, which rested on Luther's belief that scripture, and not the church hierarchy, was the only authority in matters of religion. Although the English court issued a royal letter in January 1523, addressed to the Saxon dukes, that warned the German nobility of the dangers of Luther while treating Luther's diatribe as the ridiculous insults of a madman, it remained for the king's councillor Thomas More to produce a work that would refute Luther point by point and cover him in satire. More's *Responsio* appeared in two editions printed by Pynson later in 1523, the first with the pseudonym of Baravellus, the second with the pseudonym of Rosseus.[20]

Luther responded to More's book only in the autumn of 1525, with his *Epistola ad Henricum VIII*, in which he humbly apologized to the king for the rude book he had written in 1522. Luther's *Epistola* was provoked by the exiled King Christian II of Denmark, who was keen to promote the Lutheran reformation and who sometime during 1525 had written to the Lutherans that the English king also had become so inclined. Luther had as well come under the misapprehension that Cardinal Wolsey had fallen out of favour with the king, and as a result, much of his apology was based on the premise that Wolsey was responsible for the conflict between the king and himself. Although Luther did not recant his beliefs in his *Epistola* of 1525, his tone was meek and conciliatory. Luther's *Epistola* was printed together with Henry's *Responsio* at London by Pynson in December 1526. The king's answer was curt and, making his attitude towards Luther's activities very plain, harshly dispelled any notion that he was leaning towards Protestantism: he rejected the doctrine of justification by faith and criticized Luther's denial of free will. He ended his response by informing Luther that he expected no further disputation with him.[21]

The two-month interval between the printing of Luther's *Epistola* and Henry's *Responsio*, on the one hand, and the publication of Cox's pamphlet containing the two pieces, on the other, indicates that a copy of the book must have found its way to Cracow shortly after its issue in England. It also indicates that someone at the Cracow court was interested in following the Reformation controversy and defending the orthodox position publicly in Poland. In his dedicatory letter to Szydłowiecki, Cox states that he received the book from Andrzej Krzycki, the nephew of Vice-Chancellor Piotr Tomicki and the bishop of Przemyśl (a town in southeast Poland). Furthermore, Stanislaus Hosius, in his commendatory poem following the dedicatory letter, cites Krzycki as the initiator of the publication of the pamphlet. The booklet had most likely come to Krzycki from Germany, given that the title as printed by Vietor resembles not the title on the original London edition but rather ones printed in Germany in the same year.[22]

Krzycki must have been actively interested in procuring whatever printed material existed pertaining to Reformation issues. Hosius, in his commendatory verses to the Cracow publication, praised Krzycki for his concern for the faith (*religionis amans*). Krzycki had, certainly by this time, made himself known publicly as an enemy of Lutheranism. In 1522 he had complained in his *Religionis et reipublicae querimonia* about the tendency towards religious novelty on the part of many of his countrymen. In 1523, when the king announced his edict banning the reading of Luther's works, the printed text was accompanied by a letter from Bishop Krzycki. In 1524 he published *Encomia Lutheri*, which contained his poems *In imaginem Lutheri* and *Condiciones boni Lutherani*, both of which are full of irony and sarcasm. The problem of suppressing Lutheranism may have played some part in Krzycki's criticism of Szydłowiecki for dealing too leniently with the Gdańsk rebellion of 1526.[23] In January 1527, just before Cox brought out his edition of Luther's *Epistola* and Henry's *Responsio*, Krzycki published his *De afflictione ecclesiae*, a commentary on Psalm 21, which he dedicated to Queen Bona. The book contained, on its title-page, a commendatory poem by Cox and, at the end of the book, an epigram by Stanislaus Hosius in honour of Krzycki.

By publishing Luther's *Epistola* and Henry's *Responsio*, Cox was expressing the opinions of a powerful minority of the Polish clergy and also those of the king, who with the utmost prudence sided with the clergy without persecuting his Protestant subjects and thereby avoided the bloodshed that occurred elsewhere in Europe. The need for compromise as opposed to religious militancy was accepted in a society where the Roman Church had never enjoyed a monopoly, constantly plagued as it was by pagans, dissenters, and schismatics. In the 1520s, the Reformation in Poland was limited to the cities, which had large German populations. The king, as a Catholic, aligned himself with the clergy, some of whom, like Krzycki, made an effort to compel the king to fight the movement, but most of whom did not view Lutheranism as a threat and simply expected Rome to settle the controversies and introduce a reform of its own.[24] Cox's publication assured the English (who, provoked by rumours fostered by the Habsburgs, were suspicious of Lutheran tendencies at the Polish court owing to Sigismund's demand for loyalty from the Teutonic Knights in Prussia) of the Polish court's anti-Lutheran stance.[25]

Aside from echoing the Polish royal court's anxiety to be seen as the suppressors of Lutheranism, Cox's publication of Luther's *Epistola* and Henry's *Responsio* was timely for another reason. At the end of 1526, Henry had sent a legation to Cracow not only soliciting Sigismund's promise to stop supporting the Lutherans, but also proposing the formation of an anti-Turkish league and urging Sigismund to direct his strategies and his actions towards the defence of the Hungarian kingdom and the restraint of the Turkish empire.[26] Sigismund replied by explaining that even before the Turkish invasion of Hungary the previous August, when he had lost his nephew, Louis the king of Hungary and Bohemia, on the battlefield of Mohács, he had been responsible for preserving Christianity not only from the onslaught of the Turks, but also from the Tartars, Muscovites, and other infidels and schismatics. He asked Henry to stand by his kingdom and Hungary in this time of misfortune and to exhort the other Catholic leaders to do so as well. Sigismund ended his letter cordially, referring to himself as a brother and friend.[27]

Cox's publication of Luther's *Epistola ad Henricum VIII* and Henry's *Responsio*, therefore, served as a vehicle for publicizing the friendship between Henry and Sigismund. In his prefatory letter to the publication, Cox stated that Sigismund and his court embraced Henry with sincere affection, and then linked Sigismund with Henry on the basis of their common concern for the defence of Roman Catholicism, calling Sigismund 'the second defender of the faith, in these parts of the world' (*alter in hisce mundi partibus fidei nostrae defensor*). Stanislaus Hosius's poem reiterated Cox's assertions, praising the Polish king and his court for their virtue and their upholding of the true religion.

Yet a coordinated defence of the true religion, as real an activity as it was, may have masked another reason for attracting the attention of an international audience to Sigismund's relationship with Henry. Cox's publication also projected the image of Sigismund and Henry as strong allies, and that of a tough Polish-Lithuanian presence in the face of an ever-expanding Habsburg empire. Especially at the beginning of 1527, when a Habsburg king, having just been elected to the Czech throne, was poised to take the crown of Hungary, Sigismund's court would have wanted to publish propaganda that would assert the sovereignty of Polish rule in relation to the empire.[28]

Cox's publication was an instrument for the expression of the political and social ambitions of the Polish king and his court. In his preface, Cox placed Sigismund on the same level as Henry, that is, on the first rung of European monarchs, by terming Sigismund a most noble hero and applying to him the adjective *diuus*, meaning 'exalted' and reserved for emperors and kings, and harking back to the Roman title given to a deified emperor. Moreover, Cox called Grand-chancellor Szydłowiecki an 'illustrious hero' and connected him with Henry, saying that he had recently found out that Henry had honoured Szydłowiecki with his esteem and that the grand-chancellor, in return, had become very much attached to the English king. With this statement, Cox was making public a private correspondence, for in January 1527, Szydłowiecki had written to Henry that he had received Henry's letter of thanks for the falcons he had sent the previous year as a gift to the English king, and expressed his gratitude for the king's letter, saying that should the king send his emissaries to Cracow, he would receive them kindly and send them back to him with the best falcons.[29] Hosius, in his commendatory poem, also commented on Szydłowiecki's relationship with Henry, remarking that the grand-chancellor's fame had reached to farthest Britain ('Cuius ad extremos peruenit fama Britannos'). Hosius reminded his public that Szydłowiecki had been immortalized by Erasmus's dedication of his work *Lingua* to him.[30] The flattering of Sigismund and his court with superlative descriptors, the publicizing of dynastic relationships, the acclaim for the Polish king's role in the protection of the Roman Church, and the mention of Erasmus all served to promote Sigismund before an international audience and to signal his pretensions to authority in east central Europe.

But as much as Cox's publication of Luther's *Epistola* and Henry's *Responsio* promoted Sigismund and Szydłowiecki, it also promoted Cox himself. Like Agricola Junior, Cox called attention to his role in publicizing the issues at hand and broadcasting the fame of the Polish dignitaries involved. Unlike Agricola, he does not represent himself as a Polish subject, but rather as a broker in the relationship between the London and Cracow courts. In printing Henry's *Responsio*, Cox writes in his prefatory letter, he wishes to share the 'outstanding' work of his king with 'this most fortunate Poland on account of [his, i.e. Cox's] goodwill towards the government of this country.'[31] Since Cox is introducing a work written by his king, he cannot include a modesty topos as such; it is appropriate for him only to praise the work he is publishing. The sole hint at a traditional modesty topos is in his referring to the book using a diminutive term (*libellus*) as he figuratively hands it over to Szydłowiecki at the end of the dedication. Cox's expression of modesty in this dedicatory letter relies on his lavish flattery of Krzycki, Szydłowiecki, and Sigismund. The pamphlet, by linking its editor to the highest-ranking dignitaries of the Polish kingdom, publicized Cox's relationship with the royal clique and projected an image of him as an educator sanctioned by the court. In his dedicatory preface, Cox admitted that by publishing the exchange between Luther and Henry he was hoping to gain the favour of the Cracow magnates.[32] Stanislaus Hosius, in his commendatory poem, glorified Cox as the chief hope of Polish education (*Coxus nostri spes prima Lycei*). Cox's strategy for self-promotion must have worked. A month later, at the prompting of Chancellor Szydłowiecki, Cox addressed a letter to Erasmus, the reply to which would be printed in Erasmus's *Opus epistolarum* in 1529.[33]

Rudolf Agricola Junior, Valentin Eck, and Leonard Cox were successful in exploiting the patronage system. They managed to attract the most powerful political figures of Poland and Hungary as their patrons. If they did not achieve long-lasting careers at Cracow, it is because the city's university was not receptive to humanist pedagogical trends in the early sixteenth century, nor had it undergone the process of laicization that would have welcomed the lay intellectuals as a social group. Depending as it did on ecclesiastical patrons who seemed uninterested in advancing the careers of lay humanist scholars, it was not fertile ground on which these scholar-poets might establish themselves. Although Agricola Junior and Cox were accepted as tutors at court, their work there was not satisfactory to them in the long term, as evidenced by Agricola's complaints in his letters to Vadian and Cox's return to England. In spite of working in a hostile environment, though, Agricola Junior, Eck, and Cox created effective propaganda for themselves and their pedagogical program, and they succeeded, as evidenced by the amount of literature they managed to publish and the continuance of their book dedications to highly placed individuals, in constructing their reputations as outstanding scholars and poets in the Jagiellonian regions. Through their comparisons of contemporary leaders with Roman and Greek heroes, and their display of classical and biblical erudition, they were able to communicate – to the international, multi-ethnic audience of east central Europe – the qualities of nobility and virtue as they saw them, and the value of an elite educational program that had classical learning, the writing of an elegant Latin, and Christian piety as its base.

APPENDIX 1

The Works of Rudolf Agricola Junior, Valentin Eck, and Leonard Cox: Short-Title Bibliographies

RUDOLF AGRICOLA JUNIOR[1]
(Wasserburgensis, Rhaetus, Hydroburgius)
(*c.* 1490–1521)

A. Writings

1. Prose

Habes lector hoc libello ad Ioachimum Vadianum epistolam, qua de locorum non nullorum obscuritate quaestio fit et percontatio.
Vienna: Johannes Singrenius, 1515.[2]

Ad dominum Petrum episcopum Premisliensem et regni Poloniae uicecancellarium oratio.
Printed in *Orationes Viennae Austriae ad diuum Maximilianum Caes. Aug. aliosque illustrissimos principes habitae. In celeberrimo trium Regum ad Caesarem conuentu. Anno MDXV.* Vienna: Hieronymus Vietor, 1516.

Agricola's letters to the Swiss humanist and Reformer Joachim Vadian have been edited as part of the collection of Vadian's correspondence by Emil Arbenz (see the bibliography).

2. Poetry

Pro reuerendissimo domino Matheo Langio episcopo Gurcensi siluula.
Vienna: Hieronymus Vietor, 1515.
Reprinted in *Orationes Viennae Austriae ad diuum Maximilianum Caes. Aug. aliosque illustrissimos principes habitae. In celeberrimo trium Regum ad Caesarem conuentu. Anno MDXV.* Vienna: Hieronymus Vietor, 1516.[3]

Illustrissimae reginae Bonae paraceleusis.
Cracow: Johannes Haller, 1518.

Ad magnificum dominum Sigismundum de Erberstain, ad uictoriosissimum Sigismundum Poloniae regem etc. et magnum Moschorum ducem congratulatio. Patria magnifici domini Sigismundi.

Printed with Johannes Dantiscus, *Soteria*. Cracow: Johannes Haller, 1518.
Reprinted in *Gratae posteritati Sigismundus liber baro in Herberstein, Neiperg et Guetenhag actiones suas a puero ad annum usque aetatis suae septuagesimum tertium breui commentariolo notatas reliquit*. Vienna: Raphael Hofhalter, 1558; Vienna: Raphael Hofhalter, 1560.[4]

Hymnus de diuo praesule et martyre Stanislao.
Cracow: Hieronymus Vietor, 1519.

Passio dominica per septem horas canonicas distributa.
Cracow: Hieronymus Vietor, 1520.

Miscellaneous short poems by Agricola Junior are found in the following volumes:

Johannes de Stobnica (Jan ze Stobnicy), *Introductio in Ptolomei cosmographiam.*
Cracow: Florian Ungler, 1512.
Cracow: Florian Ungler, 1513.[5]
Cracow: Hieronymus Vietor, 1519.[6]

Somnia Danielis.
Cracow: Florian Ungler, 1512.
Reprinted as *Interpretationes somniorum Danielis*. Cracow: Mathias Scharffenberg, 1533.

Johannes de Urbach (Auerbach), *Processus iudiciarius.*
Cracow: Florian Ungler, 1512–14?

Riccardus Bartholinus (Riccardo Bartolini), *Odeporicon idest itinerarium d. Mathei Sancti Angeli cardinalis Gurcensis.*
Vienna: Hieronymus Vietor, 1515.

Joachim Vadian, *Aegloga, cui titulus Faustus. De insignibus familiae Vadianorum, ad Melchiorem fratrem elegia.*
Vienna: Johannes Singrenius, 1517.
Reprinted in C. J. Solinus, *Polyhistora*. Basel: Henricus Petrus, 1557.[7]

Jodocus Ludovicus Decius, *Diarii et earum quae memoratu digna in splendidissimis, potensiss. Sigismundi Poloniae regis et sereniss. dominae Bonae Mediolani Barique ducis principis Rossani nuptiis gesta descriptio.*
Cracow: Hieronymus Vietor, 1518.

Leonard Cox, *De laudibus celeberrimae Cracouiensis Academiae oratio.*
Cracow: Hieronymus Vietor, 1518.

Michael Wratislaviensis (Michał z Wrocławia), *Epitoma figurarum in libros physicorum et de anima Aristotelis.*
Cracow: Johannes Haller, 1518.

Valentin Eck, *De antiquissima nominis et familiae Thurzonum origine.*
Cracow: Hieronymus Vietor, 1519.

Valentin Eck, *De mundi contemptu et uirtute amplectenda dialogus.*
Cracow: Hieronymus Vietor, 1519.

Cebes, *Tabula.*
Vienna: Johannes Singrenius, 1519.
Cracow: Florian Ungler, 1522.
Desiderius Erasmus Roterodamus, *Aliquot epistolae diui Eusebii Hieronymi Stridonensis.*
Cracow: Hieronymus Vietor, 1519.
Stanislaus Leopoliensis, *Salutifera Domini passionis contemplatio.*
Cracow: Hieronymus Vietor, 1520.[8]
Johannes Sacranus, *Modus epistolandi.*
Cracow: Johannes Haller, 1520.
Nicolaus Schadkovius (Mikołaj z Szadka), *Iudicium astronomicum anno Christi MDXXI.*
Cracow: Hieronymus Vietor, 1521.
Valentin Eck, *De arte uersificandi opusculum.*
Cracow: Hieronymus Vietor, 1521.
Cracow: Hieronymus Vietor, 1539.[9]
Quintus Flaccus Horatius, *De arte poetica ad Pisones.*
Cracow: Johannes Haller, 1521. (Lost.)

B. Editor or corrector

Octavius Cleophilus Phanensis (Francesco Ottavio Cleofilo), *De poetarum coetu libellus.*
Cracow: Florian Ungler, 1511.
Bonaventura, *Breuiloquium.*
Cracow: Florian Ungler, 1511 or 1512?
Proclus Diadochus, *Sphaera Thoma Linacro Britanno interprete.*
Cracow: Florian Ungler, 1512.
Filippo Beroaldo, *Modus epistolandi. Addita sunt quaedam ex elegantiis Jacobi Wimphelingii epistolae necessaria.*
Cracow: Florian Ungler, 1512.
Maffeo Vegio, *Philalethes.*
Cracow: Florian Ungler, 1512.[10]
Aristoteles, *De anima.*
Cracow: Florian Ungler, 1512.
Cracow: Johannes Haller, 1519.
Pseudo-Crates, *Epistolae cynicae.*
Cracow: Florian Ungler, 1512.
Cracow: Hieronymus Vietor, 1518.
Leonardo Bruni, *Isagoge in philosophiam moralem.*
Vienna: Hieronymus Vietor, 1515.
Cebes, *Tabula.*
Vienna: Hieronymus Vietor, 1515.
Quintus Flaccus Horatius, *Epistolarum libri duo.*

Vienna: Hieronymus Vietor, 1515.
P. Papinius Statius, *Achilleis*.
Vienna: Hieronymus Vietor, 1515.
Anselm of Canterbury, *Elucidarius dialogicus theologiae tripertitus*.
Vienna: Hieronymus Vietor, 1515.
Georg Peurbach, *Algorithmus*.
Vienna: Hieronymus Vietor, 1515.
Vienna: Johannes Singrenius, 1520.
Johannes Harmonius Marsus (Giovanni Armonio), *Comoedia Stephanium*.
Vienna: Hieronymus Vietor, 1515.
Aegidius Gallus Romanus, *Bophilaria*.
Vienna: Hieronymus Vietor, 1515.[11]
M. Tullius Cicero, *Laelius siue de amicitia*.
Vienna: Hieronymus Vietor, 1515.
Johannes Aesticampianus, *Modus epistolandi*.
Vienna: Hieronymus Vietor, 1515.
Cracow: Hieronymus Vietor, 1522.
Aurelius Prudentius, *Cathemerinon*.
Vienna: Hieronymus Vietor, 1515.
Caspar Ursinus Velius, *Epistolarum et epigrammatum liber*.
Vienna: Johannes Singrenius, 1517.
M. Tullius Cicero, *Pro Aulo Licinio Archia poeta*.
Cracow: Hieronymus Vietor, 1518.
Johannes Glogoviensis (Jan z Głogowa), *Physionomia*.
Cracow: Hieronymus Vietor, 1518.
Johannes de Nova Domo, *De constitutionibus humani corporis*.
Cracow: Hieronymus Vietor, 1518.
M. Tullius Cicero, *Pro rege Deiotaro*.
Cracow: Hieronymus Vietor, 1518.
Nicolaus de Toliszków (Mikołaj z Tuliszkowa), *Iudicium celebratissime universitatis Cracouiensis ad annum domini 1518 recollectum*.
Cracow: Johannes Haller, 1518.
Statuta prouinciae Gnesnensis.
Cracow: Johannes Haller, 1518.
Johannes de Lapide, *Resolutorium dubiorum circa celebrationem missarum occurrentium*.
Cracow: Hieronymus Vietor, 1519.
Robertus de Euremodio (Robert d'Envermeuil), *Institutiones uitae*.
Cracow: Johannes Haller, 1519.
Desiderius Erasmus Roterodamus, *De ratione studii*.
Cracow: Hieronymus Vietor, 1519.
Nicolaus de Błonie (Plove) (Mikołaj z Błonia), *Tractatus de sacramentis*.
Cracow: Johannes Haller, 1519.
Cracow: Mathias Scharffenberg, 1529.

Nicolaus de Toliszków (Mikołaj z Tuliszkowa), *Iudicium celebratissime uniuersitatis Cracouiensis ad annum 1519 recollectum.*
Cracow: Hieronymus Vietor, 1519.

C. Uncertain[12]

1. Writings

De diuo Casimiro carmen elegiacum. Venerando praeceptori suo Paulo Crosnensi florent. studii Crac. College oblatum.
Cracow: Florian Ungler, 1511.
Ad Ioachimum Vadianum epistola de locorum nonnullorum apud autores ueteres obscuritate: cum Ioachimi Vadiani epistola responsoria.
Vienna: Hieronymus Vietor, 1515.
Oratio ad dominum Petrum Tomitium. Cum carmine sapphico ad Michaelem Wratislauiensem.
Vienna: Johannes Singrenius, 1515.

2. Editor and corrector

Antonio Mancinelli, *Opusculum de componendis uersibus.*
Cracow: Florian Ungler, 1513.
Antonio Mancinelli, *Opusculum de poetica uirtute.*
Cracow: Florian Ungler, 1513.
Filippo Beroaldo, *An orator sit philosopho et medico anteponendus.*
Cracow: Florian Ungler, 1514.

D. Secondary literature

Ulrich Faber, *Epicedion siue naenia funebris in obitum Rudolphi Agricolae poetae.*
Cracow: Hieronymus Vietor, 1521.[13]

VALENTIN ECK[14]

(Eckius, Ecchius, Philyripolitanus, Lendanus Rhaetus)
(*c.* 1494–1556?)

A. Writings

1. Prose

De arte uersificandi opusculum.
Cracow: Florian Ungler, 1515.
Cracow: Hieronymus Vietor, 1521.
Cracow: Hieronymus Vietor, 1539.[15]
De mundi contemptu et uirtute amplectenda dialogus. Supellectilium fasciculus.

Cracow: Hieronymus Vietor, 1519. (Contains *Carmen de amicitiae et concordiae utilitate* and three poems to Andreas Räuber, two of which are reprinted from Eck's poem *An prudenti uiro sit ducenda uxor*, 1518.)

Cracow: Mathias Scharffenberg, 1528.

De reipublicae administratione dialogus. Epistola consolatoria, ad magnificos dominos Alexium et Ioannem Thursones, ob mortem reuerendissimi domini Ioannis Thursonis, episcopi Wratislauiensis. Epitaphia uaria pro eodem ad eosdem dominos.

Cracow: Hieronymus Vietor, 1520. (Contains Eck's poem *De amicitiae et concordiae utilitate.*)

2. Poetry

Panegyricus in laudem praestantissimi uiri doctoris Augustini Moraui praepositi Olomunczensis et Brunnensis.

Cracow: Florian Ungler, (after 8 August) 1513.

Hymnus exhortatorius.

Printed with Johannes Dantiscus, *Carmen extemporarium de uictoria insigni ex Moschis illustrissimi principis Sigismundi.* Cracow: Florian Ungler, 1514.

Reprinted in *Carmina de memorabili caede scismaticorum Moscouiorum per serenis. ac inuictis. d. Sigismundum regem Poloniae.* Rome, 1515.

An prudenti uiro sit ducenda uxor.

Cracow: Johannes Haller, 1518.

Cracow: Hieronymus Vietor, 1524. (Contains Eck's *Supellectilium fasciculus.*)

Threni neglectae religionis.

Cracow: Johannes Haller, 1518.

Carmen de amicitiae et concordiae utilitate.

Cracow: Johannes Haller, 1518. (Lost.)

Reprinted with *De mundi contemptu*, 1519 and *De reipublicae administratione*, 1520.

Supellectilium fasciculus.

Printed with *De mundi contemptu*, 1519, 1528 and *An prudenti uiro sit ducenda uxor*, 1524.

De antiquissima nominis et familiae Thurzonum origine, et singulari praestantissimi domini Alexii Thurzonis panegyris.

Cracow: Hieronymus Vietor, 1519.

Apophoreticum carmen de Christi natiuitate. Iubilus heroicus Cassouiae habitus ob aduentum reuerendissimi antistitis domini Georgii Quinqueecclesiensis episcopi. Epithalamium pro nuptiis domini Ioannis Sayslich.

Cracow: Hieronymus Vietor, 1520. (Contains *Hexastichon ad eundem dominum Alexium.*)

De diuo Alexio patricio Romano hymnus sapphicus.

Cracow: Hieronymus Vietor, (after 11 April) 1521. (Contains Eck's poems *Ad dominum Alexium de salutaris eucharistiae sacramenti mysteriis elegia* and *Domini Georgii Thursonis Augustae defuncti epitaphium.*)

Vita diui Pauli primi eremitae.

Cracow: Hieronymus Vietor, 1522.

Ad inuictissimum Ludouicum Hungariae et Bohemiae etc. regem pro bello Turcis inferendo exhortatio. Alia ad proceres Hungariae. De illustris atque magnifici domini, domini Alexii Thurzonis de Bethlemfalua etc. in regalium tauernicorum magistrum electione plausus heroicus.

Cracow: Hieronymus Vietor, 1524.

De resurrectione Dominica carmen.

Cracow: Hieronymus Vietor, 1525.

Cracow: Hieronymus Vietor, 1534.

Ad proceres Hungariae exhortatio.

Cracow: Hieronymus Vietor, 1527.

Cracow: Hieronymus Vietor, 1528.

Ad inclytum Hungariae et Bohemiae regem etc. archiducem Austriae etc. dominum Ferdinandum epistola, nomine partium superiorum Hungariae. Alia epistola ad magnificum d. Alexium Thurzonem, Regiae Curiae iudicem.

Vienna: Hieronymus Vietor, 1530. (Contains Eck's short poems *De domina Magdalena domini Thurzonis coniuge; Ad eundem dominum Thurzonem;* and *Marti militans.*)

Ad eximium uirum, Sacrae Regiae Maiestatis doctorem, dominum Ioannem Benedictum canonicum Cracouiensem epistola.

Cracow, *c.* 1550. (Contains verses by Johannes Dantiscus and Johannes Mylius.)

Cracow, *c.* 1550.

Cracow: Łazarz Andrysowic, 1561.

Miscellaneous short poems by Eck are found in the following volumes:

Octavius Cleophilus Phanensis (Francesco Ottavio Cleofilo), *De poetarum coetu libellus.*

Cracow: Florian Ungler, 1511.

Filippo Beroaldo, *Modus epistolandi. Addita sunt quaedam ex elegantiis Jacobi Wimphelingii epistolae necessaria.*

Cracow: Florian Ungler, 1512.

Henricus Scriptoris, *Algorithmus.*

Cracow: Florian Ungler, 1514.

Johannes Visliciensis (Jan z Wiślicy), *Bellum Prutenum.*

Cracow: Johannes Haller, 1516.

Pannoniae luctus.

Cracow: Hieronymus Vietor, 1544. (An anthology of poetry dedicated to the heroes of the battle of Mohács.)

Gratae posteritati Sigismundus liber baro in Herberstein, Neiperg et Guetenhag

actiones suas a puero ad annum usque aetatis suae septuagesimum tertium breui commentariolo notatas reliquit.
Vienna: Raphael Hofhalter, 1558.[16]
Vienna: Raphael Hofhalter, 1560.

B. Editor and corrector

Lucius Annaeus Florus, *Bellorum Romanorum libri quattuor.*
Cracow: Johannes Haller, 1515.
Quintus Horatius Flaccus, *De arte poetica ad Pisones.*
Cracow: Johannes Haller, 1521. (Lost.)
Quintus Horatius Flaccus, *Epistolarum libri II.*
Cracow: Johannes Haller, 1522. (Lost.)

C. Uncertain

1. Writings
De ratione legendi autores libellus. Epistola Emmanueli Reubero.
Cracow: Mathias Scharffenberg, 1523.
Epigrammatum sacrorum liber.
Cracow: Hieronymus Vietor, 1537.
Ad Ioannem Benedictum regis Poloniae medicum elegiacon.
Cracow: Hieronymus Vietor, 1545.

2. Editor and corrector
Aurelius Prudentius, *Liber peristephanon.*
Cracow: Mathias Scharffenberg, 1526.
Augustinus, *De uita christiana.*
Cracow: Hieronymus Vietor, 1529.

LEONARD COX[17]
(Coxus, Coxe, Britannus, Anglus)
(*c.* 1495–*c.* 1549)

A. Writings

1. Prose
De laudibus celeberrimae Cracouiensis Academiae oratio.
Cracow: Hieronymus Vietor, 1518.
Libellus de erudienda iuuentute.
Cracow: Hieronymus Vietor, 1526.
The art or crafte of rhetoryke.
London: Robert Redman, 1532.
London: Robert Redman, 1535?

2. Poetry

Miscellaneous short poems by Cox are found in the following volumes:

Valentin Eck, *De mundi contemptu et uirtute amplectenda dialogus.*[18]
Cracow: Hieronymus Vietor, 1519.
Cracow: Mathias Scharffenberg, 1528.

Valentin Eck, *Vita diui Pauli primi eremitae.*
Cracow: Hieronymus Vietor, 1522.

Philipp Melanchthon, *Elementa latinae grammatices.*
Cracow: Hieronymus Vietor, 1526.[19]

C. Plinius Secundus, *Liber septimus naturalis historiae, cum annotationibus M. Wolfgangi Guglinger.*
Cracow: Hieronymus Vietor, 1526.[20]

Stanisław Zaborowski, *Orthographia.*
Cracow: Hieronymus Vietor, 1526.[21]

Andreas Cricius (Andrzej Krzycki), *De afflictione Ecclesiae, commentarius in Psalmum XXI.*
Cracow: Hieronymus Vietor, 1527.

Nicolaus Schadkovius (Mikołaj z Szadka), *Iudicium astronomicum ad annum domini MDXXVII.*
Cracow: Hieronymus Vietor, 1527.

Desiderius Erasmus Roterodamus, *Epistola ad inclytum Sigismundum regem Poloniae.*
Cracow: Hieronymus Vietor, 1527.

B. Editor, corrector, translator

Desiderius Erasmus Roterodamus, *Diui Eusebii Hieronymi Stridonensis epistola ad rusticum monachum.*
Cracow: Hieronymus Vietor, 1518.

Desiderius Erasmus Roterodamus, *Diui Eusebii Hieronymi Stridonensis epistola ad Eustochium de custodia uirginitatis.*
Cracow: Hieronymus Vietor, 1519.[22]

Giovanni Pontano, *De laudibus diuinis opusculum cum argumentis Leonardi Coxi Britanni.*
Cracow: Johannes Haller, 1520.

Adriano Castellesi, *Venatio una cum scholiis non ineruditis Leonardi Coxi Britanni.*
Cracow: Hieronymus Vietor, 1524.

Desiderius Erasmus Roterodamus, *Hyperaspistes diatribae aduersus seruum arbitrium Martini Lutheri.*
Cracow: Hieronymus Vietor, 1526.

Aelius Donatus, *Grammaticae methodus et Donati de octo orationis partibus libellus … opera Glareani poetae laureati est restitutus.*
Cracow: Hieronymus Vietor, 1526.[23]

Martin Luther and Henry VIII, *Epistola Martini Lutheri ad Henricum VIII.*

Responsio dicti inuictissimi Angliae ac Franciae regis, defensoris fidei, ac domini Hyberniae etc.
Cracow: Hieronymus Vietor, 1527.
Johannes Murmellius, *Oratiunculae uariae puerorum usui expositae.*
Cracow: Hieronymus Vietor, 1527.
Quintus Horatius Flaccus, *Epodon ad Aldini exemplaris fidem recognitum Saeculari Carmine adiuncto.*
Cracow: Mathias Scharffenberg, 1527.[24]
P. Papinius Statius, *Syluae.*
Cracow: Mathias Scharffenberg, 1527. (Lost.)
Johannes Murmellius, *Dictionarius Ioannis Murmellii uariarum rerum.*
Cracow: Hieronymus Vietor, 1528.[25]
John Palsgrave, *Lesclarcissement de la langue francoyse.*
London: John Hawkins (Pynson), 1530.
Johannes Murmellius, *Lexicon in quo Latina rerum uocabula in suas singula digesta classes, cum Germanica et Hungarica interpretatione.*
Cracow: Hieronymus Vietor, 1533.[26]
Desiderius Erasmus Roterodamus, *The paraphrase of Erasmus Roterdame upon the epistle of Paule unto Titus.*
London: John Byddell, 1534.
Christopher Saint German, *A treatise concernynge divers of the constitucyons provynciall and legatines.*
London: Thomas Godfray, 1535?
William Lilly, *De octo orationis partium constructione libellus.*
London: Thomas Berthelet, 1540.
Desiderius Erasmus Roterodamus, *The second tome or volume of the paraphrase of Erasmus upon the newe testament.*
London: Edwarde Whitchurche, 1549.

C. Uncertain

1. Writings
Methodus humaniorum studiorum.
Cracow: Hieronymus Vietor, 1526.
Cracow: Mathias Scharffenberg, 1526.

2. Editor and corrector
M. Tullius Cicero, *Ad Marcum Brutum oratorem.*
Cracow: Mathias Scharffenberg, 1528.
M. Tullius Cicero, *Brutus.*
Cracow: Hieronymus Vietor, 1528.

APPENDIX 2

Variants of Personal and Place Names

Personal Names

Latin	Polish	Hungarian	Czech / Slovak / German / English / Other
Albertus de Brudzewo	Wojciech z Brudzewa (Brudzewski)		Blar, Albert
Antoninus, Johannes; Aurifex Kassoviensis, Johannes	Antonin, Jan		
Bartholinus, Riccardus			Bartolini, Riccardo
Boleslaus II	Bolesław Szczodry (Śmiały)		Boleslaus the Bold
Bovillus, Ludovicus			Öchslin, Ludwig
Callimachus, Philippus	Kallimach		Buonaccorsi, Filippo
Casimirus	Kazimierz IV Jagiellończyk		Casimir Jagiellon
Cochanovius, Johannes	Kochanowski, Jan		
Collimitius, Georgius			Tannstetter, Georg
Chahol, Franciscus	Csaholyi, Ferenc		
Coricius, Johannes			Goritz, Johann
Cricius, Andreas	Krzycki, Andrzej		
Crosnensis, Paulus	Paweł z Krosna		Paul of Krosno
Cuspinian, Johannes			Spiessheimer, Johann
Cypser, Petrus			Zipser, Peter
Dantiscus, Johannes	Dantyszek, Jan		
Decius, Justus/ Jodocus Ludovicus			Dietz, Jost
Dlugossius (Longinus), Johannes	Długosz, Jan		
Drevicius, Mathias	Drzewicki, Maciej		
Florentinus, Franciscus			Francesco Fiorentino (della Lora)
Gallus Anonymus	Gall Anonim		
Glogoviensis, Johannes	Jan z Głogowa		John of Głogów
Gloczer, Sigismundus			Glotzer, Sigismund
Hosius, Stanislaus	Hozjusz, Stanisław		
Johannes Albertus	Jan Olbracht		John Albert
Johannes de Stobnica	Jan ze Stobnicy		John of Stobnica
Kadłubek, Vincentius	Kadłubek, Wincenty		Kadłubek, Vincent
Lausman Chrysoreotanus, Nicolaus			Goldberger, Nikolaus
Lasco, Johannes à	Łaski, Jan Junior		
Logus, Georgius			Logau, Georg von
Ludovicus		Lajos II	Ludvík Jagellonský; L'udovít Jágelovský; Louis II
Matthias de Mechovia	Maciej z Miechowa		Matthias of Miechów
Moncinereus, Carolus Antonius			Monte Cinere, Carlo Antonio de

Personal Names (*Continued*)

Latin	Polish	Hungarian	Czech / Slovak / German / English / Other
Moravus, Augustinus			Augustin Olomoucký; Augustin Käsenbrot
Nicolaus de Czebinio			Nikolaus von Zeben
Nicolaus Schadkovius	Mikołaj z Szadka		Nicholas of Szadek
Nicolaus de Toliszków	Mikołaj z Tuliszkowa		Nicholas of Tuliszków
			Il Padovano (Mosca, Giammaria)
Palotzius, Lucas	Pálóczy, Lukács		
Richerius, Coelius			Ricchieri, Lodovico
Roeber/Reuber, Andreas			Räuber, Andreas
Sanocensis, Gregorius	Grzegorz z Sanoka		Gregory of Sanok
Sarbievius, Matthias Casimirus	Sarbiewski, Maciej Kazimierz		
Schidloviecz, Christophorus a	Szydłowiecki, Krzysztof		
Sebridovius, Andreas	Zebrzydowski, Andrzej		
Sigismundus	Zygmunt I (Stary)		Sigismund I (the Old)
Soos, Georgius		Soós, György	
Stanislaus, Sanctus	Św. Stanisław (Stanisław ze Szczepanowa)		St Stanislaus of Szczepanów
Taurinus, Stephanus			Stieröxel, Stefan
Tomicius, Petrus	Tomicki, Piotr		
Thurzo, Alexius		Thurzó, Elek	Thurzó, Alexius
Vadianus, Joachimus			Watt, Joachim von; Vadian, Joachim
Vincentius de Kielcza	Wincenty z Kielczy		Vincent of Kielcza
Visliciensis, Johannes	Jan z Wiślicy		John of Wiślica
Vuernerus, Georgius			Werner, Georg
	Władysław Jagiełło		Jogaila
	Władysław Jagiellończyk	Ulászló II	Vladislav II Jagellonský; Vladislav Jágelovský; Vladislav Jagiellon
Wratislaviensis, Michael	Michał z Wrocławia		Michael Falkener; Michael of Breslau
	Zapolya, Jan	Zápolya (Szapolyai), János (as king, János I)	
	Zapolya, Jan Zygmunt	Zápolya / Szapolyai, János Zsigmond	

Place Names

Hungarian	German	Slovakian	Other
Bártfa	Bartfeld	Bardejov	
Betlenfalva	Bethlemsdorf	Betlanovce	
	Bodensee		Lake Constance
	Breslau		Wrocław
	Brixen		Bressanone
	Danzig		Gdańsk
Eperjes	Preschau	Prešov	
	Ermland		Warmia
Esztergom	Gran		
Homonna	Homenau	Humenné	
	Kärnten		Koroška; Carinthia
Kassa	Kaschau	Košice	
Késmárk	Käsmark	Kežmarok	
Kisszeben	Zeben	Sabinov	
Körmöcbánya	Kremnitz	Kremnica	
Korpona	Karpfen	Krupina	
	Krain		Kranjska; Carniola
Lőcse	Leutschau	Levoča	
Mitróvicza			Sremska Mitrovica

Place Names (*Continued*)

Hungarian	German	Slovakian	Other
Nándorfehérvár			Belgrade
	Olmütz		Olomouc
Pétervárad			Petrovaradin
Pécs	Fünfkirchen		Quinque Ecclesiae
	Pless		Pszczyna
Pozsony	Pressburg	Presbork; Bratislava	
Sáros		Šariš	
Sóvár		Solivar	
	Steiermark	Štajerska	Styria
Szepes	Zips	Spiš	
Tőketerebes		Trebišov	
Varannó		Vranov	
			Walachia (Moldavia)
	Wipach		Vipava
Zágráb			Zagreb

Notes

INTRODUCTION

1 Roeck, *Kunstpatronage in der Frühen Neuzeit*, 11.

2 Price, 'Effect of Patronage,' 7. Detailed information on literary patronage in the Middle Ages is found in Moore, 'General Aspects of Literary Patronage,' and Holzknecht, *Literary Patronage in the Middle Ages.*

3 Hollingsworth, *Patronage in Renaissance Italy*, 2, 5.

4 Hollingsworth, *Patronage in Renaissance Italy*, 3–4; Pelc and Tomkiewicz, 'Rola mecenatu,' 166.

5 Roeck, *Kunstpatronage in der Frühen Neuzeit*, 29.

6 Kaufmann, *Court, Cloister, and City*, 58.

7 For Latin and vernacular variants of personal names, see appendix 2.

8 Bieńkowski, 'Naukowe środowisko krakowskie,' 21. Bieńkowski states that although the persons active in humanist education and the titles of their works are known, 'the concrete accomplishments of particular people, the educational and ideological value of books printed in Cracow, [and] the views in particular fields of knowledge characteristic of this environment have still not been investigated.'

9 Throughout their lives, Agricola Junior and Eck identified themselves, in a suffix to their names, by referring either to their towns – 'Wasserburgensis' or 'Hydroburgius' (Agricola Junior); 'Philyripolitanus' or 'Lendanus' (Eck)) – or to their region of origin – 'Rhaetus.'

10 Cox normally identified himself as either 'Britannus' or 'Anglus.'

11 Bauch, 'Valentin Eck und Georg Werner,' 40–57, and Cox, *Arte or Crafte of Rhethoryke*. Bauch's work was elaborated on by Klenner, *Eck Bálint*.

12 See the bibliography.

13 Vredeveld,'Agricola, Rudolf d. J.,' and Glomski, 'Eck, Valentin.'

14 Škoviera, *Bardejovčan Valentín Ecchius*, and Ryle, 'Cox, Leonard'

(*Oxford Dictionary of National Biography*). The commentary on Eck's handbook on versification produced by the Polish classicist Mielczarski, *Humanistyczna sztuka wierszowania*, does not take into account the biographical material supplied by Škoviera.

15 See the opposing views expressed by Jerzy Axer and Stefan Zabłocki as cited by Urbański, *Theologia Fabulosa*, 7.

16 Urbański, *Theologia Fabulosa*, 8. Polish critics traditionally dismissed the Latin writing produced at Cracow during the Renaissance as 'unoriginal' or 'foreign,' and only with the rise in popularity of neo-Latin studies in the 1970s did scholars begin to study the Latin literature of late fifteenth- and early sixteenth-century Poland with the intent of describing its own, specific aesthetic conventions, linking it to pan-European trends, and refusing to subject it to anachronistic national ideals or romantic criticism. I have in mind particularly the work of Maria Cytowska and Stefan Zabłocki, dating, in the case of Cytowska, from as early as the 1960s. Gorzkowski, *Paweł z Krosna*, 25, reports on scholarly work in Poland that continues this trend. Cytowska gives a summary of the research produced in the field of neo-Latin literature in Poland in her booklet *Studia neolatina*, 22–8. See also Ulewicz, 'Hundred Years of Philological Studies,' 935–64.

17 Urbański, *Theologia Fabulosa*, 8.

18 Aside from the mention of literary patronage in studies of the major Polish political figures of the period, I have come across only three articles that touch on the subject, and these are written from the point of view of the patron, and not the poet: Łempicki, 'Mecenat kulturalny w Polsce'; Nadolski, 'Mecenat literacki w dobie odrodzenia'; and Pelc and Tomkiewicz, 'Rola mecenatu.' See the entry for 'mecenat' by Pelc and Tomkiewicz in Michałowska, *Słownik literatury staropolskiej*, 538.

19 Bernstein, 'From Outsiders to Insiders'; Bernstein, 'Group Identity Formation'; Bernstein, 'Humanistische Standeskultur.'

20 Treml, *Humanistische Gemeinschaftsbildung;* Schirrmeister, *Triumph des Dichters.*

21 Kaufmann, *Court, Cloister, and City*, Tönnesmann, 'Anfänge der Renaissancearchitektur in Deutschland'; Farbaky, 'György Szatmári'; Popp and Suckale, *Die Jagiellonen.*

22 See the bibliography.

23 Moreover, the work of these Polish poets has already been covered in a monograph in English, Segel's *Renaissance Culture in Poland.* For information in English on the vernacular literature produced during the Renaissance in Poland, see Krzyżanowski, *History of Polish Literature*, and Miłosz, *History of Polish Literature.*

CHAPTER ONE

PATRONAGE AND HUMANIST LITERATURE AT CRACOW, 1510–1530

1 For variants of personal names, see appendix 2.

2 By 'Poland,' I mean Poland-Lithuania, two countries united through a personal union (Union of Krewo) in 1385, when the Lithuanian prince Jogaila (Jagiełło) agreed to marry the Polish princess Jadwiga and take the Polish throne. This personal association would become a political union in 1569, with the Union of Lublin.

Because the material in this book is somewhat unfamiliar to an anglophone audience, I have felt the need to accompany the text with extensive documentation. I have done this also in the hope that others may follow with research into the fascinating region of east central Europe and its history.

3 For the history of Poland in this period, I have relied on Davies, *God's Playground;* Łowmiański, *Polityka Jagiellonów;* and Halecki, *History of Poland.* Bogucka's *Dawna Polska* and *Historia Polski do 1864 roku* have also been useful, as have Johnson's *Central Europe* and the biographical sketches of the Jagiellonian kings in Duczmal, *Jagiellonowie.* Stangler and Stolot, *Polen im Zeitalter der Jagiellonen* is an excellent introduction to all aspects of sixteenth-century Polish history and culture, and is supplemented by Popp and Suckale's more recent *Die Jagiellonen.*

4 Pelc and Tomkiewicz, 'Rola mecenatu,' 173.

5 Białostocki, *Art of the Renaissance in Eastern Europe,* 10.

6 On the Polish economy of the sixteenth century, see Wyrobisz, 'Economic Landscapes'; Bogucka, 'Towns of East-Central Europe'; Mączak, 'Polish Society'; Mączak, 'Poland'; and Wyczański, *Polska w Europie XVI stulecia,* 23–72.

7 Tönnesmann, 'Anfänge der Renaissancearchitektur in Deutschland,' 301.

8 On Sigismund's patronage of the arts, see Lewalski, 'Sigismund I of Poland,' and Fabiański, 'Art and Architecture of the Renaissance in Kraków,' 141–52.

9 Białostocki, *Art of the Renaissance in Eastern Europe,* 10; Kaufmann, *Court, Cloister, and City,* 54; Miłobędzki, 'Architecture under the Last Jagiellons,' 292.

10 The rebuilding of the castle and its decoration are described by Białostocki, *Art of the Renaissance in Eastern Europe,* 18–27. Sigismund's patronage of the artefacts that filled the chapel is detailed by Bochnak, 'Mecenat Sigismunda Starego,' 131–301.

11 Kaufmann, *Court, Cloister, and City,* 54.

12 Białostocki, *Art of the Renaissance in Eastern Europe*, 35–44, describes the construction of the chapel and gives an analysis of its iconography.
13 Kaufmann, *Court, Cloister, and City*, 57.
14 Morka, 'Political Meaning of the Sigismund Chapel,' 33.
15 Lewalski, 'Sigismund I of Poland,' 59–61. Some of the expenditures on the chapel as detailed in the account books of Seweryn (Severin) Boner are given by Popiel, 'Czynności artystyczne na dworze Zygmunta I.' The most complete account of the building of the chapel has been recorded in Franaszek and Przybyszewski, *Kaplica Sigismundowska.*
16 Białostocki, *Art of the Renaissance in Eastern Europe*, 9; Rekettyés, *Stosunki polityczne*, 57–96; Tönnesmann, 'Anfänge der Renaissancearchitektur in Deutschland,' 299–300, 313.
17 Kaufmann, *Court, Cloister, and City*, 57.
18 Komornicki, 'Kultura artystyczna,' 572–3.
19 Miłobędzki, 'Architecture under the Last Jagiellons,' 294.
20 Szablowski, 'Architektura,' 41.
21 Kozakiewiczowa, 'Mecenat Jana Łaskiego,' 8; Białostocki, *Art of the Renaissance in Eastern Europe*, 45–6.
22 Schulz, *Giammaria Mosca*, 97, remarks that the former attribution of the tomb sculpture to Padovano has been effectively refuted. Still, she states, it is impossible to prove that Berrecci was the designer.
23 Białostocki, *Art of the Renaissance in Eastern Europe*, 49.
24 Schulz, *Giammaria Mosca*, 121; Białostocki, *Art of the Renaissance in Eastern Europe*, 52; Komornicki, 'Kultura artystyczna,' 561. Kieszkowski, *Kanclerz Krzysztof Szydłowiecki* gives a thorough account of Szydłowiecki's life and times, as well as his artistic patronage.
25 Lewalski, 'Sigismund I of Poland,' 67, 69; Pelc and Tomkiewicz, 'Rola mecenatu,' 171.
26 The notion of Bona herself as an active patron of the arts has been challenged by Polish historians. See Komornicki, 'Kultura artystyczna,' 550–1, and Kozakiewiczowa, 'Mecenat Jana Łaskiego,' 3.
27 For a description of the function of the royal secretary during the reign of Sigismund I, see Wyczański, *Między kulturą i polityką.*
28 Pelc and Tomkiewicz, 'Rola mecenatu,' 172–3. Although its literary criticism is now outdated, Nowak-Dłużewski, *Okolicznościowa poezja polityczna* is still useful as a reference work on the political poetry of sixteenth-century Poland. Segel, *Renaissance Culture in Poland* covers the poetry of Dantiscus and Krzycki, as well as that of the minor poets Paul of Krosno (Paulus Crosnensis) and John of Wiślica (Johannes Visliciensis).
29 The third section of Decius's work has come out in a modern edition, *De Sigismundi Regis temporibus liber, 1521*, edited by Czermak, as well as a Polish translation, Decjusz, *Księga o czaszch Króla Zygmunta*, introduction by Bieńkowski.

30 Tomkiewicz, 'Przełom renesansowy,' 13.

31 Bieńkowski, introduction to Decjusz, *Księgu o czasach Króla Zygmunta*, 10.

32 Knoll, *Rise of the Polish Monarchy*, 5–6; Michałowska, *Średniowiecze*, 105.

33 Decius, *De uetustatibus*, A2r (original 1521 edition). Decius himself stated only that he had composed the text in order to record the details of Sigismund's reign for future generations.

34 Decius, *De Sigismundi Regis temporibus liber, 1521*, ed. Czermak, 11–16.

35 Miodońska, 'Władca i państwo,' 48.

36 Gundel (1493–1567) was in Cracow at the time, having fled the plague. He had been appointed professor of poetics at Vienna after the chair was vacated by Joachim Vadian in 1518. In Cracow he began to study law, but he was back in Vienna by 1514. He then became professor of law, a post he held until his death. He also served as dean of his faculty (1530) and rector of the university (1540). He became a protégé of the Habsburg king Ferdinand I (Aschbach, *Geschichte der Wiener Universität*, 2: 319–26).

37 Tomkiewicz, 'Przełom renesansowy,' 15.

38 Miodońska, 'Władca i państwo,' 50–5.

39 Kaufmann, *Court, Cloister, and City*, 52: 'On the whole the support for monumental ... architecture, sculpture and wall paintings at fixed residences in Prague and Kraków contrasts with the patronage of the peripatetic court of Maximilian I, particularly for the graphic media and to a degree painting.'

40 Knoll, 'University Context,' 190–1. On the participation of the Polish delegates at Basel, see Knoll, 'University of Cracow and the Conciliar Movement.'

41 For a summary of Callimachus's activities in Poland, see Segel, *Renaissance Culture in Poland*, 36–82, and Kotarska, 'Poeta i historyk.' Fuller biographies are Olkiewicz, *Kallimach Doświadczony*, a popular treatment of the subject, and Paparelli, *Callimacho Esperiente.* A conference on Callimachus and his work was held in Italy in October 1985; the papers have been published as Garfagnini, *Callimaco Esperiente.*

42 For further details on the contact of the Cracow elite with Erasmus, see Glomski, 'Erasmus and Cracow (1510–1530).'

43 Among them were Justus Ludovicus Decius (in 1522), Jan Boner (in 1531), and Bishop Tomicki's great-nephew Andrzej Zebrzydowski (in 1528). For information, see Cytowska's preface and notes to Erasmus, *Korespondencja Erazma z Rotterdamu z Polakami.*

44 These were to Justus Ludovicus Decius, *Precatio Dominica* (Basel, 1523); to Hieronim Łaski, *Modus orandi Deum* (Basel, 1524) and *Institutio Christiani matrimonii* (Basel, 1526); to Johannes Antoninus (Jan Antonin), *Galen* (Basel, 1526); to Krzysztof Szydłowiecki, *Lingua* (Basel, 1525); to Jan Łaski Senior, *Diui Ambrosii opera omnia* (Basel,

1527); to Piotr Tomicki, *Senecae opera* (Basel, 1529); to Jan Boner (son of Severin) and his brother Stanisław, *Terentii comoediae* (Basel, 1532); and to Johannes Dantiscus, *Diui Basilii opus de Spiritu Sancto* (Basel, 1532). The dates given are those of the *editio princeps*. The following were reprinted at Cracow: *Modus orandi Deum* (1525); *Precatio Dominica* (1525); *Lingua* (1526).

45 A succinct explanation of the functioning of the Polish government and of the responsibilities of its officials in the sixteenth century is given by Bardach and Wyczański, 'Staat und Herrscher in Polen,' 16–28. The chancellor and vice-chancellor were in charge of the royal chancellery, which was responsible for conducting diplomatic correspondence, preparing final editions of the decisions of the Sejm (Parliament), making out legal records in the name of the king, and so on.

46 For Tomicki's biography, see Bietenholz and Deutscher, *Contemporaries of Erasmus*, 3: 327–9, and Hajdukiewicz, *Księgozbiór i zainteresowania bibliofilskie Piotra Tomickiego*. (I cite Hajdukiewicz with hesitation as it contains errors.)

47 For Szydłowiecki's biography, see Bietenholz and Deutscher, *Contemporaries of Erasmus*, 3: 304–5.

48 Szydłowiecki's patronage of the arts is covered by Kieszkowski, *Kanclerz Krzysztof Szydłowiecki*, 317–516. On Stanisław Samostrzelnik and the illuminations produced by his workshop for Tomicki and Szydłowiecki, see Miodońska, 'Buchmalerei in Polen,' 229–30, 251–4.

49 Schulz, *Giammaria Mosca*, 90; Pociecha, *Królowa Bona*, 2: 53; Quirini-Popławska, *Działalność włochów w Polsce*, 11–12, 32; Bogucka, *Bona Sforza*, 76–91.

50 A detailed history of Cracow is Bieniarzówna and others, *Dzieje Krakowa*. On the status of the German burghers at Cracow in the Renaissance, see Friedrich, 'Cives Cracoviae.' Samsonowicz, 'Gesellschaftliche Pluralität' describes the multicultural make-up of Cracow.

51 Bietenholz and Deutscher, *Contemporaries of Erasmus*, 1: 380–2; *Polski słownik biograficzny*, 5: 42–5; Bonorand, *Vadians Humanisten Korrespondenz*, 45–9.

52 See Budka, 'Bibljoteka Decjusza.'

53 On the Boner family and their associates, see Ptaśnik, 'Bonerowie.' On Severin, see Bietenholz and Deutscher, *Contemporaries of Erasmus*, 1: 167–8. Morawski, *Czasy Zygmuntowskie*, 1–32, gives examples of Severin's literary patronage. On the Bethmann family, see Ptaśnik, *Obrazki z przeszłości Krakowa*, 1–15, and *Polski słownik biograficzny*, 1: 477–8. The history of the Salomon family is given by Bukowski, 'Salomonowie herbu Łabędź.' See also Bonorand, *Vadians Humanisten Korrespondenz*, 170–3.

54 For variants of place names, see appendix 2.

55 Lambrecht, 'Communicating Europe to the Region,' 1–5.

56 On the Thurzó family, see Lambrecht, 'Aufstiegschancen und Handlungsräume'; Bathelt, 'Familie Thurzo'; Ptaśnik, 'Turzonowie w Polsce'; and Lepszy, 'Turzonowie w Polsce.'

57 For the place names of this region, I use the Hungarian versions in the text. The Slovakian and German equivalents are given in appendix 2. On the multi-ethnic composition of the Hungarian kingdom at the end of the fifteenth century, see Domonkos, 'The Multiethnic Character of the Hungarian Kingdom.'

58 Bathelt, 'Familie Thurzo,' 121.

59 Two publications, *Rudimenta grammatices Donati*, a traditional Latin grammar edited by Christopher Hegendorf and János Sylvester, and *Puerilium colloquiorum formulae*, a Latin phrasebook compiled by Sebald Heyden and János Sylvester, both printed by the Vietor press at Cracow in 1527, attest to the learning of Latin across a region of three vernaculars. Both books were printed in Latin, with German, Polish, and Hungarian explanations/translations. They have been reprinted in facsimile as Melich, *A két legrégibb magyar nyelvű nyomtatvány*.

60 Borsa, 'Polnischungarischen Beziehungen,' 117–18.

61 Kawecka-Gryczowa, *Drukarze dawnej Polski*, 327–8; a detailed account of the output of the Vietor press in Vienna is given by Bułhak, 'Wiedeńska oficyna Hieronima Wietora.'

62 For the patronage of Stanislaus Thurzó and Augustinus Moravus, see Wörster, *Humanismus in Olmütz*.

63 Eck, *Iubilus heroicus*, printed with the author's *Apophoreticum carmen de Christi natiuitate*, dedicated to Alexius Thurzó (Cracow: Hieronymus Vietor, 1520); Eck, *Panegyricus in laudem praestantissimi uiri doctoris Augustini Moraui* (Cracow: Florian Ungler, 1513).

64 See Farbaky, 'György Szatmári.'

65 Kavka, *Caroline University*, 22–3, and Pešek, 'Výuka a humanismus na pražské univerzitě,' 227–9. Vladislav moved his court from Prague to Buda in 1490, and Louis continued to govern his Czech lands remotely – he visited Prague only once during his reign (1522–3). In any case, the university at Prague, dominated by the Utraquist sect at the beginning of the sixteenth century, was too embroiled in religious matters to play host to the new intellectual movement.

66 See Domonkos, 'Ecclesiastical Patrons.' Even during the reign of the Jagiellonians' predecessor, Matthias Corvinus, at Buda, Renaissance patronage of the arts was centred not just at the royal court, but also at the courts of the bishops outside the capital.

67 Wyczański, *Między kulturą a polityką*, 96, notes that over a third of Sigismund I's secretaries wrote literature of some sort at one time or another. He claims that they were rivalled in output only by the scholar-poets connected with the university.

68 Printed subsequently in 1529, 1538, 1539. Bieńkowski, 'Naukowe

środowisko krakowskie,' 27, 30; Wyczański, *Między kulturą a polityką*, 109.

69 *Sendbrieff von der grossen schlacht ... am XXVII tag Januarii des 1527 Jars* ... (Nuremberg, 1527); *De monetae cussione* (1526); *Warum das Geld im Lande teuer werde* (1530–3). *De monetae cussione* remained in manuscript during Decius's lifetime, but was published, with a Polish translation, as Dmochowski, *Mikołaja Kopernika Rozprawy ... oraz J. L. Decjusza Traktat o biciu monety*. *Warum das Geld*, to my knowledge, has never been printed.

70 For brief biographies of Dantiscus, see Bietenholz and Deutscher, *Contemporaries of Erasmus*, 1: 377, and *Polski słownik biograficzny*, 4: 424–30. See also Segel, *Renaissance Culture in Poland*, 161–90, and Vocht, *John Dantiscus*. Nowak, *Jan Dantyszek* is a full-length biography of Dantiscus. The most recent edition of Dantiscus's work is Dantiscus, *Ioannis Dantisci Carmina*, ed. Skimina. For literary criticism, see Nowak, 'Polityk, poeta i duchowny,' 344–76.

71 For details of Krzycki's life, see *Polski słownik biograficzny*, 15: 544–9, and Bietenholz and Deutscher, *Contemporaries of Erasmus*, 2: 275–8. His *oeuvre* has been edited as Krzycki, *Andreae Cricii Carmina*, ed. Morawski; a Polish translation is Krzycki, *Poezje*, ed. Jelicz. For literary criticism, see Jelicz, 'Dichtung des Andreas Cricius,' and Gruchała, 'Zmarnowany talent – Andrzej Krzycki.'

72 Backvis, 'Fortune d'Érasme en Pologne,' 184–5, cites Erasmus's letter to Krzycki of 17 May 1527 (Allen, Ep. 1822).

73 The University of Cracow is commonly known in Poland as the Jagiellonian University because it was refounded during the reign of Władysław Jagiełło. In the early sixteenth century, it was called 'Academia Cracoviensis.' In his correspondence with Vadian (see chapter 2), Agricola Junior referred to it as 'Gymnasium Cracoviense.'

74 Bieniarzówna and others, *Dzieje Krakowa*, 19. Student life in late fifteenth- and early sixteenth-century Cracow is described by Ptaśnik, *Życie żaków krakowskich*; Karbowiak, *Mieszkania żaków krakowskich*; and Karbowiak, *Ubiory profesorów*.

75 On the early history of the University of Cracow in English, see Knoll, 'Arts Faculty at the University of Cracow'; Knoll, 'Italian Humanism in Poland'; and Knoll, 'University Context,' 189–212. In French, see Morawski, *Histoire de l'Université de Cracovie*. In German, see Pirożyński, 'Krakauer Universität in der Renaissancezeit,' and Moraw, 'Hohe Schule in Krakau.' In Polish, see Henryk Barycz, *Historja Uniwersytetu Jagiellońskiego*, and Lepszy, *Dzieje Uniwersytetu Jagiellońskiego*. The history of the study of astonomy and astrology at Cracow during the Middle Ages and Renaissance is given in Rybka, *Historia astronomii w Polsce*.

76 Markowski, 'Nauki wyzwolone i filozofia na Uniwersytecie Krak-

owskim,' 101. Hartmann Schedel referred thus to the university in his *Liber chronicarum* (Nuremberg, 1493): 'Celebre gymnasium multis clarissimis doctissimisque viris pollens, ubi plurimae ingenuae artes recitantur: studium eloquentiae, poetices, philosophiae ac physices. Astronomiae tamen studium maxime viret.'

77 The arts faculty had undergone reforms in 1449 and 1475 that enlarged the corpus of ancient authors and admitted modern, humanist authors to the curriculum. Domański, *Początki humanizmu*, 51–135, in his discussion of the reception of Italian humanist writing by the Cracow professors as evidenced by their reading and writing, questions whether these reforms were motivated by an actual change in attitude towards the literature of antiquity and of the Italian humanists (pp. 104–5). Szelińska, *Biblioteki profesorów*, 44–94, notes that the work of Italian humanists was collected by Cracow professors as early as the 1430s, and Domański (p. 100) warns that Italian humanist works were read at that time more as sources of factual knowledge than out of admiration for and a desire to imitate the new style based on classical authors. Neither Domański nor Szelińska notes real changes in the intellectual culture at the University of Cracow until the 1470s and 1480s.

78 *Poeta* is the term the scholar-poets commonly used when identifying themselves and their occupation; it was the title they gave themselves when lecturing at a university. For someone who had been crowned poet laureate, the title *poeta laureatus* was de rigueur.

79 Garbacik, 'Ognisko nauki i kultury renesansowej,' 193.

80 The situation was the same at the German universities, where an external ecclesiastical officer served as chancellor, upon whose cooperation rested the authority to grant degrees (Nauert, 'Humanist Challenge,' 292).

81 Garbacik, 'Ognisko nauki i kultury renesansowej,' 200, accuses Konarski and Tomicki of attempting to 'liquidate' the radical humanist currents at the university. The experience of Rudolf Agricola Junior, however, does not provide direct evidence of this. The ecclesiarchs did not refuse Agricola monetary support altogether; rather, they put pressure on him to take holy orders and accept a benefice. (See chapter 2.) Barycz, 'Nowa synteza,' 307–9, counters Garbacik's viewpoint, noting that Jan Łaski Senior, Jan Konarski, and Piotr Tomicki all attempted to 'modernize' the university in the first quarter of the sixteenth century.

82 Müller, 'Humanismus und Universität,' 267–8; Samsonowicz, 'Gesellschaftliche Pluralität,' 122.

83 Barycz, *Historja Uniwersytetu Jagiellońskiego*, 113–15; Janik, *Dzieje szkolnictwa polskiego*, 9. See also Karbowiak, 'Studya statystyczne z dziejów Uniwersytetu Jagiellónskiego.'

84 Bauch, *Deutsche Scholaren in Krakau*, 4–15.

85 This was typical at the German universities. See Nauert, 'Humanist Challenge,' 278–80.

86 On Celtis in Poland, see Jelicz, *Konrad Celtis*, and Segel, *Renaissance Culture in Poland*, 83–106. On his life and works in general, see Spitz, *Conrad Celtis*; Wuttke, 'Conradus Celtis Protucius'; and Robert, *Konrad Celtis und das Projekt der deutschen Dichtung*.

87 On Corvinus, see Bauch, 'Laurentius Corvinus.'

88 For a biography of Bebel and a bibliography of the early printings of his works, see Zapf, *Heinrich Bebel*, and Graf, 'Henrich Bebel.' See also Bebermeyer, *Tübinger Dichterhumanisten*, and Overfield, *Humanism and Scholasticism*, 145–51.

89 *Polski słownik biograficzny*, 25: 384–6; Segel, *Renaissance Culture in Poland*, 109–19; Cytowska, 'Twórczość Pawła z Krosna,' 512–13. See also the introduction by Kruczkiewicz to Paulus Crosnensis, *Pauli Crosnensis ... Ioannisque Visliciensis Carmina*. The most recent work on Paulus, a much needed monograph, is Gorzkowski, *Paweł z Krosna*.

90 Agricola Junior and Eck were not Swiss, a mistake that many sources continue to print. They came from Wasserburg and Lindau, respectively, on the north shore of Lake Constance. For biographical information on Agricola, I have relied on Aschbach, *Geschichte der Wiener Universität*, 141–5; Bauch, 'Rudolphus Agricola Junior'; Morawski, *Histoire de l'Université de Cracovie*, 3: 107–10; Barycz, *Historja Uniwersytetu Jagiellońskiego*, 31–7; *Polski słownik biograficzny*, 1: 32; Bonorand, *Personenkommentar II*, 216–17; and Vredeveld, 'Agricola, Rudolf d. J.,' 732–57. When referring to 'Agricola' in this book, I mean 'Agricola Junior,' and not the Dutch Rudolph Agricola (1443/4–85), author of *De inuentione dialectica* (1479). On Eck, see Bauch, 'Valentin Eck und Georg Werner'; Klenner, *Eck Bálint*; and *Polski słownik biograficzny*, 6: 198–9.

91 The conflict between humanist and anti-humanist factions at Leipzig is described by Bauch, *Geschichte des Leipziger Frühhumanismus*; Overfield, *Humanism and Scholasticism*, 222–41; and Rummel, *Humanist-Scholastic Debate*, 63–74.

92 Cox's date of birth is unknown. Although Breeze, 'Leonard Cox,' 399–410, gives his place of birth as Monmouth in Wales, Ryle, 'English Humanist in Eastern Europe,' 223–31, notes that Cox gave his place of origin as Thame in Oxfordshire on the matriculation records of both Tübingen and Cracow. For further information on Cox's life, see Zins, 'British Humanist,' and Bietenholz and Deutscher, *Contemporaries of Erasmus*, 1: 353–4. Cox is also mentioned by Morawski, *Histoire de l'Université de Cracovie*, 3: 119–20, and Barycz, *Historja Uniwersytetu Jagiellońskiego*, 45–9, and has an entry in *Polski słownik biograficzny*, 4: 98–9, and, most recently, in the *Oxford Dictionary of National Biography*,

13: 854–6, by Ryle. On Cox's time at Cracow, see also Barycz, *Szlakami dziejopisarstwa staropolskiego*, 138–44.

93 '[H]unc libellum quem olim mecum ex Germania deportaui hilaro uulto fronteque serena' (Maffeo Vegio, *Philalethes*. Cracow: Florian Ungler, 1512).

94 The date is uncertain, but is given in IISTC as 1489?–97? The edition was by Paul Schneevogel (Niavis) (*c*. 1460–*c*. 1514). See Rupprich, *Humanismus und Renaissance*, 44.

95 The edition of Cleofilo was by Andreas Boner (Arnold Woestfeld) (Overfield, *Humanism and Scholasticism*, 225). The edition of Mancinelli is recorded as VD16, M508. Agricola Junior's edition of *De componendis uersibus*, supposedly printed by the Ungler press, has apparently been lost; there is no known copy in existence (Vredeveld, 'Agricola, Rudolf d. J.,' 739).

96 Adriano Castellesi, *Venatio una cum scholiis non ineruditis Leonardi Coxi Britanni* (Cracow: Hieronymus Vietor, 1524).

97 On the bee metaphor, see Stackelberg, 'Das Bienengleichnis,' 271–93; Waszink, *Biene und Honig*; Pigman, 'Barzizza's Treatise on Imitation,' 341–52; and Domański, 'O dwu znaczeniach metafory pszczoły,' 57–72.

98 'Carmina edituro ante omnia operae pretium erit uidere libros ab optimis probatissimisque latinae linguae auctoribus editos ... Sic enim Maro uiuum quasi nobis carmen reliquit. Sic Naso in transformatis res per uera et propria epitheta expressit. Sic Horatius res uarias concinne effinxit. Id enim solum est quo uiuax et propria redditur oratio et res scripta sensibilius quasi signis lectoris animum afficit' (*De arte uersificandi opusculum*. Cracow: Florian Ungler, 1515; Cracow: Hieronymus Vietor, 1521, 1539).

99 Škoviera, *Bardejovčan Valentín Ecchius*, 121–5; Mielczarski, *Humanistyczna sztuka wierszowania*, 53–4.

100 Robertus de Euremodio, *Institutiones uitae* (Cracow: Johannes Haller, 1519). Agricola Junior relied on the edition of the sayings of Cato compiled by the fifteenth-century French monk Robertus de Euremodio (Robert d'Envermeuil). See Cosenza, *Biographical and Bibliographical Dictionary of the Italian Humanists* 4: 3068.

101 Cicero, *Pro Archia poeta* (Cracow: Hieronymus Vietor, 1518); Cicero, *Pro rege Deiotaro* (Cracow: Hieronymus Vietor, 1518).

102 *An prudenti uiro sit ducenda uxor* (Cracow: Johannes Haller, 1518; Hieronymus Vietor, 1524).

103 For a discussion of the literary tradition of this topic, see Herrmann, *Albrecht von Eyb*, 315–27, and Melczer, 'Albrecht von Eyb,' 36–7.

104 Poggio's treatise, which circulated in manuscript, was composed in 1437 but not printed until the early nineteenth century. See Bracciolini, *Poggius Bracciolini Opera omnia*, ed. Fubini, 677. Szelińska, *Biblioteki profesorów* mentions that manuscripts of Poggio's works were

owned by scholars at Cracow in the late fifteenth and early sixteenth centuries. She notes that Poggio was present at the Council of Constance, to which the Poles sent a delegation (p. 288).

105 Barbaro's treatise was composed in the early fifteenth century but first printed in Paris in 1513, five years before Eck wrote his poem (Barbaro, *Francisci Barbari De re uxoria liber*, ed. Gnesotto, 14–15, 18–20; Gothei, *Francesco Barbaro*, 88–9).

106 Antonio Bonfini spent time at Buda during the reigns of Matthias Corvinus and Vladislav II and served as court historian. His *Symposion*, whose interlocutors have the names of historical figures of the Buda court, has been dated to *c.* 1484. The work remained in manuscript until 1572, when it was printed at Basel. See Bonfinis, *Symposion*, ed. Apró.

107 Von Eyb's Latin writings, *Clarissimarum feminarum laudatio* (1459), *Inuecta in lenam* (1459), and *An uxor uiro sapienti sit ducenda* (1460), remained in manuscript, and his vernacular *Ehebuch* appeared in print first in 1471. See Herrmann, *Albrecht von Eyb*; Hiller, *Albrecht von Eyb*; and Eyb, *Ob einem manne sey zunemen ein eelichs weyb oder nicht*, ed. Weinacht.

108 On Rybisch's activities at Leipzig, see Foerster, 'Heinrich und Seyfried Ribisch,' 183–7.

109 Zabłocki, 'Poezja polsko-łacińska wczesnego renesansu,' 75, notes that Paulus was an influence specifically on Agricola.

110 'Grata Valentino praecordia, grata uoluntas / Cui uitam curae est instituisse rudem, / Qui nunquam ad Cyprias calamum conuertere fraudes, / Scribere nec luxum, mollis Asote, solet' (Cracow: Hieronymus Vietor, 1519).

111 On the values of the educational program of the German humanists, see Treml, *Humanistische Gemeinschaftsbildung*, 107–11.

112 Agricola referred to Corvinus as his teacher in his edition of Octavius Cleophilus Phanensis's *De poetarum coetu libellus* (Cracow: Florian Ungler, 1511) and his preface to Caspar Ursinus Velius's *Epistolarum et epigrammatum liber* (Vienna: Johannes Singrenius, 1517), and referred to Celtis as 'Celtis meus' in the preface to his edition of Robertus de Euremodio's *Institutiones uitae*. Eck quoted from the works of Celtis, Bebel, and Corvinus in his handbook on versification, and Cox praised all three poets in his address to the University of Cracow in December 1518 (*De laudibus celeberrimae Cracouiensis Academiae oratio*. Cracow: Hieronymus Vietor, 1518). See Glomski, 'German Role,' 31–44. Zabłocki, *Od prerenesansu do oświecenia*, 118–23, cites Celtis, for example, as the source of the stereotyped description of Poland as a northern country of eternal frost. This motif is found in Agricola's *Hymnus de diuo praesule et martyre Stanislao* (Cracow: Hieronymus Vietor, 1519).

113 Cooper, '*Mecenatismo* or *Clientelismo*?' 31.

114 I rely here on the notion of the early sixteenth-century humanists of central Europe as 'outsiders' and on the concept of their program of self-promotion as developed by Bernstein in 'From Outsiders to Insiders,' 45–64, and 'Group Identity Formation,' 375–86. Schirrmeister, *Triumph des Dichters*, also makes the point that the poets had to 'position themselves in the field of literature' by representing themselves as 'humanists' in their writing, and had to engage the help of powerful political figures through their power-legitimizing panegyrics if they were to secure economic support.

115 Boehm, 'Humanistiche Bildungsbewegung,' 327–8, 334–9; Overfield, *Humanism and Scholasticism*, 226–7, 242–4; Nauert,'Humanist Challenge,' 294, 305. The patronage of German humanist scholars differed from that of the Parisian humanists during the same period. Humanist scholars at Paris found support from French bishops and dedicated only a few of their books to influential laymen, these being mostly royal officers belonging to the new nobility. The majority of their book dedications went not to patrons but to other Parisian scholars. See Rice, 'Patrons of French Humanism,' 687–702.

116 Müller, 'Humanismus und Universität,' 249.

117 See Segel, *Renaissance Culture in Poland*, 119–26.

118 Both Dantiscus's and Eck's works would be reprinted in 1515 at Rome as part of an anthology of works on the battle, entitled *Carmina de memorabili caede scismaticorum Moscouiorum* ... (place and date supplied by Jan Łaski's dedicatory letter to the king).

119 Segel, *Renaissance Culture in Poland*, 119–26.

120 Cracow: Johannes Haller, 1518.

121 On Drzewicki, see *Polski słownik biograficzny*, 5: 409–12; on Konarski, see *Polski słownik biograficzny*, 13: 458–61; on Łaski, see Bietenholz and Deutscher, *Contemporaries of Erasmus*, 2: 296–97, and *Polski słownik biograficzny*, 18: 229–37.

122 Cracow: Vietor, 1521.

123 *Vadianische Briefsammlung* I, 11 (Cracow, 1511).

124 Johannes Aesticampianus, also referred to as Aesticampianus the Elder, is not to be confused with Johannes Rhagius Aesticampianus (the Younger). On these two scholars, see chapter 2.

125 Kawecka-Gryczowa, *Drukarze dawnej Polski*, 328.

126 *Polski słownik biograficzny*, 6: 357–8. Later generations of sixteenth-century intellectuals regarded Michael as a symbol of obscurantism. His work is now considered a bridge between scholasticism and the new learning.

127 Agricola Junior also wrote a poem to Michael, which he, Agricola, attached to the 1515 printing of his oration welcoming Piotr Tomicki to Vienna. Unfortunately, no copy of this edition is extant. See Vredeveld, 'Agricola, Rudolf d. J.,' 739.

128 *De diuo Casimiro carmen elegiacum* (Cracow: Florian Ungler, 1511).

There are now no copies extant. See *Polski słownik biograficzny,* 1: 32, and Vredeveld, 'Agricola, Rudolf d. J.,' 739.

129 The book is basically a reworking of Martin Waldseemüller's *Cosmographiae instructio* (Saint Dié, 1507), which contained the first printed map with the name 'America' on it. Stobnica's book included a smaller version (*Polski słownik biograficzny*, 10: 480). In his dedicatory preface, Stobnica stated that he wished to make known parts of the world that had been discovered by Amerigo Vespucci and others.

130 *Polski słownik biograficzny*, 10: 480–1.

131 *Polski słownik biograficzny*, 18: 81–4.

132 *Polski słownik biograficzny*, 21: 144–5.

133 *Polski słownik biograficzny*, 21: 138–40; Barycz, *Szlakami dziejopisarstwa staropolskiego*, 141–51.

134 *Vadianische Briefsammlung* II, 196, 216, 225, 240.

135 Bauch, 'Rudolphus Agricola Junior,' 12 (citing the work of the eighteenth-century Polish bibliographer Jan Daniel Janocki), lists Agricola as having, at Cracow in 1514, dedicated an edition of Filippo Beroaldo's *An orator sit philosopho et medico anteponendus* to Krzysztof Szydłowiecki. No copy of this book is extant. See Vredeveld, 'Agricola, Rudolf d. J.,' 739.

136 Vadian would serve as rector during the winter term 1516–17 and would be given the chair of rhetoric in 1516. On Vadian, see Bietenholz and Deutscher, *Contemporaries of Erasmus*, 3: 364–5. A full-length biography is Näf, *Vadian und seine Stadt*.

137 On Bartholinus, see Füssel, *Riccardus Bartholinus Perusinus*.

138 Agricola's oration may have been printed separately in Vienna in 1515, but no copy has come to light (Vredeveld, 'Agricola, Rudolf d. J.,' 739). Bauch, 'Rudolphus Agricola Junior,' 18, identifies Agricola's edition of Prudentius's *Cathemerinon* (Vienna: Hieronymus Vietor, 1515) as belonging to the publications connected with the Congress of 1515, as it was a lavish printing, complete with musical score by the organist Wolfgang Grafinger, and was dedicated to Sebastian Sprenz, the provost of Brixen (Bressanone) and secretary to Cardinal Lang.

139 Vredeveld, 'Agricola, Rudolf d. J.,' 732.

140 Bauch, 'Rudolphus Agricola Junior,' 16. The poem was printed in the collection of Ursinus Velius's verses *Epistolarum et epigrammatum liber* (Vienna: Johannes Singrenius, 1517) and reprinted in his *Poematum libri quinque* (Basel: Froben, 1522). Ursinus Velius's poems recount the convivialities organized by the humanists at Vienna; Agricola is listed as among those attending.

141 On the positive effect of the laureate's crown on a poet's career both at court and at the university in the Holy Roman Empire, see Mertens, 'Zu Sozialgeschichte und Funktion,' 327–48.

142 Printed at Cracow by the Vietor press at the end of May 1518. Evidently, a poetry competition was organized as part of the wedding festivities. Agricola participated along with Laurentius Corvinus, Caspar Ursinus Velius, Johannes Dantiscus, and others, but his epithalamium has never been found (Bauch, 'Rudolphus Agricola Junior,' 28).

143 *Vadianische Briefsammlung* I, 116. The resulting book was *Soteria*, printed by Haller at Cracow in February 1518. Agricola's contributions were entitled *Ad magnificum dominum Sigismundum de Erberstain ... congratulatio* and *Patria ... domini Sigismundi*. Herberstein's own diary of his travels has been published as Herberstein, *Sigmunds von Herberstein Selbstbiographie 1486 bis 1553*, ed. Karajan; for this particular journey, see pp. 103–33.

144 Barycz, *Szlakami dziejopisarstwa staropolskiego*, 141–4.

145 For a bibliography of Cox's works published at Cracow, see appendix 1.

146 Cox's reception as headmaster at Lőcse (Levoča) is recorded in the town annals; for the text, see Wagner, *Analecta Scepusii*, 2: 140.

147 Allen, Ep. 1803.

148 The unique extant copy of this work was destroyed during the Second World War. It is known to present-day scholars only through descriptions.

149 Zins, ' British Humanist,' 38–9.

150 Cox's activities in England are described by Carpenter in his introduction to Cox, *The Arte or Crafte of Rhetoryke*, 12–18; McConica, *English Humanists*, 140–1, 169–70, 193–4; Ryle, 'English Humanist in Eastern Europe,' 227–8; and Ryle, 'Cox, Leonard.'

151 See Glomski, 'Erasmus and Cracow (1510–1530).'

152 The group included Johannes Lang, Georg von Logau, Georg Werner, Mattheus Holnstein, Johannes Rullus, Matthias Pyrser, Anselm Ephorinus, and Stanislaus Hosius (Stanisław Hozjusz), the future bishop of Warmia.

153 On Łaski Junior, see Bietenholz and Deutscher, *Contemporaries of Erasmus*, 2: 297–301, and *Polski słownik biograficzny*, 18: 237–44.

154 Škoviera, *Bardejovčan Valentín Ecchius* gives Eck's biography based on recent archival research.

155 According to the eighteenth-century Polish bibliographer Johann Daniel Janotzky (Janocki), Eck was invited specifically to Hungary to tutor Thurzó's daughter. Polish sources also claim that Eck returned to Cracow in 1517 to succeed Paul of Krosno (Paulus Crosnensis) as a lecturer at the university. See Bauch, 'Valentin Eck und Georg Werner),' 46.

156 Bietenholz and Deutscher, *Contemporaries of Erasmus*, 3: 322–33. On Piso, see Bietenholz and Deutscher, *Contemporaries of Erasmus*, 3: 94–5.

157 For a bibliography of the works of Eck, see appendix 1.

158 That is, Matthias Pyrser and Johannes Rullus (on whom, see Barycz, *Śląsk w polskiej kulturze*, 41, 79, 123–4, 127–36), as well as Johannes Lang (*Polski słownik biograficzny*, 16: 479) and George von Logau (Georgius Logus) (Bauch, *Deutsche Scholaren in Krakau*; Bietenholz and Deutscher, *Contemporaries of Erasmus*, 2: 338–9).

159 Besides composing poetry, Werner wrote on the geography and ethnography of Hungary. On him, see Bauch, 'Beitrage zur Litteraturgeschichte des schlesischen Humanismus'; Bauch, *Deutsche Scholaren in Krakau*, 75–6; and Bietenholz and Deutscher, *Contemporaries of Erasmus*, 3: 438–9.

CHAPTER TWO
CAREERISM AT CRACOW

1 As mentioned earlier, the notion of the early sixteenth-century humanists of central Europe as 'outsiders' has been developed by Bernstein in his 'From Outsiders to Insiders,' 'Group Identity Formation,' and 'Humanistische Standeskultur'; I rely here on his analysis of the situation in which Agricola Junior, Eck, and Cox found themselves.

2 Bernstein, 'From Outsiders to Insiders,' 59–62.

3 Martin, 'Inventing Sincerity, Refashioning Prudence' discusses the notions of self-fashioning, prudence, and sincerity and their meaning in the Renaissance. See also the introduction to Woods-Marsden, *Renaissance Self-Portraiture*.

4 My findings here – that the *poetae* in general successfully exploited the patronage system – agree with the conclusion arrived at by Schirrmeister in his *Triumph des Dichters*.

5 Clough, 'The Cult of Antiquity,' 33.

6 Henderson, 'On Reading the Rhetoric of the Renaissance Letter,' 149–50.

7 McCahill, 'Finding a Job as a Humanist,' 1314.

8 I rely here on the notions of friendship expressed in humanist letter-writing as developed by Treml, *Humanistische Gemeinschaftsbildung*, 77–81. Schirrmeister, *Triumph des Dichters*, 134–5, 140–1, echoes Treml's statements, but adds that, on the other hand, an established humanist needed to have contacts with younger, less established scholars in order to hold his rank in the *respublica litteraria*.

9 In quoting from the letters of Agricola to Vadian in the notes below, I have retained the orthography used by Arbenz and Wartmann in *Vadianische Briefsammlung*.

10 Näf, *Vadian und seine Stadt*, 1: 196. I summarize Vadian's career as given by Näf.

11 Näf, *Vadianische Analekten*, 27–60, gives a list of Vadian's lectures and publications at Vienna.

12 A group of twelve unmarried masters living in the same house, which had been established by Herzog Albrecht in 1384 as the focal point of higher studies at Vienna.

13 Arbenz reprints an excerpt from Vadian's reply of 16 October 1514 and mistakenly gives it the date 1518, which is that of the first edition of Vadian's commentary on Pomponius Mela; Arbenz was unaware of the first printing of Agricola's letter and Vadian's reply as a pamphlet by Johannes Singrenius at Vienna in 1515. Agricola's letter was reprinted in Vadian's commentary on Pomponius Mela's *De orbis situ libri tres* (Vienna, 1518 and Basel, 1522), and with Dominicus Niger, *Geographiae commentariorum libri XI* (Basel, 1557, as 'Agricolae et Vadiani De nonnullis locis dissertatio'). See Vredeveld, 'Agricola, Rudolf d. J.,' 734, and Näf, *Vadian und seine Stadt*, 1: 197–8. Alicke, 'Vadians Pomponius Mela' makes no mention of either Agricola's letter or Vadian's reply.

14 Cf., for example, Agricola's phrases 'cui in omnibus sis perspicacissimo ingenio' and 'utinam ea mihi divina quadam virgula facultas daretur tecum vivendi, tecum emori vellem,' which appear in *Vadianische Briefsammlung* I, 12 (Cracow, 1511). In subsequent citations of *Vadianische Briefsammlung* in the notes to chapter 2, I use the identifying numbers only.

15 Henderson, 'Humanist Letter Writing,' 21; Henderson, 'On Reading the Rhetoric of the Renaissance Letter,' 146.

16 'Rogo te, mi Vadiane, ignoscas ineptiis meis; cum enim ad te scribo, vix manum contineo; plus enim aequo festinat et quicquid in buccam venit scribo. Elegantius et doctius tibi scriberem, si fuco delibuerem literas, a quo interdum veritas aliena est, et ipse tibi ab amicis displicet, quem non postremum esse me certo certius scio' (II, 165; Cracow, 25 August 1519); and as in his postscript to II, 240 (Cracow, 8 February 1521): 'Parce brevitati et ineptiis subitariis.' Agricola's remarks when complaining to Vadian that he does not write reveal that handing letters over to travellers was the common method of sending them: 'Ut enim mercatorum Vienna Cracoviam proficiscentium turbam taceam: quot uno mense discurrunt, quibus literas tuas facile committeres!' (I, 109; Cracow, 8 December 1517). Agricola mentions giving letters to his compatriots to carry to Vadian in II, 216 (Cracow, 17 September 1520).

17 Bernstein, 'From Outsiders to Insiders,' 59.

18 An example is I, 116 (Cracow, February 1518), where he signed himself 'Rudolfus Agricola, now a northern hunter,' and then remarked that in truth the 'e' and 'n' of the Latin word for hunter (*uenator*) should be replaced by 'o' and 'r' (which changes the word into *uora-*

tor, a 'devourer') ('Rudolfus Agricola, factus venator septentrionis; licet honestatis causa e et n adsumere loco o et r').

19 Bauch, 'Rudolphus Agricola Junior' does not suggest the possibility of Agricola's having met Aesticampianus at Leipzig, where Aesticampianus lectured as professor of rhetoric from 1508 to 1511. Johannes Rhagius Aesticampianus (1457–1520) was a wandering humanist from Sommerfeld in Lusatia who had been a pupil of Celtis at Cracow before going to study in Italy. He taught at Frankfurt a. d. Oder before coming to Leipzig, and he was forced to leave Leipzig because of a conflict with the older masters. On him, see Bauch, *Geschichte des Leipziger Frühhumanismus*, 172–83, and Overfield, *Humanism and Scholasticism*, 238–42. Agricola himself was involved in publishing Erasmus's edition of Jerome's letters by the Vietor press at Cracow in 1519, *Aliquot epistolae diui Eusebii Hieronymi Stridonensis*.

20 Corvinus was the author of three handbooks on Latin composition, *Carminum structura* (1496), *Latina idioma* (1498), and *Hortulus elegantiarum* (1503). On him, see Bauch, 'Laurentius Corvinus,' and Glomski, 'Poetry to Teach the Writing of Poetry.'

21 Agricola wrote the preface and commendatory verses for Filippo Beroaldo, *Modus epistolandi* (Cracow: Florian Ungler, 1512). On the use of Italian manuals of letter-writing at Cracow at this time, see Glomski, 'Italian Influences,' and Glomski, 'Italian Grammarians.'

22 Agricola wrote the preface for Johannes Aesticampianus, *Modus epistolandi* (Vienna: Hieronymus Vietor, 1515; Cracow: Hieronymus Vietor, 1522), and also an epitaph for this elder Aesticampianus, who is not to be confused with the younger, Johannes Rhagius Aesticampianus. The elder Aesticampianus (d. 1501), also from Sommerfeld in Lusatia, taught at Cracow from 1487 until his death, lecturing there on Aristotle and the dialectic, but also dabbling in rhetoric and the new poetics – and teaching the Italian handbooks. On him, see Mielczarski, *Między gramatyką scholastyczną a humanistyczną*. Aesticampianus's own short collection of models for letters was most likely based on Franciscus Niger's *De modo epistolandi*. See Winniczuk, 'Latin Manuals of Epistolography in Poland,' and Morawski, *Histoire de l'Université de Cracovie*, 3: 81–5.

23 Sacranus's *Modus epistolandi* (Cracow: Johannes Haller, 1520) was edited by Stanislaus de Łowicz with commendatory verses by Agricola. Johannes Sacranus Junior (Jan z Oświęcimia młodszy), a member of the faculty of theology at Cracow (from 1491), studied in Italy in the early 1470s, where he possibly attended the lectures of Filelfo. Stanislaus de Łowicz (Stanislaus of Łowicz, Stanisław z Łowicza), Sacranus's student and admirer, worked to improve the study of epistolography at Cracow, where he published an edition of Filelfo's *Epistolae familiares* in 1512 and his own *De arte componendi et resoluendi epistolas libellus*, based on the work of Celtis, in 1521. See Morawski,

Histoire de l'Université de Cracovie, 2: 250–4, 3: 101–2; Barycz, *Historja Uniwersytetu Jagiellońskiego*, 60–1, 177–9; and Winniczuk, 'Latin Manuals of Epistolography in Poland.'

24 Bernstein, 'From Outsiders to Insiders,' 60.

25 I am in agreement here with the views expressed by Henderson, 'Humanist Letter Writing,' 23.

26 McCahill, 'Finding a Job as a Humanist,' 1315–17, describes 'brokers' as powerful humanists or clerics, in intermediary positions, who could facilitate a younger humanist's search for a patron. A broker negotiated between patron and client chiefly by giving proof of the applicant's qualifications.

27 Gray, 'Finding Identity in the Middle Ages,' 17.

28 Spitz, 'Course of German Humanism,' 396.

29 'Crucem tuli puer, crucem adolescens' (realizing that he has to leave Hungary because of the political situation there) (III, 13; Esztergom, October 1514); 'Adolescens sum, multa audire, multa publice et privatim legere possum' (II, 165; Cracow, 25 August 1519).

30 '[Q]uos inter ego nycticorax ad solem, studiosissimus' (III, 11; Esztergom, 21 April? 1514).

31 'Libellus non illepidus' (I, 12; Cracow, 1511). Schirrmeister, *Triumph des Dichters*, 100, describes Agricola's actions of establishing his career by publishing the texts of the Italian humanists and of enhancing his efforts by sending a copy of his Vegio to Vadian as typical of the methods of self-advancement consciously used by the *poetae*. Schirrmeister remarks that Agricola reinforced his 'position in the literary sphere' by accompanying his editions with his own poetry.

32 'Michael testis est, non irrita esse, quae scribo'(III, 3; Cracow, 1511). If these epigrams were ever printed, they have not survived.

33 I, 120 (Cracow, 30 April 1518). This poem has never come to light. See Bauch, 'Rudolphus Agricola Junior,' 28.

34 II, 165 (Cracow, 25 August 1519). These titles were printed at Cracow by the Vietor press in 1518 and 1519, respectively.

35 In letter III, 3 (Cracow, 1511).

36 'Placet mihi Huttenus, qui a facie Lipsig mihi notus fuit' (III, 3); '[E]t ubi Glareano scripseris, nomine ipsum meo non segniter salutato, qui Rotvilae quinquennio paene meus erat condiscipulus' (II, 165; Cracow, 25 August 1519).

37 Agricola had already used the expression *respublica litteraria*, in 1511 (III, 3). The term originated in Italy in the early fifteenth century and spread through Germany. (See Bots and Waquet, *République des Lettres*, 11–13.) Although Agricola probably knew it from the panegyric that Celtis addressed to the duke of Bavaria, attached to his oration to the University of Ingolstadt (printed at Augsburg in 1492), the term might have been commonly heard in Cracow at this time. It appeared in a royal document dating from 1519 granting a stipend to

Marcus a Turri for lectures in theology at the University of Cracow (Wierzbowski, *Materyały do dziejów piśmiennictwa polskiego*, 1: 324).

38 'Tua enim diligentia et studio eos reviviscere facis auctores, qui pulvereo charteoque situ paene marcescebant ... a tetricis dialecticae studiis ferior' (I, 11; Cracow, 1511).

39 I, 11; I, 10 (Cracow, 1511); III, 11 (Esztergom, 21 April? 1514).

40 III, 3 (Cracow, 1511); II, 225 (Cracow, 11 December 1520); III, 13 (Esztergom, October 1514). On Michael Wratislaviensis, see chapter 1; on Steinhofer, who lectured on the classics at Cracow throughout the 1520s, see Bonorand, *Vadians Humanisten Korrespondenz*, 181–2; on Taurinus, a Moravian poet in the service of Cardinal Tamás Bakócz, see Bonorand, *Vadians Humanisten Korrespondenz*, 198–201, and Szörényi, 'L'influenza della Farsaglia di Lucano.'

41 On Cuspinian, see Bonorand, *Personenkommentar II*, 267; on Gundel, see Bonorand, *Joachim Vadian und der Humanismus*, 160–1.

42 'Scribe de Hadelio, quae mira Cracoviae ultra omnes doctos Viennae, quod vel mihi displicet, dicantur' (III, 30; Cracow, 4 January 1518). A couple of months later, Agricola remarked on Hadelius's nasty behaviour towards Vadian: 'Miror Hadelii ingenium, cui male numquam precatus sum, et qua occupatissimum te hominem causa adeat provocetque; quum de eo nihil unquam literis ad me tuis mali scripseris' (I, 120; Cracow, 30 April 1518). Hadelius had been crowned poet laureate in Vienna in 1517. On him, see Wiegand, 'Johannes Hadeke-Hadelius.'

43 'Nostrae farinae' (I, 109; Cracow, 8 December 1517). On Collimitius (I, 110; Cracow, 17 December 1517; I, 116; Cracow, February 1518), a Viennese mathematician and astrologer, see Bonorand, *Personenkommentar II*, 249–54. Suter (II, 150; 13 June 1519) was the director of the von Watt family enterprises in Cracow, according to Bonorand, *Vadians Humanisten Korrespondenz*, 172.

44 I, 120 (Cracow, 30 April 1518); II, 165 (Cracow, 25 August 1519).

45 II, 145 (Cracow, 1 April 1519).

46 'Caeterum scribit ad me Bovillus ex Wittenberga, quam Luther triumphet, quam vir evangelicus sit, quam papa per legatos Romam duci Lutherum vinctum anhelet et omnes libellos eius comburi, quam Fredericus hominem tutetur ...' (II, 240; Cracow, 8 February 1521). On Bovillus, who had been Agricola's student at Cracow, see Bonorand, *Vadians Humanisten Korrespondenz*, 144–5.

47 'Miror, hominem sacris occupatum mysteriis rempublicam litterariam tot iuvare lucubrationibus' (III, 3; Cracow, 1511). On Camers, an Italian who lectured at Vienna from 1497 to 1528, see Bonorand, *Personenkommentar II*, 243–6.

48 III, 3 (Cracow, 1511). On Hutten, who at that time was a guest of Augustinus Moravus in Olomouc, whence he would travel to Vienna

to join the humanist circles there, see Bonorand, *Personenkommentar II*, 315–17.

49 I, 11 (Cracow, 1511); I, 109 (Cracow, 8 December 1517); I, 116 (Cracow, February 1518).

50 'Coepi metum animo volutare, quidnam ... ad te, virum – facessat adulatio – nostrae tempestatis doctissimum politiorumque literarum professorem haud quaquam incelebrem, scripturus sim' (I, 11).

51 '[E]st enim natura insitum mihi, cum his, qui morum elegantia, litteratura, potentia mihi antecellunt, amicitiam inire' (I, 11).

52 I, 12 (Cracow, 1511). The book was printed by Florian Ungler at Cracow in 1512. Two copies are known to exist, at the University of Wrocław Library and at the British Library. It is not listed in Vredeveld, 'Agricola, Rudolf d. J.'

53 III, 3 (Cracow, 1511). This book, if it was ever printed, has never come to light. It may be that Agricola was referring to his *De diuo Casimiro carmen elegiacum* (Cracow: Florian Ungler, 1511), of which no known copy exists. See Vredeveld, 'Agricola, Rudolf d. J.,' 739.

54 'Occupatus sum; multa tibi scriberem ... Gaude interim mecum, qui meus es' (III, 30; Cracow, 4 January 1518).

55 'Consule, ut vel ante brumam egrediar' (II, 213; Cracow, 28 August 1520); 'Scribe igitur, quid agendum sit' (II, 240; Cracow, 8 February 1521).

56 Franz Gaisberg, abbot from 1504 to 1529.

57 'Aura non [autem] mihi salubris est, id quod multis, qui Cracoviae egerunt, contigit ... Tartarorum 4000 magnam Lituaniae et Poloniae partem depraedati sunt, 5000 et plures ex nostris desiderati sunt, multa milia abducta, tota Polonia maeret (II, 165; Cracow, 25 August 1519); 'Multa Poloni et magnifica pollicentur; istis ego pollicitis, vix, quo frigus abigam, habeo ... Magna scholasticorum penuria est, partim ob illud exitiale bellum, partim ob imminentis et circumquaque saevientis pestis metum' (II, 225; Cracow, 11 December 1520); '[P]assim Cracoviam prope pestis grassatur. Bella unius anni plus minus usque adeo attriverunt nos, ut vitam vix vivamus ... Aër hic insalubris est; aeger sum' (II, 240; Cracow, 8 February 1521).

58 Agricola gave no reason for his departure, but in his dedicatory letter to Nicolaus de Czebinio (Leonardus Aretinus, *Isagoge in philosophiam moralem*. Vienna: Hieronymus Vietor, 1515), he states that, having read Pliny's *Naturalis historia*, he had been in Körmöcbánya (now Kremnica in Slovakia) in 1512/13 to carry out research on mining as part of his interest in geography. In this letter, he mentions Cardinal Tamás Bakócz as his patron in Hungary. It does not seem that Agricola went to Buda to follow a further course of study, as evidenced by the surprise he expresses at finding learned men there: 'Siquidem ubi gymnasium nostrum Graccoviense [*sic*] egressus fueram, me

ipsum ex doctorum coetu ad agrestes incultosque Ungaros venire ipse coniectura mecum deprehendebam, puto me a Pallade ad Mercurium Maecenatemque illum, non Etruscum, sed Quinqueecclesiensem, immo ad viros Graecae et Latinae linguae peritissimos perrexisse' (III, 9; Buda, 1513/14). Agricola refers here to György Szatmári, the bishop of Pécs, as his patron, on whom see Farbaky, 'György Szatmári.'

59 Bauch, 'Rudolphus Agricola Junior,' 14. Agricola himself states this, saying in his dedicatory letter to Nicolaus de Czebinio (n58 above) that he turned to Nicolaus for help since his patrons in Hungary could no longer support him because of the uprising. On the uprising itself, see Baczkowski, *Zjazd wiedeński*, 148–50; Pellathy, 'Dozsa Revolt'; and Engel, *Realm of St. Stephen*, 362–4.

60 'Crucem tuli puer, crucem adolescens ... Opus erit, ut inferioris condicionis homunciones in optatum portum quietis delitescant. Eam ob rem tuae humanitatis erit, Rudolfo Agricolae providere consultius, qui propediem Viennam proficiscetur. Aut hospitium aut habitationem ... a te optat ... Id Agricola fatetur, se cum doctis malle pati, quam pauperem esse aulicum et spem sequi inanem' (III, 13; Esztergom, October 1514). According to Agricola (see nn58, 59 above), it was Nicolaus de Czebinio who provided him with funds to go to Vienna.

61 'Res in vado est; bene mecum et foeliciter agitur. Pluribus tecum agere volui, nisi eo temporis atomo patronus meus, episcopus Cracoviensis, Cracoviam venisset' (I, 110; Cracow, 17 December 1517).

62 'Occupatus sum; multa tibi scriberem. Rex venit ex Moschovia. Adsunt, quibus opus est blandiri. Gaude interim mecum, qui meus es: Agricola bene agit' (III, 30; Cracow, 4 January 1518).

63 'Perfeliciter ad nos rediit magnificus dominus Sigismundus de Erberstain, sacratissimae Caesareae Maiestatis orator ... Accersiri statim iussit tui nominis et famae duos admodum studiosos, Dantiscum et tuum Agricolam; petiit a nobis xeniolum' (I, 116; Cracow, February 1518). These poems were printed together by Haller in 1518, as *Soteria* (by Dantiscus) and *Congratulatio* (by Agricola). A second poem by Agricola was included, entitled *Patria domini Sigismundi*. (See appendix 1.)

64 'Caeterum mitto Corvini Epithalamion, donec Casparis Ursini et meum itemque Dantisci, impressum fuerit ... [M]ulta scribam, postquam stipendio meo ab episcopis satisfactum fuerit' (I, 120; Cracow, 30 April 1518).

65 Vadian had moved back to Saint Gall in June 1518. In the autumn of 1518 he made a trip to Vienna by way of Leipzig, Poznań, Wrocław, and Cracow, and reached Vienna around the end of February 1519. He stayed in Vienna until May and was back in Saint Gall by the end of that month (Näf, *Vadian und seine Stadt*, 2: 57–66). Vadian's own

move from Vienna back to Saint Gall in 1518 may have had some influence on Agricola's decision to leave Cracow, since Agricola first mentioned his intention to return to the Lake Constance region immediately after Vadian's visit to Cracow in February 1519: 'Revoca, precor, in memoriam, quae inter nos Cracoviae acta sunt' (II, 142; Cracow, 25 February 1519).

66 'Abbatem Sancti Galli Agricolae tui ergo alloquere, quod a te fieri postulat ... Votis erga immortalem deum steti, satisfeci et ultra vovi, ut post felicem in patriam nostram ingressum feliciter aliquando te intervisam' (II, 142).

67 II, 165 (Cracow, 25 August 1519); II, 225 (Cracow, 11 December 1520).

68 Vredeveld, 'Agricola, Rudolf d. J.,' 732.

69 '[N]am esse inter Polonos nec possum nec volo, utpote omnium mortalium superbissimos inconstantissimosque' (II, 196; Cracow, 9 June 1520); 'Non est Germanus, quin ipsi Iudaeis omnibus postponantur; nulla fides toti Cracoviae et praesertim polonicatis Germanis, qui nos exteros nullo amore tenent' (II, 216; Cracow, 17 September 1520). In the same letter, Agricola criticized Justus Ludovicus Decius, the royal economist, who had been a patron of Eck and Cox (see chapter 1), as a glory-seeker: 'Id tua solius gratia diligenti indagine scrutari coepissem, nisi Iodocus Decius, quem eius rei causa accesseram, his se de rebus olim nonnihil scripsisse, me coram iactitarit, ut hominem gloriolae mire cupidum nosti.' Decius had accused Agricola of the same in a letter to Vadian a year earlier (III, 44; Wieliczka, 10 February 1519).

70 'Fides ab episcopis – Posnaniensi mortuo – penes me vara est; id est, stipendium non plene exsolvunt' (II, 216).

71 'Multa Poloni et magnifica pollicentur; istis ego pollicitis, vix, quo frigus abigam, habeo ... [E]t aër et populus displicet' (II, 225; Cracow, 11 December 1520).

72 'Votis erga immortalem deum steti satisfeci et ultra vovi, ut post felicem in patriam nostram ingressum feliciter aliquando te intervisam' (II, 142; Cracow, 25 February 1519); 'Utinam ipse domi essem; quam essem tuus cum omnibus paternis rebus!' (II, 165; Cracow, 25 August 1519); 'Cura, ut tandem non procul a Sancto Gallo vivam habeamque id genus ruris deliciolas, hoc est hortum vineasque quibus ingravescente senio te mecum liberisque olim tuis, quos utinam tui similes plures cum castissima consorte tua habeas, iucunde oblectes ... Abbati insusurra, quam in patriam nostram volens ire, si sua mihi paternitas beneficio provideret' (II, 216; Cracow, 17 September 1520).

73 'Habemus ex Sancto Gallo veteris vini vas optimum; cervisiam etiam bibes' (I, 109; Cracow, 8 December 1517).

74 For example, II, 165 (Cracow, 25 August 1519), where Agricola mentions Vadian's brother Konrad and cousin Hektor. On them, see Bonorand, *Vadians Humanisten Korrespondenz*, 46–9.

75 Printed with Vadian's *Aegloga, cui titulus Faustus* (Vienna: Johannes Singrenius, 1517); the reprinting of *De insignibus familiae Vadianorum* in the volume *Commentaria in C. Iulii Solini Polyhistora*, edited by Johannes Camers (Basel: Henricus Petrus, 1557), is not noted by Vredeveld.

76 'Patrem meum, hominem sine tectorio vultus, sine felle, tibi commendatum habeas; ubi vero ex simplicitate erraverit, edoceas, quid agendum sit' (II, 165; Cracow, 25 August 1519).

77 '[E]go vero nihil ... optavi praeter stipendium, quam diu in gymnasio Cracoviensi bonas literas profitear ... Cracoviae si immorari vellem, canonicatum episcopus Posnaniensis pollicitus est' (II, 150; 13 June 1519).

78 '[E]piscopi mei maximi sunt pollicitatores et plane frigescunt. Abiturus eram, nisi Vladislaviensis me detinuisset' (II, 165; Cracow, 25 August 1519). In a later letter, Agricola repeated, 'Eram ad domuitionem capessendam in procinctu; et suis ecce pollicitationibus episcopi me detinuerunt, idque ob multa beneficia, quae dare mihi spondent et pingue salarium' (II, 196; Cracow, 9 June 1520).

79 'Si initiari sacris hic velim, mihi bene consuleretur; id tamen nunquam faciam' (II, 165).

80 'Dederunt beneficium 20 fl; resignavi, abibo' (II, 213; Cracow, 28 August 1520); 'Dabatur hic Cracoviae beneficium 50 fl.; accipere nolui' (II, 225; Cracow, 11 December 1520); 'Aura non [autem] mihi salubris est, id quod multis, qui Cracoviae egerunt contigit ... Clandestinus rumor et iam palam prorepserat de seditione Polonorum Cracoviae contra Germanos' (II, 165).

81 'Abbati insusurra, quam in patriam nostram volens ire, si sua mihi paternitas beneficio provideret; sin secus, in Lipsensi gymnasio Wittenburgensive doctissimis viris me adiungam, nisi brevi id, quod episcopi saepe literis ad me perferri curarunt, promiseruntque, ut decet, plene praestent' (II, 216; Cracow, 17 September 1520); 'Saepe te admonui, ut, quoties opportunitas offerretur, mei apud abbatem mentio fieret; certissime enim adveniente aestate domum redibo, sacris initiaturus' (II, 225); 'Aër hic insalubris est; aeger sum, quoties magnae episcoporum pollicitationes hic me tenent. Si brevi mihi esse provisum posset, Basileae interim agerem, ne otio torpescerem, vel nullo stipendio lector' (II, 240; Cracow, 8 February 1521).

82 Näf, *Vadian und seine Stadt*, 2: 60, 97–106.

83 '[S]cito: Rudolphum a festo natalis domini semper valetudinarium ac debilem fuisse, partim ut opinor, insolentia adversae fortunae, partim moerore inopiae et paupertatis ad hoc detrusus ... Libri et tota sua supellex vix 10 f. aestimatur' (II, 248; Cracow, 10 March 1521).

84 '[M]e ... in tuorum amicorum album scribito precor' (I, 11; Cracow, 1511) ; 'Et utinam ea mihi daretur facultas tecum vivendi, tecum emori vellem' (I, 12; Cracow, 1511). Agricola often closed his early

letters with a phrase such as 'vale interim et me ama et scribe' or 'vale et mutuiter me ama.'

85 'Amicitiae vinculum, quod faustiter intercessit, tam est mihi firmum, ut nec tempore nec absentia, nec denique silentio tuo longe molestissimo dissolvi ac rumpi queat' (I, 109; Cracow, 8 December 1517); 'Id siquidem animi in te mei sincerus candor et vicissarius inter nos amor, aperta utriusque simplicitas, mutua familiaritas, patriae nostrae vicinitas et ratio, indissolubilis literariae amicitiae nexus mereri non potuerunt. Nos vero, ut in amicitia officiosi simus, inter Martia tela tumultumque bellicum calamo non parcimus' (II, 225; 11 December 1520); 'Qui enim fieri posse credam, eum in amore mihi non respondere, quem inviolabilis quaedam mihi necessitudo copulavit et literae iampridem palam testatae sunt?' (II, 240; 8 February 1521).

86 'Quo tibi pacto gratas gratias agam, plane sum ignarus. Etsi nomen tuum in ore doctissimorum celebrius reddere posse me diffidam, hoc tamen a memori mea mente abolebitur numquam; quin si hactenus non stentoreum me tui nominis praeconem exhibuerim, vocalissimum eruditionis tuae buccinatorem agam' (I, 12; Cracow, 1511); 'Vides nunc, Ioachime, quanti te faciam, ut non Ioachimus vivat Cracoviae, sed in inclita patriarchae Ungari sede, in extremis Pannoniae finibus, nomen habeat famigeratum' (III, 11; Esztergom, 21 April? 1514); 'Veni, mi Vadiane, et veni, si hospitio, et eo magnificentissimo, uti volueris. Agricola dabit, ille tuus Agricola, quem absque vultus tectorio amas et amas sinceriter' (I, 110; Cracow, 17 December 1517); 'Hic tibi, Vadiane, duas ex Lituania perdices et gallum silvestrem mitto. Fruere feliciter, vescere ex septentrione avibus ultimis; propediem alia suscipies' (III, 30; Cracow, 4 January 1518).

87 Agricola's crisis had to do, in a more general sense, with a choice between the *uita actiua* and the *uita contemplatiua*, between staying at Cracow and maintaining the life of a scholar with court connections, and retiring to the Lake Constance countryside and to the quiet way of life of a parish priest. This choice was central to humanist philosophy and involved the question of how the *studia humanitatis* should relate to political and social activity. See Bernstein, 'Humanistische Standeskultur,' 124–5.

88 This section of the chapter is a slightly revised version of my article 'Careerism at Cracow.' I thank Toon Van Houdt, Jan Papy, Gilbert Tournoy, and Constant Matheeussen, the editors of *Self-Presentation and Social Identification*, for permission to reprint this material.

89 Czekajewska, 'Kultura umysłowa Polski XVI wieku,' 85.

90 Ocieczek, *Sławorodne wizerunki*, 14–15, 27. On dedicatory letters in the sixteenth century, see also Schottenloher, *Widmungsvorrede im Buch des 16. Jahrhunderts*, and Ulewicz, *Wśród impresorów krakowskich*, 95–189.

91 Czekajewska, 'Kultura umysłowa Polski XVI wieku,' 53, 76–93.

92 Schirrmeister, *Triumph des Dichters*, 152, notes that although the *poetae* normally dedicated their philological and poetic writings to members of their own academic circles or to friends of the same rank, they tended to dedicate works having a theme connected with the spheres of political and/or economic power to high-ranking patrons active in these spheres. Although Agricola Junior and Cox followed this norm, Eck did not – he dedicated nearly all his works after 1518 to Alexius Thurzó. It may be noted, though, that most of Eck's works from his life at Bártfa treated political or religious themes, and that perhaps having Thurzó as his chief patron influenced Eck's choice of theme, at least in the works he chose to publish.

93 Agricola Junior, Eck, and Cox did not, however, exploit the possibility of enhancing the images of themselves created in their book dedications by means of woodcut illustrations, as did Conrad Celtis and Jakob Locher at Vienna at the end of the fifteenth century, and Thomas Murner and Ulrich von Hutten later on; see Schirrmeister, *Triumph des Dichters*, 154–60.

94 Schirrmeister, *Triumph des Dichters*, 153–4, gives an account of how Ursinus Velius used book dedications to secure a position at the court of King Ferdinand after Maximilian's death.

95 'Non est nouum ... sed ab antiquis frequentissime usitatum ut qui litterarum studiis insudant, si quid tandem Mineruae uiribus ad suam aliorumue utilitatem sese conficere putauerint, id ad bonos principes scribant. Quod mihi fecisse uidentur non quo aliquam illis disciplinam proponant, sed quo gratitudo beneficiorum ab ipsis acceptorum; uel amor quo eis afficiuntur innotescat ac eorum ex auctoritate ad quos libri scribuntur quaedam ipsis libris accedat auctoritas' (Johannes de Stobnica, *Introductio in Ptolomei cosmographiam*. Cracow: Florian Ungler, 1512, 1513; Cracow: Hieronymus Vietor, 1519). Where multiple printings of a book exist, I quote from the first printing.

96 'Tum etiam quod pro comperto habeam compluscula cuisuis facultatis monumenta hac potissimum de causa a multis saepius legi quia uiris et litteratis et prudentibus omnique uirtute praeditis sint dedicata' (*Panegyricus in laudem Augustini Moraui*. Cracow: Florian Ungler, 1513); 'Constat enim compluscula cuiusuis facultatis monumenta, hac potissimum de causa a plerisque lectitari quia uiris et litteratis et prudentibus sunt dedicata' (*De arte uersificandi opusculum*. Cracow: Florian Ungler, 1515; Cracow: Hieronymus Vietor, 1521, 1539).

97 'Video ubique locorum ubique gentium et nationum, doctissime domine fautor, ab omnibus id passim qui litterariis monumentis posteros demerentur fieri ut eorum uel alterius eruditi hominis lucubrationes maecenatibus benemerentibus nuncupatim adscribant' (Nicolaus de Toliszków, *Iudicium ad annum 1519*. Cracow: Hieronymus Vietor, 1519).

98 '[S]ed quo pusillus iste libellus noster nomine tuo nobilissimo insignitus uendibilior redderetur' (*De arte uersificandi opusculum*).

99 Ocieczek, *Sławorodne wizerunki*, 31.

100 Ocieczek, *Sławorodne wizerunki*, 10, 26.

101 In his address to Sigismund Glotzer (Gloczer) (*Panegyricus in laudem Augustini Moraui*), to Justus Ludovicus Decius (*De arte uersificandi opusculum*), and to Alexius Thurzó (*Supellectilium fasciculus*, printed with *De mundi contemptu er virtute amplectenda dialogus*. Cracow: Hieronymus Vietor, 1519; Mathias Scharffenberg, 1528; printed with *An prudenti uiro sit ducenda uxor*. Cracow: Hieronymus Vietor, 1524). Moreover, Agricola and Eck occasionally changed the dedicatee when publishing a subsequent edition of a book. Czekajewska, 'O listach dedykacyjnych,' 32, mentions that this was a normal phenomenon in the dedications of the time, and that the writers of dedicatory letters might even mention the previous dedicatee, as does Eck in his dedication of the second edition of *De arte uersificandi opusculum* (1521).

102 *Statuta prouinciae Gnesnensis* (Cracow: Johannes Haller, 1518); Nicolaus de Błonie, *Tractatus de sacramentis* (Cracow: Johannes Haller, 1519; Cracow: Mathias Scharffenberg, 1529).

103 Ocieczek, *Sławorodne wizerunki*, 20.

104 Ocieczek, *Sławorodne wizerunki*, 15.

105 Janson, *Latin Prose Prefaces*, 145. Janson's book focuses on the classical tradition, to which Agricola Junior, Eck, and Cox adhered. Medieval formulas for the expression of an author's modesty exhibited some similiaries to the classical formulas (e.g., diminishing one's own talent or ability) but, stemming as they did from notions of Christian humility, they had their roots more in ecclesiastical literature and often stressed the spirituality of the author. See Schwietering, *Demutsformel Mittelhochdeutscher Dichter*.

106 Such vocabulary is frequent in Eck's prefaces; for instance: '[R]ogo ut hunc libellum ... hylari uultu serenaque fronte suscipias' (*Panegyricus in laudem Augustini Moraui*); 'Rogans immensam tuam magnificentiam ut hoc quantulumcunque sit hylari fronte suscipiat' (*De mundi contemptu*); 'Sed id totum acri tuae generosae magnif. iudicio humiliter subicio' (*De reipublicae administratione dialogus*. Cracow: Hieronymus Vietor, 1520); 'Quod ... humiliter subicio' (*Vita diui Pauli primi eremitae*. Cracow: Hieronymus Vietor, 1522); 'Quam humiliter dicatam offerimus magnificae dominationi tuae, cui et nostra obsequia semper paratissima commendamus' (*Ad proceres Hungariae exhortatio*. Cracow: Hieronymus Vietor, 1527, 1528). Also in Cox's dedications: 'Verum hancce praecor interea strenam qua fronte solitus es alior[s]um nunc accipe' (*De laudibus celeberrimae Cracouiensis Academiae oratio*. Cracow: Hieronymus Vietor, 1518).

107 *Illustrissimae reginae Bonae paraceleusis* (Cracow: Johannes Haller, 1518).
108 'Id uero quod maxime desiderat facile impetrabit cum nihil nisi patronicium affectat, nihil nisi in tuorum clientorum adscribi numerum postulat, rem satis illi honestam et te non indignam' (*Threni neglectae religionis.* Cracow: Johannes Haller, 1518).
109 '[Q]ui noctes atque dies huius celebritati studet, quando te sibi exoptatissimum Maecenatem feliciter adeptus sit' (Cracow: Hieronymus Vietor, 1519).
110 '[S]aepeque dum adhuc in uestra agerem Polonia, cui patriae omnia certe debeo' (Adriano Castellesi, *Venatio una cum scholiis non ineruditis Leonardi Coxi Britanni.* Cracow: Hieronymus Vietor, 1524).
111 '[U]t istud minutulum et pusillum munus ab Eckiolo (qui totus tuus est) hylari fronte suscipias' (*An prudenti uiro sit ducenda uxor.* Cracow: Johannes Haller, 1518; Hieronymus Vietor, 1524 with an afterword by Matthias Pyrser); 'cum tuae magnificentiae omnia quae possideo debeam' (*Vita diui Pauli primi eremitae*).
112 On the use of diminutives in Latin prefaces of late antiquity, see Janson, *Latin Prose Prefaces*, 145–6.
113 Janson, *Latin Prose Prefaces*, 124, notes that the request from the dedicatee for the work could function to free the writer of a certain amount of responsibility for the work, so that the author could transfer both the honour and the responsibility to the dedicatee. This strategy was popular from the late Roman Empire.
114 'Orationem quam de laudibus inclytae huius Academiae publice nuper habui iamque sic a multis mihi carissimis efflagitatam ...' (*De laudibus celeberrimae Cracouiensis Academiae oratio*).
115 *De arte uersificandi opusculum.*
116 '[I]n primis tamen Venatio tibi ista cordi fuit ... opus ipsum prae caeteris commendabas.'
117 '[Q]ui saepicule me ad scribendum de conceptione Mariae carmen hortatus sis ...' Printed together with *Passio dominica per septem horas canonicas distributa* (a compilation of sacred devotions, antiphons, and hymns with Agricola's notes) (Cracow: Hieronymus Vietor, 1520).
118 'En tuae uoluntati parui, doctissime Carole, cogebas equidem me carmen edere illud inemendatum, inconditum nec reuisum plane.'
119 Janson, *Latin Prose Prefaces*, 62–4, describes how, among the Roman writers, themes such as the request from the dedicatee and the unwillingness to write became more and more conventional, with the result that the preface was increasingly flavoured with mock modesty.
120 This prescription for modesty dated from antiquity. See Janson, *Latin Prose Prefaces*, 147–8. Thus, Eck, in his preface to *De mundi contemptu*, states that he does not have the ability to write on every-

thing concerning his topic, and refers to himself as 'ingenio longe minimus' when offering his work to Alexius Thurzó.

121 '[U]t horam praeterire non patiar, quae uel commentandis libris, uel legendis illustribus scriptoribus non impendatur' (Johannes de Lapide, *Resolutorium dubiorum circa celebrationem missarum occurrentium.* Cracow: Hieronymus Vietor, 1519).

122 'Non enim de me nihil meriti sunt, utpote qui decem retro annis in florentissimo nostro Cracouiensi gymnasio, philosophiae, reliquisque ingenuis artibus operam mecum nauarunt' (*Hymnus de beatissimae uirginis conceptu passiuo*, printed with *Passio dominica*).

123 In dedicating his poem on whether or not a wise man should take a wife, Eck comments, 'Hinc quae mea de hac disceptatione sit sententia, cum nuper Bartphae a scholasticis paulisper semotus negotiis in otio degerem, tumultuaria expressi camena' (*An prudenti uiro sit ducenda uxor*). In preparing the second edition of his handbook on versification, he writes that he has gone back to this book because he does not want to give himself up to idle leisure, and quotes Cato's comparison of human life to iron, which can be rusted by leisure (*De arte uersificandi opusculum*, 1521).

124 'Omnemque operam (quantum per me fieri potuit) impendi ut uenustissimus ille libellus qui propemodum in tenebris iacebat quam emendatissime imprimeretur ne uiderer uel alienae laudi inuidere uel studiosos iuuenes tam praeclaro opusculo defraudare' (Cracow: Florian Ungler, 1512).

125 In his prefaces to *Illustrissimae reginae Bonae paraceleusis* and Nicolaus de Toliszków's *Iudicium ad annum 1519.* In the latter Agricola writes, 'Nec tamen ab Horatiano praecepto unquam desciscam, qui nonum monet ut premantur in annum, quae memoria digna a nobis scribi uolumus.'

126 Here, of course, Cox is transferring some of his responsibility for the publication of the work to his dedicatee: 'Tuo igitur perspicatissimo iuxta ac grauissimo iudicio, nostras hasce lucubrationes subicimus.' Janson, *Latin Prose Prefaces*, 141, notes that the theme of asking for assistance from the dedicatee appeared first in epistolary prefaces in the first century.

127 Janson, *Latin Prose Prefaces*, 97, 147–8. Agricola (in his dedicatory letter to Nicolaus de Toliszków, *Iudicium ad annum 1519*) also employs the term *lucubrationes* to describe the works that authors or editors offer to their patrons.

128 Janson, *Latin Prose Prefaces*, 145–6.

129 'Hilaro itaque uultu id quantulumcunque est accipite et non quod breue pusillumque sed frugiferum utileque sit perpendite.'

130 '[E]t non donum quod certe perexiguum est sed donantis animum qui in te quam optime affectus est perpendas.' In his preface to *De mundi contemptu*, Eck writes, 'Rogans immensam tuam magnificen-

tiam ut ... mentem donantis non munus quod satis tenue est et tanto patrono indignum perpendat.'

131 'Quod etsi ... pusillum sit tuisque in me meritis multum impar, sententiarum tamen grauitate rerumque cultissimarum pondere longe maximum' (Maffeo Vegio, *Philalethes.* Cracow: Florian Ungler, 1512).

132 See Rudolf Agricola's prefaces to Johannes Glogoviensis, *Physionomia* (Cracow: Hieronymus Vietor, 1518); Cicero, *Pro rege Deiotaro* (Cracow: Hieronymus Vietor, 1518); and Nicolaus de Toliszków, *Iudicium ad annum 1519.*

133 *Epistola Martini Lutheri ad Henricum VIII. Responsio dicti inuictissimi Angliae ac Franciae regis* (Cracow: Hieronymus Vietor, 1527).

134 'Sit hoc poematum qualecumque est amoris nostri monumentum' (Cracow: Florian Ungler, 1511).

135 'Munusculum est paruum et gracile, sed certe affectu grande, quod nostrum haud dubie amorem tanquam glutino tenacissimo indissolubiliter innodabit. Dii itaque faxint ut istud sit perpetuum pignus ac monumentum meae erga te obseruantiae' (*Panegyricus in laudem Augustini Moraui*).

136 'Hinc ego inter tuos clientulos minimus, tantis tuis uirtutibus excitatus, tuam generosam praestantiam uenerari ardentissime gestio, at desunt mihi praeclara munera, desunt et opes' (*Supellectilium fasciculus*). The motif was in use at the time: Caspar Ursinus Velius stated, for example, that since he had no riches, he was offering Bishop Johann Thurzó a poem instead of a Christmas gift ('Ad eundem [Johannem Thurzonem] elegia,' in *Poematum libri quinque.* Basel: Froben, 1522). VD16, U366.

137 'Hunc igitur libellum de constitutionibus humani corporis ... accipias quem tui nominis auspicio in lucem prodire uolui ut qui uiderint plane intelligant uel tantillo fautoribus debere gratificari' (Cracow: Hieronymus Vietor, 1518).

138 This attitude towards the subject matter of the book was already present in classical antiquity. See Janson, *Latin Prose Prefaces*, 42, 151.

139 Czekajewska, 'Kultura umysłowa Polski XVI wieku,' 88.

140 For a full description of the structure of the dedicatory letter, see Czekajewska, 'O listach dedykacyjnych,' 27–8.

141 The name of the writer is also included, sometimes with a brief title (which often gives the region of origin); thus 'Rudolfus Agricola Rhaetus,' 'Rudolfus Agricola Junior poeta a Caesare laureatus,' 'Valentinus Ecchius Rhaetus,' 'Valentinus Ecchius Lendanus, Bartphensis,' 'Valentinus Eckius Bartphanae scholae moderator,' and 'Leonardus Coxus Britannus.'

142 Formulas of address, specifying the titles and epithets appropriate to persons of all ranks and professions, were taught in Renaissance letter-writing treatises (Henderson, 'On Reading the Rhetoric of the Renaissance Letter,' 153–4).

143 Vienna: Johannes Singrenius, 1517.

144 Occasionally, though, expressions of gratitude may come at the very beginning of the dedication, as in Agricola's letter to Wirtenberger and Vinerius: 'Ingratus meritissimo iure dici possem, fratres charissimi, si non egregie uestrae in me uoluntati et singulari beneuolentiae aliqua ex parte responderem' (Filippo Beroaldo, *Modus epistolandi*).

145 '[S]ed quod collata tot in me beneficia retaliare hoc chartaceo munere deceat, quod licet minutulum sit, precor tamen generosa magnificentia tua id placida fronte suscipiat, atque diu felix et incolumis uiuat' (Cracow: Hieronymus Vietor, 1521).

146 'Possum ergo diis hoc supplicare de te quod fortissimus ille Graeci exercitus dux suo de Nestore, utinam tui similes multos nostra haberet Hungaria, iam enim barbari esse desineremus, certaremus cum Graecis, uinceremus Italos, florerent litterarum studia, florerent et litterati homines' (*De mundi contemptu*).

147 Czekajewska, 'Kultura umysłowa Polski XVI wieku,' 49, 63; Ocieczek, *Sławorodne wizerunki*, 26.

148 Pseudo-Crates, *Epistolae* (Cracow: Hieronymus Vietor, 1518).

149 On Nicolaus Salomon, see Bonorand, *Vadians Humanisten Korrespondenz*, 170–1.

150 '[Q]uid dicam haesito, omnis enim sermo inferior est, quam uestrae eximie uirtutes promereantur, estis etenim omnes quales esse debetis, hoc est locupletissimis animi atque corporis dotibus felicissime exornati, nil inest uobis reprehendendum, nil deest desiderandum, sed ... omnium rerum genere donati estis' (*Apophoreticum carmen de Christi natiuitate*. Cracow: Hieronymus Vietor, 1520).

151 'Offero ergo quam optime in tuam excellentiam affectam habeo uoluntatem, et apertum mentis indicium hoc minutulo atque pusillo carmine super domestica supellectilia ... tuae modestiae et moderationi eius tenuitatem humiliter submittens, qui ex sublimi multarum dignitatum solio, humilia etiam respicere non dedignaris, ueluti immortales dii, quos (ut cum Plinio loquar) cernimus, non tam accuratis quandoque adorantium precibus quam innocentia et sanctitate laetari gratioremque existimari, qui delubris eorum puram castamque mentem quam qui meditatum aliquid carmen intulerit' (*Supellectilium fasciculus*).

152 'Unde copiosum in tuis laudibus celebrandis argumentum mihi insumere possem nisi uererer ne a pestiferis uitilitigatoribus assentandi uitium mihi ascriberetur' (*De arte uersificandi opusculum*).

153 '[U]tinam tuae dominationi, caeterisque Salomonibus, donec uixero, honeste citra tamen assentationem placere, et utilis esse possem' (*Hymnus de beatissimae uirginis conceptu passiuo*, printed with *Passio dominica*).

154 Czekajewska, 'O listach dedykacyjnych'; Ocieczek, *Sławorodne wizerunki*, 15, 28.

155 Ocieczek, *Sławorodne wizerunki*, 28.

156 Pseudo-Crates, *Epistolae* (Cracow: Florian Ungler, 1512; Cracow, Hieronymus Vietor, 1518). In 1512, Agricola tells Valentin Eck, 'Multa praeterea in his et dicta grauiter et facta constanter inuenies quae Christianae ueritati maxime astipulantur, quae quoque ad ueram religionem incitamentum copiosissimum praebent.' In 1518 he writes to Nicolaus Salomon, 'Placuit easdem iterum sub tui nominis auspicio in publicum dare, ut et studiosi litterarum haberent, quibus ad ueterum philosophorum imitationem se oblectarent.' In his letter to the young Konarskis, which follows the text, he notes that the boys accomplish their reading slowly but surely: 'Interim memoria uestra id non excidat; uelim bouem lente, sed fortius figere pedem ...'

157 'Abstinentia ergo et preces suum habent tempus. Quod in hoc sacro quadragesimali ieiunio contingit ... Proin ut ipse meos ad hoc felicissimum iter magis instigarem, hymnos Pontani legendos desumpsi, quibus uera colit numina nostram instruens religionem' (Cracow: Johannes Haller, 1520).

158 'Quotiens tenerae praesertim aetatis homines ab illustribus et primariis latinae linguae scriptoribus ad barbaros et plebeios sane praeeuntibus eorum praeceptoribus deficere audio ... quid inquam nos a uera eruditione alienos penitusque mutos facit?' (Cicero, *Pro Archia poeta*. Cracow: Hieronymus Vietor, 1518); 'Ciceronis Oratio in usum eorum seorsum impressa publicum petat, qui hactenus nouos illos libellos, absque litteraria fruge, et non sine meo planctu et gemitu legerunt. Legant et si placeat et barbari barbariem enixe amplectantur. Non esse Ciceronianos oportet, quoniam quidem Alpes non transcenderint, hoc est crassa illa barbarie eliminata, in tenera praesertim aetate meliores litteras non didicerunt' (Cicero, *Pro rege Deiotaro*).

159 'Possum ergo diis hoc supplicare de te quod fortissimus ille Graeci exercitus dux suo de Nestore, utinam tui similes multos nostra haberet Hungaria, iam enim barbari esse desineremus, certaremus cum Graecis, uinceremus Italos, florerent litterarum studia, florerent et litterati homines' (*De mundi contemptu*); 'Felix ergo hoc nostrum regnum quod eum principem est adeptum sub quo uirtutes hactenus sopitae iam tandem euigilabunt suoque titulo litterarum amatores coronabuntur: ut plane spes sit non modo foedam oris barbariem breui hinc abituram uerumetiam barbaros mores quorum temulentia hactenus adeo inebriati quam plures fuerunt ut nescierint quid rerum agerent scelesti tyrannide excaecati' (*De reipublicae administratione*).

160 Caspar Ursinus Velius, *Epistolarum et epigrammatum liber* (Vienna: Johannes Singrenius, 1517). Agricola names two dozen Germans whose work he considers to be marked by talent, elegance, discern-

ment, learning, and laboriousness, including Erasmus, Laurentius Corvinus, Ulrich von Hutten, Willibald Pirckheimer, Joachim Vadian, Beatus Rhenanus, Eobanus Hessus, Henricus Glareanus, and Johannes Dantiscus. Bernstein, 'Creating Humanist Myths' argues for von Hutten's creation of a group identity for the German humanists in his poem. See also Schirrmeister, *Triumph des Dichters*, 103–4.

161 '[P]utaui satis tutum fore id quod tuo nomine munitum exiret, eumque ita posse aemulos omnes euincere' ('Reuerendissimo ... domino Mathiae Dreuicio Vladislauiensi episcopo dignissimo Iodocus Ludouicus Decius,' in *Threni neglectae religionis*).

162 '[D]iuus Paulus, primus Anachorita, qui uel solus pie inuocatus Machometicam poterit comprimere rabiem, cum olim in terris adhuc constitutus atrocissimas etiam feras sua mitigauerit simplicitate' (*Vita diui Pauli primi eremitae*).

163 'Quod pulcherrimum illud atque omni laude dignum Principis nostri Lodouici de Turcica expeditione institutum iam tandem procedere incipit ... non tam huic regno quam uniuersae Christianae reipublicae plurimum congratulor. Futurum enim spero ut illius exemplo caeteri quoque excitati reges ... huic tam sancto operi simul se accingant' (*Ad Ludouicum Hungariae et Bohemiae regem pro bello Turcis inferendo exhortatio*. Cracow: Hieronymus Vietor, 1524).

164 'Verum ille quem adduxisti absolutissimus princeps ea praestat magnitudine qua uel hunc solum omnium mortalium huius afflictae patriae ruinam reparare posse indubie speremus omnes ... quem nos ob illius aduentum ad comunem laetitiam hac exhortamur camena' (*Ad proceres Hungariae exhortatio*).

165 'Nam cui melius dedicetur, quam illi, qui sese, serenissimo regi Sigismundo, alteri in hisce mundi partibus fidei nostrae defensori, cum in aliis negotiis omnibus, tum in hoc uere pientissimo conatu, ut omnem extirpet haeresim, apprime fidum semper Achatem praestat?' (*Epistola Martini Lutheri ad Henricum VIII. Responsio dicti inuictissimi Angliae ac Franciae regis*).

166 Most dedicatory letters do not provide enough information for us to determine whether the author/editor had the dedicatee's permission to dedicate the book to him or her before the dedication was printed, but the formula according to which the author/editor states at the end of the letter that he hopes the dedicatee will accept the work, suggests that no arrangement with the dedicatee had been made beforehand. Only occasionally, as when Agricola Junior writes in his dedicatory letter to Johannes Salomon, scholastic of Gniezno and canon of Cracow, that he is publishing *Hymnus de beatissimae uirginis conceptu passiuo* (printed with *Passio dominica*) at the request of Salomon, or as when Matthias Pyrser states in his dedication of Cox's *De erudienda iuuentute* (Cracow: Hieronymus Vietor,

1526) to Piotr Tomicki that Cox has been given the task of writing by the heads of the University of Cracow (of which Tomicki was chancellor), does the writer of the dedicatory letter indicate that the dedicatee has requested a work from the author/editor. More often than not, however, if the author/editor mentions that the dedicatee has encouraged him to write or publish a piece, he uses the formula indicating that the work is not ready and he is publishing the piece at hand in its place, while asking for time to polish or compose a piece truly worthy of its dedicatee, as Agricola Junior does in his dedication of *Illustrissimae reginae Bonae paraceleusis* to Carolus Antonius Moncinereus.

167 Williams, 'Commendatory Verses,' 1–2.

168 Voss, 'Books for Sale,' 747.

169 Hirsch, *Printing, Selling, and Reading*, 23. As Hirsch points out, this anecdote also illustrates the danger of taking prefatory material at face value – the preface was signed with Froben's name.

170 On the early sixteenth-century printing houses of Cracow, see Kawecka-Gryczowa, *Drukarze dawnej Polski.*

171 Ulewicz, *Wśród impresorów krakowskich*, 112, 124, 125, 127, 162. It is thought that Agricola Junior was working for Ungler as a corrector when he first came to Cracow.

172 Voss, 'Books for Sale,' 735, 744; Allen, '*Utopia* and European Humanism,' 91, 99.

173 The word *grammateus*, although frequently translated as 'schoolteacher,' meant a 'notary' or 'scribe' at this time. See Polska Akademia Nauk, *Lexicon mediae et infimae latinitatis polonorum.* (The term is not found in Magyar Tudományos Akadémia, *Lexicon latinitatis medii aevi Hungariae.*)

174 *De antiquissima nominis et familiae Thurzonum origine* (Cracow: Hieronymus Vietor, 1519). It appears that Carbo matriculated at Cracow in 1513 (Chmiel and others, *Album studiosorum Universitatis Cracoviensis*, 2: 149), and it is quite likely that Eck had met him there. Carbo may have been responsible for Eck's move to the Bártfa-Kassa region, and may even have introduced him to Alexius Thurzó.

175 Luther's apology appeared in September 1525, following Thomas More's *Responsio ad Lutherum* of 1523. The Cracow volume (*Epistola Martini Lutheri ad Henricum VIII*, 1527) also contains Henry VIII's *Responsio.*

176 *Ad Ludouicum Hungariae et Bohemiae regem pro bello Turcis inferendo exhortatio.*

177 Bernstein, 'From Outsiders to Insiders,' 55–6, makes this assertion in regard to the German humanists.

178 Nearly 80 per cent of them were composed in the same metre, elegiac distich. Other verse forms represented were the glyconic, iambic trimeter, and lesser asclepiadean metres, and the sapphic stanza

– all from Horace and all analysed in Eck's handbook on versification. Hendecasyllables, normally associated with the erotic poet Catullus, also made an appearance, but these are also found in the poetry of Statius, whom the Cracow poets would prefer to appear to be imitating. Cox brought out an edition of Statius's *Syluae* in 1527.

179 There is one instance of a recycled commendatory poem: an anonymous address to the reader printed at the end of Eck's *De mundi contemptu* in 1519 turned up in 1521 in the second edition of his handbook on versification, with Eck's student Georg Werner as the author. If a work was reprinted, the original commendatory verses were sometimes reprinted, although the normal case seems to be that outdated ones were dropped (and sometimes replaced by fresher, possibly more appropriate poems) even if the original dedicatory letter was retained. I note here only the initial printing of a commendatory poem since the poem would have been composed specifically for the edition in which it originally appeared.

180 Eck did write verses for Johannes Dantiscus's *Carmen extemporarium*, to which his own *Hymnus exhortatorius* (Cracow: Florian Ungler, 1514) was appended, and for his own *Threni neglectae religionis*.

181 Bernstein, 'Group Identity Formation,' 381.

182 Robertus de Euremodio, *Institutiones uitae* (Cracow: Johannes Haller, 1519).

183 *An prudenti uiro sit ducenda uxor* (1518).

184 *De arte uersificandi opusculum* (1521).

185 'Ausonias acies, praeclaraque gesta, triumphos / Insignes, cupiens condidicisse, ducum'; 'Succinctum Flori legat hoc syntagma, putetque / Diffusum Liui se retinere tomon' (Lucius Annaeus Florus, *Bellorum Romanorum libri quattuor*. Cracow: Johannes Haller, 1515).

186 'Coniugii debes sacro si foedere necti, / Tempora uel uiduo ducere casta toro'; 'Hinc igitur uatis scripta haec percurrito docti, / Paeniteas tandem ne tua facta sero' (*An prudenti uiro sit ducenda uxor*).

187 'Si cupis hoc faustam saeclo traducere uitam / Deliciis animae perpetuisque frui / Perlege' (Cracow: Hieronymus Vietor, 1518). Holnstein, from Silesia, was a student at Cracow and a member of the circle of young Erasmians who gathered around Cox. See Janotzky, *Ianociana*, 1: 124–5.

188 'Si, lector, docti non spernes, care, Georgi / Hoc breue opus, paruo tempore plura scies' (Georg Peurbach, *Algorithmus*. Vienna: Hieronymus Vietor, 1515).

189 '[P]rudens qui se uirtutis ad usum / Natum ait esse Dei notitiamque meram' (Anselm of Canterbury, *Elucidarius dialogicus theologiae tripertitus*. Vienna: Hieronymus Vietor, 1515).

190 'Semita uirtutum duris riget aspera saxis / ... / Illa sed aeternam lassis in fine quietam / Praebet ...' (*De mundi contemptu*, 1519).

191 'Alter enim prorsus temnit rudimenta Latinae ...' (*De erudienda iuuentute*). Rullus, from Silesia, was one of the young Erasmians who gathered around Cox. At about the same time as Cox left Poland, Rullus went to Wrocław, where he became a schoolmaster. On him, see Barycz, *Śląsk w polskiej kulturze*, 127–36.

192 'Ad ingenuum adolescentem Melchiorem Vadianum de Sancto Gallo iambicum protrepticum,' in Cebes, *Tabula* (Vienna: Hieronymus Vietor, 1515).

193 'Epigramma,' in Bonauentura, *Breuiloquium* (Cracow: Florian Ungler, 1511 or 1512?).

194 Agricola, 'In laudem operum diui Hieronymi,' in Erasmus, *Aliquot epistolae diui Eusebii Hieronymi* (Cracow: Hieronymus Vietor, 1519).

195 Andreas Eck, 'Octostichon,' in Robertus de Euremodio, *Institutiones uitae*. Robertus de Euremodio (Robert d'Envermeuil) was evidently a fifteenth-centry monk of Clairvaux. Cosenza, *Biographical and Bibliographical Dictionary of the Italian Humanists*, 4: 3068, notes that he wrote a commentary on Cato's *Distichs.*

196 'Calliope referens diuum uenerabilis aeui / Paulum' (Matthias Pyrser, 'Ad candidum lectorem in perpetuum Ecchianae musae decus et libelli,' in *Vita diui Pauli primi eremitae*). Pyrser was a student at Cracow, attached to the circles of Eck and Cox. He worked in the chancellery of Krzysztof Szydłowiecki, and then returned to his homeland of Silesia in the service of the bishop of Wrocław. He would later travel to Italy to study for a doctor of laws degree at Bologna. See Bauch, 'Schlesien und die Universität Krakau,' 165.

197 Stanislaus Hosius, 'Ad ... dominum Alexium Thurzonem epigramma in autoris commendationem,' in *Ad Ludouicum Hungariae et Bohemiae regem pro bello Turcis inferendo exhortatio.*

198 Bernstein, ' Group Identity Formation,' 378–83, makes the point that the humanists' proficiency in Latin was central to the creation of their 'corporate identity.'

199 Agricola, in his commendatory verses for Proclus's *Sphaera* (Cracow: Florian Ungler, 1512) and for Johannes Harmonius's *Comoedia Stephanium* (Vienna: Hieronymus Vietor, 1515), strings such laudatory adjectives together to build up his argument for buying the book. See also Eck, 'Ad lectorem,' in Filippo Beroaldo, *Modus epistolandi* (Cracow: Florian Ungler, 1512); Agricola, [no title], in Aegidius Gallus Romanus, *Bophilaria* (Vienna: Hieronymus Vietor, 1515), and Agricola, 'In laudem operum Diui Hieronymi,' in Erasmus, *Aliquot epistolae diui Eusebii Hieronymi.*

200 'Succinctum Flori legat hoc syntagma, putetque / Diffusum Liui se retinere tomon.' The book is described in Lewandowski, *Florus w Polsce*, 32–4.

201 'Ut nihil hoc breuius nil meliusque legas' (Agricola, in *De arte uersificandi arte opusculum*, 1521); 'Qui facili pinxit compendia quaeque

tabella / Nec quisquam melius talia uel breuius' (Cox, in *De mundi contemptu*, 1519).

202 'Est breuis, at multa hac ex breuitate scies' (Cracow: Hieronymus Vietor, 1527).

203 'Quis amat diebus multa paucis noscere.' Giovanni Armonio's (1477–1522) *Comoedia Stephanium*, a neo-Latin comedy based on the works of Plautus, first published at Venice about 1500, became immediately popular. See Armonio, *Ioannis Harmonii Marsi Comoedia Stephanium*, ed. Ludwig.

204 'Sic satis in paruo didicisse uolumine. Quae sit / Eloquii et morum regula, quisque modus / Haec Plato prolixo nos codice, Socraticusque / Xenocrates stilo uix meliore docet' (Andreas Eck, 'Octostichon,' in Robertus de Euremodio, *Institutiones uitae*). Eck, from Saint Gall, had studied in Vienna from 1514 to 1518, and remained in Cracow, where he was connected with Agricola Junior and his circle, until about 1520, when he entered the imperial service and began to travel across Europe. On him, see Bonorand, *Personenkommentar II*, 268–72.

205 'Sit nouus iste licet, nostro nec notus in orbe, / Is tamen excultum, crede, uolumen habet.'

206 'Quamuis breuis atque nouus sit / Hinc commoda plurima habebis.'

207 Rullus, for example, begins his poem 'En lector geminis opus hoc amplectere palmis / Si curae est pietas si nouitasque tibi' (*Vita diui Pauli primi eremitae*).

208 Bernstein, 'Group Identity Formation,' 383. August Buck states that the notion of the 'poeta eruditus' was passed down from antiquity to the Middle Ages through the *Ars poetica* of Horace and commentaries on Vergil. For the Italian humanists, who turned towards the classical poets as a source of knowledge, the notion was of extreme importance: humanist poetry was educational poetry, par excellence. See Buck, 'Begriff des "poeta eruditus."'

209 'Ecce Caballino qui proluit ora liquore / Ecchius, ambrosium fundit ab ore melos.'

210 'Qui noctesque diesque cultiori / Lima splendidulos parat libellos' (*De arte uersificandi opusculum*, 1515).

211 In an anonymous commendatory poem for Erasmus's edition of St Jerome's *Aliquot epistolae*, brought out by Agricola in 1519 at the Vietor press in Cracow.

212 'Et quamuis lacer ante fuit, mendosus et asper / Iam tamen hic Phoebi clarior orbe nitet' (Agricola, in Aristotle, *De anima*. Cracow: Florian Ungler, 1512). The 1519 printing (Cracow: Johnnes Haller) repeats Agricola's verses, but adds an anonymous commendatory poem (most likely penned by Agricola), which names the translators as 'Johannes' and 'Wolfgang.' Estreicher, *Bibliografia polska*, 12:

213, identifies them as Johannes Argyropulos and Wolfgang Mosnauer. Giovanni Argiropulo (*c.* 1415–87) was a Byzantine scholar who was active as a lecturer in Florence and Rome, and a celebrated translator of Aristotle (see *Dizionario biografico degli Italiani*, 4: 129–31). Wolfgang Mosnauer was rector of the University of Vienna in 1505 (according to Aschbach, *Geschichte der Wiener Universität*, 2: 449). Mosnauer's edition of Argiropulo's translation of *De anima* first appeared at Venice, *c.* 1500 as recorded in IISTC.

213 'Cupiens ut hoc doctore discas plenius / Christum sapere, Christum loqui, Christum insuper / Vitaque moribusque recte effingere' (Erasmus, *Aliquot epistlae diui Eusebii Hieronymi*).

214 '[H]is criticis porrige laeta nates.' Displaying one's buttocks was a gesture of contempt in the German popular culture of the time (Scribner, *For the Sake of Simple Folk*, 82–3). Furthermore, the depiction of bared buttocks in jest was a 'pervasive phenomenon in the art of the sixteenth century ... as it was earlier in medieval art' (Barolsky, *Infinite Jest*, 90). The motif of *nates nudae* in literature can also be traced through the Italian Renaissance back to the fables of Phaedrus. See Furlan and Matton, 'Baptistae Alberti *Simiae*,' 128.

215 Only one of the commendatory poems from the whole corpus accompanying the publications of Agricola, Eck, and Cox seems to refer to a specific incident. Agricola's poem 'Ad osorem,' printed with his edition of Octavius Cleophilus Phanensis's *De poetarum coetu* (Cracow: Florian Ungler, 1511), warned the critic to stop criticizing Latin writers and scorning learned poets, for if he did not, he would pay the penalty publicly. It is tempting to presume that Agricola was meeting vocal resistance to his program of introducing Italian humanist literature into Cracow, but there is no evidence in support of this hypothesis. Certainly, Agricola mentioned no such problem in his extant letters to Vadian.

216 Bernstein, 'From Outsiders to Insiders,' 56–7.

217 Treml, *Humanistische Gemeinschaftsbildung*, 107.

218 'Georgius Logus Silesius lectori,' in Caspar Ursinus Velius, *Epistolarum et epigrammatum liber*. Agricola was the author of the dedicatory epistle.

219 Johannes Antoninus from Kassa was a student at Cracow (BA, 1517) who would go on to study medicine in Italy. He travelled to Basel in 1524 and treated Erasmus for gallstones. He later became physician to King Sigismund and Bishop Tomicki. On Antoninus, see Bietenholz and Deutscher, *Contemporaries of Erasmus*, 1: 63–4.

220 'Sunt hic mystica sensa, sunt lepores, / Non spurcos Veneris iocos olentes / Sed quales puero dabis tenello / Qui primis elementa discit annis' (anonymous author, in Erasmus, *Aliquot epistolae diui Eusebii Hieronymi*).

221 'Non canit hic uates ioca, non conuiuia, ludos, / Sed diuum, cuius

Pannonia ossa fouet' (Matthias Pyrser, 'Ad candidum lectorem,' in *Vita diui Pauli primi eremitae*).

222 See also Agricola's claims for Cicero's *De amicitia* (Vienna: Hieronymus Vietor, 1515) and Aegidius Gallus Romanus's *Bophilaria*, or Antoninus's for Cox's teaching methods in *De erudienda innentute*, or Cox's for Johannes Murmellius's *Oratiunculae* (Cracow: Hieronymus Vietor, 1527).

223 See also Agricola's claims for Anselm of Canterbury's *Elucidarius*, or Cox's argument for Eck's *De mundi contemptu* (1519).

224 Treml, *Humanistische Gemeinschaftsbildung*, 111.

225 As an example, Bernardus Dantiscus Flachsbinder, 'In libellum praeceptoris': 'Fusior hic sermo, suntque hic praecepta docendi / Et bene uiuendi norma beata patet.'

226 'Esse potest uitae commodus atque phrasi' (Erasmus, *Aliquot epistolae diui Eusebii Hieronymi*).

227 'Hoc opus exigui quicunque emis aere libelli / Consulis ingenio, consulis eloquio'; 'Hunc leui, solers, pretio libellum / Compares.'

228 'Flaccus composuit. Cospus docet ista. Vietor / Impressit. Paruo grandia lector emes ... Satin haec ementi diximus, lector, tibi?' (Horace, *Epistolarum libri duo*. Vienna: Hieronymus Vietor, 1515).

229 Bernstein, 'Group Identity Formation,' 376.

230 'Si blaesae uitio linguae, calamique laboras' (Johannes Aesticampianus, *Modus epistolandi*, 1515).

CHAPTER THREE
HERO-MAKING

1 Schirrmeister, *Triumph des Dichters*, 216.

2 The process is described by Bernstein, 'From Outsiders to Insiders,' 45–64.

3 Schirrmeister, *Triumph des Dichters*, 111.

4 Buck, 'Ethik im humanistischen Studienprogramm,' 33.

5 Hardison, *Enduring Moment*, 26–7.

6 Hardison, *Enduring Moment*, 108.

7 Hardison, *Enduring Moment*, 31, 37.

8 Michałowska, *Słownik literatury staropolskiej*, 404.

9 Bieńkowski, 'Panegiryk a życie literackie w Polsce,' 184–6, 196. Bieńkowski notes that the increase in the production of panegyric poetry in sixteenth-century Poland was a result of the development of the patronage system there. He remarks that the genre was taught in humanist schools as a response to societal demand, not as an invention of the schoolmasters.

10 Hardison, *Enduring Moment*, 37.

11 *De antiquissima nominis et familiae Thurzonum origine* (Cracow: Hieronymus Vietor, 1519), ll. 15–16.

12 'Dant alii rubro lectas in littore conchas / Mygdonio quorum marmore tecta nitent; / Hic dat Idumeas ex consuetudine palmas; / Hic Siculi lautas dat modo mellis opes; / ... / Haec igitur nostrae rudiuscula carmina musae / Pontificum excellens accipe, quaeso, iubar' (*Ad dominum Mathiam episcopum Przemisliensem cancellarium regni Poloniae*, in Bonaventura, *Breuiloquium*. Cracow: Ungler, 1511 or 1512?); 'Non petis, et nequeo, rubro de littore conchas / Donare, aut gemmas aurifer Herme tuas. / Hoc igitur laeto paruum rogo pectore carmen / Suscipe Thespiadum fautor amice domus' (*Panegyricus in laudem doctoris Augustini Moraui ... praefatio*, in *Panegyricus in laudem Augustini Moraui* Cracow: Florian Ungler, 1513).

13 See chapter 2, n113. Curtius, *European Literature and the Latin Middle Ages*, 83–89, gives an overview of the traditional topics of modesty, especially in the exordium.

14 'En tua tam celebris fama est tantusque tuarum / Virtutum splendor iustitiaeque decus / Ut ... infantiles subrustica carmina linguas / Impellat tenui concelebrare sono' (*Praefatio in Threnos neglectae religionis*, in *Threni neglectae religionis*. Cracow: Johannes Haller, 1518).

15 'Te quoque Korp[o]ninae pastor dignissime plebis / Chartaceo suadet uenerari munere Phoebus' (*Ad Korponensis ecclesiae protomystam dominum Nicolaum Lausman Chrysoreotanum [uulgo Goldberger])*, in *De arte uersificandi opusculum*. Cracow: Hieronymus Vietor, 1521, 1539). Korpona (the ethnic German town of Karpfen) is now Krupina, located in Slovakia. Eck would use the same argument some thirty years later, when writing in honour of the king's doctor, Johannes Benedictus Solfa (*Ad eximium uirum, Sacrae Regiae Maiestatis doctorem, dominum Ioannem Benedictum canonicum Cracouiensem epistola*. Cracow, *c.* 1550).

16 'Nulla tamen potuit me uis arcere negoti / Quin canerem famae nomina clara tuae.' In German, he would most likely have been called Nikolaus von Zeben, from what is now the Slovakian town Sabinov, located south of Bardejov (Bártfa), near Prešov (Eperjes). Nicolaus was a parish priest at Körmöcbánya (Kremnitz), now Kremnica, in central Slovakia, just west of Banská Bystrica. Agricola's poem *Ad magistrum Nicolaum de Czebinio contionatorem Cremnicziensem* was printed in his edition of Proclus Diadochus, *Sphaera* (Cracow: Florian Ungler, 1512).

17 'Sed generosae tuae Thurzo quae stirpis origo / Sit uideo multos addubitare senes / ... / Hanc igitur dubio tollam de pectore nubem / Et referam generis quae sit origo tui' (*De antiquissima nominis et familiae Thurzonum origine*). Curtius, *European Literature and the Latin Middle Ages*, 87, terms this a 'topic of the exordium.'

18 *Ad Sigismundum Gloczer canonicum Olomunczensem* and *Ad Ioannem Tulner uicarium Olomunczensem*, in *Panegyricus in laudem Augustini Moraui; Ad dominum Iodocum Decium*, in *An prudenti uiro sit ducenda*

uxor (Cracow: Johannes Haller, 1518); *Ad dominum Lucam Palotzii, castellanum castri, Makowiitza,* in *Vita diui Pauli primi eremitae* (Cracow: Hieronymus Vietor, 1522). Makovica castle, located near Bártfa (Bardejov), is now referred to as Zborov castle. It was destroyed in the eighteenth century and remains in ruins.

19 'In tuas quamuis mea musa laudes / Torpeat praesul teneris sub annis' (*Ad dominum Ioannem Lubranskii episcopum Posnaniensem,* in Johannes de Stobnica, *Introductio in Ptolomei cosmographiam.* Cracow: Florian Ungler, 1512, 1513; Hieronymus Vietor, 1519).

20 'Nostra tuis impar titulis Polyhymnia, non dum / Digna est in laudes pandere uela tuas / Nam de Pimpleo tenuissima rure fluenta / Hausit et incultos promit ab ore sonos' (*Ad dominum Franciscum Chahol episcopum Zagrauiensem,* in *De arte uersificandi opusculum.* Cracow: Florian Ungler, 1515).

21 'Praeterea quidam pudor ingens nostra relidit / Ora tuum quoties attento promere nomen, / ... / Quodque infantiles horret uenerabile uersus, / Quales nos blaeso uix sic effundimus ore' (*Ad dominum Nicolaum Lausman Chrysoreotanum [uulgo Goldberger]*). Eck would repeat this motif in his poem to the king's doctor, Johannes Benedictus Solfa (*Ad eximium uirum, Sacrae Regiae Maiestatis doctorem, dominum Ioannem Benedictum canonicum Cracouiensem epistola*).

22 'Et quamquam gelido trepident mea corda timore / Cum cerno uultum praesulis ipse sacrum' (*Ad dominum Mathiam Dreuicium Vladislauiensem praesulem,* in *Threni neglectae religionis*).

23 'Aeger enim clarios nequeo calcare Penates / Et mea Castalio labra rigare fauo' (*Ad Sebastianum Steinhoffer Hallanum,* in *De arte uersificandi opusculum,* 1515).

24 'Cumque leo igniuomis saeuiret rictibus ardens, / ... Cererem et messor in arua petit. / ... / Sed me dentata segetes abscindere falce / Sydera uulnifici prohibuere canis ...' (*Panegyricus in laudem doctoris Augustini Moraui ... praefatio*).

25 Curtius, *European Literature and the Latin Middle Ages,* 88–9.

26 'Sed nunc tempus erit grauiori insurgere cantu / Et de fluctifrago trepidantem pellere nauem / Litore et antennis ualidas firmare triremes' (*Panegyricus in laudem Augustini Moraui*).

27 'Sic ego turgidulos si coner scindere fluctus / Linter in undosis obrueretur aquis' (*Ad dominum Franciscum Chahol episcopum Zagrauiensem*).

28 'Essem confiteor multum temerarius, ante et / Cogerer incoeptum sistere forte gradum, / Namque puer tepidos nimium dum tendit ad axes / Icarus, Icareis nomen inuirit aquis, / Sic ego turgidulos si coner scindere fluctus, / Linter in undosis obrueretur aquis. / ... / Paruula namque leuem faciunt praeludia cursum / Ad grauiora, labor primus abhorret onus' (*Ad dominum Franciscum Chahol episcopum Zagrauiensem*).

29 'Sic quondam tepido liquefactis aere pennis / Icarus in uitreum corruit ipse mare, / Et Phaeton patrium iuuenili remige currum / Conscendens subito praecipitatur iners; / Atque ego praeruptos ausim si radere fluctus / Alnus in aequoreis obrueretur aquis, / Hinc decet, haec tenui ludat tantisper in amne / Donec caeruleos discat obire lacus' (*Ad dominum Mathiam Dreuicium Vladislauiensem praesulem*).
30 'Nostra nimis gracilis sub tantis musula rebus / Deficit, atque illo pondere pressa gemit. / ... / Attamen hos fragiles dum spiritus incolat artus, / Et calor in membris palpitet ipse suis, / Thurzonis laudes uersu quocunque tonabo, / Et referam meritis carmina digna suis' (*De antiquissima nominis et familiae Thurzonum origine*).
31 'Quos nunc pacato uir quam doctissime uultu / Suscipe, dona tibi mox meliora dabo / ... / Quare age combustos placido nunc pectore flores / Accipe; in autumno dulcia uina dabo' (*Panegyricus in laudem doctoris Augustini Moraui ... praefatio*).
32 'Quod petimus laeto capias Thurzo inclyte uultu, / Quo sumes tandem meliora magis' (*De antiquissima nominis et familiae Thurzonum origine*).
33 'Istic magne tuam praesul stirpemque domumque / Et famam digna celebratam laude uidebis, / ... / Interea modicos ubi res tempusque requirent / Conscribam uersus, et te nostrumque patronum / Thurzonem magnum merito uenerabor honore' (*Ad Georgium episcopum ecclesiae Quinqueecclesiensis et secretarium et cancellarium Regiae Maiestatis*, printed with *Iubilus heroicus* and *Apophoreticum carmen de Christi natiuitate.* Cracow: Hieronymus Vietor, 1520).
34 'Sis igitur paucis contentus uersibus oro / Illico suscipies grande poema' (*Ad Sebastianum Steinhoffer Hallanum*).
35 'Accipe qui ueniunt uersus de paupere seruo / Nam tibi multa breui tempore metra canam' (*Ad dominum Mathiam episcopum Przemisliensem cancellarium regni Poloniae*).
36 *Ad Nicolaum Salomonem,* in pseudo-Crates, *Epistolae* (Cracow: Hieronymus Vietor, 1518); *Nicolao Salomoni Agricola bene agere,* in Robertus de Euremodio, *Institutiones uitae* (Cracow: Johannes Haller, 1519).
37 *Pro nobili iuuene, domino Georgio Soos,* in *Vita diui Pauli primi eremitae.* The Soós family held the castle at Sóvár (Solivar), east of Eperjes (Prešov).
38 The poem to Eysenberger is a double acrostic; the initial letters of each line spell 'Jesus,' and the final letters of each line, 'Maria.' In the poem Eck gives Eysenberger the clues to the solution.
39 'Maxime rex, alto diuorum sanguine crete' (*Praefatio in Threnos neglectae religionis*).
40 'Maxima Pannoniae praesul dignissime gentis / Gloria perspicuum pontificumque decus' (*Ad dominum Franciscum Chahol episcopum Zagrauiensem*).
41 'Inclyta pontificum lux, et clarissima gentis / Gloria Pannonicae' (*Ad*

Georgium episcopum ecclesiae Quinqueecclesiensis et secretarium et cancellarium Regiae Maiestatis).

42 'Gentis Antistes decus es potentis / ... patriaeque splendor' (*Ad dominum Ioannem Lubranskii episcopum Posnaniensem*).

43 *Ad dominum Nicolaum Lausman Chrysoreotanum (uulgo Goldberger).*

44 'Iamque uale Pylios praesul uicture per annos' (*Ad dominum Franciscum Chahol episcopum Zagrauiensem*); 'Unde suum crescit decus et sua gloria uiuet / ... / Et suus aethereas tandem migrabit ad aedes / Spiritus et summi paradisi gaudia cernet' (*Panegyricus in laudem Augustini Moraui*); 'Nulla uoluntati est similis (mihi crede) papyrus / Pectoris affectum qua reserare queam' (*Panegyricus in laudem doctoris Augustini Moraui ... praefatio*).

45 'Sic tibi longaeuam bifrons fortuna senectam / Contribuet faustos Iuppiter atque dies' (*Ad dominum Mathiam Dreuicium Vladislauiensem praesulem*); 'Det Deus ut iusta populos sic lance gubernes / Per multos annos, ut tandem rite peracta / Hac uita, decimi subeas fastigia coeli' (*Ad dominum Nicolaum Lausman Chrysoreotanum [uulgo Goldberger]*).

46 'Sic tibi pro uoto ueniant felicia quaeque / Nec te unquam grauius sors inimica premat' (*Ad dominum Thurzonem*, printed with *Ad Hungariae et Bohemiae regem Ferdinandum epistola* and *Alia epistola ad dominum Alexium Thurzonem Regiae Curiae iudicem*. Vienna: Hieronymus Vietor, 1530.)

47 'Diue sacerdoti faueas rogo supplice uoce / Quem decorat Crocae pontificalis honor / Magnus Ioannes natus de gente Konarski / Hic pater est, pro quo nuncupo uota tibi. / Hic mihi Maecenas meus est, hic Pollio, quicquid / In me est id totum debeo nempe uiro' (*Ad diuum Ioannem Baptistam pro Ioanne Konarski*, in Giovanni Pontano, *De laudibus diuinis opusculum, cum argumentis Leonardi Coxi Britanni*. Cracow: Johannes Haller, 1520).

48 'Quid sit iam minime poteris dubitare, Iodoce / Uxor felicem te generosa facit. / Quam precor in Pylios seruet tibi Iuppiter annos / Ut faustum multo pignore te faciat' (*Ad dominum Iodocum Decium*). Decius was to marry Anna Krupka in 1519. In this short poem, as in the main work, Eck characterized the good wife as a faithful helpmate ('Et tibi fida comes, custosque fidelis adhaeret / Et te prae reliquis condecorare solet') and painted the marital life as one of happiness, with children.

49 'Ergo occurre meae praesul uenerande iuuentae / Ut possim studium continuare meum, / Turpiter in medio gressum ne sistere campo / Cogar et inceptam dis[s]eruisse uiam / Nam te munificum cunctis ostendis amicis / Tristibus afflictis es pius usque parens' (*Ad dominum Franciscum Chahol episcopum Zagrauiensem*).

50 'Thurzo, precor, patrone faue, quo regia tandem / Te duce proueniat pensio, grata mihi.'

51 Helpful in identifying these strategies was Lausberg, *Handbook of Literary Rhetoric*.

52 'Ipse uirtutes sequeris beatas / ... / Diceris clemens, pius et benignus, / Atque doctorum facilis uirorum / Soter et fautor ...' (*Ad dominum Ioannem Lubranskii episcopum Posnaniensem*).

53 '... cui lumbos zona pudoris / Constringit, galeamque timor, thoraca fidesque, / Loricam constans Astrea, obacutaque uerba / Vibrantem gladium praestant, quibus acribus armis, / Vallatus, munisque greges ...' (*Ad Nicolaum Lausman Chrysoreotanum [uulgo Goldberger]*).

54 The figure of *exemplum*, or example, can be traced back to Aristotle's *Rhetoric*, where it was cited as a means of persuasion. In the Middle Ages, *exemplum* was associated only with narration. The Renaissance, while allowing *exemplum* to embrace narrative, returned the notion to its classical meaning of a comparison that demonstrates a general truth (Lyons, *Exemplum*, 4, 6, 11–12).

55 An exemplum used as an example of conduct was a familiar Renaissance notion (Lyons, *Exemplum*, 13).

56 'Praedicat hermetem Memphetica terra uetustum / Niliaco primas qui tulit orbe notas; / Cecropidae ficto non laudant carmine Cadmum / Carmentemque tonat Ausonis ora suam' (*Ad dominum Mathiam episcopum Przemisliensem cancellarium regni Poloniae*).

57 *Panegyricus in laudem Augustini Moraui* (l. 128).

58 'Non igitur famosa tuae nunc stemmata gentis / Dicam uel clarum nobilitate genus. / Praetereo duplices dotes animi atque nitentis / Corporis ingenii munera clara tui, / Nec quoque diuitias magnas titulosue potentes, / Nec uirtute tua nomina parta canam' (*Ad dominum Franciscum Chahol episcopum Zagrauiensem*).

59 'Quare magna tuae iam non ego stemmata gentis / Dicam uel studiis nomina parta tuis / Corporis obticeo dotes et mentis opimae; / Nec non ingenii pondera clara tui, / Hinc quoque diuitias amplas titulosque superbos / Praetereo, et quidquid te decore solet' (*Ad dominum Mathiam Dreuicium Vladislauiensem praesulem*).

60 'Sed quid imprimis dubius recensem / Cum decus, uirtus, honor et uenustas / Non inaequali tua corda luce / Iamque decorant. / Ergo ne tantum gracili decoris / Voce defoedam, reprimo camenas' (*Ad Ioannem Tulner uicarium Olomunczensem*); 'Sed quid ego dubius rerum preponere censem / In te uirtutum cum micat omne decus. / ... / Quare ego ne gracili defoedam carmine tantas / Virtutes, cesso scribere plura tibi' (*Ad dominum Iodocum Decium*).

61 'Ast ego cum uideam praedictis omnibus unum / Te mire celebrem, dubito clarissime Luca / Quid primum referam, uel quid posterius' (*Ad dominum Lucam Palotzii, castellanum castri, Makowiitza*).

62 In the Middle Ages, the *exemplum* became associated with narration, so that the term came to be used to mean any narration in an oratori-

cal situation, not just the specific, narrow 'exemplary' narration (Lyons, *Exemplum*, 11). Here, of course, the poets are using narration in that specific, didactic sense – 'a narrative with a claim to a particular form of truth' – an aspect of exemplum accepted in the Renaissance (Lyons, *Exemplum*, 12).

63 '[V]anos coepit contemnere ludos / Quos iuuenes ardent primis tractare sub annis / Ligneolo placuit nec tunc equitare caballo / ... / Ac eadem bibulis cupiens inarare bacillo / Pulueribusque notas passim formare rotundas / Coeperat, et si quos priscorum forte libellos / Occlusos reperit uatum, reserare solebat / Atque per ignotos rudibus discurrere labris / Codiculos ...' (*Panegyricus in laudem Augustini Moraui*).

64 Giovanni Bonzagno (Johannes Baptista Bonzagnus) (?–1537) was an Italian from Reggio who had come to Hungary in 1512 and who served the bishops of Eger from 1516. He went on to become the royal ambassador to Venice and the provost of Várad (now Oradea in Romania). *Querela pacis*, in which the figure of Peace comes down to earth, was first published by Froben at Basel in December 1517. It was printed at Cracow by Hieronymus Vietor in April 1518.

65 'Applausus mirata nouos dea, pone cohortem / Substitit, et tales hausit ab aure sonos. / Viuat, io, multos Bonzagnus uiuat in annos, / Et numeret Pylii saecula grata senis, / Qui solus decreta patrum, legesque sacratas, / Atque fidem, merita relligione colit ... (*Ad reuerendum dominum Ioannem Baptistam Bonzagnum custodem, canonicum et uicarium in spiritualibus ecclesiae Agriensis atque causarum auditorem generalem*, in *Vita diui Pauli primi eremitae*).

66 On the transmission of classical and late-antique rhetorical norms, see Murphy, *Rhetoric in the Middle Ages*.

67 Schirrmeister, *Triumph des Dichters*, 216.

68 The tradition comes from Quintilian. Cf. Lausberg, *Handbook of Literary Rhetoric*, 106. The extent to which the humanist poets valued the idea of *nobilitas* is shown by their adoption of Latin names, which in many cases served to mask their lower-class origins. See Bernstein, 'Group Identity Formation,' 381–2, and Bernstein, 'Humanistische Standeskultur,' 103–4.

69 The importance of the family line would furthermore be signalled by poems in Eck's book to the physician Johannes Benedictus Solfa (*Ad eximium uirum, Sacrae Regiae Maiestatis doctorem, dominum Ioannem Benedictum, canonicum Cracouiensem epistola*) that describe the family crest of Benedictus and interpret the symbols contained in it.

70 *Ad Ioachimum von Watt, alias Vadianum*. Vadian's elegy was printed in his *Aegloga, cui titulus Faustus. De insignibus familiae Vadianorum, ad Melchiorem fratrem elegia* (Vienna: Johannes Singrenius, 1517). Agricola's poem and Vadian's elegy were reprinted in *Commentaria*

in C. Iulii Solini Polyhistora (Basel: Petrus, 1557). See chapter 2, n75.

71 'Gentis, antistes, decus es potentis / Ipse Lubranae' (*Ad dominum Ioannem Lubranskii episcopum Posnaniensem*).

72 'Bina homini prosunt coelesti praestita nutu / Virtutis clarum sanguinis atque decus; / Quae duo si fuerit quisquam fortitus, ab unde / Faustus, et ad normam rite beatus erit' (*Ad Ioachimum von Watt, alias Vadianum*).

73 'Nobilitas duplici completur munere uera, / Virtute eximia, sanguine et egregio' (*De antiquissima nominis et familiae Thurzonum origine*).

74 North, 'Canons and Hierarchies,' 165–83.

75 Wilckens, *Albrecht Dürer*, 129–51; Delmarcel, *Los Honores*, 18–28.

76 'Cui miranda pio renitet clementia uultu, / Quemque fouet pietas, atque sacrata fides ...' (*Praefatio in Threnos neglectae religionis*).

77 'Pubescens uitulum, mox crescens robore et annis, / Quo uoluit taurum sustulit ipse Milo' (*De antiquissima nominis et familiae Thurzonum origine*).

78 'Virtutum omne decus quod raro in corpore pulchro / cernitur. Et coruo uirtus est rarior albo / Incolit ingenuos pulchri quae corporis artus' (*Panegyricus in laudem Augustini Moraui*).

79 Magdolna was the widow of Tamás Széchy, the lord lieutenant (*supremus comes*) of Vas county. Through his marriage to her, Thurzó increased his wealth by obtaining some of the Széchy estates in Vas and Zala counties. See Erdélyi, 'Elek Thurzó of Bethlenfalva,' 35.

80 *De formosissima atque pudicissima domina Magdalena, domini Thurzonis coniuge*, in *Ad Hungariae et Bohemiae regem Ferdinandum epistola*.

81 'Hinc est qui nulli priscorum carmine uatum / cedit, sed cunctos quotquot ueneranda uetustas / Laudibus extollit, superat modulamine suaui' (*Panegyricus in laudem Augustini Moraui*).

82 'Magno atque eloquii micantis haustum / Altis Castalii iugi sub antris / Mentem percupidus tuam replesti; / Ardenterque sitim grauem leuasti / Tantis cum studiis tuis' (*Ad dominum Petrum Cypser Leusthouianum, parochianum et archidiaconum Bartphensem*, in *An prudenti uiro*, 1518).

83 'Christicolumque doces in relligione popellum / Quo teneat superi iussa uerenda dei' (*Ad magistrum Nicolaum de Czebinio contionatorem Cremnicziensem*).

84 '[V]igilans pastor ... / Nunc tam prudenti moderaris pectore, ut ipsas / Nunc Korpona queat noctes dormire, diesque / Ablatis curis laetos deducere ...' (*Ad dominum Nicolaum Lausman Chrysoreotanum [uulgo Goldberger]*).

85 'Hinc pietate Titum superat quoque lance fideli / Traianum, aut priscis qui modo iura dedit.' *In nouo magistratu praestantissimi uiri domini Andreae Reuber, septenarum artium Baccalaurei celebratissimi iudicis Bartphensis dignissimi 1517, Pro quartodecimo magistratu Andreae Reuber anno 1518*, and *Pro quintodecimo magistratu eiusdem anno mille-*

simo quingentesimo 19 were printed in *De mundi contemptu* (Cracow: Hieronymus Vietor, 1519). The first two had previously been printed in *An prudenti uiro* (1518).

86 'Quaerite Baptistam legum, rectique patronum, / Hic semper cunctis arbiter aequus adest' (*Ad reuerendum dominum Ioannem Baptistam Bonzagnum custodem, canonicum et uicarium in spiritualibus ecclesiae Agriensis atque causarum auditorem generalem*). In his poems to Johannes Benedictus Solfa (*Ad eximium uirum, Sacrae Regiae Maiestatis doctorem, dominum Ioannem Benedictum canonicum Cracouiensem epistola*), Eck praised him for completing his medical studies in Italy and noted that he had been singled out by King Sigismund because of his expertise.

87 Hardison, *Enduring Moment*, 30.

88 'Nemo etenim ignorat quantas uirtute pararit / diuitias' (*Panegyricus in laudem Augustini Moraui*).

89 'Nam dat diuitias multis ut uiuere fausti / Rite queant, inopem pulchre et deducere uitam' (*Panegyricus in laudem Augustini Moraui*).

90 'Quem uirtus, quem cana fides, industria solers, / Terrenis longe praeposuere uiris'; 'Ungarus unde capit magna incrementa colonus, / Diuitiis multum crescit et ipse suis'; 'Verum quicquid id est diuini muneris, omne / Thurzoni debet Pannonis ora suo' (*De antiquissima nominis et familiae Thurzonum origine*).

91 'Ille poetarum fautor celeberrimus omnem / Qui tollit maesta de sollicitudine mentem / Unde suum crescit decus et sua gloria uiuet' (*Panegyricus in laudem Augustini Moraui*).

92 'Doctus es et doctos uero tibi nectis amore / Ut te fautorem iure uocare queant' (*Ad magistrum Nicolaum de Czebinio contionatorem Cremnicziensem*).

93 'Erigis structis benefacta muris / Moenia ut uita queat in quieta / Ante non tutus placido sacerdos / Psallere Christo / ... / Et tibi cordi est studiosa pubes / Unde complures alis in palaestris / saepe sacratis' (*Ad dominum Ioannem Lubranskii episcopum Posnaniensem*).

94 'Nam te munificum cunctis ostendis amicis / Tristibus afflictis es pius usque parens / Auxiliatricem non cessas tendere dextram / In miserorum usum at diligis usque bonos' (*Ad dominum Franciscum Chahol episcopum Zagrauiensem*).

95 'Vos igitur diui uates, ... / ... / Hunc tantum nostri studii communis et artis / Fautorem, uestris concelebrate modis' (*De antiquissima nominis et familiae Thurzonum origine*).

96 Bernstein, 'Group Identity Formation,' 382.

97 See Treml, *Humanistische Gemeinschaftsbildung*, 108–13, for an outline of the German humanists' views on the *studia humanitatis*, morality, and behaviour.

98 The year of publication is not known (the book contains no colophon, and Eck ended his dedicatory letter only with the date 8 August) but

has been determined as either 1512 (the year in which Johannes Benedictus Solfa, who is termed *magister* at the head of the preliminary verses that he contributes, received his MA degree) or 1513 (the year in which Augustinus Moravus died, in November). See Bauch, 'Valentin Eck und Georg Werner,' 44–5; Wörster, *Humanismus in Olmütz*, 100–1. Kawecka-Gryczowa, *Polonia typographica*, 3: 27, dates the printing as 1513.

99 Bauch, 'Valentin Eck und Georg Werner,' 44 ; Macůrek, 'Humanismus v oblasti moravsko-slezské,' 348; Harder, 'Zentren des Humanismus in Böhmen und Mähren,' 159; Wörster, *Humanismus in Olmütz*, 46.

100 On Moravus, Stanislaus Thurzó, and the promotion of humanism and the arts at Olomouc, see Wörster, *Humanismus in Olmütz*, 101; Hlobil and Petrů, *Humanismus a raná renesance na Moravé*, 27–38; Bietenholz and Deutscher, *Contemporaries of Erasmus*, 3: 322–5; Harder, 'Zentren des Humanismus in Böhmen und Mähren,' 157–69; and Macůrek, 'Humanismus v oblasti moravsko-slezské,' 332–55.

101 Wörster, *Humanismus in Olmütz*, 101.

102 Wörster, *Humanismus in Olmütz*, 43.

103 Bauch, 'Valentin Eck und Georg Werner,' 45; Wörster, *Humanismus in Olmütz*, 101.

104 *Polski słownik biograficzny*, 6: 198; Bauch, 'Valentin Eck und Georg Werner,' 45; Wörster, *Humanismus in Olmütz*, 101.

105 Hammer, *Latin and German Encomia of Cities*, 12. See also Ludwig, 'Darstellung südwestdeutscher Städte,' 39–76.

106 Wörster, *Humanismus in Olmütz*, 101.

107 Wörster, *Humanismus in Olmütz*, 101.

108 *Pentametrum elegiacum ... in Alma Academia Cracouiensi*, *Ode sapphica de Polonia et Cracouia*, ... *In natale solum quod Nouumforum perhibetur*, and *Slesiae descriptio compendiosa* were printed in Corvinus's *Cosmographia* (Basel, 1496); *Oda sapphica de Polonia et eius metropoli Cracouia* in his *Hortulus elegantiarum* (first printed at Cracow, 1502, but also printed at Leipzig at least half a dozen times before 1510, so that Eck would have known it as a student there); and *Carmen ... quo ualedicit Prutenos* ... in Copernicus's translation of the letters of Theophylactos Simocattes (Cracow, 1509). On these poems, see Buszewicz, *Cracovia in litteris*, 51–3, 118, 155–6, 166–7, 211–12; Harder, 'Die Landesbeschreibung in der Literatur des schlesischen Frühhumanismus,' 36–8; and Krókowski, 'Laurentius Corvinus,' 160–2. On the publication of the letters of Theophylactos Simocattes, see Segel, *Renaissance Culture in Poland*, 127–37.

109 See Thomson, 'Scholar as Hero,' 197–212.

110 According to tradition, Eck began to tutor Thurzó's daughter in

1517. Bauch, 'Valentin Eck und Georg Werner,' 46, gives Janocki as the source of this information.

111 It is possible that Eck was introduced to Thurzó by Valentin Carbo, the town clerk of Kassa. See chapter 4.

112 For the biography of Alexius Thurzó, see Bietenholz and Deutscher, *Contemporaries of Erasmus*, 3: 322–3; Lambrecht, 'Aufstiegschancen und Handlungsräume,' 343; and Erdélyi, 'Elek Thurzó of Bethlenfalva.'

113 In the title to *De antiquissima nominis et familiae Thurzonum origine*, Thurzó is named as *camerarius Cremnicensis* (controller of the mining revenues at Körmöcbánya) and *liber dominus Plesnensis* (free lord of Pszczyna). According to Lepszy, 'Turzonowie w Polsce,' 474, it was Alexius's younger brother who held Pszczyna. The town is found in Silesia, now southwest Poland, near Katowice.

114 Erdélyi, 'Elek Thurzó of Bethlenfalva,' 7.

115 Vienna, 1509; printed in Paulus Crosnensis, *Pauli Crosnensis Rutheni Carmina*, ed. Cytowska, 81–103.

116 Gorzkowski, *Paweł z Krosna*, 237, notes that Paulus was following in the footsteps of the fifth-century poet Sidonius, who popularized the motif of the labours of Hercules. In *Carm.* 13, he compared Emperor Majorian with Hercules. On Paulus's poem, see also Segel, *Renaissance Culture in Poland*, 110–11.

117 Müller, *Gedechtnus*, 169–74.

118 Wörster, *Humanismus in Olmütz*, 35; Bauch, *Caspar Ursinus Velius*, 32–3. Ursinus Velius published his *Praeludium* along with other poems to his patrons Johann and Stanislaus Thurzó in *Poematum libri quinque* (Basel, 1522).

119 Müller, *Gedechtnus*, 239.

120 Lausberg, *Handbook of Literary Rhetoric*, 106; Murphy, *Rhetoric in the Middle Ages*, 41; Crane, *Wit and Rhetoric*, 61–75; Clark, 'Rise and Fall of Progymnasmata,' 259–63.

121 Percival, 'Renaissance Grammar,' 69–71, and Padley, *Grammatical Theory*, 15–20.

122 Škoviera, *Bardejovčan Valentín Ecchius*, 90, 112–13.

123 Hardison, *Enduring Moment*, 30.

124 Macůrek, 'Humanismus v oblasti moravsko-slezské,' 347.

125 Lambrecht, 'Aufstiegschancen und Handlungsräume,' 326, cites the probable origin of the name as 'Turzen.' The family emigrated from Lower Austria (Niederösterreich) into the Tatra mountains in the early fifteenth century.

126 Johann Thurzó (1437–1508) arrived in Cracow from the Szepes (now the Spiš in eastern Slovakia) in 1462, and there he married into a wealthy German burgher family. As a town councillor he took an active part in cultural affairs, especially in the embellishment of St

Mary's church on the city's main square. He lent money to the Polish king. He expanded his business with the establishment of a copper smelting mine in Mogiła, at the time a village near Cracow, today part of the city itself. In 1493 he created one of the first trading companies in Poland. In 1495 the Thurzós associated themselves with the Fugger business (Lambrecht, 'Aufstiegschancen und Handlungsräume,' 332–3).

127 'Verum quicquid id est diuini muneris, omne / Thurzoni debet Pannonis ora suo' (*De antiquissima nominis et familiae Thurzonum origine*, ll. 93–4).

128 'Heroas magnos, mundi duo sidera, uirtus / In quorum diuo pectore tota sedet' (*De antiquissima nominis et familiae Thurzonum origine*, ll. 105–6).

129 '[P]roceres magno tres nomine claros' (*De antiquissima nominis et familiae Thurzonum origine*, l. 107).

130 'Turba nouennarum sua crura manusque ligarunt / Fasciolis'; 'Hic etiam fama est Charites cunabula circum / Proiecisse rosas' (*Panegyricus in laudem Augustini Moraui*, ll. 28–9, 32–3).

131 'Daphneam Dryades tibi mox neuere corollam, / Quam capiti imposuit Calliopea tuo' (*De antiquissima nominis et familiae Thurzonum origine*, ll. 147–8).

132 Müller, *Gedechtnus*, 366.

133 'Ligneolo placuit nec tunc equitare caballo / siue Morae per aquas tumidi meditarier altas / Piscibus insidias lento tunc uimine inanes' (*Panegyricus in laudem Augustini Moraui*, ll. 40–2).

134 'Ac eadem bibulis cupiens inarare bacillo / Pulueribusque notas passim formare rotundas / Coeperat, et si quos priscorum forte libellos / occlusos reperit uatum, reserare solebat / Atque per ignotos rudibus discurrere labris / Codiculos' (*Panegyricus in laudem Augustini Moraui*, ll. 49–54).

135 Thomson, 'Scholar as Hero,' 208.

136 'Dumque uiam incautus properas tirunculus altam / Delibans artes sedulitate nouas' (*De antiquissima nominis et familiae Thurzonum origine*, ll. 153–4).

137 Galinsky, *Herakles Theme*, 101–3, 196–202.

138 Galinsky, *Herakles Theme*, 199; Panofsky, *Hercules am Scheidewege*, 68–76, 83–5. Panofsky notes that Locher relied on Silius Italicus, *Punica* 14.18–128 for his *Concertatio*.

139 The play was printed in Grünpeck's *Comoediae utilissimae* (Augsburg, after 16 November 1497). The political background to Maximilian's identification with Hercules is given by McDonald, 'Maximilian of Habsburg and the Veneration of Hercules.'

140 Printed as *Virtus et uoluptas* (Augsburg, 1511).

141 Chelidonius's play was performed in February 1515 and printed in

May of that year in Vienna. For further details on these theatre pieces, see Wuttke, *Histori Herculis*, 207–14.

142 'Nulla carent duro sublimia facta labore' (*De antiquissima nominis et familiae Thurzonum origine*, l. 197).

143 'Non aliter sapidi quam mellis prouida nutrix / Arboream subiens uernali tempore syluam / Singula purpurei depraedans germina ueris / Iamque rosas graciles, uiolas nunc flore rubentes / Delibans, donec castas impleuerit alas' (*Panegyricus in laudem Augustini Moraui*, ll. 101–5). The idea here is not just one of industriousness, but also that Moravus will use the models of classical literature (pollen) in the production of his own writing (honey).

144 Eck is probably referring here to Aelius Melissus, the grammarian, comic poet, and librarian to Augustus and not to Gaius Maecenus Melissus, the freedman of Maecenas, who invented a form of light drama (*fabula trabeata*) and compiled a collection of jokes.

145 'Non aliter sapidi quam mellis sedula nutrix, / Vere nouo tacitum cum subit ipsa nemus. / Singula purpurei depraedans germina floris, / Nunc has nunc illas aduolat ore dapas, / Dum liquido castas succo compleuerit alas / Quo posset dulcem parca replere domum' (*De antiquissima nominis et familiae Thurzonum origine*, ll. 253–8). On the antique origins of the metaphor of the bee and its popularity in Renaissance literature, see Waszink, *Biene und Honig*; Pigman, 'Barzizza's Treatise on Imitation'; Domański, 'O dwu znaczeniach metafory pszczoły'; Maleszyński, 'Pszczoła-"archipoeta,"' 47–72.

146 'O Thurzo felix, o terque, quaterque beate / Qui tam multiplici nobilitate micas. / Quippe in te uirtus, solertia, gloria fama, / Nam praecellenti iuncta nitore latent' (*De antiquissima nominis et familiae Thurzonum origine*, ll. 269–72; in the Jagiellonian Library copy, Cim. Qu. 4228, 'Nam' has been corrected, in an old hand, to 'Tam').

147 'E quibus eximiis uirtutibus auguror ipse / Quae sit decrepiti uita futura senis. / Ipse tuos primo tritauos iam flore iuuentae, / Es praetergressus nobilitate tua' (*De antiquissima nominis et familiae Thurzonum origine*, ll. 281–4).

148 The term is explained by Murphy, *Rhetoric in the Middle Ages*, 41.

149 '[N]am docta tuos melioribus astris / Posteritas patres superat' (*Panegyricus in laudem Augustini Moraui*, ll. 250–1).

150 'Nam dat diuitias multis ut uiuere fausti / Rite queant, inopem pulchre et deducere uitam / Ille poetarum fautor celeberrimus omnem / Qui tollit maesta de sollicitudine mentem' (*Panegyricus in laudem Augustini Moraui*, ll. 276–9).

151 Thomson, 'Scholar as Hero,' 200.

152 Wörster, *Humanismus in Olmütz*, 101.

153 Bauch, 'Valentin Eck und Georg Werner,' 49, quoting Szalay, *Geschichte Ungarns*, 2: 257.

CHAPTER FOUR
THE NEED FOR THE IMMEDIATE PRODUCTION OF POETRY

1 Silver, 'Prints for a Prince,' 13, 15, 17, 20; Füssel, 'Dichtung und Politik um 1500,' 803–4, 822–31; Tanner, *Last Descendant*, 100–9, 124–6. Müller, *Gedechtnus* covers in detail Maximilian's program of self-promotion through literary works. See especially chapters 4 and 7 ('Maximilians Ruhmeswerk,' 'Hof, Herrscher, Öffentlichkeit: zur Funktion des Ruhmeswerks').

2 Tazbir, *Polska przedmurzem Europy*, 21–54, discusses the origin of the concept and the discrepancies in its interpretation in Poland and in the West. Western political opinion was, for example, much keener to have Poland take up arms against the Turks than Poland was itself. The Poles complained of lack of support in their struggles against the Tartars and the Muscovites.

3 Nowak-Dłużewski was the author of a series of books on the history of Polish political poetry from the Middle Ages to the seventeenth century under the title *Okolicznościowa poezja polityczna w Polsce* (Warsaw: Instytut Wydawniczy Pax, 1963–72). Because of its breadth, the work is still useful in spite of its outdated critical slant. The question of how to interpret a work of literature as a historical source was important enough to provoke the organization of a conference by the Polish Academy of Sciences in 1976; see the resulting book, Stefanowska and Sławiński, *Dzieło literackie jako źródło historyczne*.

4 Martin, 'Inventing Sincerity, Refashioning Prudence.'

5 See, for example, Urbański's analysis of 'information' in the poetry of Sarbievius, in Urbański, *Theologia Fabulosa*, 145–59.

6 Schirrmeister, *Triumph des Dichters*, 217, states that monarchal rule in the early modern period could be realized on a long-term basis only if it were represented in panegyrics.

7 Łowmiański, *Polityka Jagiellonów*, 450, 455.

8 Füssel, 'Kaiserliche Repräsentation,' 359–68.

9 On the expansionist politics of the Jagiellons at the end of the fifteenth century, see Łowmiański, *Polityka Jagiellonów*, and Baczkowski, *Zjazd Wiedeński*, on whom I rely for this information.

10 On the origins of this conflict, see Davies, *God's Playground*, 87–91.

11 Baczkowski, *Zjazd Wiedeński*, 66.

12 However, by deciding to save his possessions in the east, Sigismund resigned from his interests in the west, a development that would cost the Poles their influence in the Danube region (Łowmiański, *Polityka Jagiellonów*, 428, 451).

13 Füssel, 'Kaiserliche Repräsentation,' 361; Nowak-Dłużewski, *Okolicznościowa poezja polityczna*, 61–7.

14 Füssel, 'Kaiserliche Repräsentation,' 366.

15 Füssel, *Riccardus Bartholinus Perusinus*, 75–139, gives a detailed analysis of *Odeporicon*.

16 Dantiscus's poetic contributions to the publicity surrounding the Congress are analysed by Milewska-Waźbińska, 'Poetry of Joannes Dantiscus in the Diplomatic Service.'

17 Vienna: Johannes Singrenius, 1515. The title-page to the first edition reads 'Congressus ac celeberrimi conuentus Caesaris Max. et trium regum Hungariae, Boemiae, et Poloniae ... descriptio,' but the work has become known by the title immediately preceding the text (*Diarium ...*).

18 Cuspinian (1473–1529), from Schweinfurt in Franconia, had studied at Leipzig and Vienna. He qualified as a doctor and held the post of professor of poetics at Vienna University, as the successor to Conrad Celtis, before entering the imperial service as a diplomat. On him, see Bonorand, *Personenkommentar II*, 267, and Ankwicz-Kleehoven, *Wiener Humanist Johannes Cuspinian*.

19 Füssel, 'Kaiserliche Repräsentation,' 365.

20 *Carmina ... de felicissimo redito ex Vienna* was dedicated to the grand-chancellor, Krzysztof Szydłowiecki. On the poem, see Gorzkowski, *Paweł z Krosna*, 173–6, and Gryczowa, 'Wokół Kongresu Wiedeńskiego,' who prints the text.

21 In 1519, Lang would become the archbishop himself. He was an ambitious man known for displays of power and pomp (as reflected in Agricola's poem). Lang was recognized as a patron of humanists, and Erasmus sought out his acquaintance. His portrait was drawn by Dürer. See Bietenholz and Deutscher, *Contemporaries of Erasmus*, 2: 289, and Obersteiner, *Die Bischöfe von Gurk*, 272–88. Lang's life and work have been covered in detail in a monograph, Sallaberger, *Kardinal Matthäus Lang*.

22 *Oratio ad reuerendissimum dominum Matheum cardinalem Gurcensem coadiutorem et successorem Salisburgensem* (Vienna: Hieronymus Vietor, 1515). VD16, W3474. Winderl's oration would be reprinted in the anthology of orations given in July.

23 Bauch, 'Rudolphus Agricola Junior,' 16–17. There was also a printing dated 29 February. See Vredeveld, 'Agricola, Rudolf d. J.,' 734. The poem was reprinted, with minor alterations to suit the occasion, together with Agricola's oration in honour of Bishop Piotr Tomicki, in the anthology of orations given by members of the university in July. This reprinting is not cited by Vredeveld.

24 Agricola hints at the *Siluae* of Statius, a collection of occasional poems.

25 'Quam diuum et sophiae quam sit probitatis et aequi / Cultor, ubi excoluit te, satis edocuit'; 'Haec tua, summe pater, probitas in herile redundat / Grande decus repetens fluxerat unde caput' (*Pro reuerendissimo domino Matheo Langio*. Vienna: Hieronymus Vietor, 1515.

Reprinted in *Orationes Viennae Austriae ad diuum Maximilianum Caes. Aug. aliosque illustrissimos principes habitae*. Vienna: Hieronymus Vietor, 1516. VD16, K2559. Ll. 65–6, 91–2).

26 'Discere uis animi mores quoque principis? Aulam / Et prius in famulum lumina flecte gregem' (*Pro reuerendissimo domino Matheo Langio*, ll. 93–4).

27 'Dent fugitiua alii tibi xenia, nostra papyrus / Quod dabit a tineae dentibus exul erit' (*Pro reuerendissimo domino Matheo Langio*, ll. 109–10).

28 Vredeveld, 'Agricola, Rudolf d. J.,' 732.

29 Schirrmeister, *Triumph des Dichters*, 62–6.

30 *Orationes Viennae Austriae ad diuum Maximilianum.*

31 Janotzky, *Ianociana*, 1: 10; Vredeveld, 'Agricola, Rudolf d. J.,' 739. A poem by Agricola in honour of his teacher at Cracow, Michael Wratislaviensis, was apparently included in the publication.

32 Kieszkowski, *Kanclerz Krzysztof Szydłowiecki*, 189–208.

33 '[Q]uando enim diuina potius quaedam res quam humana uidetur, modestius est de ea silere quam tenuiter loqui' (*Ad dominum Petrum episcopum Premisliensem et regni Poloniae uicecancellarium oratio*, in *Orationes Viennae Austriae ad diuum Maximilianum*, fol. Q3v).

34 Treml, *Humanistische Gemeinschaftsbildung*, 108, 111–13.

35 Füssel, *Riccardus Bartholinus Perusinus*, 138.

36 For the background to the Polish-Lithuanian conflict with Muscovy, see Łowmiański, *Polityka Jagiellonów*, 402–30 (here, however, the date for the battle of Orsha is incorrectly given as 8 December); Nowak-Dłużewski, *Okolicznościowa poezja polityczna*, 49–50; and, most recently, Dróżdż, *Orsza 1514*.

37 Historians attribute the victory to mercenary troops (Łowmiański, *Polityka Jagiellonów*, 427).

38 Dantiscus's collected works have been published in a modern edition, Dantiscus, *Ioannis Dantisci Carmina*, ed. Skimina.

39 The dates are according to Kawecka-Gryczowa, *Polonia typographica*, vol. 4, nos 106, 114.

40 Wapowski had, for a short time, fallen out of favour with the king. His contribution of a panegyric to this publication was a successful attempt at returning himself to the king's good graces. On Wapowski, see Modelska Strzelecka, 'Bernard Wapowski.'

41 For publication details and an analysis of the poems contained therein, see Nowak-Dłużewski, *Okolicznościowa poezja polityczna*, 52–9. There is also the problem of a poem by Caspar Ursinus Velius, *Ad Sigismundum Regem Poloniae Moschorum uictorem poema heroicum*, supposedly printed at Cracow by Ungler in November 1514, but which for an unknown reason was not included in the Rome volume. The 1514 printing of Ursinus Velius's poem was recorded by Janotzky, but neither Bauch (*Caspar Ursinus Velius*) nor Karol Estreicher (*Bib-*

liografia polska, 32: 64) was able to locate it; nor, more recently, was Bułhak, the editor of volume 3 of Kawecka-Gryczowa, *Polonia typographica*. The poem was reprinted in Ursinus Velius's collection of poems at Basel in 1522 (*Poematum libri quinque*), published as *In inclytum regem Sigismundum Poloniae ob Moschos debellatos epinicion.*

42 Nowak-Dłużewski, *Okolicznościowa poezja polityczna*, 58.

43 In the 1515 Rome printing, the poem was entitled simply *Silua*. In the historiography of Polish literature the poem is known as *Sylua*, *Syluula*, or *De uictoria Sigismundi*. I shall refer to it as *Silua* here. I quote from the 1515 printing of both *Silua* and Eck's *Hymnus exhortatorius*.

44 'Qui fuerat nuper metuendus nunc timet ipse' (*Silua*, l. 42).

45 '[C]adebant / Innumeri, qui nunc per iugera lata putrescunt / Innumeri, qui nunc liquidis uersantur in undis' (*Silua*, ll. 70–2).

46 '[N]am paucula turma / Nostrorum innumerae disiecit Moschica turbae / Agmina et execuit furibundos hostis aceruos' (*Hymnus exhortatorius*, ll. 25–7).

47 The Hercynian Forest was a late-classical name for the wooded heights ranging from Bohemia through Moravia and Hungary.

48 'In densis qui se siluis altaque palude / Attonitis similes ceruis auibusque recondunt, / Quaeruntur tamen ad poenas, nec silua palusue / Securos faciet' (*Silua*, ll. 74–7).

49 'Exanimes passim modo qui per rura feruntur / Et canibusque lupis lacerandi, lumina namque / Effodiunt uolucrum rostri' (*Hymnus exhortatorius*, ll. 28–30).

50 'Ergo age pone metum' (*Hymnus exhortatorius*, l. 9).

51 'Ergo solue metum niditissima Croca, iocosque / Suscipe pro ueteri iam sollicitudine mentis' (*Hymnus exhortatorius*, ll. 32–3); 'Mens solet in placido defessis aequore reddi / Qualis nunc cunctis animus datur' (*Silua*, ll. 97–8).

52 'Fac plausus hylares resonent per compita; et omnis / laetetur pubes circumque incendia flammae / Prosiliet, cytharae ad sonitum ducantque choreas / Nymphae (*Hymnus exhortatorius*, ll. 34–7); 'Omnes arctoi qui sunt sub sidere coeli / Extollant tensas laeto de pectore palmas / Et laudes hylares animis et carmina Christo / Per plateas, uicos, regiones, compita cantent'; 'Ferte faces pueri, celsis de turribus ignis / Luceat'; 'Dulcia qui sequitur formosae castra Diones / In gyrum ducat dignum modulando choreas / Victori carmen' (*Silua*, ll. 52–5, 88–9, 100–2).

53 On Dantiscus's life and writings, see Nowak, *Jan Dantyszek*, and Skimina, *Twórczość poetycka Jana Dantyszka*. On his career at court, see Wyczański, 'Dantiscus as a Representative of the New Class of King's Secretaries in Europe.'

54 'Quos subito potui numeros conflare calore / Excudi, tanti testes utcumque triumphi' (*Silua*, ll. 107–8).

55 '[S]uper aethera regem / Sismundum atque duces tollam' (*Hymnus exhortatorius*, ll. 65–6).

56 Rome, although claiming that Poland was the 'bulwark of Christendom,' had been supporting the Teutonic Knights in Prussia and also wthholding support from the Poles in their struggle against the Tartars. See Tazbir, *Polska przedmurzem Europy*, 26–7.

57 Łowmiański, *Polityka Jagiellonów*, 428–30; Nowak-Dłużewski, *Okolicznościowa poezja polityczna*, 50. Herberstein himself describes his mission in his autobiography, Herberstein, *Sigmunds von Herberstein Selbstbiographie*,' ed. Karajan. On his life, see also Pferschy, *Sigismund von Herberstein*. Besides his autobiography, Herberstein would compose an account of his travels through Russia, *Rerum Moscouiticarum commentarii*, first published in 1549 and reprinted many times in the original and in translation, which would become a classic work on the geography and culture of sixteenth-century Russia. See Kämpfer and Frötscher, *450 Jahre Sigismund von Herbersteins Rerum Moscoviticarum Commentarii*.

58 A recent Slovenian-Russian tribute to Herberstein is Rugel, *Žiga Herberstein*.

59 For a discussion of the other poems in the cycle not mentioned here, including Johannes Visliciensis, *Bellum Prutenum*, see Nowak-Dłużewski, *Okolicznościowa poezja polityczna*, 49–60, and Segel, *Renaissance Culture in Poland*, 119–26.

60 Nowak, *Jan Dantyszek*, 110–11.

61 Herberstein, *Sigmunds von Herberstein Selbstbiographie*, 106.

62 Agricola describes the occasion of Herberstein's visit in a letter to Joachim Vadian (*Vadianische Briefsammlung* I, 116) written in February 1518. Agricola states that he and Dantiscus were summoned by Herberstein and asked for a gift; but since they had only a day in which to write the poems, the result, Agricola confesses, was rather crude.

63 Nowak-Dłużewski, *Okolicznościowa poezja polityczna*, 60.

64 Skimina, *Twórczość poetycka Jana Dantyszka*, 41–3.

65 The book was reprinted at Vienna in 1560. There exists also at Budapest a fragment of a 1556 edition, but too little remains of it to ascertain whether Dantiscus's *Soteria* and Agricola's *Congratulatio* were included. Quotations of both poems here are from Cracow: Johannes Hallter, 1518.

66 'Unde tibi torquem et fasces donauit equestres' (*Soteria*, l. 35).

67 'Ille tibi, Sigismunde, dedit per tanta uiarum / Interualla animum inuictum, quo semper in omnem / Euentum contra rerum discrimina mille, / Et casus uarios iuisti pectore forti' (*Soteria*, ll. 12–15).

68 'Te, Sigismunde, inquam forti quem pectore nunquam / Rebus in aduersis fortunae deicit aestus' (*Congratulatio*, ll. 65–6).

69 Skimina, *Twórczość poetycka Jana Dantyszka*, 44, notes that Dantiscus's

mention of the 'Pythagorean letter' refers to the shape of the letter Y as the fork in the road of life, the choice between the path of virtue and the path of vice.

70 'Alexander, Macedum fortissimus heros, / ... / Ilion ingressus, Troianaque pergama uisit / Inferiasque uiris ducibus, quos sustulit acre / Bellum utrinque duo Troiae per lustra, parabat' (*Congratulatio*, ll. 6–10).

71 'Hic amor, haec eadem uirtus cognata poetis / Res celebrare uirum magnas, praeclaraque gesta / Scribere, et immortale decus laudemque uenustis / Diuulgare modis' (*Congratulatio*, ll. 31–6).

72 'Accipe Moscorum uenienti e finibus olim / Quae nec cocta quidem, tibi, nec bene culta notam / Carmina. Si tempus foret, et uberiora dedissem' (*Congratulatio*, ll. 89–91).

73 Bauch, 'Valentin Eck und Georg Werner,' 48.

74 'Id uero quod maxime desiderat facile impetrabit cum nihil, nisi patrocinium, affectat, nihil, nisi in tuorum clientulorum adscribi numerum postulat, rem satis illi honestam et te non indignam' (*Reuerendissimo domino Mathiae Dreuicio Vladislauiensi episcopo Iodocus Ludouicus Decius*, in Eck, *Threni neglectae religionis*. Cracow: Johannes Haller, 1518).

75 Nowak-Dłużewski, *Okolicznościowa poezja polityczna*, 41.

76 *Polski słownik biograficzny*, 5: 409–12; Łowmiański, *Polityka Jagiellonów*, 352.

77 Wiesflecker, *Kaiser Maximilian I.*, 4: 227–30. Wiesflecker also makes mention of a very detailed memorandum authored by Maximilian and preserved in *Acta Tomiciana*, 4: 350–4. The date is sometime in 1518.

78 'Itaque cum pridie Eckii Lindani carmen de neglecta religione ... legissem ... hominem compellare coepi hortarique ut illud daret in lucem' (*Reuerendissimo domino Mathiae Dreuicio Vladislauiensi episcopo Iodocus Ludouicus Decius*).

79 '[P]utaui satis tutum fore id quod tuo nomine munitum exiret, eumque ita posse aemulos omnes euincere' (*Reuerendissimo domino Mathiae Dreuicio Vladislauiensi episcopo Iodocus Ludouicus Decius*).

80 Scullard, *Scipio Africanus*, 109, 168.

81 According to Horace, the *querimonia* was the primary function of the elegy, but in practice the elegy was used for amatory poetry in Roman literature, and almost never for poems of mourning. In the sixteenth century, however, Ovid's *Tristia* were considered examples of *querimonia*. Sixteenth-century poetic theory would try to bridge the gap between *querimonia* and *amores* with the hypothesis that the transition from mourning for the dead to the expression of unhappy love (*querimonia amantium*) had to do with common characteristics of the mourner and the unhappy lover (Ludwig, 'Petrus Lotichius Secundus,' 175–7, 183). Erasmus was most likely inspired by Seneca's essay

De clementia, on the need for clemency in a ruler (Bainton, 'The Querela Pacis of Erasmus,' 36). Cytowska, in her introduction to Erasmus, *Erazm z Rotterdamu Wybór pism*, cxx, suggests the connection between Eck and Erasmus.

82 The political realities behind Erasmus' claims are discussed by Letocha, 'Quand Érasme se fait politique.'

83 Such associations came down to the Renaissance from medieval literature and can be seen early on in the poem *Carmen ad Nicolaum Papam V in Thurcum Mahomet*, composed in about 1453 by the Florentine Leonardo Dati. See Bisaha, *Creating East and West*, 161–6.

84 Bauch, 'Valentin Eck und Georg Werner,' 47.

85 'Anthiocena colit sedes Idolia uana / Clauigeri ridens dogmata sancta ducis' (*Threni neglectae religionis*, ll. 25–6).

86 'Illaque Byzanti quondam clarissima praebet / Expulso scrophis sordida tecta deo' (*Threni neglectae religionis*, ll. 27–8).

87 'Haec quoque quae Solymis, et quae super ostia Nili / Floruit, immundae spurcida seruit harae' (*Threni neglectae religionis*, ll. 29–30).

88 'Othomannus Thracia regna / Occupat. Arctoum Moschica dextra latus, / Impinguat saeuos Euxini ripa Valachos / Hippophagus Scythicis Tartarus alget agris' (*Threni neglectae religionis*, ll. 31–4).

89 'Et recutita cohors quamquam dispersa per orbem / Lucro inhiat, Solymas incolit ipsa domos, / Et fera Sultani trepidat mandata tyranni, / Qui retinet nostro regna sacrata deo' (*Threni neglectae religionis*, ll. 35–8).

90 'Nam segnes populos ciuilem ducere uitam / Edocuit summa relligione sua' (*Threni neglectae religionis*, ll. 67–8).

91 Schirrmeister, *Triumph des Dichters*, 216. Schirrmeister notes that Bartholinus portrayed Maximilian as such in his *Austrias* (1516).

92 Quoting Aristotle, Eck states, '[N]ecesse est, si quis honeste uiuere cupiat, cum prudentia iustitiam possideat' (*De reipublicae administratione dialogus*. Cracow: Hieronymus Vietor, 1520. Fol. B2v). The dialogue has been analysed with reference to Eck's reliance on classical sources by Škoviera, 'Dialóg *De reipublicae administratione*,' and has been translated into Polish by Kazikowski as Walenty Eck, 'Dialog o rządzeniu rzecząpospolitą.'

93 'Hinc capiunt dulces tua regia dona poetae / Qui tua uiuaci carmine gesta canunt' (*Threni neglectae religionis*, ll. 125–6).

94 Morka, 'Political Meaning of the Sigismund Chapel,' 32–3. Moreover, the virtues of Sigismund presented by Eck in his poem conform with the ones Cytowska lists as in the portait of Sigismund generally presented in the Polish-Latin literature of the period. (Cytowska does not discuss Eck's poem in her article.) See Cytowska, 'Król Zygmunt Stary,' 11–18.

95 Once again, Eck elaborates on these virtues and their importance for the ideal leader in his dialogue *De reipublicae administratione*.

96 'Non opus est Italos, Gallos, aut Theutona castra / Implores; tua gens sufficit una tibi'; 'Attamen, ut cupias, uicinas iungere turmas, / His ualidis populis rex generose tuis / Maximus arma tibi feret auxiliaria Caesar' (*Threni neglectae religionis*, ll. 179–80, 197–9).

97 Milewska-Waźbińska, 'Turks in the Renaissance Latin Poetry of Poland,' 438.

98 Lausberg, *Handbook of Literary Rhetoric*, 277–8.

99 Zabłocki, 'Poezja polsko-łacińska wczesnego renesansu,' 76.

100 Zabłocki, 'Poezja polsko-łacińska wczesnego renesansu,' 77; Miłosz, *History of Polish Literature*, 19.

101 On the legend of Stanislaus, its medieval sources, and the significance of the saint's cult, see Gustaw, *Hagiografia polska*, 2: 419–55. Although the legend of St Stanislaus resembles that of Thomas Becket, it has been demonstrated that the latter did not influence the formation of the Stanislaus story in the Middle Ages. See Uruszczak, 'Répercussions de la mort de Thomas Becket en Pologne,' 115–25.

102 Michałowska, *Średniowiecze*, 167–80.

103 Zabłocki, 'Poezja polsko-łacińska wczesnego renesansu,' 77; Walczak, 'The Jagiellonian Saints,' 139–50; Nowakowska, 'Papacy and Piety in the Career of Cardinal Fryderyk Jagiellon,' 170–83.

104 Kieszkowski, *Kanclerz Krzysztof Szydłowiecki*, 131–5; Stangler and Stolot, *Polen im Zeitalter der Jagiellonen*, 252–4.

105 '[E]piscopi mei maximi sunt pollicatores et plane frigescunt. Abiturus eram, nisi Vladislaviensis me detinuisset. Aura non [autem] mihi salubris est ... Bis aegerrime laborabam ... Tartarorum 4000 magnam Lituaniae et Poloniae depraedati sunt ... Molitur nescio quid magister Prussiae; occisi sunt aliquot Elbingenses cives et negotiatores ... Clandestinus rumor et iam palam prorepserat de seditione Polonorum Cracoviae contra Germanos' (*Vadianische Briefsammlung* II, 165).

106 Agricola stated that he was sending two copies of the poem – one for Vadian and the other for the abbot of Saint Gall, who Agricola hoped would provide a benefice for him so that he could leave Cracow. See chapter 2.

107 Zabłocki, 'Poezja polsko-łacińska wczesnego renesansu,' 78.

108 A modern edition of the text is found in volume 1 of Długosz, *Joannis Dlugossii senioris Canonici Cracoviensis Opera*, ed. Przezdziecki.

109 For a summary of Callimachus's activities in Poland, see Segel, *Renaissance Culture in Poland*, 36–82, and Kotarska, 'Poeta i historyk.' Fuller biographies are Olkiewicz, *Kallimach doświadczony*, a popular treatment of the subject, and Paparelli, *Callimacho Esperiente*. A conference on the subject of Callimachus and his work was held in Italy in October 1985; the papers have been published as Garfagnini, *Callimaco Esperiente*.

110 Date of composition uncertain; printed by the Haller press at Cra-

cow, *c.* 1521 (Kawecka-Gryczowa, *Polonia typographica*, vol. 4, no. 193).

111 Printed in his collection *Panegyrici et alia carmina*. Second printing at Cracow, by the Ungler press, 1513. Most recently printed in Paulus Crosnensis, *Pauli Crosnensis Rutheni Carmina*, ed. Cytowska, 103–15. For the genesis and analysis of the humanist poems in honour of St Stanislaus, see Stawecka, 'Humanistyczne panegiryki łacińskie,' 5–34.

112 Stawecka, 'Humanistyczne panegiryki łacińskie,' 17; Zabłocki, 'Poezja polsko-łacińska wczesnego renesansu,' 77.

113 Lines 49–72 of Agricola's poem, which include the invocation to the saint and a description of his birthplace, are especially reminiscent of ll. 5–24 of Paulus's *Panegyricus ad diuum Stanislaum*.

114 Gorzkowski, *Paweł z Krosna*, 230–6. Stawecka, 'Humanistyczne panegiryki łacińskie,' 22, also remarks on the similarities between Paulus's and Agricola's poems.

115 Stawecka, 'Humanistyczne panegiryki łacińskie,' 23–4.

116 Although Stawecka, 'Humanistyczne panegiryki łacińskie,' 22–3, admits that Agricola's opening lines form an 'original' part of his poem, she does not analyse these verses and gives no reason why Agricola would have begun his poem in such a manner. Instead, she argues that Agricola abides by his opening statement in the remainder of the poem by claiming that it does not contain much mixing of pagan images with Christian.

117 'Poscis insanum precibus furorem, / Dum furis spurcis nimium camenis'; 'Hi mouent plectrum, fidibusque gaudent / Et ... / ... meliora nobis / Carmina dictant' (*Hymnus de diuo Stanislao*. Cracow: Hieronymus Vietor, 1519. Ll. 21–2, 45–8).

118 Łowmiański, *Polityka Jagiellonów*, 428.

119 'Saepe uexatum fidei cruentis / Hostibus regnum repares, iuuesque / Fata Sismundi faueant triumphis / Prospera regis. / Arua fecundos habeant liquores / Quos suo Phoebus moderetur igne, / Facque ne morbus [*sic*] fugitiua nobis / Astra minentur' (*Hymnus de diuo Stanislao*, ll. 233–40).

120 Birnbaum, *Humanists in a Shattered World*, 70–1; Łowmiański, *Polityka Jagiellonów*, 455–9.

121 Benedictine Monks, *Book of Saints*, 26; Klaniczay, *Holy Rulers*, 157; Klaniczay, 'Fortuna della leggenda di S. Alessio,' 8; Odenkirchen, *Life of St. Alexius*, 11; Farmer, *Oxford Dictionary of Saints*, 16; Gieysztor, 'Pauvreté dans les textes hagiographiques,' 126–7, 129; Vrtel-Wierczyński, *Staropolska Legenda o św. Aleksym*, 66–90, 216–34.

122 Gieysztor, 'Pauvreté dans les textes hagiographiques,' 131. For a detailed discussion of the medieval German manuscript tradition, which covers variants in both Latin and the vernacular, see Joret, 'Légende de Saint Alexis en Allemagne.' The legend had already

been printed in Germany many times beginning in the 1470s as part of Jacob de Voragine's *Legenda aurea* (see IISTC database), but it did not come into print at Cracow until 1529, and then in a vernacular version (Vrtel-Wierczyński, *Staropolska Legenda o św. Aleksym*, 252–8).

123 'At pater nati tacitum recessum / Ingemens, totum famulos in orbem / Illico emisit, patrias referrent / Hunc ut ad aedes. / Qui licet tandem Syrios in agros / Venerint, trita iuuenem reuinctum / Veste, non norunt, inopi stipem sed / Contribuerunt' (*De diuo Alexio*. Cracow: Hieronymus Vietor, 1521. Ll. 101–8).

124 'Audiens natum genitrix fuisse / Hunc suum, actutum super insepultum / Corpus immenso gemituque fletu / Maesta ruebat. / Hoc idem consors thalami relicta, / Et pater maerens faciebat, ullus / Nec modus crebris lachrymis dabatur / Nocte dieque' (*De diuo Alexio*, ll. 185–92).

125 For a comparison of medieval and Renaissance notions of contempt for the world, see Domański, 'Uwagi o średniowiecznej i renesansowej "pogardzie świata" i "nędzy człowieka."'

126 'Quippe nunc nostrum ueniunt in orbem, / Non ut hic regnent, iugulent sed omnes / Quotquot excelsi colimus tonantis / Numina Christi' (*De diuo Alexio*, ll. 209–12).

127 Łowmiański, *Polityka Jagiellonów*, 459.

128 Habermann, *Catholic Encyclopedia*, 11: 590–1; Farmer, *Oxford Dictionary of Saints*, 393.

129 Rebenich, 'Kirchenvater Hieronymus als Hagiograph'; Cherf, 'Latin Manuscript Tradition.' For the early printed versions, see German STC, IISTC, and VD16.

130 For details, see Elm, 'Eremiten und Eremitenorden des 13. Jahrhunderts.'

131 Klaniczay, *Holy Rulers*, 366.

132 These same monks came to Poland in 1382 and founded the monastery of Jasna Góra ('Bright Hill') near Częstochowa, which housed a miraculous icon of the Virgin Mary. Jasna Góra was a site of continual pilgrimage, but following an attempted robbery in 1430, in which the criminals slashed the painting, its fame grew. In 1655 the monastery was attacked by the Swedes. The victory of a small number of Poles over the Swedish army, after a siege of forty days, was attributed to the Virgin, and the monastery and its icon have been symbols of the Polish nation, and its protection by the Virgin, ever since.

133 Engel, *Realm of St. Stephen*, 171; Zombori and others, *Thousand Years of Christianity in Hungary*, 331–2. Bauch, 'Valentin Eck und Georg Werner,' 52, suggests that Louis Jagiellon's bringing back of the head of St Paul from Prague to the Pauline monastery at Buda might have influenced Eck's choice of a saint about whom to compose his

poem. A contemporary account of King Louis's discovery of the head at Karlštejn (Karlstein), where it had been hidden by the Bohemians, is Gyöngyönsi, *Vitae fratrum eremitarum Ordinis Sancti Pauli primi eremitae*, ed. Hervay, 181–3. See also Szalay, *Geschichte Ungarns*, vol. 3, pt 2, p. 217.

134 'Ut solet exortis cum tempestatibus aequor / Vexatur, dubia trepidans in puppe magister'; 'Instar ouis tenerae, saeuos quae forte luporum / Euasit rictus, aegre pauitantia sedat / Corda, sed a tergo semper formidat atroces / Insidiatorum dentes, morsusque malignos'; '[T]orui de more colubri / Inter fallaces scopulos, terrenaque saxa, / Ignauam linquens pellem' (*Vita diui Pauli primi eremitae*. Cracow: Hieronymus Vietor, 1522. Ll. 41–2, 46–9, 75–7).

135 On the events leading up to Mohács and the crisis in the Hungarian government, see Łowmiański, *Polityka Jagiellonów*, 456–9, and Engel, *Realm of St. Stephen*, 368–9.

136 See the analysis under 'The War with Muscovy' earlier in this chapter.

137 It appears that Eck was not inspired by Andrzej Krzycki's (Cricius) *Religionis et reipublicae querimonia* (Cracow, 1522), in which 'Religio' complains of persecution by a certain group of evil men. Krzycki's poem was directed against the growing Lutheran movement. Moreover, 'Religio' does not address the king directly, but is assured at the end by 'Respublica' that the pious king (*pius princeps*) will protect them both. See Krzycki, *Andreae Cricii Carmina*, ed. Morawski, 89–96.

138 'Nanque potes, quia praeforti tua robore dextra / Emicat, et ualida populum dicione gubernas / Cui Mahometaeam semper proscindere gentem / Dulce fuit' (*Ad Ludouicum Hungariae et Bohemiae regem pro bello Turcis inferendo exhortatio*. Cracow: Hieronymus Vietor, 1524. Ll. 32–5).

139 'Atque ego commemini, nec adhuc celeberrima facta / Ad coitus uitrei Saui atque binominis Istri / Quando Capistranus precibus, Ianusque potenti / Huniades dextra, Phrygias fudere phalanges' (*Ad Ludouicum Hungariae et Bohemiae regem pro bello Turcis inferendo exhortatio*, ll. 36–9).

140 'Quod faxit pater omnipotens qui fortibus ausis / Annuat usque tuis, qui te feliciter olim / Hoste triumphato uictorem reddet Olympo' (*Ad Ludouicum Hungariae et Bohemiae regem pro bello Turcis inferendo exhortatio*, ll. 60–2).

141 Engel, *Realm of St. Stephen*, 348.

142 'Dedecet ista quies uos non minus ac colus olim / Lydius Alciden, uel Scyria lana potentem / Pelei genitum' (*Ad proceres Hungariae*. Cracow: Hieronymus Vietor, 1524. Ll. 16–18).

143 '[E]t praeda sumus laceranda cruento / Turcarum rictu, rictu improbiore canino' (*Ad proceres Hungariae*, ll. 51–2).

144 Milewska-Waźbińska, 'Turks in the Renaissance Latin Poetry of Poland,' 439–40.
145 Bisaha, *Creating East and West*, 135–6, 161–6.
146 Jankovics, 'Image of the Turks in Hungarian Renaissance Literature,' 270.
147 Imre, 'Ungarische Türkenkrieg,' 93–103.
148 Milewska-Waźbińska, 'Turks in the Renaissance Latin Poetry of Poland,' 441.
149 Bisaha, *Creating East and West*, 41–60.
150 On the battle of Mohács and the incidents leading to the Habsburg succession, see Alföldi, 'Battle of Mohács, 1526'; Domonkos, 'Battle of Mohács'; Birnbaum, *Humanists in a Shattered World*, 99–100; Erdélyi, 'Elek Thurzó of Bethlenfalva,' passim; Łowmiański, *Polityka Jagiellonów*, 459–64; and Engel, *Realm of St. Stephen*, 367–71.
151 On Alexius Thurzó's support of Ferdinand, see Erdélyi, 'Elek Thurzó of Bethlenfalva,' 20–43.
152 Erdélyi, 'Elek Thurzó of Bethlenfalva,' 25–6.
153 Škoviera, *Bardejovčan Valentín Ecchius*, 24.
154 The date is uncertain.
155 Soltész and others, *Az Országos Széchényi Könyvtár 16. századi nyomtatványainak katalógusa*, E64 and E65.
156 After Hieronymus Vietor moved his business from Vienna to Cracow at the end of 1517, he kept a press running at Vienna. His brother, Benedikt Büttner, managed it until his death in 1523, whereupon it was overseen by agents until Vietor gave it to his son Florian in 1531. The output of this press was negligible – from 1528 to 1532, for example, it published only about a dozen books. See Kawecka-Gryczowa, *Drukarze dawnej Polski*, 329.
157 'Achillem / Corde refert magnum, tetrica grauitate Catonem, / Consilio Fabium, prudenter rebus agendis / Pompeium, bonitate Titum, rectum statuendo / Traianum' (*Ad proceres Hungariae exhortatio*. Cracow: Hieronymus Vietor, 1527, 1528. Ll. 55–9).
158 '[I]lla lues patriae quae tempore longo / Protrusit miseros in aperta pericula ciues'; 'Non illum Solometh turpissima foedera Turcae / Christigenum in mortem iamdudum turpiter icta / Nec coniurati nuper timida agmina fratres / In male suscepta stabilem dicione tueri / Eualuere, iacet regali pulsus ab aula' (*Ad proceres Hungariae exhortatio*, ll. 28–9, 42–6).
159 It is likely no coincidence that Eck used this image; a wolf appeared on Zápolya's coat of arms.
160 'Sed quid perstringere conor / Quae sunt magniloquo grauiter dicenda Maroni, / Vix equidem agrestis modicum caprile Menalcae / Ludere sufficio, grauidas aut lacte capellas' (*Ad proceres Hungariae exhortatio*, ll. 74–7).
161 'Leaders of Hungary, beat your breasts, which were recently sad; a

happy sky, the clouds pushed away, hangs over you now' ('Plaudite Pannonii proceres maestissima nuper/ Pectora, depulsis iucundus nubibus aether / Prominet').

162 '... qui Castaliis nutritus in aruis / Inter Pierios uates quibus augur Apollo / Praesidet' (*Ad proceres Hungariae exhortatio*, ll. 94–6).

163 Domonkos, 'Battle of Mohács,' 212, 215.

164 The title *iudex* was given to the mayor of a town in the Hungarian kingdom at this time (Engel, *Realm of St. Stephen*, 252).

165 'Illa inquam uariis quam tristi factio Marte / Reddidit afflictam Zapolitana modis' (*Ad regem Ferdinandum epistola*. Vienna: Hieronymus Vietor, 1530. Ll. 3–4).

166 'At deus ex alto gemitus et uota suorum / Respiciens, gratam contulit almus opem, / Victus ab Austriaco, duce te, propellitur orbe / Turca, o quam merita clade cruentus abit' (*Ad regem Ferdinandum epistola*, ll. 17–20).

167 'Hic alii Turcae sunt, monstra domestica, foede / Coeperunt patriam qui temerare fidem'; 'Sum quippe, heu, bello nimium contrita perenni / Viribus in totum debilitata meis'; 'Ut cum priuatis aeraria publica cistis / Undique sint nummis euacuata suis' (*Ad regem Ferdinandum epistola*, ll. 37–8, 49–50, 53–4).

168 'Tanti mi obsequium, tanti obseruantia constat, / Et tanti per me non uiolata fides'; 'Atque pius tandem me tot tantisque periclis / Durius afflictam fortiter eripias' (*Ad regem Ferdinandum epistola*, ll. 65–6, 69–70).

169 'E multis tamen expediam paucissima, nollem / Carmine te incompto detinuisse diu. / Nulla foris pax, nulla domi, foris errat in armis/ Mars ferus, ast intra moenia taetra lues' (*Ad Alexium Thurzonem epistola*. Vienna: Hieronymus Vietor, 1530. Ll. 7–10).

170 '[C]alet undique corpus, / Aetnaeo dicas uiscera in igne coqui' (*Ad Alexium Thurzonem epistola*, ll. 23–4).

171 'Iamque adit, haec etenim dum scribo, en nuntius intrat / Qui rapidum iamiam clamat adesse lupum'; 'Vera loquor, vidi his oculis, ait, oppida circum / Varano et Terebes, castra locare trucem' (*Ad Alexium Thurzonem epistola*, ll. 53–4, 57–8).

172 'Haec, arma ut propere ferat auxiliaria nobis, / Effice apud regni Thurzo precor dominum' (*Ad Alexium Thurzonem epistola*, ll. 65–6).

173 'Iucunda coniunx faciat te prole parentem, / Cum peraget cursum luna nouena suum / Ut sit qui uultu referat uos, certus et haeres / Succedat patriis lege fauente bonis' (*Ad Alexium Thurzonem epistola*, ll. 81–4). Thurzó's second wife, Magdolna Székely (d. 1556), was the widow of Tamás Széczy, lord lieutenant (*supremus comes*) of Vas county (Erdélyi, 'Elek Thurzó of Bethlenfalva,' 35). Their marriage took place most likely in the autumn of 1528.

174 *Ad inclytum Ferdinandum Pannoniae et Bohemiae regem inuictissimum hendecasyllabi, elegiae, et epigramma* (Vienna: Hieronymus Vietor,

1529) is mentioned by Bauch, 'Valentin Eck und Georg Werner,' 54. On Logau (d. 1553), a protégé of the Thurzó family who studied in Italy after leaving Cracow, see Bietenholz and Deutscher, *Contemporaries of Erasmus*, 3: 338–9.

175 See Kulcsár, 'Der Humanismus in Ungarn'; Balogh, 'Die ungarischen Mäzene der Renaissance'; Kadić, 'Croatian Humanists at the Hungarian Court'; Feuer-Tóth, *Art and Humanism in Hungary*; and Klaniczay and Jankovics, *Matthias Corvinus and the Humanism in Central Europe*.

176 Rázsó, 'Mercenary Army of King Matthias Corvinus,' 125–6.

177 Rekettyés, *Stosunki polityczne*, 19–56; Engel, *Realm of St. Stephen*, 345–9. On Louis's rule and the Czech lands, see Macek, *Jagellonský věk v českých zemích*, 1: 292–318.

178 Engel, *Realm of St. Stephen*, 366–7.

179 Birnbaum, *Humanists in a Shattered World*, 79–80.

180 Vladislav moved his court to Buda in 1490 and Louis continued to govern his Czech lands remotely – he visited Prague only once during his reign (1522–3). On Vladislav's and Louis's relationship with the Czech lands, see Macek, *Jagellonský věk v českých zemích*, 1: 180–225, 292–318. On the sponsorship of the arts in Bohemia during the reigns of Vladislav and Louis, see Goleniszczew-Kutuzow, *Odrodzenie włoskie i literatury słowiańskie*, 201–9; Kaufmann, *Court, Cloister, and City*, 59–67; and Fajt, 'Late Gothic Sculpture in Bohemia,' 256–60. In the provincial centres of Olomouc and Wrocław, the bishops Stanislaus and Johann Thurzó cultivated the arts at their courts. See Wörster, 'Breslau und Olmütz als humanistische Zentren vor der Reformation,' and Lambrecht, 'Communicating Europe to the Region.'

181 Kulcsár, 'Der Humanismus in Ungarn,' 62–5; Neagu, *Servant of the Renaissance*, 25–35.

182 For the details of Szatmári's life and patronage of art, see Farbaky, 'György Szatmári,' 213–78.

183 Farbaky, 'György Szatmári,' passim.

184 The only known copy of the book is at the Russian National Library in Saint Petersburg. The text of *Iubilus heroicus* has been reprinted by Farbaky, *Szatmári György, a mecénás*, 166–70.

185 Farbaky, 'György Szatmári,' 220.

186 'Interea modicos ubi res tempusque requirent / Conscribam uersus, et te nostrumque patronum / Thurzonem magnum merito uenerabor honore' (*Ad Georgium episcopum ecclesiae Quinqueecclesiensis et secretarium et cancellarium Regiae Maestatis*, printed with *Apophoreticum carmen de Christi natiuitate* and *Iubilus heroicus*. Cracow: Hieronymus Vietor, 1520. Ll. 28–30).

187 See chapter 2 for a discussion of this topos.

188 'Illa sed in lucem non sic fundenda camena est / Illico, quin potius

decimum limanda per annum' (*Ad Georgium episcopum ecclesiae Quinqueecclesiensis*, ll. 26–7).

189 'Quae si non uincet grandissima plectra Maronis / Attamen hanc faciem sublimibus inseret astris / Cui nostro similem duo uel tres tempore uates / Effingent nunquam quamuis sua tempora laurus / Cingat' (*Ad Georgium episcopum ecclesiae Quinqueecclesiensis*, ll. 19–23).

190 *Ad Korponensis ecclesiae protomystam dominum Nicolaum Lausman Chrysoreotanum (uulgo Goldberger)*, in *De arte uersificandi opusculum* (Cracow: Hieronymus Vietor, 1521, 1539).

191 Wick, *Kassa története és műemlékei*, 49–52. See also Török, *Matthias Corvinus und die Renaissance in Ungarn*, 527.

192 In the town records of Kassa, his name appears as 'Hans Saytzlich,' or 'Sayczlich' (Kemény, *Kassa város régi számadáskönyve*, 61, 77). The closest approximation in modern German would be Seislig. Eck notes that his surname in Latin is 'Catacallus,' and refers to him, in the text of the poem, as 'Ianus,' the Latin equivalent of the Hungarian 'János.'

193 There is no exact English translation for this title, which denotes a sort of royal treasury official.

194 The matriculation book of the University of Cracow records, in the winter semester 1513, a certain 'Valentinus Stephani de Casschouia, dioc. Agriensis,' which could have been Valentin Carbo. See Chmiel and others, *Album studiosorum Universitatis Cracoviensis*, 2: 149. Carbo may have been responsible for Eck's introduction to Alexius Thurzó.

195 Eck's mention of the Hungarian peasant uprising and King Sigismund's victory at Orsha in the *Epithalamium* would date the composition of the poem to the end of 1514 or early 1515, and thus while Eck was still resident at Cracow. The crusade against the Turks called by Bishop Tamás Bakócz in the spring of 1514 had resulted in an uprising of the peasant recruits against the nobility, which forced the magnates of Hungary to gather their own armies in order to quell the rebellion. The uprising was finally put down in July of that year, but retaliations on the part of the peasants took place for months afterwards. See Engel, *Realm of St. Stephen*, 362–4. King Sigismund's victory at Orsha against the Muscovites took place in September 1514.

196 'Dum mea uix humiles bene lambit cymbula fluctus / Et refugit tumidos anchora nostra lacus / Attamen ausa nimis nunc soluit carbasa, et undis / Expaciata uagis sub tua tecta uenit' (*Epithalamium pro nuptiis domini Ioannis Sayslich ... prooemium*, printed with *Apophoreticum carmen de Christi natiuitate*, ll. 7–10).

197 'Et si non digno cupido tamen ipsa relatu, / Iane, tuas ardet concelebrare faces, / Connubiumque tuum gestit transmittere in annos / Longos, quod forsan saecla futura legent. / Sunt pia uota

quidem; quis enim non magna camenis / Promittat uates osque futura suis' (*Epithalamium pro nuptiis domini Ioannis Sayslich ... prooemium*, ll. 11–16).

198 Brożek, 'Epitalamia Zygmuntowskie,' 61–2.

199 'Huc adsis graciles hilari; te uoce puellae / Ducturae choreas terque quater vocantque / Tecum adduc cytharas, dextram resonabile plectrum / Exornet, Thyasos quisquis inibit ouans' (*Epithalamium pro nuptiis domini Ioannis Sayslich*, ll. 7–10).

200 'Quo nihil utilius, nil sanctius, aptius, unquam / Terrenis poterat contribuisse uiris'; 'Humanos iusta sensus quod lege refrenat, / Affectus hominum quod regit usque pios'; 'Hinc magus illicito conceptus semine, turpes / Persarum ritus indicat atque faces' (*Epithalamium pro nuptiis domini Ioannis Sayslich*, ll. 25–6, 29–30, 43–4). Eck was not embarrassed to recycle his poetry. This whole section (ll. 23–48) is identical to lines 195–220 of his *An prudenti uiro sit ducenda uxor* (Cracow: Johannes Haller, 1518; Hieronymus Vietor, 1524), where he argued for the 'utility of marriage.' In the prefatory letter to its first printing, dated 2 January 1518, Eck stated that he had recently composed the work. It seems, therefore, that these lines originally belonged to *Epithalamium pro nuptiis domini Ioannis Sayslich*. The 1524 printing of Eck's *An prudenti uiro* would be linked to Erasmus by the Cracow humanist Matthias Pyrser, who, in his afterword to the book, quoted from Erasmus's *Encomium matrimonii* (*editio princeps*, March 1518).

201 'Thespiades igitur nunc huc properate puellae / Dum uester nimio feruet amore cliens' (*Epithalamium pro nuptiis domini Ioannis Sayslich*, ll. 55–6).

202 'Et subeat fausta thalamos Iunone iugales / Inque suo timidus sit pudor usque toro / Nam sine lege Venus scelus est, sine lege libido / Foeda manet, sacer est cum ratione torus' (*Epithalamium pro nuptiis domini Ioannis Sayslich*, ll. 69–72).

203 The first printing was by Haller, the second by Vietor. See chapter 1 for the possible influences on Eck in the writing of this poem.

204 *Supellectilium fasciculus* was printed first with Eck's *De mundi contemptu et uirtute amplectenda dialogus* (Cracow: Hieronymus Vietor) in 1519, then with *An prudenti uiro sit ducenda uxor* (Cracow: Hieronymus Vietor) in 1524, and finally with *De mundi contemptu* (Cracow: Mathias Scharffenberg) in 1528.

205 Bergman, 'Polsko-łacińskie epitalamium,' 193.

206 Bergman, 'Polsko-łacińskie epitalamium,' 187, 203; Bieńkowski, 'Panegiryk a życie literackie w Polsce,' 192; Mroczek, *Epitalamium staropolskie*, 116–22.

207 'Ianus Palladiae Catacallus magna cohortis / Gloria, Pierios qui fouet usque uiros' (*Epithalamium pro nuptiis domini Ioannis Sayslich*, ll. 51–2).

208 'Ipse etenim quondam Phoebi quoque castra subibat, / Dum non tam magna mole grauatus erat'; '... qui nocteque dieque / Sudauit uestris doctus alumnus agris'; 'In quibus in tantum hic uester profecit alumnus / Ut magno possit cum Cicerone loqui' (*Epithalamium pro nuptiis domini Ioannis Sayslich*, ll. 53–4, 57–8, 63–4).
209 'Et generare sacro pulcherrima pignora partu / Nobile quae gemino stemma parente trahant' (*Epithalamium pro nuptiis domini Ioannis Sayslich*, ll. 87–8).
210 For the career of Alexius Thurzó, I rely on Birnbaum, *Humanists in a Shattered World*, 43; Bietenholz and Deutscher, *Contemporaries of Erasmus*, 3: 322; Erdélyi, 'Elek Thurzó of Bethlenfalva,' 10–17; Lambrecht, 'Aufstiegschancen und Handlungsräume,' 332–3; Kalus, *Die Fugger in der Slowakei*, 117–24, 163–7; and Engel and others, *Magyarország története 1301–1526*, 418–19.
211 Erdélyi, 'Elek Thurzó of Bethlenfalva,' 15.
212 'Non dignior illo / Inuentus, populo qui iura Tauernica possit / Huniaco iusta lance exhibere magister'; '... nec quisquam promptior unquam / Ad commune bonum curandum, propria quamuis / Interea utilitas cesset' (*De electione*, in *Ad Ludouicum Hungariae et Bohemiae regem pro bello Turcis inferendo exhortatio*, ll. 80–2, 91–3).
213 '[T]utore bonum Thurzone redibit / Omne illis, priscum sollemnia iura uigorem / Seruabunt, procul hinc linguarum murmura uana' (*De electione*, ll. 99–101).
214 'Nil habuit uirtus maius, nil Rex Lodouicus, / Thurzonem poterant quo condecorare potentem' (*De electione*, ll. 115–16).
215 'Immundam meruit lepram Gecchzea cupido, / Rex aconita bibit Ptolomaeus'; 'Hannibalem Campanus uincit Iacchus' (*De electione*, ll. 41–2, 54).
216 Schirrmeister, *Triumph des Dichters*, 216.

CONCLUSION

1 On Bona, see Bietenholz and Deutscher, *Contemporaries of Erasmus*, 1: 165–6. Her family, childhood, and betrothal to Sigismund are covered in volume 1 of Pociecha, *Królowa Bona*.
2 Nowak-Dłużewski, *Okolicznościowa poezja polityczna*, 75, dates the poem at the end of 1517 or the beginning of 1518. It must have been written after March 1518, when Sigismund gave orders for the group of the five men to meet Bona and accompany her back to Cracow. Otherwise, how would Agricola have known the composition of this group? See Pociecha, *Królowa Bona*, 1: 224. Yet the date given by Malicki and Zwinogrodzka, *Katalog poloników XVI wieku*, no. 21, as after 18 V 1518 (most likely an error for 18 IV 1518, the date of Sigismund and Bona's wedding) is too late. (Kawecka-Gryczowa, *Polonia typographica*, vol. 4, no. 159, dates the poem as after 18 IV

1518.) In his (unfortunately undated) dedicatory letter to Bishop Ciołek's secretary, Agricola's remarks on the haste with which he composed the piece at the request of the secretary seem to place the poem before the wedding, and indeed at the time of the reception in Olomouc.

3 *Illustrissimae reginae Bonae paraceleusis* (Cracow: Haller, 1518). A *paraceleusis*, a 'calling out' or 'cheering address,' is similar to a *propempticon*, good wishes to someone setting off on a journey. See Nowak-Dłużewski, *Okolicznościowa poezja polityczna*, 75.

4 Agricola apparently wrote an epithalamium for the wedding and the coronation of Bona, which took place in Cracow on 18 April 1518, but this poem, mentioned by Agricola in his letter to Joachim Vadian (*Vadianische Briefsammlung* I, 120) of 30 April 1518, is not extant. He also penned a commendatory poem, 'Connubii sacra regalis, magnumque paratum / Et causam, ingressum, principiumque leges ...,' for the description of the wedding festivities by Justus Ludovicus Decius, *Diarii et earum quae memoratu digna in splendidissimis, potentiss. Sigismundi Poloniae regis et sereniss. dominae Bonae Mediolani Barique ducis principis Rossani nuptiis gesta* (Cracow: Hieronymus Vietor, 1518). Other marriage poems were written by Caspar Ursinus Velius, Andrzej Krzycki, Joachim Vadian, Johannes Dantiscus, Hieronymus Balbus, Celio Calcagnini, Johannes Hadelius, and Laurentius Corvinus. See Nowak-Dłużewski, *Okolicznościowa poezja polityczna*, 73–83; Mroczek, *Epitalamium staropolskie*, passim; and Ryle, 'Celebrations for the Marriage of Sigismund I.'

5 On Lubrański, see *Polski słownik biograficzny*, 18: 81–4.

6 'Cuius ad expensas Musae migrare latinae / Plenaque Sarmatiae uisere regna solent' (*Illustrissimae reginae Bonae paraceleusis*, ll. 53–4). See Nowak-Dłużewski, *Okolicznościowa poezja polityczna*, 76.

7 On Ciołek, see *Polski słownik biograficzny*, 4: 78–81, and Bietenholz and Deutscher, *Contemporaries of Erasmus*, 1: 304–5. His oration against the Turks, delivered at Augsburg in August 1518, was published by Jakob Spiegel with a dedication to Erasmus (Allen, Ep. 863)

8 Ciołek was sent to Rome by Alexander (previously grand duke of Lithuania, then king of Poland) in 1501, to deliver a speech against the Turks to Pope Alexander VI, and 1505, to pay respects to Julius II on behalf of the Polish king. Both missions were considered great successes.

9 'Plocensis sedulo aerias qui construit aedes / Et sumptu reficit tecta uetusta graui' (*Illustrissimae reginae Bonae paraceleusis*, ll. 57–8).

10 Nowak-Dłużewski, *Okolicznościowa poezja polityczna*, 75, remarks that it is strange Agricola omits Krzysztof Szydłowiecki, who was among the group, but Bauch, 'Rudolphus Agricola Junior,' 28, says that Agricola does refer to Szydłowiecki in the poem. The lines '... palatinus pleno quem pectore princeps / Diligit et lateri iussit adesse suo' (*Illus-*

trissimae reginae Bonae paraceleusis, ll. 65–6), as the description of someone so close to the king, fit Szydłowiecki and not Górka, whom Agricola calls 'ille palatinus Lucas' (l. 71), and the description of the palatine as the king's Achates in lines 65–8 (see n11 below) fit Szydłowiecki. Moreover, the expression '*ille* palatinus' differentiates Górka from the 'palatinus' named earlier on, in line 65 (i.e., Szydłowiecki).

11 'Inde palatinus pleno quem pectore princeps / Diligit et lateri iussit adesse suo / Atque adeo incaluit uirtutum ardore suarum / Tractus ut Aeneam traxit Achatis amor' (*Illustrissimae reginae Bonae paraceleusis*, ll. 65–8). The lines from *Siluula* read '... te lateri iussit adesse suo. / Atque adeo incaluit uirtutum ardore tuarum/ Tractus, ut Aeneam traxit Achatis amor' (ll. 52–4). Leonard Cox would use the same comparison when addressing Szydłowiecki in his dedicatory letter to him for his publication of Martin Luther's *Epistola ad Henricum VIII* and Henry's *Responsio* (Cracow: Hieronymus Vietor, 1527).

12 On Górka, see *Polski słownik biograficzny*, 8: 409–12.

13 If this is more than a modesty topos, then Agricola may be referring to the lost epithalamium that was written for Sigismund and Bona's wedding. As Bauch, 'Rudolphus Agricola Junior,' 28, points out, Agricola refers to his epithalamium in his letter to Vadian of 30 April 1518 (*Vadianische Briefsammlung* I, 120).

14 'Ad laudes torpent carmina nostra tuas' (*Illustrissimae reginae Bonae paraceleusis*, l. 28).

15 'Haec ego non humili referam dicenda cothurno / Maxima tu nostra pars eris historiae' (*Illustrissimae reginae Bonae paraceleusis*, ll. 39–40).

16 Bauch, 'Rudolphus Agricola Junior,' 29–31.

17 'Hac de re brevi multa scribam, postquam stipendio meo ab episcopis satisfactum fuerit' (*Vadianische Briefsammlung* I, 120; 30 April 1518). In April 1519 he signed a letter to Vadian, for the first time, *lector ordinarius* (*Vadianische Briefsammlung* II, 142; 25 February 1519). Bauch, 'Rudolphus Agricola Junior,' 30, quoting *Liber diligentiarum*, notes Agricola's activity at the Collegium Maius as starting in the winter semester of 1518–19 and theorizes that his post must have given him 'half-official' status at the university, since his name appeared neither on the list of the Collegium Maius or Collegium Minus, nor on that of *extranei de facultate* or *extranei non de facultate* (even though Wisłocki lists him in his appendix as *extraneus non de facultate*). In the list of lectures and exercises, Agricola's academic title is given as *poeta* (Wisłocki, *Liber diligentiarum*, 137, 140, 146).

18 In August 1519, Agricola titled himself *camerariorum Italorum reginae praeceptor* in the signature to his letter to Vadian (*Vadianische Briefsammlung* II, 165; 25 August 1519).

19 Cox is listed last in the timetable of the university lectures for the winter semester 1526–7 (Wisłocki, *Liber diligentiarum*, 178), where his academic title is given as *poeta*.

20 For details on the controversy, see More, *Complete Works of St. Thomas More*, 715–31.

21 Doernberg, *Henry VIII and Luther*, 47–60.

22 The London title reads 'Literarum quibus inuictissimus princeps Henricus octauus rex Angliae et Franciae, dominus Hyberniae ac fidei defensor respondit ad quandam epistolam Martini Lutheri ad se missam et ipsius Lutheranae quoque epistolae exemplum.' The edition printed at Cologne in February 1527 reprints this title, whereas versions printed at Dresden, Hagenau, and Ingolstadt in 1527 have on the title-page 'Epistola Martini Lutheri ad Henricum VIII Angliae ac Franciae regem etc. In qua ueniam petit eorum quae prius stultus ac praeceps in eundem regem effuderit, offerens palinodiam se cantaturum. Responsio dicti inuictissimi Angliae ac Franciae regis defensoris fidei ac domini Hyberniae etc. ad singula praefatae epistolae capita. 1527' (VD16, L4620–4623).

23 Gruchała, 'Zmarnowany talent – Andrzej Krzycki,' 290–1, 294–9.

24 When the Counter-Reformation did come to Poland, after the establishment of Calvinism and Arianism in the country, it would be led by none other than Stanislaus Hosius, who would bring the Jesuit order to Poland in 1564 (Davies, *God's Playground*, 166; Miłosz, *History of Polish Literature*, 28–35). The authority on Protestantism in Poland is Tazbir; see his *Reformacja w Polsce*.

25 On the English reaction to the Polish settlement of the Prussian question, see Jasnowski, *England and Poland*, 9, and Zins, *Polska w oczach Anglików*, 55–6; on the affair of the Gdańsk citizens accused of Lutheranism while on business in London, see Jasnowski, *England and Poland*, 8–9, and Zins, *Polska w oczach Anglików*, 56.

26 Henry had initially proposed the forming of an anti-Turkish league to Sigismund in 1523. For the exchange of letters between the two kings concerning the Turkish problem, see Zins, *Polska w oczach Anglików*, 54–5.

27 The letters are found in *Acta Tomiciana*, 8: 288–9. Henry's letter is dated 1 November 1526, and Sigismund's is dated only late in the year 1526. (The text is from copies in the Polish archives.) In Brewer and others, *Letters and Papers Foreign and Domestic*, vol. 4, no. 3102, Sigismund's letter is given the date 7 May 1527. Sigismund also sent a letter to Cardinal Wolsey at the same time, reiterating their shared concern for protecting the Christian religion against infidels (*Acta Tomiciana*, 8: 291; Brewer and others, *Letters and Papers Foreign and Domestic*, vol. 4, no. 3103).

28 Henry VIII and Cardinal Wolsey would become involved in the dispute between Ferdinand and Zápolya for the crown of Hungary, with Zápolya seeking Henry's express support. See Jasnowski, *England and Poland*, 9–10, and Zins, *Polska w oczach Anglików*, 56–7.

29 In January 1527, Krzysztof Szydłowiecki sent off two letters to

England, one to Cardinal Wolsey and the other to Henry VIII himself. The letter to Wolsey was formal, explaining that although he had not met Wolsey in person, he would like to offer his services to him, and was taken up mostly with political news concerning the events taking place in Hungary. The letters are found in *Acta Tomiciana*, 9: 42–3, and in Brewer and others, *Letters and Papers Foreign and Domestic*, vol. 4, nos 2823 and 2824. On the story of Szydłowiecki and the falcons, see Jasnowski, *England and Poland*, 8.

30 'Quem saeuae eripuit morti immortalis Erasmus, / Cuius non patitur te sacra lingua mori' (*Epistola Martini Lutheri ad Henricum VIII*, fol. A3r).

31 '[C]upiens tam egregium opus mei principis ... felicissimae huic Poloniae, pro meo erga prouinciam studio, communicare, statim Hieronymo Vietori typographo tradidi imprimendum' (*Epistola Martini Lutheri ad Henricum VIII*, fol. A2r).

32 'Certo etenim mihi persuaseram hac opera non exiguam me gratiam initurum ab inclytae huius patriae optimatibus' (*Epistola Martini Lutheri ad Henricum VIII*, fol. A2r).

33 Allen, Ep. 1803; Erasmus, *Korespondencja Erazma*, ed. Cytowska, no. XIV (Cracow, 28 March 1527). Erasmus's reply is Allen, Ep. 1824; Erasmus, *Korespondencja Erazma*, ed. Cytowska, no. XX. In May 1527, King Sigismund had addressed to him a specially composed letter from Erasmus (Allen, Ep. 1819; Erasmus, *Korespondencja Erazma*, ed. Cytowska, no. XVI), which was printed in Cracow in the same year in a pamphlet to which Cox would contribute a commendatory verse, and reprinted in a collection of Erasmus's letters at Basel in 1529.

APPENDIX 1

1 Based on Vredeveld, 'Agricola, Rudolf d. J.,' and supplemented by my own research. See Vredeveld for detailed bibliographical information.

2 Reprinted as *Ad Ioachimum Vadianum epistola* (or *Rudolfus Agricola Iunior Ioachimo Vadiano*) in various printings of Joachim Vadian's edition of Pomponius Mela's *De orbis situ libri tres* (Vienna, 1518; Basel, 1522, 1557). See Vredeveld, 'Agricola, Rudolf d. J.,' for details. Agricola Junior's dedicatory letter to Caspar Ursinus Velius was also reprinted in *De orbis situ libri tres* (Paris: Christian Wechel, 1540).

3 VD16, K2559. Not recorded by Vredeveld.

4 VD16, H2201. Not recorded by Vredeveld.

5 Malicki and Zwinogrodzka, *Katalog poloników XVI wieku*, no. 1249. Not recorded by Vredeveld.

6 Malicki and Zwinogrodzka, *Katalog poloników XVI wieku*, no. 1250. Not recorded by Vredeveld.

7 VD16, S6970. Not recorded by Vredeveld.
8 Attribution of authorship according to Bauch, 'Rudolfus Agricola Junior,' 36.
9 Malicki and Zwinogrodzka, *Katalog poloników XVI wieku*, no. 673. Not recorded by Vredeveld.
10 Not recorded by Vredeveld. Copies at the British Library, London, and the University of Wrocław Library.
11 The author, Aegidius Gallus Romanus (Egidio Gallo) (1475–1521), is not to be confused with Aegidius Columna Romanus. On Gallus Romanus, see Cosenza, *Biographical and Bibliographical Dictionary of the Italian Humanists*, 2: 1536.
12 Recorded in bibliographical sources, but no known copy exists.
13 Malicki and Zwinogrodzka, *Katalog poloników XVI wieku*, no. 765.
14 For further details, including bibliographical references, see Glomski, 'Eck, Valentin.'
15 The 1521 printing is a revised, expanded edition. The 1539 printing is a reprint of the 1521 edition.
16 There exists a fragment of an earlier edition, dated 1556?, at the National Széchenyi Library (Budapest), which may have contained Eck's poetry. See Soltész and others, *Az Országos Széchényi Könyvtár 16. századi nyomtatványainak katalógusa*, H228.
17 Based on Breeze, 'Leonard Cox,' and Ryle, 'Cox, Leonard,' and supplemented by my own research. For bibliographical details of Cox's London publications, see ESTC.
18 Not recorded by Breeze.
19 Copy at Universitetsbibliotek Uppsala. Not recorded by Breeze.
20 Malicki and Zwinogrodzka, *Katalog poloników XVI wieku*, no. 1929. Not recorded by Breeze.
21 Copy at the Czapski Library (Muzeum im. Emeryka Hutten Czapskiego), Cracow. Not recorded by Breeze.
22 The title-page and the dedication by Cox to Henri Estienne are now lost.
23 Copy at Universitetsbibliotek Uppsala. Not recorded by Breeze.
24 The unsigned commendatory verse appearing at the end of the text is attributed to Cox.
25 Reprinted throughout the sixteenth century by Vietor, Ungler, and Scharffenberg, in editions retaining Cox's prefatory verses. For details, see Cygal-Krupowa, *Szesnastowieczne edycje 'Dictionarii Ioannis Murmellii,'* 21–37.
26 A revised, Hungarian version of *Dictionarius Ioannis Murmellii uariarum rerum*. Breeze, 'Leonard Cox,' 409, relying on Magyar Tudományos Akadémia, *Régi magyarországi nyomtatványok 1473–1600*, 79–80, notes that Cox's prefatory poem appears in this edition with the word *sarmatico* (Polish) changed to *pannonico* (Hungarian).

Bibliography

ABBREVIATIONS

Acta Tomiciana = Adam Tytus Działyński, W. Kętrzyński, Z. Celichowski, and W. Pociecha, eds. *Epistole. Legationes. Responsa. Actiones. Res gestae ... Sigismundi ... Regis Poloniae ... Per S. Górski collecte et in tomos XXVII digeste.* Poznań, Wrocław, Cracow: Various publishers, 1852– .

Allen = P.S. Allen and others, eds. *Opus epistolarum Desiderii Erasmi Roterodami.* 12 vols. Oxford: Clarendon, 1906–58.

ESTC = British Library and ESTC / North America. *English Short Title Catalogue.* Online database (RLG Eureka). CD-ROM. 3rd ed. [Detroit and London]: Thomson Gale, in association with the British Library, 1981–2005.

German STC = A.F. Johnson and Victor Scholderer, comps. *Short-Title Catalogue of Books Printed in the German-Speaking Countries and German Books Printed in Other Countries from 1455 to 1600 now in the British Museum.* London: British Museum, 1962; D.L. Paisey, comp. *Supplement.* London: British Library, 1990.

IISTC = British Library. *Illustrated Incunabula Short-Title Catalogue.* 2nd ed. CD-ROM. Reading and Woodbridge, CT: Primary Source Media, 1998.

Ossoliński = Zakład Narodowy imienia Ossolińskich

PAN = Wydawnictwo Polskiej Akademii Nauk

PIW = Państwowy Instytut Wydawniczy

PWN = Państwowe Wydawnictwo Naukowe

Vadianische Briefsammlung = Emil Arbenz and Hermann Wartmann, eds. *Die Vadianische Briefsammlung der Stadtbibliothek St. Gallen*, published in seven instalments in the journal *Mitteilungen zur Vaterländischen Geschichte*, 24 (1891), 25 pt 2 (1894), 27 (1897), 28 (1902), 29 (1903), 30 (1908), and 30a (1913). The letters of Rudolf Agricola Junior to Joachim

Vadian are found in vols 24, 25, and 27. In the citations from *Vadianische Briefsammlung*, the roman numeral refers to the number of the instalment (I, II, or III), and the arabic to the number of the letter.
VD16 = Bayerische Staatsbibliothek, Munich and Herzog August Bibliothek, Wolfenbüttel. *Verzeichnis der im deutschen Sprachbereich erscheinenen Drucke des XVI. Jahrhunderts*. Stuttgart: Anton Hiersemann, 1983–2000.

Alföldi, László M. 'The Battle of Mohács, 1526.' In Bak and Király, *From Hunyadi to Rákóczi*, 189–202.
Alicke, Gerhard. 'Vadians Pomponius Mela – ein Stück Buchgeschichte.' *Daphnis* 29 (2000): 379–412.
Allen, Peter R. '*Utopia* and European Humanism: The Functions of the Prefatory Letters and Verses.' *Studies in the Renaissance* 10 (1963): 91–107.
Ankwicz-Kleehoven, Hans. *Der Wiener Humanist Johannes Cuspinian. Gelehrter und Diplomat zur Zeit Kaiser Maximilans I.* Graz and Cologne: Hermann Böhlaus, 1959.
Armonio, Giovanni. *Ioannis Harmonii Marsi Comoedia Stephanium*. Ed. Walther Ludwig. Munich: Wilhelm Fink, 1971.
Aschbach, Joseph von. *Geschichte der Wiener Universität*. Vol. 2, *Die Wiener Universität und ihre Humanisten im Zeitalter Kaiser Maximilians I.* Vienna: Wilhelm Braumüller, 1877. Repr. Farnborough, Hants: Gregg, 1967.
Backvis, Claude. 'La fortune d'Érasme en Pologne.' In *Colloquium Erasmianum: Actes du Colloque International réuni à Mons du 26 au 29 octobre 1967 à l'occasion du cinquième centenaire de la naissance d'Érasme*, [no editor given], 173–202. Mons: Centre Universitaire de l'État, 1968.
Baczkowski, Krzysztof. 'Kallimachs Stelle in der Kulturgeschichte Polens.' In *Der polnische Humanismus und die europäischen Sodalitäten. Akten des polnisch-deutschen Symposions vom 15.–19. Mai 1996 im Collegium Maius der Universität Krakau*, ed. Stephan Füssel and Jan Pirożyński, 73–90. Wiesbaden: Harrassowitz, 1997.
– *Zjazd wiedeński 1515. Geneza, przebieg i znaczenie*. Warsaw: PWN, 1975.
Baczkowski, Krzysztof, Waldemar Bukowski, Mariusz Markiewicz, Krzysztof Ożóg, Maciej Salamon, Franciszek Sikora, and Stanisław Szczur, eds. *Cracovia, Polonia, Europa. Studia z dziejów średniowiecza ofiarowane Jerzemu Wyrozumskiemu w sześćdziesiątą piątą rocznicę urodzin i czterdziestolecie pracy naukowej*. Cracow: Wydawnictwo i drukarnia 'Secesja,' 1995.
Bainton, Roland H. 'The Querela Pacis of Erasmus, Classical and Christian Sources.' *Archiv für Reformationsgeschichte* 42 (1951): 32–48.
Bak, János M., and Béla K. Király, eds. *From Hunyadi to Rákóczi: War and Society in Late Medieval and Early Modern Hungary*. Brooklyn, NY: Brooklyn College Press, 1982.

Balogh, Jolán. 'Die ungarischen Mäzene der Renaissance.' In Török, *Matthias Corvinus und die Renaissance in Ungarn*, 73–80.

Barbaro, Francesco. *Francisci Barbari De re uxoria liber in partes duas*. Ed. Attilio Gnesotto. Padua: Tipografia Giovanni Battista Randi, 1915.

Bardach, Juliusz, and Andrzej Wyczański. 'Staat und Herrscher in Polen zur Zeit der Jagiellonen.' In Stangler and Stolot, *Polen im Zeitalter der Jagiellonen*, 16–28.

Barolsky, Paul. *Infinite Jest: Wit and Humor in Italian Renaissance Art*. Columbia, MO: University of Missouri Press, 1978.

Barycz, Henryk. *Historja Uniwersytetu Jagiellońskiego w epoce humanizmu*. Cracow: Polska Akademja Umiejętności, 1935.

– 'Nowa synteza dziejów Uniwersytetu Jagiellońskiego. Rozważania krytyczne.' *Przegląd historyczno-oświatowy* 9 (1966): 283–329.

– *Śląsk w polskiej kulturze umysłowej*. Katowice: Wydawnictwo 'Śląsk,' 1979.

– 'Sycylijski pionier kultury renesansowej w Polsce.' In *W blaskach epoki Odrodzenia*, 161–209. Warsaw: PIW, 1968.

– *Szlakami dziejopisarstwa staropolskiego. Studia nad historiografią w. XVI–XVIII*. Wrocław: Ossoliński, 1981.

– 'Z krakowskiego Parnasu w początkach wieku XVI.' *Biuletyn Biblioteki Jagiellońskiej* 30 (1980): 15–27.

Bathelt, Kurt. 'Die Familie Thurzo in Kunst und Kultur Ost-Mitteleuropas (1450–1650).' *Deutsche Monatshefte*, NF, vol. 7 (1940/41): 115–25.

Bauch, Gustav. 'Beiträge zur Litteraturgeschichte des schlesischen Humanismus. IV.' *Zeitschrift des Vereins für Geschichte und Altherthum Schlesiens* 32 (1898): 82–104.

– *Caspar Ursinus Velius. Der Hofhistoriograph Ferdinands I. und Erzieher Maximilians II*. Budapest: Friedrich Kilian, 1886.

– *Deutsche Scholaren in Krakau in der Zeit der Renaissance, 1460–1520*. Breslau [Wrocław]: M. und H. Marcus, 1901.

– *Geschichte des Leipziger Frühhumanismus*. Beihefte zum Centralblatt für Bibliothekswesen 22. Leipzig: Otto Harrassowitz, 1899.

– 'Laurentius Corvinus, der Breslauer Stadschreiber und Humanist.' *Zeitschrift des Vereins für Geschichte Schlesiens* 17 (1883): 230–302.

– 'Rudolphus Agricola Junior. Ein Beitrag zur Geschichte des Humanismus im deutsch-polnisch-ungarischen Osten.' In *Evangelische höhere Bürgerschule II. Wissenschaftliche Abhandlung zum Jaresbericht der Evangelischen höheren Bürgerschule II in Breslau Ostern 1892*. Breslau [Wrocław]: Grass, Barth und Co., 1892.

– 'Schlesien und die Universität Krakau in XV. und XVI. Jahrhundert.' *Zeitschrift des Vereins für Geschichte und Altertum Schlesiens* 41 (1907): 99–180.

– 'Valentin Eck und Georg Werner. Zwei Lebensbilder aus der Zeit der Besitzergreifung Ungarns durch die Habsburger.' *Ungarische Revue* 14 (1894): 40–57.

– 'Die Vertreibung des Johannes Rhagius Aesticampianus aus Leipzig.' *Archiv für Litteraturgeschichte* 13 (1885): 1–33.

Baumgart, P. 'Humanistische Bildungsreform an deutschen Universitäten des 16. Jahrhunderts.' In *Humanismus im Bildungswesen des 15. und 16. Jahrhunderts*, ed. W. Reinhard, 171–97. Weinheim: Acta Humaniora, 1984.

Baxandall, Michael. 'Rudolf Agricola on Patrons Efficient and Patrons Final: A Renaissance Discrimination.' *Burlington Magazine* 124, no. 952 (July 1982): 424–5.

Bebermeyer, G. *Tübinger Dichterhumanisten. Bebel/Frischlin/Flayder*. Tübingen: H. Laupp, 1927. Repr. Hildesheim: Olms, 1967.

Benedictine Monks of St Augustine's Abbey, Ramsgate, comp. *The Book of Saints*. 6th ed. London: A. and C. Black, 1989.

Bergman, Michał. 'Polsko-łacińskie epitalamium.' *Pamiętnik literacki* 25 (1928): 185–204.

Bernstein, Eckhard. 'Creating Humanist Myths: Two Poems by Ulrich von Hutten.' In *Acta Conventus Neo-Latini Torontonensis: Proceedings of the Seventh International Congress of Neo-Latin Studies*, ed. Alexander Dalzell, Charles Fantazzi, and Richard J. Schoeck, 249–60. Binghamton, NY: Medieval and Renaissance Texts and Studies, 1991.

– 'From Outsiders to Insiders: Some Reflections on the Development of a Group Identity of the German Humanists between 1450 and 1530.' In *In Laudem Caroli: Renaissance and Reformation Studies for Charles G. Nauert*, ed. James V. Mehl, 45–64. Kirksville, MO: Thomas Jefferson University Press, 1998.

– 'Group Identity Formation in the German Renaissance Humanists: The Function of Latin.' In *Germania Latina. Latinitas teutonica. Politik, Wissenschaft, humanistische Kultur vom späten Mittelalter bis in unsere Zeit*, ed. Eckhard Keßler and Heinrich C. Kuhn, 1: 375–86. Munich: Wilhelm Fink, 2003.

– 'Humanistische Standeskultur.' In Röcke and Münkler, *Die Literatur im Übergang*, 97–129.

– 'Vom lateinischen Frühhumanismus bis Conrad Celtis.' In Röcke and Münkler, *Die Literatur im Übergang*, 54–76.

Białostocki, Jan. *The Art of the Renaissance in Eastern Europe: Hungary, Bohemia, Poland*. Ithaca, NY: Cornell University Press, 1976.

Bieniarzówna, Janina, Jan M. Małecki, and Józef Mitkowski, eds. *Dzieje Krakowa*. Vol. 2, *Kraków w wiekach XVI–XVIII*, ed. Janina Bieniarzówna and Jan M. Małecki. Cracow: Wydawnictwo Literackie, 1984.

Bieńkowski, Tadeusz. 'Naukowe środowisko krakowskie w początkach XVI wieku (1500–1530).' *Studia i materiały z dziejów nauki polskiej*, series A, no. 13 (1975): 21–73.

– 'Panegiryk a życie literackie w Polsce XVI i XVII w.' In *Z dziejów życia literackiego w Polsce XVI i XVII wieku*, ed. Hanna Dziechcińska, 181–96. Wrocław: Ossoliński / PAN, 1980.

Bietenholz, Peter G., and Thomas B. Deutscher, eds. *Contemporaries of Erasmus*. 3 vols. Toronto: University of Toronto Press, 1985–7.

Birnbaum, Marianna D. *Humanists in a Shattered World: Croatian and Hungarian Latinity in the Sixteenth Century*. Columbus, OH: Slavica, 1986.

Bisaha, Nancy. *Creating East and West: Renaissance Humanists and the Ottoman Turks*. Philadelphia: University of Pennsylvania Press, 2004.

Bochnak, Adam.'Mecenat Sigismunda Starego w zakresie rzemiosła artystycznego.' *Studia do dziejów Wawelu* 2 (1960): 131–301.

Boehm, Laetitia. 'Humanistische Bildungsbewegung und mittelalterliche Universitätsverfassung: Aspekte zur frühneuzeitlichen Reformgeschichte der deutschen Universitäten.' In *The Universities in the Late Middle Ages*, ed. Jozef IJsewijn and Jacques Paquet, 315–46. Louvain: Leuven University Press, 1978.

Bogucka, Maria. *Bona Sforza*. 2nd ed. Wrocław: Ossoliński, 1998.

– *Dawna Polska. Narodziny, rozkwit, upadek*. Warsaw: Wydawnictwo TRIO and Wyższa Szkoła Humanistyczna w Pułtusku, 1998.

– *Historia Polski do 1864 roku*. Wrocław: Ossoliński, 1999.

– 'The Towns of East-Central Europe from the Fourteenth to the Seventeenth Century.' In Mączak and others, *East-Central Europe in Transition*, 97–108.

Bohonos, Maria, comp. *Katalog starych druków Biblioteki Zakładu Narodowego im. Ossolińskich*. Wrocław: Ossoliński, 1965.

Bonfinis, Antonius. *Symposion de virginitate et pudicitia coniugali*. Ed. Stephanus Apró. Budapest: K.M. Egyetemi Nyomda, 1943.

Bonorand, Conradin. *Joachim Vadian und der Humanismus im Bereich des Erzbistums Salzburg*. Vadian-Studien 10. Saint Gall: Fehr'sche Buchhandlung, 1980.

– *Personenkommentar II zum Vadianischen Briefwerk*. In *Die Dedikationsepisteln von und an Vadian*, ed. Conradin Bonorand and Heinz Haffter. Vadian-Studien 11. Saint Gall: VGS Verlagsgemeinschaft, 1983.

– *Vadians Humanisten Korrespondenz mit Schülern und Freunden aus seiner Wienerzeit: Personenkommentar IV zum Vadianischen Briefwerk*. Vadian-Studien 15. Saint Gall: VGS Verlagsgemeinschaft, 1988.

Borsa, Gedeon. 'Die polnischungarischen Beziehungen auf dem Gebiete der Buchdruckerkunst im 16. Jahrhundert.' In *Studia z dziejów polsko-węgierskich stosunków literackich*, ed. István Csapláros, 117–23. Warsaw: Wydawnictwo Uniwersytetu Warszawskiego, 1978.

Bots, Hans, and Françoise Waquet. *La République des Lettres*. Paris: Belin; Brussels: De Boeck, 1997.

Bracciolini, Poggio. *Poggius Bracciolini Opera omnia. Tomus Secundus. Opera miscellanea edita et inedita*. Ed. Riccardo Fubini. Torino: Bottega D'Erasmo, 1966.

Breeze, Andrew. 'Leonard Cox, a Welsh Humanist in Poland and Hungary.' *National Library of Wales Journal* 25 (Winter 1988): 399–410.

Breeze, Andrew, and Jacqueline Glomski. 'An Early British Treatise upon Education: Leonard Cox's *De erudienda iuventute* (1526).' *Humanistica Lovaniensia* 40 (1991): 112–67.

Brennan, Michael. *Literary Patronage in the English Renaissance: The Pembroke Family*. London: Routledge, 1988.

Brewer, J.S., James Gairdner, and R.H. Brodie, comps. *Letters and Papers Foreign and Domestic of the Reign of Henry VIII*. 21 vols. London: Various publishers, 1862–1920.

Brożek, Mieczysław. 'Epitalamia Zygmuntowskie.' In *Łacińska poezja w dawnej Polsce*, ed. Teresa Michałowska, 39–62. Warsaw: Instytut Badań Literackich, 1995.

Buck, August. 'Der Begriff des "poeta eruditus" in der Dichtungstheorie der italienischen Renaissance.' In *Die humanistische Tradition in der Romania*, 227–43. Bad Homburg: Dr Max Gehlen, 1968.

– 'Die Ethik im humanistischen Studienprogramm.' In *Ethik im Humanismus*, ed. Walter Rüegg and Dieter Wuttke, 31–44. Boppard: Harald Boldt Verlag, 1979.

Buck, August, Georg Kauffman, Blake Lee Spahr, and Conrad Wiedemann, eds. *Europaïsche Hofkultur im 16. und 17. Jahrhundert. Kongress des Wolfenbütteler Arbeitskreises für Renaissanceforschung und des Internationalen Arbeitskreises für Barockliteratur 1979*. 3 vols. Wolfenbütteler Arbeiten zur Barockforschung 8–10. Hamburg: Dr Ernst Hauswedell und Co., 1981.

Budka, W. 'Bibljoteka Decjuszów.' *Silva rerum* 4 (1928): 110–26.

Budzisz, Andrzej. 'Portret literacki Zygmunta Starego w epigramacie polsko-łacińskim XVI wieku.' In *Epigram grecki i łaciński w kulturze Europy. Konferencja ogólnopolska. Poznań, 11–12 grudnia 1995*, ed. Krystyna Bartol and Jerzy Danielewicz, 225–34. Poznań: Uniwersytet im. Adama Mickiewicza, 1997.

Bukowski, Waldemar. 'Salomonowie herbu Łabędź. Ze studiów nad patrycjatem krakowskim wieków średnich.' In Baczkowski and others, *Cracovia, Polonia, Europa*, 113–45.

Bułhak, Henryk. 'Wiedeńska oficyna Hieronima Wietora.' In *Z Badań nad dawną książką. Studia ofiarowane Profesor Alodii Kaweckiej-Gryczowej w 85-lecie urodzin*, ed. Paulina Buchwald-Pelcowa and others, 2: 297–432. Warsaw: Biblioteka Narodowa, 1991–3.

Burke, Peter. 'Representations of the Self from Petrarch to Descartes.' In *Rewriting the Self: Histories from the Renaissance to the Present*, ed. Roy Porter, 17–28. London and New York: Routledge, 1997.

Burmeister, Karl Heinz. 'Humanisten aus der Bodenseeregion an der Universität Krakau in ersten Viertel des 16. Jahrhunderts.' *Polska Akademia Umiejętności. Prace Komisji Historii Nauki* 2 (2000): 31–43.

– 'Zwei gelehrte Dichter in Krakau: Rudolf Agricola (†1521) aus Wasserburg und Valentin Eck (†1550) aus Lindau.' *Jahrbuch des Landkreises Lindau* 13 (1998): 85–7.

Buszewicz, Elwira. *Cracovia in litteris. Obraz Krakowa w piśmiennictwie*

doby Odrodzenia. Cracow: Towarzystwo Autorów i Wydawców Prac Naukowych UNIVERSITAS, 1998.
Chądzyński, Sergiusz, and Cyprian Mielczarski. 'Seminarium Zakładu Badań Kopernikańskich.' *Kwartalnik historii nauki i techniki* 16 (1981): 733–4.
Cherf, John Frank. 'The Latin Manuscript Tradition of the *Vita Sancti Pauli.*' In *Studies in the Text Tradition of St. Jerome's Vitae Patrum*, ed. William Abbott Oldfather, 65–142. Urbana, IL: University of Illinois Press, 1943.
Chmiel, Adam, Karol Lewicki, Ignacy Żegota Pauli, Józef Sebastian Pelczar, Bolesław Ulanowski, and Jerzy Zathey, eds. *Album studiosorum Universitatis Cracoviensis.* Vol. 2, *Ab anno 1490 ad annum 1551.* Cracow: Academia Litterarum Cracoviensis, 1892.
Clark, Donald L. 'The Rise and Fall of Progymnasmata in Sixteenth- and Seventeenth-Century Grammar Schools.' *Speech Monographs* 19 (1952): 259–63.
Clough, Cecil H. 'The Cult of Antiquity: Letters and Letter Collections.' In *Cultural Aspects of the Italian Renaissance: Essays in Honour of Paul Oskar Kristeller*, 33–67. Manchester: Manchester University Press; New York: Alfred F. Zambelli, 1976.
Conrady, Karl Otto. *Lateinische Dichtungstradition und deutsche Lyrik des 17. Jahrhunderts.* Bonn: H. Bouvier, 1962.
Cooper, Tracy E. '*Mecenatismo* or *Clientelismo?* The Character of Renaissance Patronage.' In *The Search for a Patron in the Middle Ages and the Renaissance*, ed. David G. Wilkins and Rebecca L. Wilkins, 19–32. Lewiston, NY: Edwin Mellen, 1996.
Cosenza, Mario Emilio. *Biographical and Bibliographical Dictionary of the Italian Humanists and of the World of Classical Scholarship in Italy, 1300–1800.* 6 vols. 2nd ed. Boston: G.K. Hall, 1962–7.
Cox, Leonard. *The Arte or Crafte of Rhethoryke. A Reprint.* Ed. Frederic Ives Carpenter. Chicago: University of Chicago Press, 1899. Repr. New York: AMS, 1973.
Coxe, Leonard. 'Książecka o nauczaniu młodzieży.' Trans. Janina Czerniatowicz. In *Filozofia i myśl społeczna XVI wieku*, ed. Lech Szczucki, 82–101. 700 [Siedemset] lat myśli polskiej 2. Warsaw: PWN, 1978.
Crane, William G. *Wit and Rhetoric in the Renaissance: The Formal Basis of Elizabethan Prose Style.* New York: Columbia University Press, 1937.
Curtius, Ernst Robert. *European Literature and the Latin Middle Ages.* Trans. Willard R. Trask. 7th printing. Princeton, NJ: Princeton University Press, 1990.
Cygal-Krupowa, Zofia. *Szesnastowieczne edycje 'Dictionarii Ioannis Murmellii variarum rerum ...'* Zeszyty naukowe Uniwersytetu Jagiellońskiego 505. Warsaw: PWN, 1979.
Cytowska, Maria. 'Król Zygmunt Stary w poezji polsko-łacińskiej XVI wieku.' In *W łacińskiej Polsce i w cesarskim Rzymie*, ed. Zofia Głombiow-

ska, 11–18. Gdańsk: Wydawnictwo Uniwersytetu Gdańskiego, 2000.

– *Od Aleksandra do Alwara. Gramatyki łacińskie w Polsce w XVI w.* Wrocław: Ossoliński/PAN, 1968.

– *Studia neolatina. Pięć odczytów.* Wrocław: Wydawnictwo Uniwersytetu Wrocławskiego, 1983.

– 'Twórczość Pawła z Krosna na tle ówczesnej literatury humanistycznej.' *Meander* 16 (1961): 502–15.

Czekajewska, Anna. 'Kultura umysłowa Polski XVI w. w świetle listów dedykacyjnych.' *Studia i Materiały z Dziejów Nauki Polskiej*, series A., pt 7 (1965): 47–109.

– 'O listach dedykacyjnych w polskiej książce XVI wieku.' *Roczniki Biblioteczne* 6 (1962): 21–56.

Dąbrowski, Jan. 'Les relations de Cracovie et son Université avec la Hongrie à l'époque de l'humanisme.' In *La Renaissance et la Réformation en Pologne et en Hongrie. Renaissance und Reformation in Polen und in Ungarn (1450–1650)*, ed. György Székely and Erik Fügedi, 451–64. Budapest: Akadémiai Kiadó, 1963.

– 'Związki początków i rozwoju odrodzenia w Krakowie z odrodzeniem na Węgrzech.' In *Krakowskie odrodzenie. Referaty z konferencji naukowej Towarzystwa Miłośników Historii i Zabytków Krakowa z września 1953*, 138–157. Cracow: Wydawnictwo Literackie, 1954.

Dantiscus, Ioannes. *Ioannis Dantisci poetae laureati Carmina.* Ed. Stanislaus Skimina. Cracow: Polonica Academia Litterarum et Scientiarum, 1950.

Davies, Norman. *God's Playground: A History of Poland.* Vol. 1, *The Origins to 1795.* Oxford: Clarendon, 1981; New York: Columbia University Press, 1982.

Decius, Jodocus Ludovicus. *De Sigismundi Regis temporibus liber, 1521.* Ed. Wiktor Czermak. Cracow: Nakładem Akademii Umiejętności, 1901.

– *De uetustatibus Polonorum. Liber I. De Iagellonum familia. Liber II. De Sigismundi Regis temporibus. Liber III.* Cracow: Hieronymus Vietor, 1521.

Decjusz, Jodok Ludwik. *Księga o czasach Króla Zygmunta.* Trans. Zespół Koła Naukowego Studentów Filologii Klasycznej UW under the direction of Prof. Kazimierz Kumaniecki. Introduction by Tadeusz Bieńkowski. Warszawa: PWN, 1960.

Delmarcel, Guy. *Los Honores: Flemish Tapestries for the Emperor Charles V.* Trans. Alastair Weir. Antwerp: Pandora/SDZ, 2000.

Denis, Johann Nepomuk Cosmas. *Wiens Buchdruckergeschichte.* 2 vols. Vienna: Christian Friedrich Wappler, 1782, 1793.

Dizionario biografico degli Italiani. Rome: Istituto della Enciclopedia Italiana, 1960– .

Długosz, Jan [Dlugossius, Ioannes]. *Joannis Dlugossii senioris Canonici Cracoviensis Opera.* Ed. Alexander Przezdziecki. Vol. 1, *Vita Sancti*

Stanislai, ed. Ignatius Polkowski and Ignatius Żegota Pauli. Cracow: Kluczycki, 1887.

Dmitrieva, Marina, and Karen Lambrecht, eds. *Krakau, Prag und Wien. Funktionen von Metropolen im frühmodernem Staat*. Stuttgart: Franz Steiner Verlag, 2000.

Dmochowski, Jan, ed. *Mikołaja Kopernika Rozprawy o monecie i inne pisma ekonomiczne oraz J.L. Decjusza Traktat o biciu monety*. Warsaw: Nakład Begethnera i Wolffa, 1924.

Dobrowolski, Tadeusz, and Władysław Tatarkiewicz, eds. *Historia Sztuki Polskiej*. 3 vols. Cracow: Wydawnictwo Literackie, 1962.

Doernberg, Erwin. *Henry VIII and Luther: An Account of Their Personal Relations*. London: Barrie and Rockliff, 1961.

Domański, Juliusz. 'O dwu znaczeniach metafory pszczoły.' *Archiwum historii filozofii i myśli społecznej* 42 (1997): 57–72.

– *Początki humanizmu*. Wrocław: Ossoliński, 1982.

– 'Uwagi o średniowiecznej i renesansowej "pogardzie świata" i "nędzy człowieka" (Lotariusz – Poggio Bracciolini – Erazm z Rotterdamu).' *Odrodzenie i Reformacja w Polsce* 36 (1991): 5–52.

Domonkos, Leslie S. 'The Battle of Mohács as a Cultural Watershed.' In Bak and Király, *From Hunyadi to Rákóczi*, 203–24.

– 'Ecclesiastical Patrons as a Factor in the Hungarian Renaissance.' *New Review of East-European History* 14 (December 1974): 100–16.

– 'The Multiethnic Character of the Hungarian Kingdom in the Later Middle Ages.' In *Transylvania: The Roots of Ethnic Conflict*, ed. John F. Cadzow, Andrew Ludanyi, and Louis J. Elteto, 41–60. Kent, OH: Kent State University Press, 1983.

Dreher, Derick F.W. 'Dürer's Portrait of Ulrich Varnbüler: The Monumental Woodcut and "Gedechtnus" in the German Renaissance.' In *Artibus. Kulturwissenschaft und deutsche Philologie des Mittelalters und der frühen Neuzeit. Festschrift für Dieter Wuttke zum 65. Geburtstag*, ed. Stephan Füssel, Gert Hübner, and Joachim Knape, 273–92. Wiesbaden: Harrassowitz, 1994.

Dróżdż, Piotr. *Orsza 1514*. Warsaw: Bellona, 2000.

Duczmal, Malgorzata. *Jagiellonowie. Leksykon biograficzny*. Cracow: Wydawnictwo Literackie, 1996.

Dupriez, Bernard. *A Dictionary of Literary Devices*. Trans. and adapted by Albert W. Halsall. New York: Harvester Wheatsheaf, 1991.

Eberhard, Winfried, and Alfred A. Strnad, eds. *Humanismus und Renaissance in Ostmitteleuropa vor der Reformation*. Cologne: Böhlau, 1996.

Eck, Walenty. 'Dialog o rządzeniu rzecząpospolitą.' Trans. Stefan Kazikowski. *Studia i materiały z dziejów nauki polskiej*, series A, pt 13 (1975): 3–19.

Egg, Erich. *Ausstellung Maximilian I. Innsbruck*. Innsbruck: Land Tirol, Kulturreferat, 1969.

Eisenstein, Elizabeth L. *The Printing Press as an Agent of Change: Commu-*

nications and Cultural Transformations in Early-Modern Europe. 2 vols. Cambridge: Cambridge University Press, 1979 [1980].

Ellinger, Georg. *Geschichte der Neulateinischen Literatur Deutschlands im Sechzehnten Jahrhundert.* 3 vols. Berlin and Leipzig: Walter de Gruyter und Co., 1929–33. Repr. Berlin: de Gruyter, 1969.

Elm, Kaspar. 'Eremiten und Eremitenorden des 13. Jahrhunderts.' In Elm, *Beiträge zur Geschichte des Paulinerordens*, 11–22.

– ed. *Beiträge zur Geschichte des Paulinerordens.* Berlin: Duncker und Humblot, 2000.

Engel, Pál. *The Realm of St. Stephen: A History of Medieval Hungary, 895–1526.* Trans. Andrew Ayton. London: I.B. Taurus, 2001.

Engel, Pál, Gyula Kristó, and András Kubinyi. *Magyarország története 1301–1526.* Budapest: Osiris Kiadó, 2001.

'Erasmiana Cracoviensia. W 500-lecie urodzin Erazma z Rotterdamu (1469–1536).' Special issue, *Zeszyty naukowe Uniwersytetu Jagiellońskiego* 250; *Prace historyczne* 33 (1971).

Erasmus, Desiderius. *Erazm z Rotterdamu Wybór pism.* Introduction by Maria Cytowska. Trans. M. Cytowska, E. Jędrkiewicz, and M. Mejor. Wrocław: Ossoliński, 1992.

– *Korespondencja Erazma z Rotterdamu z Polakami.* Ed. Maria Cytowska. Warsaw: PIW, 1965.

Erdélyi, Gabriella. 'Elek Thurzó of Bethlenfalva – a Model of a King-maker: On the Beginnings of Ferdinand of Habsburg's Rule as King of Hungary, 1526–1532.' M.A. thesis in Medieval Studies, Central European University, Budapest, 1997.

Estreicher, K. *Bibliografia polska.* 34 vols. Cracow: Drukarnia Uniwersytetu Jagiellońskiego, 1870–1951.

Eyb, Albrecht von. *Ob einem manne sey zunemen ein eelichs weyb oder nicht.* Ed. Helmut Weinacht. Darmstadt: Wissenschaftliche Buchgesellschaft, 1982.

Fabiański, Marcin. 'Art and Architecture of the Renaissance in Kraków, 1500–1550: An Introduction.' In *Polish and English Responses to French Art and Architecture: Contrasts and Similarities*, ed. Francis Ames-Lewis, 141–54. London: Birkbeck College, University of London, Department of History of Art, 1995.

Fajt, Jiří. 'Late Gothic Sculpture in Bohemia during the Reign of Wladislaw II (1471–1516): The Present State of Knowledge and Questions of Future Research.' In Popp and Suckale, *Die Jagiellonen*, 251–62.

Farbaky, Péter. 'György Szatmári (*c.* 1457–1524), Patron of Renaissance Architechture in Early Sixteenth-Century Hungary.' *Acta Historiae Artium Academiae Scientiarum Hungaricae (An Art-Historical Journal of the Hungarian Academy of Sciences)* 41 (1999/2000): 213–78.

– 'Renaissance Art and Architecture in Hungary.' *Bulletin of the Society for Renaissance Studies* 14 (May 1997): 7–14.

– *Szatmári György, a mecénás.* Budapest: Akadémiai Kiadó, 2002.

Farmer, David Hugh. *The Oxford Dictionary of Saints.* 5th ed. Oxford: Oxford University Press, 2003.

Feuer-Tóth, Rózsa. *Art and Humanism in Hungary in the Age of Matthias Corvinus.* Budapest: Akadémiai Kiadó, 1990.

Fiszman, Samuel, ed. *The Polish Renaissance in Its European Context.* Bloomington, IN: University of Indiana Press, 1988.

Fitch Lytle, Guy, and Stephen Orgel, eds. *Patronage in the Renaissance.* Princeton, NJ: Princeton University Press, 1981.

Foerster, Richard. 'Heinrich und Seyfried Ribisch.' *Zeitschrift des Vereins für Geschichte Schlesiens* 41 (1907): 181–240.

Franaszek, Antoni, and Bolesław Przybyszewski, eds. *Kaplica Sigismundowska. Materiały źródłowe, 1517–1977.* Cracow: Nakładem Ministerstwa Kultury i Sztuki, 1991.

Friedrich, Karin. 'Cives Cracoviae: Bürgertum im frühneuzeitlichen Krakau zwischen Stadtpatriotismus und nationaler Pluralität.' In Dmitrieva and Lambrecht, *Krakau, Prag und Wien,* 143–61.

Furlan, F., and S. Matton. 'Baptistae Alberti *Simiae* et de nonnullis eiusdem Baptistae Apologis qui nondum in vulgus prodiere: Autour des *intercenales* inconnues de Leon Battista Alberti.' *Bibliothèque d'Humanisme et Renaissance* 55 (1993): 125–35.

Füssel, Stephan. 'Dichtung und Politik um 1500. Das "Haus Österreich" in Selbstdarstellung, Volkslied und panegyrischen Carmina.' In *Die Österreichische Literatur. Ihr Profil von den Anfängen im Mittelalter bis ins 18. Jahrhundert* (1050–1750), ed. Herbert Zeman with Fritz Peter Knapp, 2: 803–32. Graz: Akademische Druck- und Verlagsanstalt, 1986.

– 'Kaiserliche Repräsentation bein "Weiner Kongreß" 1515 im Spiegel der zeitgenössischen Darstellungen.' In Buck and others, *Europaïsche Hofkultur,* 2: 359–68.

– *Riccardus Bartholinus Perusinus. Humanistische Panegyrik am Hofe Kaiser Maximilians I.* Baden-Baden: Walentin Koerner, 1987.

– ed. *Deutsche Dichter der frühen Neuzeit (1450–1600). Ihr Leben und Werk.* Berlin: Erich Schmidt Verlag, 1993.

Galinsky, G. Karl. *The Herakles Theme: The Adaptations of the Hero in Literature from Homer to the Twentieth Century.* Oxford: Basil Blackwell, 1972.

Garbacik, Józef. 'Ognisko nauki i kultury renesansowej (1470–1520).' In Lepszy, *Dzieje Uniwersytetu Jagiellońskiego,* 189–220.

Garfagnini, Gian Carlo, ed. *Callimaco Esperiente poeta e politico del '400.* Florence: Leo S. Olschki, 1987.

Gerlo, A. 'The *Opus de conscribendi epistolis* of Erasmus and the Tradition of the *Ars epistolica.*' In *Classical Influences on European Culture, A.D. 500–1500,* ed. R.R. Bolgar, 103–14. Cambridge: Cambridge University Press, 1971.

Gieysztor, Alexander. 'La pauvreté dans les textes hagiographiques.' In *Études sur l'histoire de la pauvreté,* ed. Michel Mollat, 125–39. Paris: Sorbonne, 1974.

Glomski, Jacqueline. 'Careerism at Cracow: The Dedicatory Letters of Rudolf Agricola Junior, Valentin Eck, and Leonard Cox (1510–1530).' In Van Houdt and others, *Self-Presentation and Social Identification*, 165–82.
– 'Early Humanism at Cracow (1510–1530).' *Bulletin of the Society for Renaissance Studies* 14 (October 1996): 1–7.
– 'Eck, Valentin.' In *Die deutsche Literatur des Mittelalters. Verfasserlexikon.* Suppl. vol., *Deutscher Humanismus 1480–1520*, ed. Franz Josef Worstbrock, 1: 589–600. Berlin: de Gruyter, 2005– .
– 'Erasmus and Cracow (1510–1530).' *Erasmus of Rotterdam Yearbook* 17 (1997): 1–18.
– 'The German Role in the Reception of Italian Neo-Latin Literary Currents at Cracow (1510–1525).' In Guthmüller, *Deutschland und Italien in ihren wechselseitigen Beziehungen*, 31–44.
– 'Humanizm renesansowy w Krakowie a znaczenie włoskiego piśmiennictwa nowołacińskiego.' *Terminus* 2 (2000): 27–36.
– 'The Imitation of Non-Classical Models in the Renaissance: Italian Neo-Latin Writing and the Early Cracow Humanists.' In *Acta Conventus Neo-Latini Abulensis: Proceedings of the Tenth Congress of the International Association for Neo-Latin Studies (Ávila, 1997)*, ed. Rhoda Schnur, Jenaro Costas Rodriguez, Roger Green, Antonio Iurilli, Elizabeth McCutcheon, Antonio Moreno Hernández, Monique Mund-Dopchie, and Hermann Wiegand, 293–99. Tempe, AZ: Medieval and Renaissance Texts and Studies, 2000.
– 'The Italian Grammarians and Early Humanism at Cracow.' *Studi Umanistici Piceni* 19 (1999): 47–53.
– 'Italian Influences on Early Humanist Educational Theory at Cracow (1495–1530).' In *Acta Conventus Neo-Latini Bariensis: Proceedings of the Ninth Congress of the International Association for Neo-Latin Studies (Bari 1994)*, ed. Rhoda Schnur, J.F. Alcina, John Dillon, Walther Ludwig, Colette Nativel, Mauro de Nichilo, and Stephen Ryle, 285–92. Tempe, AZ: Medieval and Renaissance Texts and Studies, 1998.
– 'Kraków i *ars versificandi*.' *Ruch literacki* 38 (1997): 451–63.
– 'Poetry to Teach the Writing of Poetry: Laurentius Corvinus's *Carminum structura* (1496).' In *Poets and Teachers. Fifth Annual Symposium of the Cambridge Society for Neo-Latin Studies, September 1996*, ed. Yasmin Haskell and Philip Hardie, 157–68. Kleos. Estemporaneo di studi e testi sulla fortuna dell'antico 4. Bari: Levante Editori, 1999.
Goleniszczew-Kutuzow, Ilja N. *Odrodzenie włoskie i literatury słowiańskie wieku XV i XVI.* Trans. W. and R. Śliwowski. Introduction by Julian Krzyżanowski. Warsaw: PIW, 1970.
Gorzkowski, Albert. *Paweł z Krosna. Humanistyczne peregrynacje krakowskiego profesora.* Cracow: Księgarnia Akademicka / Wydawnictwo Naukowe, 2000.
– 'Paweł z Krosna i jego twórczość w świetle dotychczasowych badań.' *Pamiętnik literacki* 89 (1998): 143–54.

– '*Societas litterarum*. Oblicza humanizmu Akademii Krakowskiej.' *Zeszyty Naukowe Uniwersytetu Jagiellońskiego* 1218 (1998): 47–61.

Gothei, Percy. *Francesco Barbaro. Früh-Humanismus und Staatskunst in Venedig*. Berlin: Die Runde, 1932.

Graciotti, Sante, and Amedeo Di Francesco, eds. *L'eredità classica in Italia e Ungheria fra tardo Medioevo e primo Rinascimento*. Rome: Il Calamo, 2001.

Graf, Klaus. 'Henrich Bebel.' In Füssel, *Deutscher Dichter der frühen Neuzeit*, 281–95.

– 'Heinrich Bebel (1472–1518). Wider ein barbarisches Latein.' In *Humanismus im deutschen Südwesten. Biographische Profile*, ed. Paul Gerhard Schmidt, 179–94. Sigmaringen: Jan Thorbecke, 1993.

Gray, Douglas. 'Finding Identity in the Middle Ages.' In *Sixteenth-Century Identities*, ed. A.J. Piesse, 9–33. Manchester: Manchester University Press, 2000.

Gray, Hanna H. 'Renaissance Humanism: The Pursuit of Eloquence.' *Journal of the History of Ideas* 24 (1963): 497–514.

Greenblatt, Stephen. *Renaissance Self-Fashioning: From More to Shakespeare*. Chicago: University of Chicago Press, 1980.

Grimal, Pierre. *The Dictionary of Classical Mythology*. Trans. A.R. Maxwell-Hyslop. Oxford: Basil Blackwell, 1996.

Gruchała, Janusz S. 'Zmarnowany talent – Andrzej Krzycki.' In Grzeszczuk, *Pisarze staropolscy*, 256–305.

Gryczowa, Alodia. 'Wokół Kongresu Wiedeńskiego. Nieznany utwór Pawła z Krosna.' *Pamiętnik literacki* 42 (1951): 885–907.

Grzeszczuk, Stanisław, ed. *Pisarze staropolscy. Sylwetki*. Vol. 1. Warsaw: Wiedza Powszechna, 1991.

Gustaw, Romuald, gen. ed. *Hagiografia polska. Słownik bio-bibliograficzny*. 2 vols. Poznań: Księgarnia Św. Wojciecha, 1971–2.

Guthmüller, Bodo, ed. *Deutschland und Italien in ihren wechselseitigen Beziehungen während der Renaissance*. Wiesbaden: Harrassowitz, 2000.

Guthmüller, Bodo, and Wilhelm Kühlmann, eds. *Europa und die Türken in der Renaissance*. Tübingen: Max Niemeyer, 2000.

Gyöngyönsi, Gregorius. *Vitae fratrum eremitarum Ordinis Sancti Pauli primi eremitae*. Ed. Franciscus L. Hervay. Budapest: Akadémiai Kiadó, 1988.

Habermann, Charles G., gen. ed. *The Catholic Encyclopedia*. 16 vols. New York: Various publishers, 1907–14.

Hajdukiewicz, Leszek. *Księgozbiór i zainteresowania bibliofilskie Piotra Tomickiego na tle jego działalności kulturalnej*. Wrocław: Ossoliński/PAN, 1961.

Halecki, O. *A History of Poland*. New ed. with additional material by A. Polansky and Thaddeus V. Grommada. New York: Dorset, 1992.

Hammer, William. *Latin and German Encomia of Cities*. [Chicago:] University of Chicago Libraries, 1937.

Harder, Hans-Bernd. 'Die Landesbeschreibung in der Literatur des schlesischen Frühhumanismus.' In *Landesbeschreibungen Mitteleuropas vom 15. bis 17. Jahrhundert. Vorträge der 2. internationalen Tagung des 'Slawenkomitees' im Herder-Institut Marburg a. d. Lahn 10.–13. November 1980*, 29–48. Cologne: Böhlau, 1983.

– 'Zentren des Humanismus in Böhmen und Mähren im 16. Jahrhundert.' In Buck and others, *Europaïsche Hofkultur*, 2: 157–69.

Hardison, O.B., Jr. *The Enduring Moment: A Study of the Idea of Praise in Renaissance Literary Theory and Practice.* Chapel Hill, NC: University of North Carolina Press, 1962.

Harth, Helene. 'Poggio Bracciolini und die Brieftheorie des 15. Jahrhunderts. Zur Gattungsform des humanistischen Briefs.' In *Der Brief im Zeitalter der Renaissance*, ed. Franz Josef Worstbrock, 81–99. Weinheim: Acta Humaniora, 1983.

Helbig, Herbert. *Die Reformation der Universität Leipzig im 16. Jahrhundert.* Gütersloh: C. Bertelsmann, 1953.

Henderson, Judith Rice. 'Humanist Letter Writing: Private Conversation or Public Forum.' In Van Houdt and others, *Self-Presentation and Social Identification*, 17–38.

– 'On Reading the Rhetoric of the Renaissance Letter.' In *Renaissance-Rhetorik. Renaissance Rhetoric*, ed. Heinrich F. Plett, 143–62. Berlin: Walter de Gruyter, 1993.

Henning, Edward B. 'Patronage and Style in the Arts: A Suggestion Concerning Their Relations.' *Journal of Aesthetics and Art Criticism* 18 (1959–60): 464–71.

Herberstein, Sigismund von. *Sigmunds von Herberstein Selbstbiographie 1486 bis 1553.* Ed. T.G. von Karajan. Fontes Rerum Austriacarum, pt 1, vol. 1, pp. 67–396. Wien: Kaiserl. Königl. Hof- und Staatsdrukerei, 1855.

Herrmann, Max. *Albrecht von Eyb und die Frühzeit des deutschen Humanismus.* Berlin: Weidmannsche Buchhandlung, 1893.

Hiller, Joseph Anthony. *Albrecht von Eyb, Medieval Moralist.* Washington, DC: Catholic University of America Press, 1939.

Hirsch, Rudolf. *Printing, Selling, and Reading, 1450–1550.* 2nd ed. Wiesbaden: Harrassowitz, 1974.

Hirschberg, Aleksander. *O życiu i pismach Justa Ludwika Decyusza, 1485–1545.* Lwów: Nakładem autora, 1874.

Hlobil, Ivo, and Eduard Petrů. *Humanism and the Early Renaissance in Moravia.* Trans. Jana and Michael Stoddart. Ed. Marek Perůtka. Olomouc: Votobia, 1999. [Translation of the following item.]

– *Humanismus a raná renesance na Moravě.* Prague: Academia, 1992.

Hollingsworth, Mary. *Patronage in Renaissance Italy from 1400 to the Early Sixteenth Century.* London: John Murray, 1994.

Holotík, L'udovít, gen. ed. *Dejiny Bardejova.* Košice: Východoslovenské vydavatel'stvo, 1975.

Holotík, L'udovit, and Anton Vantuch, eds. *Humanizmus a renesancia na Slovensku v 15.–16. storočí.* Bratislava: Vydavatel'stvo Slovenskej akadémie vied, 1967.

Holzknecht, Karl Julius. *Literary Patronage in the Middle Ages.* Philadelphia [Menasha, WI]: Collegiate Press, 1923.

Hornblower, Simon, and Antony Spawforth, eds. *The Oxford Classical Dictionary.* 3rd ed. Oxford: Oxford University Press, 1996.

IJsewijn, Jozef, and Dirk Sacré. *Companion to Neo-Latin Studies.* 2 vols. Louvain: Leuven University Press, 1990, 1998.

IJsewijn, Jozef, and W. Bracke, eds. *Joannes Dantiscus (1485–1548): Polish Ambassador and Humanist.* Brussels: Koninklijke Academie voor Wetenschappen, 1996.

Imre, Mihály. 'Der ungarische Türkenkrieg als rhetorisches Thema in der Frühen Neuzeit.' In *Deutschland und Ungarn in ihren Bildungs- und Wissenschaftsbeziehungen während der Renaissance,* ed. Wilhelm Kühlmann and Anton Schindling, 93–108. Stuttgart: Franz Steiner Verlag, 2004.

Irmscher, Johannes, ed. *Renaissance und Humanismus in Mittel- und Osteuropa.* 2 vols. Berlin: Akademie-Verlag, 1962.

Janik, Michał. *Dzieje szkolnictwa polskiego.* 2nd ed. Częstochowa: A. Gmachowski, 1924.

Jankovics, József. 'The Image of the Turks in Hungarian Renaissance Literature.' In Guthmüller and Kühlmann, *Europa und die Türken,* 267–73.

Janotzky, Johann [Janocki, Jan]. *Ianociana sive clarorum atque illustrium Poloniae Auctorum Maecenatumque Memoriae Miscellae.* 2 vols. Warsaw and Leipzig: Apud Michaelem Groellium, 1776, 1779.

Janson, Tore. *Latin Prose Prefaces: Studies in Literary Conventions.* Stockholm: Almqvist and Wiksell, 1964.

Jardine, Lisa. *Worldly Goods: A New History of the Renaissance.* London: Macmillan, 1996.

Jasnowski, Jozef. *England and Poland in the Sixteenth and Seventeenth Centuries (Political Relations).* Newtown, Wales: Montgomeryshire Printing Co., 1948.

Jelicz, Antonina. 'Die Dichtung des Andreas Cricius.' In Irmscher, *Renaissance und Humanismus in Mittel- und Osteuropa,* 2: 131–8.

– *Konrad Celtis na tle wczesnego Renesansu w Polsce.* Warsaw: PWN, 1956.

Johnson, Lonnie R. *Central Europe: Enemies, Neighbors, Friends.* Oxford: Oxford University Press, 1996.

Joret, Charles. 'Le légende de Saint Alexis en Allemagne.' *Annales de la Faculté des Lettres de Bordeaux* 2 (1880): 286–304, 410–16.

Kadić, Ante. 'Croatian Humanists at the Hungarian Court.' *East European Quarterly* 22 (1988): 129–46.

Kalus, Peter. *Die Fugger in der Slowakei.* Augsburg: Wissner, 1999.

Kämpfer, Frank, and Reinhard Frötscher, eds. *450 Jahre Sigismund von*

Herbersteins Rerum Moscoviticarum Commentarii, 1549–1999. Weisbaden: Harrassowitz, 2002.

Karbowiak, A. *Mieszkania żaków krakowskich w XIV–XVI wieku*. Lwów: Towarzystwo Nauczycieli Szkół Wyższych, 1887.

– 'Studya statystyczne z dziejów Uniwersytetu Jagiellónskiego, 1433/4–1509/10.' *Archiwum do dziejów literatury i oświaty w Polsce* 12 (1910): 1–82.

– *Ubiory profesorów i uczniów w Uniwersytecie Jagiellońskim w związku z współczesnymi zwyczajami (1364–1889)*. Cracow: Druk Wł. L. Anczyca i Spółki, 1889.

Kaufmann, Thomas DaCosta. *Court, Cloister, and City: The Art and Culture of Central Europe, 1450–1800*. London: Weidenfeld and Nicolson, 1995.

Kavka, František. *The Caroline University of Prague: A Short History*. Prague: Universita Karlova, 1962.

Kawecka-Gryczowa, Alodia. *Rola drukarstwa polskiego w dobie odrodzenia*. Warsaw: PIW, 1954.

– ed. *Drukarze dawnej Polski od XV do XVIII wieku*. Vol. 1, *Małopolska*. Pt 1, *Wiek XV–XVI*. Wrocław: Ossoliński, 1983.

– gen. ed. *Polonia typographica saeculi sedecimi*. 11 fasc. to date. Warsaw: Ossoliński/PAN, 1959– .

Kemény, Lajos. *Kassa város régi számadáskönyvei, 1431–1533*. Košice: Gusztáv Bernovits, 1892.

Kieszkowski, Jerzy. *Kanclerz Krzysztof Szydłowiecki. Z dziejów kultury i sztuki Zygmuntowskich czasów*. 2 vols. Poznań: J.K. Żupański, 1912.

Klaniczay, Gábor. 'La fortuna della leggenda di S. Alessio, ovvero l'antichità cristiana nell'Ungheria del Medioevo.' In Graciotti and Di Francesco, *L'eredità classica in Italia e Ungheria fra tardo Medioevo e primo Rinascimento*, 1–20.

– *Holy Rulers and Blessed Princesses: Dynastic Cults in Medieval Central Europe*. Trans. Éva Pálmai. Cambridge: Cambridge University Press, 2002.

Klaniczay, Tibor, and József Jankovics, eds. *Matthias Corvinus and the Humanism in Central Europe*. Budapest: Balassi Kiadó, 1994.

Klenner, Aladár. *Eck Bálint, Thurzó Elek humanista pártfogoltja*. Pestszenterzsébet: Rajkai Lajos Könyvnyomdája, [1939].

Klingová, Erika. 'Porovnanie učebníc metriky Valentína Ecchia a jeho vzoru Konráda Celtisa.' *Slovenská literatúra* 44 (1996): 161–8.

Knoll, Paul W. 'The Arts Faculty at the University of Cracow at the End of the Fifteenth Century.' In *The Copernican Achievement*, ed. Robert S. Westman, 137–56. Berkeley, CA: University of California Press, 1975.

– 'Italian Humanism in Poland: The Role of the University of Kraków in the Fifteenth and Early Sixteenth Centuries.' In *Renaissance Culture in Context: Theory and Practice*, ed. Jean R. Brink and William F. Gentrup, 164–75. Aldershot, Hants: Scolar Press, 1993.

– *The Rise of the Polish Monarchy: Piast Poland in East Central Europe, 1320–1370*. Chicago: University of Chicago Press, 1972.
– 'The University Context of Kochanowski's Era: Humanism and the Academic Culture of the Early Renaissance in Poland.' In Fiszman, *Polish Renaissance in Its European Context*, 189–212.
– 'The University of Cracow and the Conciliar Movement.' In *Rebirth, Reform, and Resilience: Universities in Transition, 1300–1700*, ed. James M. Kittelson and Pamela J. Transue, 190–212. Columbus, OH: Ohio State University Press, 1984.
Komornicki, Stefan S. 'Kultura artystyczna w Polsce czasów odrodzenia.' In *Kultura staropolska*, [no editor given], 533–605. Cracow: Nakładem Polskiej Akademji Umiejętności, 1932.
Kotarska, Jadwiga. 'Poeta i historyk – Filip Kallimach.' In Greszczuk, *Pisarze staropolscy*, 174–207.
Kozakiewiczowa, Helena. 'Mecenat Jana Łaskiego.' *Biuletyn historii sztuki* 23 (1961): 3–17.
Krókowski, Jerzy. 'Laurentius Corvinus und seine Beziehungen zu Polen.' In Irmscher, *Renaissance und Humanismus in Mittel- und Osteuropa*, 2: 152–72.
Krpelec, Bartolomej. *Bardejov a jeho okolie dávno a dnes*. Bardejov: Miestny odbor Matice Slovenskej, 1935.
Krzycki, Andrzej. *Andreae Cricii Carmina*. Ed. Casimirus Morawski. Cracow: Typis Universitatis Jagellonicae, 1888.
– *Poezje*. Ed. Antonina Jelicz. Trans. Edwin Jędrkiewicz. Warsaw: PIW, 1962.
Krzyżanowski, Julian. *A History of Polish Literature*. Warsaw: PWN – Polish Scientific Publishers, 1978.
Kubinyi, András. 'Alltag und Fest am ungarischen Königshof der Jagellonen 1490–1526.' In *Alltag bei Hofe. 3. Symposium der Residenzen-Kommission der Akademie der Wissenschaften in Göttingen*, ed. Werner Paravicini, 197–215. Sigmaringen: Jan Thorbecke, 1995.
Kulcsár, Péter. 'Der Humanismus in Ungarn.' In Török, *Matthias Corvinus und die Renaissance in Ungarn*, 55–65.
Kuzmík, Jozef. *Slovník autorov slovenských a so slovenskými vzt'ahmi za humanizmu*. Martin: Matica slovenská, 1976.
Lachs, Jan. 'Anselmus Ephorinus.' *Archiwum historji i filozofji medycyny* 4 (1926): 40–54.
Lambrecht, Karen. 'Aufstiegschancen und Handlungsräume in ostmitteleuropäischen Zentren um 1500. Das Beispiel der Unternehmerfamilie Thurzó.' *Zeitschrift für Ostmitteleuropa-Forschung* 47 (1998): 317–46.
– 'Communicating Europe to the Region: Breslau in the Age of the Renaissance.' *German History* 20 (2002): 1–19.
Lausberg, Heinrich. *Handbook of Literary Rhetoric: A Foundation for Literary Study*. Foreword by George A. Kennedy. Trans. M.T. Bliss, A.

Jansen, and D.E. Orton. Ed. D.E. Orton and R. Dean Anderson. Leiden: Brill, 1998.

Łempicki, Stanisław. 'Mecenat kulturalny w Polsce.' In *Studja staropolskie. Księga ku czci Aleksandra Brücknera*, [no editor given], 273–99. Cracow: Nakładem Krakowskiej Spółki Wydawniczej, 1928.

Lepszy, Kazimierz, ed. *Dzieje Uniwersytetu Jagiellońskiego w latach 1364–1764*. Cracow: PWN, 1964.

Lepszy, L. 'Turzonowie w Polsce.' *Przegląd polski* 96 (1890): 461–77.

Letocha, Danièle. 'Quand Érasme se fait politique: la première lettre à Sigismond 1er le Vieux.' *Renaissance and Reformation / Renaissance et Réforme* 24 (1988): 251–71.

Lewalski, Kenneth F. 'Sigismund I of Poland: Renaissance King and Patron.' *Studies in the Renaissance* 14 (1967): 49–72.

Lewandowski, Ignacy. *Florus w Polsce*. Wrocław: Ossoliński/PAN, 1970.

Łowmiański, Henryk. *Polityka Jagiellonów*. Ed. Krzysztof Pietkiewicz. Poznań: Wydawnictwo Poznańskie, 1999.

Ludwig, Walther. 'Die Darstellung südwestdeutscher Städte in der lateinischen Literatur des 15. bis 17. Jahrhunderts.' In *Stadt und Repräsentation*, ed. Bernhard Kirchgässner and Hans-Peter Becht, 39–76. Sigmaringen: Thorbecke, 1995.

– 'Petrus Lotichius Secundus and the Roman Elegists: Prolegomena to a Study of Neo-Latin Elegy.' In *Classical Influences on European Culture, A.D. 1500–1700*, ed. R.R. Bolgar, 171–90. Cambridge: Cambridge University Press, 1976.

Lyons, John D. *Exemplum: The Rhetoric of Example in Early Modern France and Italy*. Princeton, NJ: Princeton University Press, 1989.

Macek, Josef. *Jagellonský věk v českých zemích (1471–1526)*. 4 vols. Prague: Academia, 1992–9.

Macůrek, Josef. 'Humanismus v oblasti moravsko-slezské a jeho vztahy ke Slovensku ...' In Holotík and Vantuch, *Humanizmus a renesancia na Slovensku*, 332–55.

Mączak, Antoni. 'From Aristocratic Household to Princely Court: Restructuring Patronage in the Sixteenth and Seventeenth Centuries.' In *Princes, Patronage, and the Nobility: The Court at the Beginning of the Modern Age, c. 1450–1650*, ed. Ronald G. Asch and Adolf M. Birke, 315–27. London: German Historical Institute / Oxford University Press, 1991.

– 'Poland.' In *The Renaissance in National Context*, ed. Roy Porter and Mikuláš Teich, 180–96. Cambridge: Cambridge University Press, 1992.

– 'Polish Society and Power System in the Renaissance.' In Fiszman, *Polish Renaissance in Its European Context*, 17–33.

Mączak, Antoni, Henryk Samsonowicz, and Peter Burke, eds. *East-Central Europe in Transition: From the Fourteenth to the Seventeenth Century*. Cambridge: Cambridge University Press, 1985.

Magocsi, Paul Robert. *Historical Atlas of Central Europe from the Early Fifth Century to the Present.* Rev. ed. London: Thames and Hudson, 2002.

Magyar Tudományos Akadémia. *Lexicon latinitatis medii aevi Hungariae. A magyarországi középkori latinság szótára.* Budapest: Akadémiai Kiadó, 1987– .

– *Régi magyarországi nyomtatványok 1473–1600. Res litteraria Hungariae vetus operum impressorum 1473–1600.* Budapest: Akadémiai Kiadó, 1971.

Maleszyński, Dariusz Cezary. 'Pszczoła-"archipoeta" (teoria *mimesis* w dawnej metaforze).' In *Człowiek w tekście. Formy istnienia według literatury staropolskiej*, 47–72. Poznań: Wydawnictwo Naukowe Uniwersytetu im. Adama Mickiewicza w Poznaniu, 2002.

Malicki, Marian, and Ewa Zwinogrodzka, eds. *Katalog poloników XVI wieku Biblioteki Jagiellońskiej. Catalogus Librorum Polonicorum saeculi XVI qui in Bibliotheca Iagellonica asservantur.* With contributions from Małgorzata Gołuszka, Wanda Ptak-Korbel, Zofia Wawrykiewicz, and Ewa Szczawińska. 3 vols. Cracow: Nakładem Uniwersytetu Jagiellońskiego, 1992–5.

Markowski, Mieczysław. 'Nauki wyzwolone i filozofia na Uniwersytecie Krakowskim w XV wieku.' *Studia mediewistyczne* 9 (1968): 91–116.

Marosi, Ernő. 'Die Corvinische Renaissance in Ungarn und ihre Ausstahlung in Ostmitteleuropa.' In Eberhard and Strnad, *Humanismus und Renaissance in Ostmitteleuropa*, 173–87.

Martin, John. 'Inventing Sincerity, Refashioning Prudence: The Discovery of the Individual in Renaissance Europe.' *American Historical Review* 102:5 (December 1997): 1309–42.

Mayer, Anton. *Wiens Buchdrucker-Geschichte, 1482–1882.* 2 vols. Vienna: Wilhelm Frick, 1883–7.

McCahill, Elizabeth May. 'Finding a Job as a Humanist: The Epistolary Collection of Lapo da Castiglionchio the Younger.' *Renaissance Quarterly* 57 (2004): 1308–45.

McConica, J.K. *English Humanists and Reformation Politics under Henry VIII and Edward VI.* Oxford: Clarendon, 1965.

McDonald, William C. *German Literary Patronage from Charlemagne to Maximilian I: A Critical Commentary with Special Emphasis on Imperial Promotion of Literature.* Amsterdam: Rodopi, 1973.

– 'Maximilian of Habsburg and the Veneration of Hercules: On the Revival of Myth and the German Renaissance.' *Journal of Medieval and Renaissance Studies* 6 (1967): 139–54.

Melczer, William. 'Albrecht von Eyb (1420–1475) et les racines italiennes du premier humanisme allemand.' In *L'Humanisme allemand (1480–1540). XVIIIe Colloque International de Tours*, ed. Joël Lefebvre and Jean-Claude Margolin, 31–44. XVIIIe colloque international de Tours. Munich: Fink Verlag; Paris: Librairie Vrin, 1979.

Melich, János, ed. *A két legrégibb magyar nyelvű nyomtatvány. I. Hegendorf*

– *Sylvester: Rudimenta grammatices Donati. Cracoviae 1527. II. Heyden – Sylvester: Puerilium colloq. formulae. Cracoviae 1527.* Budapest: Magyar nyelvtudományi társaság, 1912.
Mertens, Dieter. 'Zu Sozialgeschichte und Funktion des poeta laureatus im Zeitalter Maximilans I.' In *Gelehrte im Reich. Zur Sozial- und Wirkungsgeschichte akademischer Eliten des 14. bis 16. Jahrhunderts*, ed. Rainer Christoph Schwinges, 327–48. Berlin: Duncker und Humblot, 1996.
Michałowska, Teresa, ed. *Słownik literatury staropolskiej. Średniowiecze. Renesans. Barok.* With assistance from Barbara Otwinowska and Elżbieta Sarnowska-Temeriusz. 2nd ed. Wrocław: Ossoliński, 1998.
– *Średniowiecze.* Warsaw: PWN, 1997.
Mielczarski, Cyprian. *Humanistyczna sztuka wierszowania na Uniwersytecie Krakowskim. Podręcznik De arte versificandi Walentego Ecka (Kraków 1515).* Warsaw: Uniwersytet Warszawski, 2004.
– *Między gramatyką scholastyczną a humanistyczną. Komentarz Jana Sommerfelda starszego do traktatu gramatycznego Eberharda Hiszpańskiego (Strasburg 1499).* Warsaw: Uniwersytet Warszawski, 2003.
Milde, Wolfgang. 'Zur Druckhäufigkeit von Niccolò Perottis "Cornucopiae" und "Rudimenta grammatices" im 15. und 16. Jahrhundert.' *Studi Umanistici Piceni* 2 (1982): 29–42.
Milewska-Waźbińska, Barbara. 'The Poetry of Joannes Dantiscus in the Diplomatic Service.' In IJsewijn and Bracke, *Joannes Dantiscus*, 109–14.
– 'The Turks in the Renaissance Latin Poetry of Poland.' In Guthmüller and Kühlmann, *Europa und die Türken*, 437–42.
Miłobędzki, Adam. 'Architecture under the Last Jagiellons in Its Political and Social Context.' In Fiszman, *Polish Renaissance in Its European Context*, 291–300.
Miłosz, Czesław. *The History of Polish Literature.* 2nd ed. Berkeley, CA: University of California Press, 1983.
Miodońska, Barbara. 'Die Buchmalerei in Polen zur Zeit der Jagiellonen.' In Stangler and Stolot, *Polen im Zeitalter der Jagiellonen*, 224–59.
– 'Władca i państwo w krakowskim drzeworycie ksiażkowym XVI w.' In *Renesans. Sztuka i ideologia*, ed. Tadeusz Stefan Jaroszewski, 45–96. Warsaw: PWN, 1976.
Miziołek, Jerzy. 'L'ideale classico nelle raffigurazioni dei re di Polonia come capitani (secoli XVI–XVII).' In *Il 'perfetto capitano'. Immagini e realtà (secoli XV–XVII)*, ed. Marcello Fantoni, 401–47. Rome: Bulzoni, 2001.
Modelska Strzelecka, Bożena. 'Bernard Wapowski.' In *The Cracow Circle of Nicholas Copernicus*, ed. Józef Gierowski, 23–60. Warsaw and Cracow: Polish Scientific Publishers, 1973.
Moore, Samuel. 'General Aspects of Literary Patronage in the Middle Ages.' *The Library*, 3rd series, vol. 4 (1913): 369–92.
Moraw, Peter. 'Die Hohe Schule in Krakau und das europäische Universitätssystem um 1400.' In *Studien zum 15. Jahrhundert. Festschrift für*

Erich Meuthen, ed. Johannes Helmrath and Heribert Müller, 1: 521–39. Munich: R. Oldenbourg, 1994.

Morawski, Casimir [Kazimierz]. *Histoire de l'Université de Cracovie. Moyen Age et Renaissance*. 3 vols. Paris: A. Picard et Fils; Cracow: G. Gebethner, 1900–5.

Morawski, Kazimierz. *Czasy Zygmuntowskie na tle prądów odrodzenia*. Warsaw: PIW, 1965.

More, Saint Thomas. *The Complete Works of St. Thomas More*. Vol. 5, ed. John M. Headley and trans. Sister Scholastica Mandeville. New Haven: Yale University Press, 1969.

Morka, Mieczysław. 'The Political Meaning of the Sigismund Chapel.' *Polish Art Studies* 10 (1989): 21–34.

Mroczek, Katarzyna. *Epitalamium staropolskie między tradycją literacką a obrzędem weselnym*. Wrocław: Ossoliński/PAN, 1989.

Müller, Jan-Dirk. 'Deutsch-lateinische Panegyrik am Kaiserhof und die Entstehung eines neuen höfischen Publikums in Deutschland.' In Buck and others, *Europaïsche Hofkultur*, 2: 133–40.

– *Gedechtnus. Literatur und Hofgesellschaft um Maximilian I*. Munich: Wilhelm Fink, 1982.

Müller, Rainer. 'Humanismus und Universität im östlichen Mitteleuropa.' In Eberhard and Strnad, *Humanismus und Renaissance in Ostmitteleuropa*, 245–72.

Murphy, James J. *Rhetoric in the Middle Ages: A History of the Rhetorical Theory from Saint Augustine to the Renaissance*. MRTS Reprint Series 4. Tempe, AZ: Arizona Center for Medieval and Renaissance Studies, 2001.

Näf, Werner. *Vadian und seine Stadt St. Gallen*. 2 vols. Saint Gall: Fehr'sche Buchhandlung, 1944, 1957.

– *Vadianische Analekten*. Vadian-Studien 1. Saint Gall: Fehr'sche Buchhandlung, 1945.

Nadolski, B. 'Mecenat literacki w dobie odrodzenia.' In *Odrodzenia w Polsce. Materiały sesji naukowej PAN 25–30 października 1953 roku*. Vol. 5, *Historia sztuki*, ed. Ksawery Piwocki, 374–79. Warsaw: PIW, 1958.

Nauert, Charles G., Jr. 'Humanism as Method: Roots of Conflict with the Scholastics.' *Sixteenth Century Journal* 29 (1998): 427–38.

– 'The Humanist Challenge to Medieval German Culture.' *Daphnis: Zeitschrift für mittlere deutsche Literatur* 15 (1986): 277–306.

– 'Humanist Infiltration into the Academic World.' *Renaissance Quarterly* 43 (Winter 1990): 799–812.

Neagu, Cristina. *Servant of the Renaissance: The Poetry and Prose of Nicolaus Olahus*. Oxford and Bern: Peter Lang, 2003.

North, Helen F. 'Canons and Hierarchies of the Cardinal Virtues in Greek and Latin Literature.' In *The Classical Tradition: Literary and Historical Studies in Honor of Harry Caplan*, ed. Luitpold Wallach, 165–83. Ithaca, NY: Cornell University Press, 1966.

Nowak, Zbigniew. *Jan Dantyszek. Portret renesansowego humanisty.* Wrocław: Ossoliński, 1982.

– 'Polityk, poeta i duchowny Jan Dantyszek.' In Grzeszczuk, *Pisarze staropolscy*, 344–76.

Nowak-Dłużewski, Juliusz. *Okolicznościowa poezja polityczna w Polsce. Czasy Zygmuntowskie.* Warsaw: Instytut Wydawniczy Pax, 1966.

Nowakowska, Natalia. 'Papacy and Piety in the Career of Cardinal Fryderyk Jagiellon, Prince of Poland, 1468–1503.' D.Phil. thesis, University of Oxford, 2003.

Obersteiner, Jakob. *Die Bischöfe von Gurk 1072–1822.* Klagenfurt: Verlag Geschichtsvereines für Kärnten, 1969.

Ocieczek, Renarda. *Sławorodne wizerunki. O wierszowanych listach dedykacyjnych z XVII wieku.* Katowice: Uniwersytet Śląski, 1982.

Odenkirchen, Carl J. *The Life of St. Alexius in the Old French Version of the Hildesheim Manuscript.* Brookline, MA: Classical Folia Editions, 1978.

Olkiewicz, Joanna. *Kallimach doświadczony.* Warsaw: Ludowa Spółdzielnia Wydawnicza, 1981.

– *Polscy medyceusze.* Warsaw: Ludowa Spółdzielnia Wydawnicza, 1985.

Overfield, James H. *Humanism and Scholasticism in Late Medieval Germany.* Princeton, NJ: Princeton University Press, 1984.

Ożóg, Jan. *Katalog poloników XVI w. Biblioteki Uniwersyteckiej we Wrocławiu.* 2 vols. Wrocław: Wydawnictwo Uniwersytetu Wrocławskiego, 1988–91.

Padley, G.A. *Grammatical Theory in Western Europe: The Latin Tradition.* Cambridge: Cambridge University Press, 1976.

Panofsky, Erwin. *Hercules am Scheidewege und andere antike Bildstoffe in der neuen Kunst.* Studien der Bibliothek Warburg 18. Berlin and Leipzig: B.G. Teubner, 1930. Repr. with an afterword by Dieter Wuttke, Berlin: Gebr. Mann Verlag, 1997.

Paparelli, Gioacchino. *Callimacho Esperiente.* Salerno: Edizioni Beta, 1971.

Paulus Crosnensis. *Pauli Crosnensis Rutheni atque Ioannis Visliciensis Carmina.* Ed. B. Kruczkiewicz. Cracow: Sumptibus Academiae Litterarum Cracoviensis, 1887.

– *Pauli Crosnensis Rutheni Carmina.* Ed. Maria Cytowska. Warsaw: PWN, 1962.

Pelc, Janusz, ed. *Problemy literatury staropolskiej. Seria druga.* Wrocław: Ossoliński, 1973.

Pelc, Janusz, and Władysław Tomkiewicz. 'Rola mecenatu w rozwoju kultury i literatury polskiej w czasach renesansu.' In Pelc, *Problemy literatury staropolskiej*, 165–236.

Pellathy, Gabriel S. 'The Dozsa Revolt: Prelude and Aftermath.' *East European Quarterly* 21 (1987): 275–95.

Percival, W. Keith. 'Renaissance Grammar.' In *Renaissance Humanism: Foundations, Forms, and Legacy*, ed. Albert Rabil, Jr, 3: 67–83. Philadelphia: University of Pennsylvania Press, 1988.

Pešek, Jiří. 'Výuka a humanismus na pražské univerzitě doby předbělohorské.' In *Dějiny Univerzity Karlovy, 1348–1990*, ed. František Kavka and Josef Petráň. Vol. 1, *1347/48–1622*, ed. Michal Svatoš, 227–39. Prague: Univerzita Karlova, 1995.

Pferschy, Gerhard, ed. *Sigismund von Herberstein. Kaiserlicher Gesandter und Begründer der Rußlandkunde und die europaïsche Diplomatie*. Graz: Akademische Druk- und Verlagsanstalt, 1989.

Pigman, G.W. 'Barzizza's Treatise on Imitation.' *Bibliothèque d'Humanisme et Renaissance* 44: (1982): 341–52.

Pirożyński, Jan. 'Die Krakauer Universität in der Renaissancezeit.' In *Der polnische Humanismus und die europäischen Sodalitäten. Akten des polnisch-deutschen Symposions vom 15.–19. Mai 1996 im Collegium Maius der Universität Krakau*, ed. Stephan Füssel and Jan Pirożyński, 13–38. Pirckheimer Jahrbuch 12. Wiesbaden: Harrassowitz, 1997.

Pociecha, Władysław. *Królowa Bona (1494–1557). Czasy i ludzie odrodzenia*. 4 vols. Poznań: Various publishers, 1949–58.

Polska Akademia Nauk. *Lexicon mediae et infimae latinitatis polonorum. Słownik łaciny średniowiecznej w Polsce*. Wrocław: Ossoliński/PAN, 1953– .

Polski słownik biograficzny. Cracow: Various publishers, 1935– .

Popiel, Paweł. 'Czynności artystyczne na dworze Zygmunta I wedle zapisów Seweryna Bonera.' *Sprawozdania komisyi do badania historyi sztuki w Polsce* 1, pt 2 (1878): 25–32; pt 3 (1879): 63–72.

Popp, Dietmar, and Robert Suckale, eds. *Die Jagiellonen. Kunst und Kultur einer europaïschen Dynastie an der Wende zur Neuzeit*. Nuremberg: Germanisches Nationalmuseum, 2002.

Price, B.B. 'The Effect of Patronage on the Intellectualization of Medieval Endeavors.' In *The Search for a Patron in the Middle Ages and the Renaissance*, ed. David G. Wilkins and Rebecca L. Wilkins, 5–18. Lewiston, NY: Edwin Mellen, 1996.

Ptaśnik, Jan. 'Bonerowie.' *Rocznik krakowski* 7 (1905): 1–134.

– *Obrazki z przeszłości Krakowa. Serya druga*. Cracow: Towarzystwo Miłośników Historyi i Zabytków Krakowa, 1903.

– *Obrazki życia żaków krakowskich w XV i XVI wieku*. Cracow: Towarzystwo Miłośników Historyi i Zabytków Krakowa, 1900.

– 'Turzonowie w Polsce i ich stosunki z Fuggerami.' *Przewodnik naukowy i literacki* 33 (1905): 829–38, 927–34, 1020–8, 1115–24.

– *Życie żaków krakowskich*. 2nd ed., ed. Mieczysław Ptaśnik. Warsaw: Wiedza Powszechna, 1957.

Quirini-Popławska, Danuta. *Działalność włochów w Polsce w I połowie XVI wieku na dworze królewskim, w dyplomacji i hierarchii kościelnej*. Wrocław: Ossoliński/PAN, 1973.

Rázsó, Gyula. 'The Mercenary Army of King Matthias Corvinus.' In Bak and Király, *From Hunyadi to Rákóczi*, 125–40.

Rebenich, Stefan. 'Der Kirchenvater Hieronymus als Hagiograph. Die

Vita Sancti Pauli primi Eremitae.' In Elm, *Beiträge zur Geschichte des Paulinerordens*, 23–40.

Rekettyés, Maria. *Stosunki polityczne i kulturalne polsko-węgierskie za Władysława Jagiellończyka*. Wroclaw: Signum, 1999.

Rice, Eugene F., Jr. 'The Patrons of French Humanism, 1490–1520.' In *Renaissance Studies in Honor of Hans Baron*, ed. Anthony Molho and John A. Tedeschi, 687–702. Dekalb, IL: Northern Illinois University Press, 1971.

Ritoókné Szalay, Ágnes. *'Nympha super ripam Danubii.' Tanulmányok a XV–XVI. századi magyarországi művelődés köréből*. Budapest: Balassi Kiadó, 2002.

Ritoók-Szalay, Ágnes. 'Erasmus und die ungarischen Intellektuellen des 16. Jahrhunderts.' In *Erasmus und Europa*, ed. August Buck, 111–28. Wiesbaden: Otto Harrassowitz, 1988.

Robert, Jörg. *Konrad Celtis und das Projekt der deutschen Dichtung. Studien zur humanistischen Konstitution von Poetik, Philosophie, Nation und Ich*. Tübingen: Max Niemeyer, 2003.

Röcke, Werner, and Marina Münkler, eds. *Die Literatur im Übergang vom Mittelalter zur Neuzeit*. Hansers Sozialgeschichte der deutschen Literatur vom 16. Jahrhundert bis zur Gegenwart 1. Munich: Carl Hanser, 2004.

Roeck, Bernd. *Kunstpatronage in der Frühen Neuzeit. Studien zur Kunstmarkt, Künstlern und ihren Auftraggebern in Italien und im Heiligen Römischen Reich (15.–17. Jahrhundert)*. Göttingen: Vandenhoeck und Ruprecht, 1999.

Rugel, Just, ed. *Žiga Herberstein, 1486–1566*. Bilje: Humar; Moscow: Belye al'vy, 2000.

Rummel, Erika. *The Humanist-Scholastic Debate in the Renaissance and Reformation*. Cambridge, MA: Harvard University Press, 1995.

Rupprich, Hans. *Humanismus und Renaissance in den deutschen Städten und an den Universitäten*. Leipzig: Philipp Reclam, 1935.

Rybka, Eugeniusz, ed. *Historia astronomii w Polsce*. Vol. 1, by Jerzy Dobrzycki, Mieczysław Markowski, and Tadeusz Przypkowski. Wrocław: Ossoliński/PAN, 1975.

Ryle, S.F. 'The Celebrations for the Marriage of Sigismund I of Poland and Bona Sforza, Duchess of Bari.' In *Acta Conventus Neo-Latini Bariensis: Proceedings of the Ninth International Congress of Neo-Latin Studies*, ed. Rhoda Schnur, J.F. Alcina, John Dillon, Walther Ludwig, Colette Nativel, Mauro de Nichilo, and Stephen Ryle, 525–32. Tempe, AZ: Medieval and Renaissance Texts and Studies, 1998.

– 'Cox, Leonard.' In *Oxford Dictionary of National Biography*, ed. H.C.G. Matthew and Brian Harrison, 13: 854–6. Oxford: Oxford University Press, 2004.

– 'An English Humanist in Eastern Europe: Leonard Cox (*c*. 1495–*c*. 1550).' *Studi Umanistici Piceni* 12 (1992): 223–31.

– 'Leonard Cox.' In *British Rhetoricians and Logicians, 1500–1660. Second Series*, ed. Edward A. Malone, 58–67. Dictionary of Literary Biography 281. Detroit: Thomson-Gale, 2003.

Sallaberger, Johann. *Kardinal Matthäus Lang von Wellenburg (1468–1540). Staatsmann und Kirchenfürst im Zeitalter von Renaissance, Reformation und Bauerkriegen*. Salzburg: Anton Pustet, 1997.

Samsonowicz, Henryk. 'Gesellschaftliche Pluralität und Interaktion in Krakau.' In Dmitrieva and Lambrecht, *Krakau, Prag, und Wien*, 117–29.

Sarnowska-Temeriusz, Elżbieta. *Droga na Parnas. Problemy staropolskiej wiedzy o poezji*. Wrocław: Ossoliński/PAN, 1974.

Schirrmeister, Albert. *Triumph des Dichters. Gekrönte Intellektuelle im 16. Jahrhundert*. Cologne: Böhlau, 2003.

Schottenloher, Karl. *Die Widmungsvorrede im Buch des 16. Jahrhunderts*. Münster Westfalen: Aschendorffsche Verlagsbuchhandlung, 1953.

Schulz, Anne Markham. *Giammaria Mosca Called Padovano: A Renaissance Sculptor in Italy and Poland*. 2 vols. University Park, PA: Pennsylvania State University Press, 1998.

Schwietering, Julius. *Die Demutsformel mittelhochdeutscher Dichter*. Berlin: Weidmannsche Buchhandlung, 1921. Repr. Göttingen: Vandenhoeck und Ruprecht, 1970.

Scribner, R.W. *For the Sake of Simple Folk: Popular Propaganda for the German Reformation*. 2nd ed. Oxford: Clarendon, 1994.

Scullard, H.H. *Scipio Africanus: Soldier and Politician*. London: Thames and Hudson, 1970.

Sedlar, Jean W. *East Central Europe in the Middle Ages, 1000–1500*. Seattle: University of Washington Press, 1994.

Segel, Harold B. *Renaissance Culture in Poland: The Rise of Humanism, 1470–1543*. Ithaca, NY: Cornell University Press, 1989.

Seznec, Jean. *The Survival of the Pagan Gods: The Mythological Tradition and Its Place in Renaissance Humanism and Art*. Princeton, NJ: Princeton University Press, 1972. Repr. of 1953 edition (New York, Pantheon Books). Originally published in French, *Studies of the Warburg Institute* 11 (1940).

Silver, Larry. 'Prints for a Prince: Maximilian, Nuremberg, and the Woodcut.' In *New Perspectives on the Art of Renaissance Nuremberg: Five Essays*, ed. Jeffrey Chipps Smith, 7–21. Austin, TX: Archer M. Huntington Art Gallery, University of Texas, 1985.

Skimina, Stanisław. *Twórczość poetycka Jana Dantyszka*. Cracow: Polska Akademia Umiejętności, 1948.

Škoviera, Daniel. *Bardejovčan Valentín Ecchius a jeho učebnica* Ars versificandi. Bratislava: Stimul, 2002.

– 'Dialóg *De reipublicae administratione* od humanistu Valentína Ecchia.' *Slovenská literatúra* 41 (1994): 274–84.

– 'Zeitgenössische Vorbilder des Humanistischen Lehrbuches der

Metrik von Valentinus Ecchius Lindaviensis.' *Zborník Filosofickej Fakulty Univerzity Komenského* 21/22 (1992): 5–20.

Ślaski, Jan. 'Italia – Germania – Polonia.'In *Il Rinascimento in Polonia. Atti dei Colloqui italo-polacchi, 1989–1992*, ed. Jolanta Żurawska, 301–14. Napoli: Bibliopolis, 1994.

Śnieżyńska-Stolot, Ewa. 'Pojęcie mecenatu artystycznego.' *Folia historiae artium* 17 (1981): 5–14.

Soltész, E., K. Velenczei, and Á.W. Salgó, comps. *Az Országos Széchényi Könyvtár 16. századi nyomtatványainak katalógusa. Catalogus librorum sedecimo saeculo impressorum, qui in Bibliotheca Nationali Hungariae Széchényiana asservantur.* Budapest: Bibliotheca Nationalis Hungariae Széchényiana, 1990.

Spitz, Lewis W. *Conrad Celtis: The German Arch-Humanist*. Cambridge, MA: Harvard University Press, 1957.

– 'The Course of German Humanism.' In *Itinerarium Italicum: The Profile of the Italian Renaissance in the Mirror of Its European Transformations*, ed. Heiko A. Oberman with Thomas A. Brady, Jr, 371–436. Leiden: E.J. Brill, 1975.

Stackelberg, J. von. 'Das Bienengleichnis: Ein Beitrag zur Geschichte der literarischen *Imitatio*.' *Romanische Forschungen* 68 (1956): 271–93.

Stangler, Gottfried, and Franciszek Stolot, eds. *Polen im Zeitalter der Jagiellonen, 1386–1572*. Schallaburg 1986. Vienna: Amt der Nö. Landesregierung, 1986.

Stawecka, Krystyna. 'Humanistyczne panegiryki łacińskie ku czci św. Stanisława ze Szczepanowa.' *Roczniki humanistyczne* 9 (1960): 5–34.

Stefanowska, Zofia, and Janusz Sławiński, eds. *Dzieło literackie jako źródło historyczne*. Warsaw: Czytelnik, 1978.

Strnad, Alfred A. 'Die Rezeption von Humanismus und Renaissance in Wien.' In Eberhard and Strnad, *Humanismus und Renaissance in Ostmitteleuropa*, 71–135.

Szablowski, Jerzy. 'Architektura.' In *Historia sztuki polski*, ed. Tadeusz Dobrowolski and Władysław Tatarkiewicz, 2: 28–104. Cracow: Wydawnictwo Literackie, 1962.

Szalay, László [Ladislaus von]. *Geschichte Ungarns*. 3 vols. Pest [Vienna]: Wilhelm Lauffer, 1866–75.

Szelińska, Wacława. *Biblioteki profesorów Uniwersytetu Krakowskiego w XV i początkach XVI wieku*. Wrocław: Ossoliński/PAN, 1966.

Szörényi, László. 'L'influenza della Farsaglia di Lucano sull'epopea tardoumanista latina in Ungheria: la *Stauromachia* di Stephanus Taurinus.' In Graciotti and Di Francesco, *L'eredità classica in Italia e Ungheria fra tardo Medioevo e primo Rinascimento*, 241–60.

Tanner, Marie. *The Last Descendant of Aeneas: The Hapsburgs and the Mythic Image of the Emperor*. New Haven: Yale University Press, 1993.

Tazbir, Janusz. *Polska przedmurzem Europy*. Warsaw: Twój Styl, 2004.

– *Reformacja w Polsce*. Warsaw: Książka i Wiedza, 1993.

Thomson, Ian. 'The Scholar as Hero in Ianus Pannonius' Panegyric on Guarinus Veronensis.' *Renaissance Quarterly* 44 (1991): 197–212.

Tomiak, Janusz J. 'The University of Cracow in the Period of Its Greatness.' *Polish Review* 16 (Spring 1971): 25–94.

Tomkiewicz, Władysław. 'Przełom renesansowy w świadomości ówczesnego społeczeństwa polskiego.' In *Renesans. Sztuka i ideologia*, ed. Tadeusz Stefan Jaroszewski, 9–18. Warsaw: PWN, 1976.

Tönnesmann, Andreas. 'Anfänge der Renaissancearchitektur in Deutschland: Interesse und Intention der Auftraggeber.' In Guthmüller, *Deutschland und Italien*, 299–318.

Török, Gyöngyi, ed. *Matthias Corvinus und die Renaissance in Ungarn 1458–1541*. Schallaburg 1982. Vienna: Amt der Nö. Landesregierung, 1982.

Treml, Christine. *Humanistische Gemeinschaftsbildung. Sozio-kulturelle Untersuchung zur Entstehung eines neuen Gelehrtenstandes in der frühen Neuzeit*. Hildesheim: Georg Olms, 1989.

Ulewicz, Tadeusz. 'A Hundred Years of Philological Studies on Humanism and the Latin Renaissance in Poland.' In *La Filologia medievale e umanistica greca e latina nel secolo XX*, [no editor given], 935–64. Rome: Università di Roma 'La Sapienza,' 1993.

– 'Przed przyjściem Kallimacha. Pierwsze zwiastuny humanizmu w złotej jesieni polskiego średniowiecza.' In *Studia slavistica et humanistica in honorem Nullo Minissi*, ed. Ireneusz Opacki, Aleksander Wilkoń, and Jolanta Żurawska, 59–74. Katowice: Wydawnictwo Uniwersytetu Śląskiego, 1997.

– *Wśród impresorów krakowskich doby renesansu*. Cracow: Wydawnictwo Literackie, 1977.

Urbański, Piotr. *Theologia Fabulosa. Commentationes Sarbievianae*. Szczecin: Uniwersytet Szczeciński, 2000.

Ursyn z Krakowa, Jan. *Modus epistolandi cum epistolis exemplaribus et orationibus annexis. O sposobie pisania listów wraz z wzorami listów i mowami*. Ed. and trans. with an introduction and notes by Lidia Winniczuk. Wrocław: Ossoliński/PAN, 1957.

Uruszczak, Wacław. 'Les répercussions de la mort de Thomas Becket en Pologne (XIIe–XIIIe siècles).' In *Thomas Becket. Actes du Colloque international de Sédières. 19–24 août 1973*, ed. Raymonde Foreville, 115–25. Paris: Beauchesne, 1975.

Van Houdt, Toon, Jan Papy, Gilbert Tournoy, and Constant Matheeussen, eds. *Self-Presentation and Social Identification: The Rhetoric and Pragmatics of Letter Writing in Early Modern Times*. Louvain: University of Leuven Press, 2002.

Vocht, H. de. *John Dantiscus and His Netherlandish Friends*. Louvain: Librairie Universitaire, 1961.

Voss, Paul J. 'Books for Sale: Advertising and Patronage in Late Elizabethan England.' *Sixteenth Century Journal* 29 (1998): 733–56.

Vredeveld, H. 'Agricola, Rudolf d. J.' In *Die Deutsche Literatur. Biographisches und bibliographisches Lexikon*. No. 2, *Die Deutsche Literatur zwischen 1450 und 1620*, ed. Hans-Gert Roloff. Pt A, *Autorenlexikon*. Vol. 1, *A–Al*, 732–57. Bern: Peter Lang, 1991.

Vrtel-Wierczyński, Stefan. *Staropolska legenda o św. Aleksym*. Poznań: Poznańskie Towarzystwo Przyjaciół Nauk, 1937.

Wagner, Carolus, ed. *Analecta Scepusii sacri et profani*. 4 vols. Viennae, Posonii et Cassoviae [Vienna, Pozsony, and Kassa], 1773–8.

Walczak, Marek. '"The Jagiellonian Saints": Some Political, National and Ecclesiastical Aspects of Artistic Propaganda in Jagiellonian Poland.' In Popp and Suckale, *Die Jagiellonen*, 139–50.

Waquet, Françoise. 'Qu'est-ce que la République des Lettres? Essai de sémantique historique.' *Bibliothèque de l'École des Chartes* 147 (1989): 473–502.

Waszink, J.H. *Biene und Honig als Symbol des Dichters und der Dichtung in der griechisch-römischen Antike*. Opladen: Westdeutschen Verlag, 1974.

Weissman, Ronald. 'Taking Patronage Seriously: Mediterranean Values and Renaissance Society.' In *Patronage, Art, and Society in Renaissance Italy*, ed. F.W. Kent and Patricia Simons, with J.C. Eade, 25–45. Canberra: Humanities Research Centre; Oxford: Clarendon, 1987.

Wick, Béla. *Kassa története és műemlékei*. Košice: Wicko, 1941.

Wiegand, Hermann. 'Johannes Hadeke-Hadelius. Ein niedersächsischer Wanderhumanist in Rostock, Krakau und Wien.' In *Humanismus im Norden. Frühneuzeitliche Rezeption antiker Kultur und Literatur an Nord- und Ostsee*, ed. Thomas Haye, 105–34. Amsterdam: Rodopi, 2000.

Wierzbowski, Teodor. *Materyały do dziejów piśmiennictwa polskiego*. 2 vols. Warsaw: L. Szkaradziński, 1900; Drukarnia Estetyczna, 1904.

Wiesflecker, Hermann. *Kaiser Maximilian I. Das Reich, Österreich und Europa an der Wende zur Neuzeit*. 5 vols. Vienna: Verlag für Geschichte und Politik, 1971–86.

Wilckens, Leonie von, ed. *Albrecht Dürer, 1471–1971. Ausstellung des Germanischen Nationalmuseums*. Munich: Prestel-Verlag, 1971.

Williams, Franklin B., Jr. 'Commendatory Verses: The Rise of the Art of Puffing.' *Studies in Bibliography* 19 (1966): 1–14.

Winniczuk, Lidia. *Epistolografia. Łacińskie podręczniki epistolograficzne w Polsce w XV–XVI wieku*. Warsaw: Ministerstwo Szkołnictwa Wyższego, 1952.

– 'The Latin Manuals of Epistolography in Poland in the Fifteenth and Sixteenth Centuries.' *Acta Conventus Neo-Latini Sanctandreani. Proceedings of the Fifth International Congress of Neo-Latin Studies*, ed. I. D. McFarlane, 549–59. Binghamton, NY: Medieval and Renaissance Texts and Studies, 1986.

Wisłocki, Wladislaus. *Liber diligentiarum Facultatis Artisticae Universitatis Cracoviensis. Pars I (1487–1563)*. Cracow: Sumptibus Academiae Litterarum, 1886.

Woods-Marsden, Joanna. *Renaissance Self-Portraiture: The Visual Construction of Identity and the Social Status of the Artist*. New Haven: Yale University Press, 1998.

Worstbrock, Franz Josef . 'Die Brieflehre des Konrad Celtis. Textgeschichte und Autorschaft.' In *Philologie als Kulturwissenschaft. Studien zur Literatur und Geschichte des Mittelalters. Festschrift für Karl Stackmann zum 65. Geburtstag*, ed. Ludger Grenzmann, Hubert Herkommer, and Dieter Wuttke, 242–69. Göttingen: Vandenhoeck und Ruprecht, 1987.

Wörster, Peter. 'Breslau und Olmütz als humanistische Zentren vor der Reformation.' In Eberhard and Strnad, *Humanismus und Renaissance in Ostmitteleuropa*, 215–27.

– *Humanismus in Olmütz. Landesbeschreibung in der ersten Hälfte des 16. Jahrhunderts*. Marburg: N.G. Elwert, 1994.

Wuttke, Dieter. 'Conradus Celtis Protucius.' In Füssel, *Deutsche Dichter der frühen Neuzeit*, 173–99.

– *Die Histori Herculis des Nürnberger Humanisten und Freundes der Gebrüder Vischer, Pangratz Bernhaubt, gen. Schwenter*. Cologne: Böhlau, 1964.

Wyczański, Andrzej. 'Dantiscus as a Representative of the New Class of King's Secretaries in Europe.' In IJsewijn and Bracke, *Joannes Dantiscus*, 87–94.

– *Między kulturą a polityką. Sekretarze królewscy Zygmunta Starego (1506–1548)*. Warsaw: PWN, 1990.

– *Polska w Europie XVI stulecia*. Poznań: Wydawnictwo Poznańskie, 1999.

Wyrobisz, Andrzej. 'Economic Landscapes: Poland from the Fourteenth to the Seventeenth Century.' In Mączak and others, *East-Central Europe in Transition*, 36–46.

Zabłocki, Stefan. *Od prerenesansu do oświecenia. Z dziejów inspiracji klasycznych w literaturze polskiej*. Warsaw: PWN, 1976.

– 'Poezja polsko-łacińska wczesnego renesansu.' In Pelc, *Problemy literatury staropolskiej*, 7–102.

Zapf, Georg Wilhelm. *Heinrich Bebel nach seinem Leben und Schriften*. Augsburg: Braun, 1802. Repr. Leipzig: Zentralantiquariat des Deutschen Demokratischen Republik, 1973.

Zins, Henryk. 'A British Humanist and the University of Kraków at the Beginning of the Sixteenth Century: A Chapter in Anglo-Polish Relations in the Age of the Renaissance.' *Renaissance Studies* 8 (March 1994): 13–39.

– *Polska w oczach Anglików XIV–XVI wiek*. 2nd ed. Lublin: Wydawnictwo Uniwersytetu Marii Curie-Skłodowskiej, 2002.

Ziomek, Jerzy. *Renesans*. 5th ed. Warsaw: PWN, 1995.

Zombori, István, Pál Cséfalvay, and Maria Antonietta De Angelis, eds. *A Thousand Years of Christianity in Hungary*. Budapest: Hungarian Catholic Episcopal Conference, 2001.

Index

Erasmus Studies

A series of studies concerned with Erasmus and related subjects

1 *Under Pretext of Praise: Satiric Mode in Erasmus' Fiction*
Sister Geraldine Thompson

2 *Erasmus on Language and Method in Theology*
Marjorie O'Rourke Boyle

3 *The Politics of Erasmus: A Pacifist Intellectual and His Political Milieu*
James D. Tracy

4 *Phoenix of His Age: Interpretations of Erasmus, c. 1550–1750*
Bruce Mansfield

5 *Christening Pagan Mysteries: Erasmus in Pursuit of Wisdom*
Marjorie O'Rourke Boyle

6 *Renaissance English Translations of Erasmus: A Bibliography to 1700*
E.J. Devereux

7 *Erasmus as a Translator of the Classics*
Erika Rummel

8 *Erasmus'* Annotations on the New Testament: *From Philologist to Theologian*
Erika Rummel

9 *Humanist Play and Belief: The Seriocomic Art of Desiderius Erasmus*
Walter M. Gordon

10 *Erasmus: His Life, Works, and Influence*
Cornelis Augustijn

11 *Interpretations of Erasmus, c1750–1920: Man on His Own*
Bruce Mansfield

12 *Rhetoric and Theology: The Hermeneutic of Erasmus*
Manfred Hoffmann

13 *Conversing with God: Erasmus' Pastoral Writings*
Hilmar M. Pabel

14 *Holy Scripture Speaks: The Production and Reception of Erasmus'* Paraphrases on the New Testament
Hilmar M. Pabel and Mark Vessey (eds)

15 *Erasmus in the Twentieth Century: Interpretations c1920–2000*
Bruce Mansfield

16 *Patronage and Humanist Literature in the Age of the Jagiellons: Court and Career in the Writings of Rudolf Agricola Junior, Valentin Eck, and Leonard Cox*
Jacqueline Glomski